REINVENTING
the FRESHMAN
WRITING & RESEARCH
course

A Text for All *Freshman,* Co-Requisite and *Writing Across the Curriculum* Courses

PATRICIA SEHULSTER
S.U.N.Y. Westchester Community College

Kendall Hunt
publishing company

Dedication

© Bildagentur Zoonar GmbH/Shutterstock.com

Like the eagle in flight, I have the good fortune of experiencing many winds beneath my wings. Their currents keep me afloat when I need uplift, send me soaring with inspiration, and bring me to safe landings whenever I might lose my way. They have served as my teachers and my writing supporters. I dedicate this text to all of them: My husband, Chuck, and my son, Chris; my late grandmother, Loretta Long; my late parents, Mary and Leo Schaefer; my siblings, Mary Lee and T.J., Terri, Maureen, Ruthie and Lenny, Julia and Brenda, Jeanie, and Russ and Kathy; and my nieces and nephews, Tara Jean, Scott, Devin, Keira, Wayne, Josh, Jay, Ryan, Justin, Danielle, Sarah, and Rachel. I add to this list all the teachers who have come before me and mentored me, my current teaching colleagues, and all the future teachers I hope will gain something from this book. Lastly, I dedicate this text to my students, past, present, and to come; they shape my days and add meaning to my life. They have written this book with me, for every day they teach me about teaching and learning, about new perspectives, and about the life-altering power of education.

Contents

Preface

I write this book, but I have not composed it alone. As I repeatedly tell my colleagues, "Good teaching is good stealing, and we put our own individual marks upon that which we borrow from others." My ideas certainly represent reinventions and adaptations of what has come before me—many of them so integral a part of my repertoire now that I cannot name or separate their sources. We teach and learn not in a vacuum, but in a community of other scholars as pedagogical informants, teachers as sources, our students as teachers, our institutions as gatekeepers, and our world as context. Yet, we possess our individual proclivities, styles, histories, strengths, weaknesses, etc. We can no more simply assume someone else's lesson plans or learning styles than we can don comfortably someone else's suit of clothing two sizes too big or too small. In this text, then, I offer only frameworks from which my readers can build, adapting and modifying what fits their own styles of teaching and learning. As I frequently note to my own students, I provide merely a toolbox, and sometimes students will choose the hammer, but at other times, they might select the chisel. Sometimes, they may even use a combination I had not envisioned but that works for them, for writing is at its core a *process*, and that process is as individual as the writers who compose and as varied as the genres and audiences we target.

The tools I offer here target three very specific types of courses: the required freshman writing and research course, its co-requisite course, and the Writing Across the Curriculum approach course for teaching both.

Many students come to these courses baffled by the fact that after four years of high school writing, they must take yet another writing class. They come to college hoping for challenge and difference, and immediately we require of them a course they think they have already studied. *Our* challenge becomes offering them something new: an expanded definition of writing as a way of engaging with reading, discovering, thinking and rethinking, dialoguing with others, and making meaning of our own. In this conception of writing, we must focus on interaction and collaboration, writer in relation to others (as opposed to just the teacher), writing as opportunity for informed self-expression for specific audiences, and writing as self-directed learning.

While these broad course definitions offer an ideal sense of our expectations as teachers and learners, we cannot hope to meet those ideals without first setting specific and measurable learning outcomes. This text's plan envelops the following course objectives:

Students will:

1. Demonstrate an understanding of writing as a multistage process, devising strategies for pre-writing, composing, revising, editing, and proofreading and using writing for inquiry, learning, thinking, and communicating.

2. Produce texts that present ideas effectively and fluently:

   a. Include a clear focus, controlling idea, or question.
   b. Support ideas with reasoning and evidence.
   c. Summarize others' ideas clearly, accurately, thoroughly, and concisely.
   d. Integrate their own ideas with those of others.

e. Organize ideas to clarify and support the controlling idea or question and to best suit the targeted audience.

f. Write with adequate command of language and its grammatical and mechanical conventions.

3. Use appropriate research methods.

a. Develop and refine a research topic and question.
b. Evaluate the credibility, reliability, and applicability of sources.
c. Identify, analyze, and evaluate arguments in sources.
d. Document where information and ideas come from in the style appropriate for the discipline.

4. Develop the foundations for creative, independent, and critical thinking that considers a multiplicity of perspectives and disciplines.

Meeting these rigorous and complex objectives will require the full course, for no single lesson or topic will encompass all of them. Rather, students will build the skill sets throughout the term, scaffolding not only the assignments, but also the tools necessary to complete those assignments successfully.

Bearing this approach to skills-acquisition in mind, I organize this text according to a fifteen-week semester comprised of five units. These divisions include a unit to assist students in discovering their own abilities to learn, think, read, and write on a college level ("Entering the Academic World," weeks 1–3); a unit to introduce students to the cycle of choosing a research topic and question and then creating a research proposal ("Finding a Research Topic and Question," weeks 4–6); a unit to engage students in finding and evaluating various types of sources and designing their own claims based on them ("Finding and Assessing Existing Academic Dialogues," weeks 7–9); a unit to develop students' abilities to add their own voices through synthesis, drafting, and revising ("Formalizing Our Contributions to the Dialogue," weeks 10–14); and a final unit to develop students' skills in and comfort with presenting in various formats to varying audiences their discoveries ("Presenting Our Discoveries and Conclusions," week 15/Final Exam Period). Each of these units also outlines the objectives.

I present this entire text as a conversation between me and its users. In fact, the predominant metaphor of the book encompasses an academic dialogue—the conversation of students with peers (class dialogue and peer review), of students with professors (information and feedback), of students with and as scholars (research and talking back), and of students with themselves (reflection). I have designed each *feature* of the text to envelop one or more of these types of dialogues, sometimes in writing and sometimes in speech.

- **In-Class Activities**: These low-stakes writing and talking activities get students thinking about and applying the particular concepts and skills discussed in each unit. I have designed them to utilize individual, small group, and large group work, and teachers can use them in whatever configuration they like. (See Appendix for information on Achieving the Dream's recommended "Active Learning Strategies.") The text includes enough activities to use two each week. Frequently, these activities incorporate a kind of models of practice—templates, of sorts—that students will ultimately use in their research writing.

- Journal Entries: These low-stakes writing assignments serve as preparation for and reflection upon the unit writing assignments. Students will always write them on their own, but students may complete them in or outside of class, as the teacher chooses, and they may or may not share them with peers (in class or online through discussion forums, blogs, etc., again, as the teacher chooses).

- Assignments/Assessments: Each unit works toward a culminating assignment: a full essay of a particular type, and complete with its evaluation rubric. For each of these assignments, I recommend the use of three drafts: two reviewed by peers and the "final" copy submitted only to the teacher.

- Readings and Resources: In each unit, I provide related readings and resources. I have concentrated the bulk of the readings in Chapters 1 and 2, and many of these readings make use of the Internet, for today's students often prefer that way of reading and can practice their search techniques in finding these texts online. Chapter 2's readings provide texts within five categories: "On the Environment"; "On Technology and Us"; "On Negotiating Cultural, Political, and Other Differences"; "On a College Education"; and "On Food." I intend these texts to serve as catalysts for thinking about possible research topics and questions, though teachers and students might certainly narrow to a single area of focus or expand to others not included but of interest. These readings also provide common texts to introduce students to the process of analysis and evaluation, the next unit's focus.

- Grammar Skills: The end of each unit targets a particular grammatical concept. I have selected these topics based upon the most common trouble spots I see among my students, so the book does not actually offer a full grammar handbook. The information provided offers only an understanding; students need to apply the rules in the actual work that they do, for grammar lasts only if put in context. In each section, I offer some tips regarding how students and teachers might utilize the concept.

- Co-Requisite Course Material: Each unit provides additional—or follow-up—activities for the co-requisite course that may be paired with the writing and research course. These activities serve to clarify and reinforce lessons as well as to target both the noncognitive and skill-level issues these students must address.

- WAC/WID (Writing Across the Curriculum/Writing in the Disciplines) Activities: Each unit offers suggestions and tips for WAC/WID activities within the given unit. I note here that frequently, WAC/WID courses encompass side-by-side learning community courses, with the writing course paired with a discipline-specific course. In this model, each course remains a separate entity but may share some readings or discussions. I, however, envision a day in which the WAC/WID course makes the discipline-specific course the primary class—the topic, if you will—and the writing course the stepsister that lives and breathes within that other course as a kind of writing lab. I imagine a day in which writing and research skills are taught only in context—the context of the required major courses students must—and want to—take. I have designed this text to work with either model.

While all of the lessons and units within this book have succeeded in my own writing and research classrooms, I know well that with each different set of students, we reconstitute our teaching strategies; the very nature of teaching and learning demands these adjustments of us. I offer here but a template of what can work, and I hope teachers and learners will take from it whatever they can and then reinvent and adapt it to fit themselves.

**A Note Regarding Online Classes

This text certainly can work with online classes, though a few structural necessities must accompany that use. Teachers must post class activities as discussion forums, so that students can interact. Students must conduct peer review in such forums too. Journal entries may remain private or shared, become part of discussion forums or journals or blogs, and not every entry must be done in the same way. Using the e-text will actually facilitate its application for students.

Acknowledgments

Through forty years of teaching, I have learned that there really are no new ideas about teaching, only new names to call them and new ways to implement them. All of us owe a great many of our ideas and methods to others.

I owe a debt of gratitude to a host of contributors to the ideas evidenced in this book. They number too many to name, for in a long career, I have assimilated much from scholars and colleagues. I include on the following list only those who have had the largest impact on this text's design and methodology. (For a full list of sources, please see the bibliography at the end of this book.)

- All of my SUNY Westchester Community College colleagues, who have in one way or another contributed to the making of this text, for every time I discuss teaching with them, I learn something
- My colleagues, Professors Erich Werner, Ellen Wasserman, and Jacqueline Reichman, who experimented with and shared the sequence of this plan first and then graciously allowed me to tinker with it
- Professor Peter Adams and the Community College of Baltimore County, who designed and shared the ALP (Accelerated Learning Program) used all over the United States
- Thomas Baily, Shana Smith Jaggars, and Davis Jenkins, who presented a plethora of ideas in their *Redesigning America's Community Colleges*
- CCC (Conference on College Composition and Communication) Executive Committee, who researches and then releases policy and position statements about the teaching of writing on the college level
- Michelle Cox, Jeffrey Galin, and Dan Melzen, who have offered many insights about WAC (Writing Across the Curriculum) courses
- Carol S. Dweck, PhD, who has championed the concept of growth mindset
- Peter Elbow, who for decades has offered ideas and strategies for the effective teaching of writing
- Gerald Graff and Cathy Bickenstein, who promoted the idea of the "They say/I say" approach to teaching research writing
- Jessica Kester, who has added much to the discussion of WAC and WID courses
- Ken Macrorie, who invented and shared his concept of the i-search paper
- Mike Rose, whose books about teaching in the community college have inspired me for years
- Howard Tinberg and Jean-Paul Nadeau, whose book, *The Community College Writer Exceeding Expectations,* provides concrete advice for creating success in the college writing classroom
- Cia Verschelden, who has helped innumerable teachers and students negotiate bandwidth recovery

- Kathleen Yancy, who has pioneered great strides in the studies of teaching college writing to developmental and non-developmental students alike
- Larry Edgerton, for my use of some of his pages from his *The Less-is-More Handbook*
- Eric Drown and Kathy Sole, for use of some of their pages from *Writing College Research Papers*

This book could never have become a reality without my Kendall Hunt editors, Beth Trowbridge and Sue Saad. They came to me to ask me to write a book and then, while still allowing me free reign to create what I wanted to design, guided me in *everything*. Thank you!

CHAPTER 1

Entering the Academic World
Weeks 1–3

Learning Objectives

Students will:

- Demonstrate an understanding of writing as a multistage process.
- Produce texts that present ideas effectively and fluently.
- Think critically.
- Understand growth mindset, grit, and multiple intelligences.

Congratulations! You have chosen to begin your foray into the academic world! Welcome to the journey!

You are thinking, "Well, haven't I been in that world for the past twelve years, since the day I started kindergarten?" Yes, you have, but now you step from those essential training grounds into the field of transference and expansion, depth and breadth, and honing and meaning-making.

© potowizard/Shutterstock.com

© Sapunkele/Shutterstock.com

The college-level academic world asks you to utilize the skills and knowledge you have already gained through education and experience and advance them in a myriad of ways. Perhaps some of the biggest differences you will find in college expectations include those encountered in *reading, writing, research, and thinking.* These skills apply to every discipline you will study in college, and for that reason, colleges almost always start students with a writing and research course.

In this course, I ask you to think of your learning experience in three vital ways:

- It is indeed *a journey*; you will not always know the way or an answer, but the learning comes in the *process of discovery.* (You did not walk the day you entered this world. First you crawled. Then you stumbled and even fell, and only then did you learn to run. Why should college-level learning differ?)

- You have entered into a *conversation or dialogue with your peers* (conversation and peer review), *with your professors* (instruction and feedback), *with other scholars* (research), and *even with yourself* (reflection).
  - ▶ You *should* talk back!
  - ▶ You *should* consider opposing and new ideas and perspectives!
  - ▶ You *should* form your own contribution to the dialogue!

- *Writing can serve as your way into and through the journey.* It offers you a path to engage with reading; to discover, learn, think, and rethink; to dialogue and interact with others; and to express your own ideas. It serves as an essential tool for your success.

During this journey, you will at times feel frustrated or even lost, but these responses constitute only a small part of your travel. Along the way, you will have the guidance of professors, peers, and academic support centers. Yet, the first and most important key to the success of your journey will come from you.

A. Considering Our Own Frame of Mind and Determination

Perhaps your experience has made you believe that you and others around you have a built-in, natural capacity for learning that nothing you do can alter. Perhaps you believe some people possess intelligence, and others do not, so you doubt my assertion that *you* have the power to determine your academic success level.

Everyone *does* have that power, and it develops from each individual's beliefs and attitudes. Carol S. Dweck, PhD, calls this power *growth mindset* (as opposed to fixed mindset). She contends that those with a growth mindset believe that their "basic qualities are things [they] can cultivate through [their] efforts, [their] strategies, and help from others. [. . .] Everyone can change and grow through supplication and experience."[1]

What exactly does she mean by "cultivate"? She claims that all of us can actually follow patterns that will keep us growing intellectually, and conversely, we can repeat patterns that can stop us from growing too.

---

1. Carol S. Dweck, PhD, *mindset THE NEW PSYCHOLOGY OF SUCCESS* (New York: Random House, 2006), 7.

Growth Mindset

- I can learn anything I want to
- When I'm frustrated, I persevere
- I want to challenge myself
- When I fail, I learn
- Tell me I try hard
- If you succeed, I'm inspired
- My effort and attitude determine everything

Fixed Mindset

- I'm either good at it, or I'm not
- When I'm frustrated, I give up
- I don't like to be challenged
- When I fail, I'm no good
- Tell me I'm smart
- If you succeed, I feel threatened
- My abilities determine everything

© desdemona72/Shutterstock.com

Let's take some time to think about this idea for awhile.

IN-CLASS ACTIVITY 1A

1. As a whole class, or individually on your phones, laptops, tablets, or classroom computer, watch the following two videos:

   "Psychologist Carol Dweck and Educator Sal Khan Talk About Mindset":

   https://www.mindsetkit.org/practices/13MJygtBNRRxN26s

   "Explanation of Mindset By Sprouts":

   https://www.youtube.com/watch?v=KUWn_TJTrnU

2. Fill in your own answers on the following chart.

CATEGORY	MY STRONGEST SKILL	MY WEAKEST SKILL
In School		
Everyone has always told me . . .		
Outside of School		
In Writing		

My Own Example:

CATEGORY	MY STRONGEST SKILL	MY WEAKEST SKILL
In School	Writing, reading, researching	Math
Everyone has always told me . . .	I am a studious and well-organized student.	I do not have good spatial concepts.
Outside of School	I am a good listener, good mediator, good leader, and good athlete.	Balancing work and life outside of work
In Writing	I am creative, can write a lot, know grammar and vocabulary.	I cannot type at all well; I always have to cut words because I am verbose.

3. Now answer the following questions.

    a. In what ways do these categories, "Strongest" and "Weakest," correlate to growth mindset and fixed mindset? Explain.

    b. What effect has what others have judged you to be strongest and weakest in had on you? For example, did it make you engage in that activity more than other types of activities? Did you shy away from that which you thought you did not do well or might fail at doing? Explain.

    c. How willing are you to try something new to you and that you might not initially succeed in doing? Explain.

    d. In what ways do you think the *process* of writing—brainstorming, drafting, and revising—relates to mindset theory?

4. Now, turn to your nearest two neighbors to form a group of three. Make certain to introduce yourselves to one another. Take turns sharing your ideas/answers to the questions a–d.

5. Based on your discussion, create a single statement that completes the following sentence:

   Mindset has a _____ effect on a person's academic success. It

   matters _____ one's beginning intellectual abilities
                 (as much as, less than, the same amount as)

   because _____.

6. Send someone from your group to the whiteboard/blackboard to post your group's conclusion for all to see. Be prepared to defend it.

© iQoncept/Shutterstock.com

Growth mindset has a close relationship with a concept another psychologist, Angela Duckworth, discusses a great deal: *grit*. She and most dictionaries define grit as the quality of perseverance, an unwillingness to quit. She contends that students with grit succeed, regardless of their abilities because they keep working to overcome obstacles and any type of barriers to success. Her claim tells us that *grit stands as the tool that helps you practice the principles of growth mindset.* If you think of anything you have ever learned to do particularly well and that you desired to do particularly well—playing a sport, playing a video game, playing a musical instrument, sewing a garment, gardening, etc.—you will find you probably used grit to become as good at it as you have become. You did not perform it well from the very start; you had to work at the skill set required to improve and hone those skills. How much of that kind of grit have you transferred to your academic world?

JOURNAL ENTRY 1: MINDSET, GRIT, AND MY OWN ACADEMIC JOURNEY

Read the pages below, from psychologist Carol Dweck's website.

"What is Mindset?":

https://www.mindsetworks.com/science/

"How Does Mindset Affect Success?":

https://www.mindsetworks.com/science/Impact

"Test Your Mindset" (the full, four-page evaluation):

http://blog.mindsetworks.com/what-s-my-mindset?view=quiz

Watch Angela Duckworth's "The Key to Success? Grit" *TED Talk Education*, April 2013

http://www.ted.com/talks/angela_lee_duckworth_the_key_to_success_grit?language=en

Take Angela Duckworth's "Grit Scale Test":

https://angeladuckworth.com/grit-scale/

In your Journal entry:

- Discuss the results of your Mindset Test and your Grit Scale Test. What did the results tell you about yourself that you already knew, and what surprised you? Did the results of one test seem compatible with the other? Why/why not?
- Think about what these texts convey about mindset and grit in general. How do you think they might apply to writing specifically?
- Discuss whether or not you have a growth mindset or fixed mindset toward writing and whether or not you have grit when it comes to writing. Do you feel that people can improve their writing ability with effort? Or are people born being good writers or bad writers, and no amount of effort can change that condition? What writing experiences have you had that confirm (or challenge) this mindset?

**Use at least 250 words in your response. Use at least one quote from the readings to help explain or support your ideas. You might choose to use any of the readings about mindset or grit. (See this chapter's "Readings and Resources" for a complete list.)

Journal Entry Rubric

CATEGORY AND SLO ADDRESSED	EXCEEDS STANDARDS (2.5 POINTS)	MEETS STANDARDS (2 POINTS)	APPROACHES STANDARDS (1.5 POINTS)	DOES NOT MEET STANDARDS (0–1 POINT)
Response answers the questions with clarity of expression.	Writer addresses all parts of the question thoroughly in clear, understandable prose.	Writer addresses the question with reasonable clarity.	Writer does not fully answer the question and lacks some clarity.	Writer does not address the question or barely addresses it and lacks any clarity.
Response demonstrates critical thinking.	Writer demonstrates thoughtful and critical analysis and utilizes engaged consideration of others' ideas to form his/her own.	Writer demonstrates some analysis and some consideration of others' ideas to form her/his own.	Writer demonstrates little thoughtful and critical analysis and does not utilize consideration of others' ideas to form her/his own.	Writer demonstrates no critical analysis and mostly merely summarizes others' ideas and does not form his/her own.
Response demonstrates originality and creativity.	Writer creates his/her own thoughtful, original ideas.	Writer attempts to create his/her own ideas.	Writer mostly parrots others' ideas with little creation of his/her own ideas.	Writer merely summarizes others' ideas.
Response incorporates or addresses in some way others' perspectives.	Writer incorporates others' positions in her/his discussion.	Writer acknowledges at least one other person's position in her/his discussion.	Writer attempts to reference at least one other person's position in her/his discussion but fails to acknowledge that contribution or position her/his own argument against it.	Writer does not even acknowledge others' positions in her/his discussion.
OVERALL SCORE:	EXCEEDS STANDARDS	MEETS STANDARDS	APPROACHES STANDARDS	DOES NOT MEET STANDARDS

As we contemplate mindset and grit, let us consider too whether or not the academic world requires a particular kind of intelligence. Until about the 1980s, most people thought so, and they labeled that capacity IQ (Intelligence Quotient). They even designed a test for it. But in the 1980s and throughout the 1990s, Howard Gardner, relying initially on some earlier work done by others, expanded that single concept to include what he called *multiple intelligences,* each of which encompassed "the ability to solve problems or create products that are valued within one or more cultural settings."[2] Gardner considered these intelligences to envelop eight different areas, though he has admitted that as human beings and society change, and as psychologists continue to research, these eight categories could expand yet again.

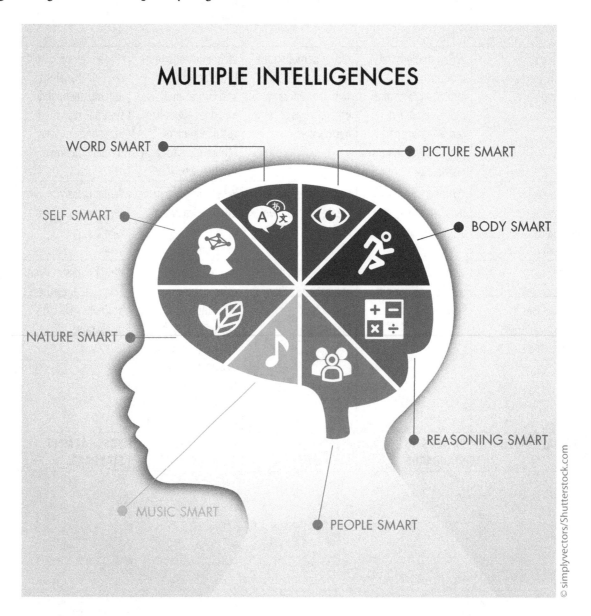

MULTIPLE INTELLIGENCES

WORD SMART

PICTURE SMART

SELF SMART

BODY SMART

NATURE SMART

REASONING SMART

MUSIC SMART

PEOPLE SMART

© simplyvectors/Shutterstock.com

---

2. Howard Gardner, *Frames of Mind The Theory of Multiple Intelligences* (New York: Basic Books, 1993), xxviii.

One key point Gardner makes when he discusses these multiple intelligences includes his emphasis that *they do not constitute separate entities*, but, rather, *work in concert*, and that every human being possesses *a unique combination* of these multiple intelligences. If we agree with this hypothesis, then what does it mean for our own concept of academic intelligence and the standard IQ number that has made so many of us believe that we either possess academic abilities, or we do not, and that only certain kinds of professionals are intelligent? In addition, if we think about Gardner's premise that these various intelligences all share the capacity to solve problems and create the two highest levels of another psychologist's (Bloom's) taxonomy for learning, what can we conclude about anyone's—including our own—power to learn?

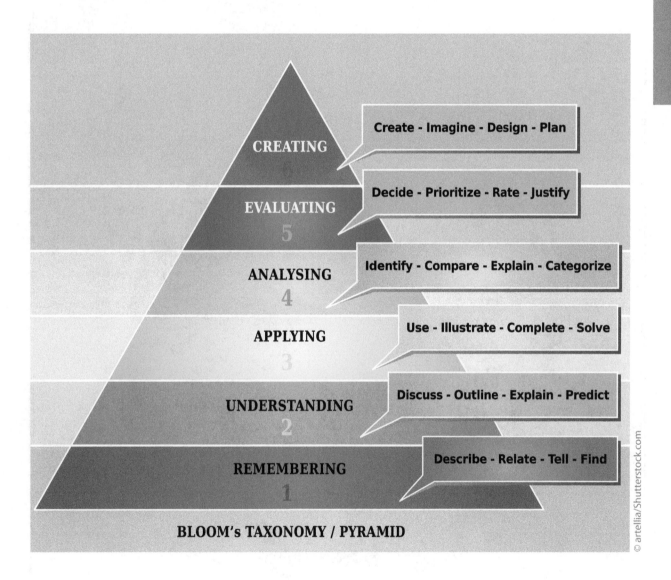

BLOOM's TAXONOMY / PYRAMID

© artellia/Shutterstock.com

IN-CLASS ACTIVTY 1B

**Revisit (or even keep in front of you) your assigned reading of "Gardner's Theory of Multiple Intelligences," by Kendra Cherry.

1. Consider what you have learned about multiple intelligences. Fill in the pie chart below with an example of the way *you* exhibit each one. Then, feel free to change the percentages to reflect *your* ratios, or to leave them equal as they are now.

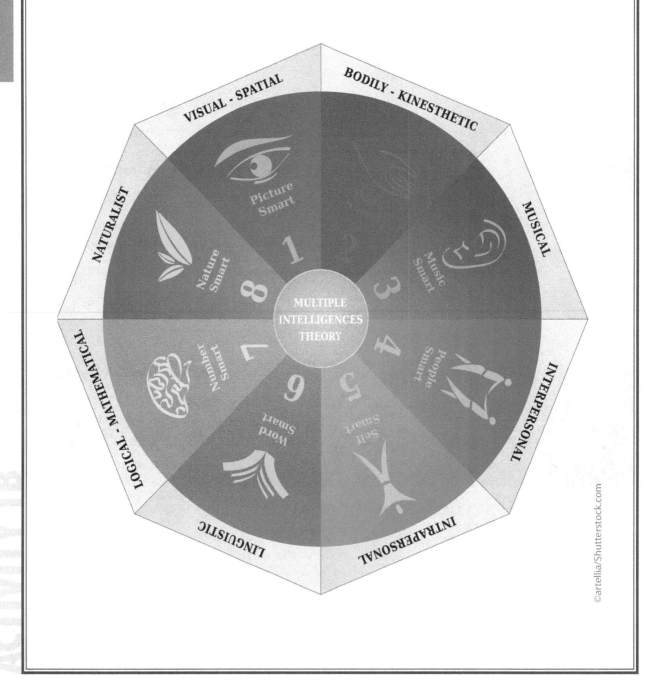

©artellia/Shutterstock.com

2. Do you see any overlapping? Do you see any way one form of intelligence can influence or advance another? Explain.

3. Form a group of three to four students. Discuss your different individual charts and your answers to question 2. What conclusions can you reach about the ways Gardner's theories make sense and the ways they might not make sense?

4. In what ways do these theories fit with what Carol Dweck says about growth mindset and with what Duckworth says about grit?

5. As a group, fill in the following sentence:

Carol S. Dweck tells us _____,

and Gardner proclaims, _____; taking these theories together,

we can conclude that _____

_____.

6. Share your sentence with another group, and read that group's sentence. Discuss their similarities and differences. Can you reach a consensus on another sentence? If so, write that new sentence here. If not, state why you cannot do so.

B. Defining College-Level Writing, Reading, and Thinking

So what does any of this information about growth mindset, grit, and multiple intelligences have to do with college-level writing? Let's take a moment to reflect on our own experiences with writing. Some of us have written since our early childhoods, while others of us have avoided writing, if we could. Some of us think of ourselves as daily writers, while others of us think of ourselves not as writers, but as writing-assignment-completers. *All* of us probably label ourselves as some kind of writer: good, competent, mediocre, or poor. But how have we learned to evaluate our own and others' writing? Can a blog or social media post, for example, stand out as "good writing" just as a Pulitzer-Prize-winning novel can? Do we believe that anyone who produces text of any kind fits the definition of a writer?

IN-CLASS ACTIVITY 1C: WHAT MAKES "GOOD" WRITING?

Part 1

1. Right now, at this very moment, what assumptions do you hold about what makes "good" writing and a "good" writer? Fill in just the first column of the following chart.

	WHAT I ASSUME	WHAT MALERMAN SAYS	WHAT WILLENS SAYS	WHAT CONSOL SAYS LAMOTT SAYS	WHAT 8 WRITERS SAY
Who can and does write?					
What's it look like?					
How does it get that way?					
Why write?					

2. Turn to the person to your right and compare your answers. Did you have anything in common?

Part 2

1. Perhaps one answer many of you might have noted in the "How does it get that way?" column included the idea of *drafting and rewriting*. Let's take a look at that concept through the eyes of other writers, who speak in the following quick video clips.

   "Enough about the first draft: Don't fear 1st attempts" on May 14, 2019, by John Malerman for *Daily Fuel*:

   > https://dailyfuel.com/2019/05/14/enough-about-the-first-draft/

   "Writers Speak to Kids: Mo Willens for NBC News Learn" on September 17, 2012:

   > https://www.nbclearn.com/writers-speak-to-kids/cuecard/60820

   "Mike Consol on Ann Lamott on those horrible first drafts that all writers produce" on August 23, 2015:

   > https://www.youtube.com/watch?v=Vr44UV2vCMg

   "8 Writers on Facing the Blank Page" on August 17, 2016, for Louisiana Channel:

   > https://www.youtube.com/watch?v=dGwSqy_27X8

2. Now go back to the chart, and fill in the remaining columns based on what you heard in the video clips.

3. As you examine your chart and compare your initial assumptions to those of the other writers, what stands out to you? Write below one sentence about how your thinking about writing has or has not changed as a result of this activity.

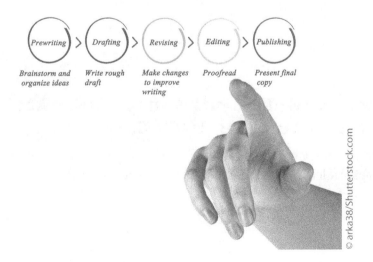

Writing Process

Prewriting > Drafting > Revising > Editing > Publishing

Brainstorm and organize ideas | Write rough draft | Make changes to improve writing | Proofread | Present final copy

© arka38/Shutterstock.com

JOURNAL ENTRY 2: "SHITTY FIRST DRAFTS": REFLECTION AND RESPONSE

Read "Shitty First Drafts" by Anne Lamott, presented by University of Kentucky on August 6, 2012, at:

https://wrd.as.uky.edu/sites/default/files/1-Shitty%20First%20Drafts.pdf

Respond to each of the numbered questions below, but do so in paragraphs, not in numbered sections. Address them in any order you choose.

1. Using your own words, describe (summarize) Lamott's "mindset" toward writing. How does she think and feel about writing, and about herself as a writer? (Apply/use the growth/fixed mindset concepts we have examined as you consider and describe Lamott's attitudes toward writing.)

2. What strategies does she use to manage her doubts and fears? Does she demonstrate grit, use of multiple intelligences, and/or a specific process?

3. Lamott is an accomplished, published writer. Do her thoughts and feelings about writing and her writing process surprise you?

4. Compare Lamott's writing mindset to your own. Do you have similar thoughts and feelings about your writing?

5. Compare Lamott's writing PROCESS to your own. Are the practical steps you take similar or different? Explain.

**Use at least 250 words in your response. Use at least one quote from the reading to help explain and support your own ideas.

See page 7 for the journal evaluation rubric.

◇◇

Common Myths about Writing and Which You Should Not Let Get in Your Way Because They Are but Myths, NOT to Be Believed

Here we consider some widely held beliefs about *writing*. If you have any of the following beliefs, you will want to guard against letting them get in the way of your writing work.

Myth 1: Writing is a talent that people are born with, and I do not have it.

Writing is a skill that can be learned, and everyone can learn how to write. No matter what your current writing skills, you can learn to write better if you are willing to invest some time and effort. When people say, "I cannot write!" they often mean that they do not know how to engage in a specific type of writing and are intimidated by the prospect of looking foolish in front of their peers or teachers. The solution to this problem is not just to sit down and start writing with the hope of producing something that readers will expect. Instead, ask for (or find) samples of the kind of writing you must do and model your own writing on them. Later in this chapter, we will discuss what your teachers and readers of research essays expect to see in your paper. For now, be confident that no matter what your previous experience writing research papers, you can write this one.

Myth 2: I have to know everything I want to say before I can start writing.

Many emerging writers wonder how they can get started writing if they do not know what they want to communicate. They fear that time spent writing without a clear sense of what is to be communicated is time wasted. So they spend time trying meticulously to plan everything they want to include so that they can write efficiently, only to find that they are no clearer on what they want to say than they were when they sat down to figure things out. Part of the problem is that preplanning tends to stifle the open-mindedness you need in order to forge connections among your sources. According to cognitive psychologist Dr. David Galbraith, people who write with few expectations about final outcomes tend to enhance their personal understanding of the topic and develop ideas of their own far more often than do people who meticulously plan their writing (1999). Galbraith explains that planners tend to use writing simply to express what they already know. Because of this, their understanding of the topic tends not to be developed or enhanced by the act of writing. To embrace an exploratory approach to drafting, you do not need to write fully crafted sentences and paragraphs. You can make concept maps, tables, index cards, sticky notes, or sketches. Whichever forms of exploration you choose, the important thing is that you spend time playing around with the ideas you have encountered in your research without the pressure to produce the final word.

Myth 3: My first draft should be as good as it can be, so I will only have to "clean it up" in revision.

People who want to plan their writing down to the last detail also tend to want their first draft to be as close to their final draft as possible for the sake of efficiency. In order to meet their goal, such writers sacrifice depth and complexity for efficiency. They tend to oversimplify the complicated issues at the heart of their research. But in order to meet the expectations of academic readers, you must wrestle with the complexities and nuances of a topic. Even experienced academic writers write multiple drafts, finding their ideas and analyses emerging as they write. You too should expect that your first draft will be messy, and that in subsequent revisions, you will add and subtract large chunks of text. We will explain the details of revision later. For now, you should start thinking about revision as more than just cleaning and polishing your text. Expect to reconsider your ideas and arguments as your thinking develops through the work of drafting. If you start your first draft with the knowledge that much will change in revision, you free yourself to write whatever comes and find your best ideas.

Myth 4: I have one more source to read before I can start writing.

You may have only a short time to write your research paper, which means you need to start writing. Today. And you will need to continue writing tomorrow. And the next day. And the day after that. There is always going to be one more source you could read. But you cannot let the desire to find it interfere with your need to write. Start writing early in your research process and continue writing daily until you are done. Between your draft and your revision, you may well go read that source. But because the only way to think effectively about your sources is to write about them, you cannot postpone writing until you have everything in hand and perfectly understood. In fact, it may be a good idea to set a time limit on your initial phase of research. Commit to the idea that at a certain point you will stop collecting research and start writing about it. Start writing with what you have and be willing to revise as you consider further evidence later in the process.

Myth 5: If I could just find the perfect source, I would understand exactly what I want to say about my topic.

Many writers of research papers believe that there is one perfect source out there that will make everything fall into place, clear up every confusion, and enable them to breeze through the writing stage of the research project. This belief stems from the mistaken notion that their job as a researcher is simply to find and present information. However, your most important work is to make information meaningful by thinking carefully about what it tells you in regard to the problem you are trying to solve or the issue you are trying to resolve. Information only matters when you use it to advance discussion about a topic. So, when you are confused and do not know what to think, do not go looking for a source. Instead, try writing about your confusion. Describe the source of your confusion. Do you not know the meaning of technical terms? Do you need help interpreting statistics? Is the relationship between ideas or data and conclusions not clear? Is the structure of the piece of writing unfamiliar? By explaining to yourself exactly what it is you do not understand, you can identify the strategies that you can try to overcome your difficulty. You may need to consult a specialized dictionary or get the help of someone who has an analytical skill that you do not yet have. Or you might just need to ask a question of your instructor or teaching assistant.

Myth 6: There is nothing that can be done about "writer's block."

Every writer periodically experiences moments when getting words on a page becomes a struggle. When that happens, blinking cursors on empty pages seem to mock the writer's effort. But when you are writing a research paper in a short time, you cannot afford to give in to what is popularly known as *writer's block*. It can help to know that writer's block is partially a manifestation of fear and anxiety about completing an unfamiliar task. Studies of what researchers call "reluctance to write" indicate that it can be overcome by using many of the strategies that have been recommended to you in this book: committing to a schedule of work, measuring your output by word count rather than time spent, and using multiple writing techniques to relieve the pressure to produce perfect prose in early drafts.

Myth 7: I cannot figure out my introduction, so I cannot write the paper.

It is true that the introduction is a particularly important part of the essay. It is the place where you introduce your reader to your topic and the questions driving research about it. It is the place where you identify the particular parts of the research conversation you find useful and problematic, and to which you want to respond. And it is the place where you define and justify your thesis. You need to have command of your research project to write an effective introduction. It is no wonder that writing an introduction at the start of your drafting process can be particularly daunting. If you can write your introduction, go ahead. But expect it to be highly provisional and subject to change. And do not struggle too much with it. If your introduction will not come, skip ahead and write a low-risk section of the body of your essay. Try describing and answering one of your supporting questions. Define and illustrate an important concept. Present the view of a writer whose ideas you want to build on or counter. In other words, start by writing small two- to three-paragraph chunks of your essay. When you have enough of these chunks, start stringing them together in an argument about your topic. Doing this kind of detail work on the nuances of your topic enhances your understanding of what other researchers are saying, and helps you develop well-founded judgments about the uses and limits of their ideas and data. Do enough of it, and you will find yourself developing stronger opinions about the central questions of your topic, and your thesis and argument will become clearer. Having worked with the conceptual and informational materials of your topic long enough to decide what you think about it, you should be in position to write a stronger, but still preliminary, version of your introduction.

© Jean-Christian Bourcart/Contributor/ Getty Images Entertainment/Getty Images

While you should not succumb to writer's block, you may be interested to hear that feeling stuck at first is common to many writers. Author Kurt Vonnegut is often thought to have said, "When I write, I feel like an armless, legless man with a crayon in his mouth."

From *Writing College Research Papers, Second Edition* by Eric Drown and Kathy Sole. Copyright © 2013 by Bridgepoint Education Inc. Reprinted by permission.

◇◇

While we can always simply sit and write, reading material can help to inspire us, force us to consider new ideas and perspectives different from our own, and in general, serve as a catalyst for our own writing. The two processes connect to one another, each one circling back to the other in an endless cycle. Whether you read a textbook for a course, an article from the Internet, or a news story, you should practice some specific critical reading and note-taking skills.

Critical Reading and Note-Taking Strategies

Let us take some time to understand the differences between reading for information and reading to write about a topic. Along the way, we will collect some concrete strategies for reading critically.

To get the most out of your time spent reading, you should set ambitious reading goals; Table 1.1 lays out some of the key differences between basic and advanced reading goals.

Table 1.1   Basic and Advanced Reading Goals

BASIC READING GOALS	ADVANCED READING GOALS
Read to store and retrieve information	Read to be conversant—to be able to speak about the details (and the relationships among them) and general effect of a text without referring to it
Read passively	Read actively—take notes, ask questions, make connections, paraphrase key points
Read to absorb	Read to explore, inquire, consider, question, criticize, analyze
Read to understand	Read to do something to/with the text—evaluate, synthesize, create, write
Read for the gist	Read to understand nuances and to assess views, to locate gaps in the conversation, to find places to comment and respond
Read each text in isolation	Read texts as part of an intertextual dialogue or field
Read impressionistically	Read systematically
Read to agree or disagree	Read to understand a position that is different from one's own

Analyzing and Interpreting

In order to read to fulfill these more advanced goals, you may need to alter your reading habits. In particular you will need to take an *analytical* approach to reading texts in order to interpret them. By *interpretation*, we mean the process by which you have come to see the significance, meaning, or implications of the ideas, data, and questions with which you are working. Analysis and interpretation are notoriously fuzzy terms. But it is not hard to be concrete about the process used to do these activities. Let us begin by understanding what it means to read analytically. To read analytically is to attend to, understand, assess, and comment on

1. The sequence of moves a writer uses to make an argument;
2. The relationship between claims made and the evidence and logic used to support them;
3. The significance and implications of specific keywords or phrases a writer chooses to convey a view;
4. Patterns in data, ideas, methods, or perspectives;
5. Anomalous data, ideas, methods, or perspective once a pattern has been established; and
6. The explicit or tacit organizing binaries or oppositions in the piece.

Reading analytically also means

7. To uncover and reveal the tacit values and assumptions that anchor a writer's perspective;
8. To understand the larger contexts in which specific data or phenomenon are relevant; and
9. To explore and reveal the implications of the data, ideas, or methods.

While it may seem that reading analytically requires you to pay attention to a lot, the following sections provide you with some strategies for a step-by-step reading and note-taking process that will maximize your chances of reading analytically.

Approaching the Text With the Right Mindset in the Right Environment

It can be easy to check out of a reading that on first blush seems dull or irrelevant, is hard to follow, or is on complex subject matter. Do not let yourself take the easy way out! It will make your life as a writer considerably more difficult if you do. So, try to focus hard, knowing that the work you put in up front will pay off with time saved, less stress, and better results at the end of the project. Work actively to pay attention, understand, and respond to the material being presented. Concentrate on understanding what is being conveyed, whatever the deficiencies of the piece of writing. Try to connect what you are reading to what you already know (through personal experience or other reading you have done on the subject). Think about how what you are reading possibly changes what you think about the topic on which you are working. Assess the uses and limits of the ideas which you are reading for your own writing project.

Using Pre-Reading Strategies

Survey the reading and develop questions and interests to guide your reading. Activate what you already know about the topics, whether from other reading or life experiences. When you *survey* a text, you scan the table of contents, introduction, chapter introductions, headings, or summaries to pick up a shallow overview of the text. From your survey, develop a small set of initial questions or thoughts that you will to try to answer or think through as you read. Also, locate areas of particular interest (topics or subtopics, but also specific page ranges) to which you will give your best attention.

Before reading the text carefully, consider what you already know (or think you know) about the topic of the text. By creating expectations about what you are reading, you will notice when the writer's line of thought diverges from your expectations and see those moments as interesting, puzzling, troubling, ambiguous, or suggestive—as moments about which you will need to write.

Marking Up Your Texts

The simple act of making marks on a reading focuses your attention and promotes an active and dynamic approach to your reading that is absolutely essential if you are to write effectively about what you read. Unless you have a late model tablet that accepts input from a stylus, and a good piece of "ink on PDF" software (such as PDFill's PDF Ink), it is best to mark up a reading using a pencil or pen.

The next paragraph will describe some basic marks and types of margin comments. Notice how they focus your attention more on the flow of the intellectual conversation, rather than on the specific pieces of information or materials the writers use to have the conversation. Remember, you are reading to further the conversation, not merely to acquire and retain information. To participate in the conversation, you have to be able to use the words on the page to map the *exchange* of ideas embedded in the text.

Use the following marks and margin comment types to help you make the conversation in your set of research texts come to life (see *Marked Up Text: Sam Anderson, "In Defense of Distraction"* for an example):

- Underline essential and supporting questions and label which supporting questions go with each essential question;

- Circle key concepts, and then define concepts and terms in your own words in the margin;

- Double-underline compelling passages and make margin notes about how you could use them in your own project;

Marking up a source helps reinforce your engagement with it, regardless of which method you choose to make notes and annotations.

- Draw a block around passages that are complicated, challenging, or hard to understand, and then on a separate sheet of paper, try to paraphrase them until you understand them;

- Jot down the ideas, examples, and lines of inquiry that occur to you as you read;

- Draw lines or make cross-references to forge connections and comparisons between sections of the reading, or between the current reading and others you have read previously; and

- Make margin notes about the uses and limits of particular concepts or passages for your own work.

It is particularly important to track the *writerly moves* the writer is making. When you track a writer's moves, you are paying as much attention to the purpose of each paragraph as to the content of it. When you attend to the writer's purpose of a paragraph, you better understand how that writer wants you to synthesize the ideas, exhibits, and arguments presented into a larger argument. When you understand how a writer is making the argument, you can better evaluate it. Table 1.2 below presents some common writerly moves for which to be on the lookout.

Table 1.2 Common Writerly Moves

Offering background	Countering another writer's argument	Analyzing an exhibit
Making an argument	Interpreting an exhibit	Defining terms
Borrowing expert authority	Describing a method	Extending another writer's argument
Criticizing another writer's method	Presenting another writer's argument	Revealing tacit values or assumptions

Keeping track of a writer's moves will enable you to better see the conversation in the writer's text. By understanding how the author is making use of sources, you can distinguish between what the sources say and what the author is saying in response. Then you can consider your response to all the voices in the text.

CHAPTER 1

Q – Can Distraction be useful?

Simon, Meyer, Gallagher

PURPOSE: THEIR OWN EVIDENCE SHOWS THEY'VE MISSED SOMETHING VALUABLE ABOUT DISTRACTION

The prophets of total attention meltdown sometimes invoke, as an example of the great culture we are going to lose as we succumb to e-thinking, the canonical French juggernaut Marcel Proust. And indeed, at seven volumes, several thousand pages, and 1.5 million words, *Á la Recherche du Temps Perdu* is in many ways the anti-Twitter. (It would take, by the way, exactly 68,636 tweets to reproduce.) It's important to remember, however, that the most famous moment in all of Proust, the moment that launches the entire monumental project, is a moment of pure distraction: when the narrator, Marcel, eats a spoonful of teasoaked madeleine and finds himself instantly transported back to the world of his childhood: Proust makes it clear that conscious focus could never have yielded such profound magic. Marcel has to abandon the constraints of what he calls "voluntary memory," the kind of narrow, purpose-driven attention that Adderall, say, might have allowed him to harness in order to get to the deeper truths available by the distraction. That famous cookie is a kind of hyperlink: a little blip that launches an associative cascade of a million other subjects. This sort of free-associative wandering is essential to the creative process; one moment of judicious unmindfulness can inspire thousands of hours of mindfulness.

ANALYSIS

INTERRPRETATION

DISTRACTION CAN REVEAL TRUTH?

I NEED TO TRY TO PARAPHRASE THIS

EXHIBIT

DISTRACTION CAN BE a PRECURSOR TO CREATIVITY

My favorite focusing exercise comes from William James: Draw a dot on a piece of paper, then pay attention to it for as long as you can. (Sitting in my office one afternoon, with my monkey mind swinging busily across the lush rain forest of online distractions, I tried this with the closest dot in the vicinity: the bright-red mouse-nipple at the center of my laptop's keyboard. I managed to stare at it for 30 minutes, with mixed results.) James argued that the human mind can't actually focus on the dot, or any unchanging object, for more than a few seconds at a time: It's too hungry for variety, surprise, the adventure of the unknown. It has to refresh its attention by continually finding new aspects of the dot to focus on: subtleties of its shape, its relationship to the edges of the paper, metaphorical associations (a fly, an eye, a hole). The exercise becomes a question less of pure unwavering focus than of your ability to organize distractions around a central point. The dot, in all other words, becomes only the hub of your total dot-related distraction.

BORROWING a CONCEPT

PARADOX? NEED TO FIGURE THIS OUT

This is what the web-threatened punditry often fails to recognize: Focus is a paradox; it has distraction built into it. The two are symbiotic; they're the systole and diastole of consciousness. Attention comes from the Latin "to stretch out" or "reach toward," distraction from "to pull apart." We need both. In their extreme forms, focus and attention may even circle circle back around and bleed into one another. Meyer says there's a subset of Buddhists who believe that the most advanced monks become essentially "world-class multitaskers," that all those years of meditation might actually speed up their mental processes enough to handle the kind of information overload the rest of us find crippling.

ARGUMENT

The truly wise mind will harness, rather than abandon, the power of distraction. Unwavering focus the inability to be distracted can actually be just as problematic as ADHD. Trouble with "attentional shift" is a feature common to a handful of mental illnesses, including schizophrenia and OCD. Its been hypothesized the ADHD might even be an advantage in certain change-rich environments.

ARGUMENT

ITS HARD TO SEE HOW. I SUPPOSE YOU MIGHT BE MORE AWARE OF DIVERSE STIMULI, BUT HOW WELL COULD YOU RESPOND TO IT?

You should also keep track of your intellectual response to the reading: Are you skeptical of some of the ideas or arguments presented? Does some way of approaching a problem or object of analysis seem particularly interesting or puzzling? Is something confusing or suddenly particularly clear? Write it all down. Keep track of the questions, ideas, problems, potential forwards/counters, and personal experiences that percolate in your brain as you read. These will be the foundations on which you come to terms with the piece.

When you are finished reading, immediately write a healthy paragraph right on your printout (or on the first or last page of your chapter, right in the book if you own it) documenting both the basic substance of the writer's contribution to the conversation and your initial intellectual responses to it. Record the essential ideas, concepts, or claims that you want to forward or counter, and explain how and why. Describe how reading this text changed your thinking (furthered it? nuanced it? redirected it? complicated it? confused it?).

Transfer your margin notes to a word-processing program or note-taking program (such as Evernote) after reading. Transferring notes only after you read, rather than as you go, because the act of transferring your notes from the page to the word processor helps solidify your encounter with the text. You will remember more of what you read and develop a deeper, more sophisticated response to the text by revisiting your margin notes in the act of transfer.

You do not need to transfer everything. In fact, you want to be selective to start winnowing important stuff from trivial (even if interesting) stuff. Start by transferring everything that went into your "healthy paragraph." When you wrote that paragraph, you started to develop your own response to the material. You began to integrate new ideas and information with old, and started to think about how your own project will be impacted by engaging this particular text in conversation. As you revisit your notes in light of other readings and further work on your own piece of writing, you will add to, revise, rethink, and respond to this initial response (so be sure to record the date of your initial reading, and each time you revisit your notes). By tracking the development of your thought as you revisit and rethink your response to a reading in light of further readings and thinking, you will have a history of your engagement with the ideas and lines of thought that are the substance of the conversation you and all the other writers are having. When you write your paper, you will rely on the history of your encounter with other conversationalists to formulate your own entry into the conversation.

After transferring that first "healthy paragraph," transfer only the most important concepts (especially ones named with specialized terms), conversation-changing insights, passages, examples, and lines of thought you might want to emulate or deploy in your own writing projects. Do not worry about capturing data or statistics—they are on paper and easily retrievable. If you need one or two specific pieces of information, go back and make a note on the first page of the reading indicating where exactly in the essay the data is (page number) and—here is the crucial step—explaining the meaning and implications of the data. Unless you write down what the data means to you, you will surely forget what you found interesting, useful, or troubling about the data.

This intensive approach to reading is necessary because you are not just reading to understand a fact, remember it, and select the right option on a multiple-choice exam. You are reading to respond to this text (and others) in writing. You need to cultivate and record a complex intellectual response to the text in order to write about it in an interesting and compelling way.

Let's practice these skills with some visual texts and some of our assigned reading.

IN-CLASS ACTIVITY 1D: ANALYZING THE STRUCTURE OF ARGUMENTS

PRELIMINARY INFORMATION:

The Structure of an Argument:

COMPONENT	DEFINITION	EXAMPLE
Claim	The position for which one argues; the conclusion one has reached about an argument.	Attending community college offers students an excellent way to begin their college educations
Reasons	Statements that answer the question "why?" (and often begin with "because . . .")	because doing so saves money and still provides the necessary education.
Evidence	Specifics (facts, data, etc.) that support, explain, and prove the reasons	Community colleges cost only a quarter of what four-year colleges cost, and they provide all the general education requirements of any degree program.

Types of Supporting Evidence:

TYPES OF SUPPORT (PREFACTS)	MEANING
P—Personal Experience	Personal experience or observation to help support a claim/thesis/premise/nutshell idea.
R—Reasons	The explanation for your statements.
E—Examples	Specific samples or instances that help to illustrate the claim/thesis/premise/nutshell idea.
F—Facts, Data, Statistics, Studies	Statements that can be proven true or false; concrete and verifiable numbers or proofs.
A—Analogies	Showing similarities between two unlike entities to clarify a point or example.
C—Concrete Images	Using a combination of narrating (telling) and painting a mental picture with images and figurative language (showing). e.g., "Telling": I saved money. "Showing": Instead of paying $30,000 through a loan I would have to repay, I withdrew only $5,000 from my bank account to pay the tuition bill in full for the same 30 credits.
T—Testimonials	Quotations from people in authority/experts/ researchers (e.g., criminologist, scientists, Census Bureau, etc.)

Qualifiers:

A **qualifier** is a word, phrase, or added condition that changes how absolute, certain, or generalized a statement [claim/thesis/premise/nutshell idea] is.

Qualifiers may include:

Qualifiers of quantity: some, most, all, none, several, etc.
Qualifiers of time: occasionally, sometimes, usually, always, never, etc.

Example:

- CLAIM: People should strive not to take opioids like Oxycontin to relieve pain.
  - ▶ REASON: People become easily addicted to opioids.
    - EVIDENCE: According to the National Institute of health, "Misuse of prescription opioids and heroin affects more than 2 million Americans and an estimated 15 million people worldwide each year."
  - ▶ REASON: Addiction can easily lead to overdosing and death.
    - EVIDENCE: According to the National Institute on Drug Abuse, "130 people a day die in the United States because of opioid abuse."
    - EVIDENCE: Studies show that opioids are more addictive than many drugs, and when their cost increases or the prescriptions run out, people use unsafe street drug versions.
  - ▶ QUALIFIER: Exceptions can be made for people with terminal illnesses that cause excruciating pain, so they can ease their final days.

AND NOW THE ACTIVITY:

Work in groups of three to four people to analyze and answer the questions about the following examples. Prepare to discuss your responses with the rest of the class.

A. Identify the structure of this argument:

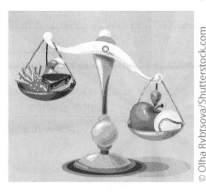

- ▶ CLAIM:

- ▶ REASONS (at least two):

- ▶ EVIDENCE (at least two items):

B. Now, reexamine—and even put in front of you—your assigned reading, "Blue Collar Brilliance" by Mike Rose. If you have not already done so, practice the critical reading and note-taking skills on the article. THEN, identify its . . .

- ▶ CLAIM:

- ▶ REASONS (at least two):

- ▶ EVIDENCE (at least two items):

C. Now, write a three-sentence summary of his argument.

D. Discuss and record your answers to the following questions:

1. How does Rose organize his argument? For example, where do you find his claim? What types of evidence does he use? What sequence does he follow? Do you find this organization effective? Why or why not?

2. Do the workers Rose discusses demonstrate a growth mindset, grit, and/or multiple intelligences? Explain.

3. Do you think what Rose labels "blue-collar brilliance" can transfer or in any way become applicable to an academic setting such as college? Explain.

4. Do you agree with Rose's argument? Why or why not?

5. In what ways does Rose's essay mesh with, contradict, or enhance the arguments in your assigned reading, "Gardner's Theory of Multiple Intelligences" by Kendra Cherry?

C. Entering the Class Academic Dialogue and Peer Review

As you move from reading to thinking and writing, you engage in a process that actually inserts you into a dialogue. First, you converse with the writer of the reading by listening to the author's words. Then, in your interpretations of the text, you rewrite the piece in your own way. Finally, you produce your own contribution by speaking or writing about that reading. When others listen to you or read your writing, the process begins again.

You then stand out as both a dialogue-receiver and a dialogue-starter. Whether you read and respond to a friend's text message, peruse an advertisement and draw a conclusion about the product, or read and summarize a chapter of your sociology textbook, in every case, you engage in a dialogue.

© Creative Stall/Shutterstock.com

JOURNAL ENTRY 3: A DIALOGUE WITH MIKE ROSE

Reread "Blue-Collar Brilliance" by Mike Rose, June 1, 2009, for *The American Scholar*:

https://theamericanscholar.org/blue-collar-brilliance/#.XDNbjfx7lN0

Respond to the following questions in a few paragraphs. Try to write about 300 words, but do not concern yourself with spelling or grammar and mechanics; just write.

- How do you use intelligence in settings other than school? Be specific by giving examples and illustrations.

- How do your family and friends display intelligence in nonacademic settings? Again, be specific by giving examples and illustrations.

- Based on these ideas and examples, draw a conclusion about "nonacademic intelligence" and "academic intelligence." Feel free to add a quote from Mike Rose or from Howard Gardner.

See page 7 for the journal evaluation rubric.

In college, the dialogue in which you engage follows certain conventions. That academic dialogue asks you to participate in a kind of formal call and response activity in which you examine what a scholar has to say; identify its primary claims, points, and evidence; and call back with your own reasoned response to that material. Sometimes, you might quote the expert directly, while at other times, you might only paraphrase or summarize, but *always, you will work toward your own contribution to that dialogue*; you will talk back!

© Gustavo Frazao/Shutterstock.com

IN-CLASS ACTIVITY 1E: TALKING BACK TO TARA BAHRAMPOUR WITH SUMMARY AND RESPONSE

PART 1: Work in groups of three to four students to complete the following exercise.

1. Reexamine—and even put in front of you—your assigned reading, "'Find your passion?' That's bad advice, scientists say" by Tara Bahrampour (for *The Washington Post*, July 23, 2018).

2. Identify the idea or belief that Tara Bahrampour has concluded is mistaken. Write it word-for-word.

3. Use the following formula to summarize that mistaken idea or belief. Offer a fair and thorough representation by using at least three sentences.

Many people believe that _____. They believe this

idea because _____. They see evidence for their

their claim in _____.

4. Now, like Tara Bahrampour, respond to that idea by disagreeing and providing the reasons for that counterclaim. Use at least three sentences and the following formula.

However, this idea is mistaken because _____. I believe

_____ because _____.

5. Meet with another group and share, compare, and discuss your answers. Decide whether or not you want to make any changes, and explain why you would or would not do so.

PART 2: This time, work quietly on your own.

1. Think of any idea or belief that you think is mistaken.

2. State/identify the idea you believe is mistaken.

3. Use the following formula to summarize that mistaken idea or belief. Offer a fair and thorough representation by using at least three sentences.

Many people believe that _____. They believe this

idea because _____. They see evidence for their

claim in _____.

4. Now, respond to that idea by disagreeing and providing the reasons for that counterclaim. Use at least three sentences and the following formula.

However, this idea is mistaken because _____. I believe

_____ because _____.

5. Examine the work you just completed. Notice the patterns. Write a rule for engaging in a summary-response dialogue with an idea with which you do not agree.

D. My Writing Mindset Reflective Letter Assignment

Now that you have experimented with and practiced with your initial foray into an academic dialogue about mindset, grit, and multiple intelligences, you have readied yourself for your first assignment: to reflect on your own experiences with these concepts and to contribute your own ideas about them.

ASSIGNMENT 1: MY WRITING MINDSET REFLECTIVE LETTER

PRELIMINARY INFORMATION:

The Formal Letter: Conventions and Formatting:

- Date [May go here or after the Sender's Address]
- Sender's Address [Address only, NO name]
- Inside Address (To Whom the Letter is Going—Your professor, in this case)
- Salutation:
- Body of Letter/Body Paragraphs
- Closing Paragraph/Call to Action/Reiteration of Main Point
- Valediction/Complimentary Closing
- Blank Block for Signature
- Typed Signature/Name

See the following links:

"Rules and Layout of Formal Letters" from NVTC:

http://www.nvtc.ee/e-oppe/Varkki/layout/rules_for_writing_formal_letters.html

"Video on Writing the Formal Letter":

https://www.youtube.com/watch?v=Ns_Fxn-0z_E

Journal Entry 4: DRAFT of the Assignment [500–700 words]

Using Anne Lamott's approach to writing first drafts, write a quick draft of your "My Writing Mindset Reflective Letter." Remember what Lamott has said about drafts:

"The first draft is the child's draft, where you let it all pour out and then let it romp all over the place, knowing that no one is going to see it and that you can shape it later. You just let this childlike part of you channel whatever voices and visions come through and onto the page. If one of the characters wants to say, "Well, so what, Mr. Poopy Pants?," you let her. No one is going to see it. If the kid wants to get into really sentimental, weepy, emotional territory, you let him. Just

get it all down on paper, because there may be something great in those six, crazy pages that you would never have gotten to by more rational, grown-up means."[3]

DIRECTIONS: "My Mindset Reflective Letter" Essay—700 words (2–2.5 pages)

Reflect on your own beliefs about *yourself as writer*. How have your experiences as writer affected those beliefs? How have those views changed over time and as a result of the work we have been engaged in during these first couple of weeks of class?

Write a letter to me, your teacher, describing your mindset about writing. What is your own mindset toward writing—and especially toward academic writing—and how can you improve that mindset? Discuss how specific readings (Dweck, Duckworth, Rose, Gardner, and/or Lamott) have influenced how you think about your own writing abilities and how you might cultivate new ways of thinking about yourself as a writer. How might those ways of thinking affect your experience of this course and of college in general?

Your letter should be . . .

- *In first-person:* This letter is about your mindset, so you will use "I."
- *Organized chronologically:* Begin by describing how you thought about your writing before this semester, and then explain how specific readings and exercises have influenced your thinking. End the essay by describing the way you think now and what influence you believe that thinking will have on your college/academic writing experience.
- *Addressed to me, your teacher*: Follow the outlined conventions and formatting of a formal letter, and adopt a formal (or semi-formal) tone. Your purpose is to convince me, your teacher and reader, that you have thought seriously about the material and about how you might use it to improve your learning. For a sample, see the model at the end of this chapter.
- *Well-documented:* Integrate the ideas and information from at least two of the readings of this unit. (See a complete list at the end of this chapter.) Use signal phrases such as "According to Carol S. Dweck," or "Mike Rose notes that," etc., to acknowledge where ideas, information, and borrowed words come from. Enclose all borrowed words in quotation marks ("").

You will write this journal entry as draft 1.

After your first peer review, you will revise the essay. Then you will meet with peers again.

After that discussion, you will revise the essay a third and final time to submit for a grade.

---

3. Anne Lamott, "Shitty First Drafts," University of Kentucky, August 6, 2012, https://wrd.as.uky.edu/sites/default/files/1-Shitty%20First%20Drafts.pdf.

MY MINDSET REFLECTIVE LETTER ESSAY EVALUATION RUBRIC

CATEGORY	EXCEEDS STANDARDS [20–25 POINTS]	MEETS STANDARDS [17.5–19.75 POINTS]	APPROACHES STANDARDS [15–17 POINTS]	DOES NOT MEET STANDARDS [14 POINTS AND BELOW]
Reflection Writer's thinking shows depth and rigor.				
Integration Writer integrates ideas/info from readings.				
Focus Writer stays on task and on topic.				
Organization Writer organizes ideas effectively.				
Documentation Writer uses signal phrases and quotation marks.				
Correctness Writer avoids errors that confuse or distract.				

Because you exist as part of a community of learners inside the classroom, you actually have a built-in, live academic dialogue mechanism: *the peer review*. Peer review offers you the opportunity to rehearse your written contribution in front of an audience that will give you feedback. This kind of interactive conversation about your writing offers you the chance to hear what others think you mean and to determine how closely those thoughts match your own intentions. Peer review can even help you to think about new ideas to include and new ways of saying what you mean. Peer review also gives you a window to see other ways your peers have approached the same assignment, an impression that can sometimes assist you in reshaping your own essay.

Regardless of your skill-level or fears, every one of you has something vital to offer your peers because you provide a reader or sounding board, someone who can respond to how your peer's dialogue strikes you. Peers neither judge nor evaluate; they converse. Peers guide you to see what you cannot see yourself, because all of us writers sit too closely to and grow too attached to our own words.

IN-CLASS ACTIVITY 1F: PEER REVIEW 1

1. Form a group of three. [Each member of the group will have come prepared with three copies of the draft.]
2. Circulate your drafts, assigning each one a number.
3. Read the draft from writer number 1.
   a. ON THE DRAFT ITSELF: Highlight/underline/circle in blue the parts of the essay that seem strong.
   b. ON THE DRAFT ITSELF: Highlight/underline/circle in red the parts of the essay about which you have questions/concerns or that confuse you.
4. In turn, discuss the essay and your comments with the writer and the rest of your group.
5. Repeat steps 4 and 5 with next writer, until everyone's draft has been discussed.

Peer review encompasses another step in the process of writing, but it does not serve as the final step. Writing functions as both a social and anti-social act. In its initial stages, as you read and discuss ideas, you work with others. Then, alone, you play with your first draft. You work with others again in peer review, and then you must reflect upon that dialogue on your own and revise again by yourself.

JOURNAL ENTRY 5: REFLECTION ON PEER REVIEW

Reflect on what you learned from your peer review session.

1. Explain what you learned from the feedback others gave you on your draft.

2. Explain what you learned from reading your peers' drafts.

3. Write a three-step plan of action for your revision of your first draft. What three specific changes—additions, deletions, changes in sequence, etc.—will you make to improve the draft before the next peer review? Why will you make these alterations? What specific effect do you hope they will have?

Once you have revised, you can experience peer review again, and then at last you will write your final draft—or at least the draft you will submit as complete and its best version at that moment.

IN-CLASS ACTIVITY 1G: PEER REVIEW 2

1. Form a group of three. [Each member of the group will have come prepared with three copies of the draft.]
2. Circulate your drafts, assigning each one a number.
3. Read the draft from Writer #1.
   a. ON THE DRAFT ITSELF: Make annotations. Make certain to address how or where the author:
      - Does or does not follow the conventions of a formal letter,
      - Makes a specific claim about the writer's mindset toward writing, especially academic writing,
      - Uses and quotes the readings as part of the argument, and
      - Follows a chronological and logical organization.
4. Fill out the essay rubric below, by checking the appropriate column and filling in some comments in each category. Tear it off to give to the writer.
5. In turn, discuss each essay as a group.
6. Repeat steps 4 and 5 with next writer, until everyone's draft has been reviewed and discussed.

CATEGORY	EXCEEDS STANDARDS [20–25 POINTS]	MEETS STANDARDS [17.5–19.75 POINTS]	APPROACHES STANDARDS [15–17 POINTS]	DOES NOT MEET STANDARDS [14 POINTS AND BELOW]
Reflection Does the writer's thinking show depth and rigor?				
Integration Does the writer integrate ideas/info from readings?				
Focus Does the writer stay on task and on topic?				
Organization Does the writer organize ideas effectively?				
Documentation Does the writer use signal phrases and quotation marks?				
Correctness Does the writer avoid errors that confuse or distract?				

E.   Defining College-Level Research

The activities in which you have engaged so far in this unit—reading, responding, talking, thinking, and writing—have paralleled exactly the skills you will need to succeed at college-level research writing. You have begun to make the move from mere reporting of research to entering and contributing to the academic conversation.

WHAT IS RESEARCH?

Before we get started, you should understand that the academic environment is not the only environment that values research. Research skills are also highly valued in policy settings, as well as in the professions and trades. According to Dr. David Jonassen (2000), director of the University of Missouri Center for the Study of Problem Solving, "Virtually everyone, in their everyday and professional lives, regularly solves problems. Few, if any, people, are rewarded in their professional lives for memorizing information and completing examinations" (p. 63). Research is primarily a problem-solving activity. When you conduct research, you must define and clarify problems, ask answerable questions, locate and evaluate resources, and use sources to make persuasive arguments and actionable recommendations. By learning to conduct research, you will get more out of your education, enhance your career, and contribute to the success of the civic and business organizations to which you belong.

As a researcher, your most basic task will be to identify problems of interest and ask the right questions.

You Already Do Research

At the most basic level, research satisfies our need to answer questions, solve problems, make choices, or figure out what things mean. Sometimes our questions are simple or of personal consequence. In those cases, our answers depend simply on gathering information or weighing opinions and evaluating what we find in terms of our taste or preference. For example, when we browse the Internet to find restaurants for a special dinner next weekend, we are in fact conducting simple informal research. When we read everything we can find about different types of automobiles to help us make a decision about what type of car to purchase, we are seeking reliable expert testimony to help us make sense of the vast amount of information available to us.

Critical Thinking in Everyday Research

Even though the research is simple in these cases, we are still using some critical thinking skills. In fact, we are using some of the same ones that inform academic research. Professional researchers always approach their sources of information skeptically. They know that their conclusions depend on having high-quality, reliable information to think carefully about. So they need to ensure that they are not misled by irrelevant, inaccurate, or out-of-date information, or by the arguments of sloppy or unscrupulous thinkers. The same goes for everyday researchers. In order to avoid a bad meal or being dissatisfied with our new car, we need to evaluate whether our sources are **relevant**, **credible**, and **timely**; understand their *motivation* and *bias*; and make judgments about how *representative* a particular review is in light of what other reviewers write. You can draw on your experience with everyday research to understand that a review of a Chinese restaurant is *irrelevant* or of no use if you want to eat Thai food.

Criteria for Evaluating Sources

- Relevant
- Credible
- Timely
- Representative
- Appropriate motivation and controlled for bias

A review written by the cousin of the owner of the restaurant is not *credible*, or believable, because you cannot be sure that the reviewer is writing to tell the truth. Perhaps the reviewer means to drive more customers to the restaurant with an excellent review, and therefore overlooks significant problems in service or quality. This reviewer is *motivated* by the relationship with the owner, and therefore this evaluation is *biased* in favor of the restaurant. This review would not then be trustworthy. A review of the restaurant written five years ago may no longer accurately reflect the dining experience; in order to get a more accurate picture, you will need a more recent, or *timely*, review. Finally, you may have had the experience of reading one or two negative reviews of a place among a hundred positive reviews. Those negative reviews do not represent or stand for the general opinion of the place. To say that a review is not *representative* is not to say that it is untrue necessarily—merely that it is does not fall in line with the consensus. With a nonrepresentative source, it is good practice to ask why it dissents from the consensus. A source may be nonrepresentative because its writer has idiosyncratic or personal preferences, uses a different method of arriving at conclusions, looks at things from a different viewpoint, or perhaps has made some mistake. You will use these same criteria to evaluate sources in the research you will conduct.

The Differences between Academic or Professional Research and Everyday Research

This text is meant to prepare you to use research to answer more complicated questions: the kind that you will encounter in academic and workplace environments. In those settings, questions can be very complex, and expert testimony may not provide clear guidance. Answers may be partial, not definitive, or dependent on multiple variables or on the values of the researcher. Moreover, the stakes can be considerably higher than choosing a restaurant or car.

Consider these questions:

- In the last two decades, honeybee populations have been decimated by Honeybee Colony Collapse Disorder (CCD). Since honeybees pollinate our food crops, the collapse of millions of colonies is a threat to the world food supply. What is causing this disorder? What can be done to prevent CCD and restore the honeybee population?

- The United States continues to experience high levels of unemployment despite an uptick in the economy. Why has job growth not kept pace with the increasing gross domestic product (a standard measure of the productivity of our national economy)? What factors influence unemployment? What can the government do to help businesses create good, well-paying jobs?

- Your company wants to develop a new product or line of business. How will consumers respond to your product, service, or marketing? What variables will influence their purchasing decisions for the foreseeable future? How can you mitigate risk?

It is not just complexity that distinguishes these questions from the research questions we tend to ask and answer in our daily life. It is that they are emerging, not-yet-fully-understood problems. There are no simple, clear-cut, definitive answers out there waiting to be found. Reasonable people in full possession of available data might reasonably disagree as to what the data mean, or what the appropriate course of action should be.

Yet these are pressing matters. We simply cannot wait for all the information to become available, and for unclear matters to resolve themselves before taking action. That is where research—our most effective means of solving complex problems—comes in. In such cases, researchers use a systematic approach that enables them to begin to ask and answer these emerging questions. As a result, the work of research is not always to provide clear and definitive solutions to problems. Research can also clarify issues, bring forward new variables or alternative perspectives for consideration, reduce uncertainty, or reveal tacit values.

The Cumulative, Ongoing, and Critical Nature of Research

Because of the nature of the problems researchers need to solve, research tends to be *cumulative* and *ongoing*, which is to say that researchers consider the results of the past and expect that future research may extend, revise, or refute their own work. That is why researchers tend to start their work by reviewing what is already known or believed to be true. They read journal articles, conference proceedings, and other forms of scholarly publication to ground themselves in the ideas and perspectives of other researchers. As they read these sources, they want to know:

- What questions other researchers have pursued,
- How other researchers have framed their questions,
- What data exist,
- What concepts and ideas previous researchers have used or created to make sense of their data,
- What related problems, issues, or phenomenon need to be taken into account,
- What false starts others have encountered, and
- What remains to be understood about the problem.

The work of review is more than a simple gathering of useful information, however. Researchers look *critically* at earlier work to evaluate its strengths and weaknesses, as well as its utility for their own work. As they read the works of other researchers, they

- Check for errors,
- Look for ideas to refute, borrow, or build on,

- Browse for suggestive data, cases, or examples,
- Seek out unexplored questions or unrecognized implications,
- Uncover problematic assumptions or bias, and
- Consider alternative explanations or perspectives.

As you start to review sources for use in your own research, you will need to approach them just as critically. To do so, it is important to have an idea of what makes sources trustworthy.

Trustworthy Research Is Selective

Every research study is *selective*, in the sense that researchers must focus their study on a limited number of questions. As a result, researchers tend to specialize and coordinate their work. For example, because the problem of Honeybee Colony Collapse Disorder is so complex, there are several overlapping communities of researchers trying to solve it. Some teams of researchers are trying to isolate an environmental cause of CCD. Others are looking at causes in biological pathogens. Still others are trying to improve methods for gathering and analyzing relevant data. Yet even others are looking to the past to find analogous events that might help us see the problem in a more familiar light. Each of these teams comprises experts with different skills and knowledge, bringing different methods of generating and interpreting data to the work of solving the problem of CCD. Without specialization and focused studies of constituent elements of the problem, key aspects of the problem would go unstudied.

Trustworthy Research Tends to Be Peer-Reviewed

With specialization, however, comes the prospect of conflicting results. For example, one study may show that eating beef has health benefits for humans, while another study shows that eating beef is detrimental to our health in some way. For consumers looking for guidance, this apparent contradiction can be frustrating because they presume that one study must be right and the other wrong. Someone must have gotten the facts wrong. However, researchers know that each research study develops different research questions, studies different populations of people or different types of beef, or conducts research in a different manner. So results may vary even when a study's facts and fact handling are correct. In the future, results and the conclusions drawn from them may vary as more data are gathered, alternative perspectives or explanations are considered, and new ways of framing questions are developed. That is why researchers' work is subject to review by other experts in their field. *Peer review* certifies that the research has been carried out carefully and systematically and that interpretations and conclusions are reasonably drawn. This constant, critical peer review process is one reason research is so reliable, and such a powerful tool for constructing knowledge.

Research Must Be Synthesized to Be Useful

Over time, as fields of study mature, researchers start the important work of synthesizing the current state of knowledge. In *synthesis*, researchers assemble the diverse work on different aspects of the problem and try to create a bigger, more useful picture of what the research community knows. But synthesis is more than simple summary. It is the critical interpretative act of making meaning out of information. This makes research useful. As we have seen in the CCD case, it often takes multiple strands of research to help us solve complex problems. In synthesis, researchers attempt to weave these strands together into a more comprehensive explanation for the purpose of resolving conflicts or contradictions, and exploring the implication of what has been learned. Much of the work you will do in research projects will be to synthesize the current state of knowledge in your field and explore its implications for an argument you wish to make.

Research as Conversation

This text focuses on a research process that begins with a systematic review of the literature produced by other researchers. In a *literature review* or *annotated bibliography*, your role is primarily to synthesize, assess, and interpret the existing research in order to increase clarity,

The goal of research is not to make a definitive final statement on a subject but to engage in discussion with existing research in order to pose new questions and further impel the dialogue.

reduce uncertainty, locate areas for further research or discussion, and possibly to make actionable recommendations. Ordinarily we think of "literature" as referring to the works of creative writers: poems, plays, stories, and novels. In research settings, "the literature" means the set of articles, books, reports, conference presentations, and other publications that contain the current state of knowledge. "Reviewing the literature" means finding and reading those publications to see what is known, what questions and issues are currently being discussed, and where you can make a contribution to the discussion.

Before we get started understanding the research process you will use in this text, it is important to make a subtle shift in the way you think about research. Most of us tend to think about research primarily in terms of *information* and what we *do* with it: We gather information, evaluate it, analyze it, summarize it. However, such a view of research tends to make student researchers passive conduits of information produced by others. Furthermore, it encourages them to see the presentation of information itself as their chief work in writing. In professional settings, researchers make progress by constantly exchanging and testing ideas and building on one another's work. In order for their work to be useful to others, researchers must do more than just deliver information. One point of research is to contribute to the collective work of problem solving. Researchers must demonstrate the relevance and utility of their ideas by showing how it relates to previous work, whether by adding nuance, altering conclusions, or provoking reconsideration of issues once thought settled. Throughout this text, you will be expected to take a more active role in research, one that approximates what researchers do. You will be asked to go beyond collecting and reporting facts, to formulate your own researched response to what researchers have written.

Research as an Evidence-Based Conversation Among People

In order to take a more active approach to research, it can be helpful to think of your purpose in research as joining the *conversation* of an established community of thinkers. Here is how philosopher, critic, and researcher Kenneth Burke (1973) describes what it is like to join the conversation of other thinkers:

> Imagine that you enter a parlor. You come late. When you arrive, others have long preceded you, and they are engaged in a heated discussion, a discussion too heated

for them to pause and tell you exactly what it is about. In fact, the discussion had already begun long before any of them got there, so that no one present is qualified to retrace for you all the steps that had gone before. You listen for a while, until you decide that you have caught the tenor of the argument; then you put in your oar. Someone answers; you answer him; another comes to your defense; another aligns himself against you, to either the embarrassment or gratification of your opponent, depending upon the quality of your ally's assistance. However, the discussion is interminable. The hour grows late, you must depart. And you do depart, with the discussion still vigorously in progress. (pp. 110–111)

Part of what is so compelling about this passage is the way that it captures the persistent exchange of ideas and positions that is characteristic of research. It also suggests that in order to join the conversation, it is *your* responsibility to figure out *for yourself* what others are saying, why they are saying it, and what importance it has for you.

Research Articles Make Contributions to a Conversation

One implication of seeing research as a conversation that preexists you, and that will continue on after you, is that you must approach a piece of researched writing with a seeing eye toward understanding what *work* that piece of writing is doing in the conversation. Instead of an article standing on its own and simply reporting information, you must make an effort to see how an article fulfills a researcher's intent to make some specific contribution to the conversation: to support another's view, to resolve an open question, to add a new dimension to the problem, to correct an error or misinterpretation, or to argue that the conversation itself is based on faulty assumptions.

Another implication of this conversational view of research is that it relieves you of the pressure and responsibility of having the final word, or to base your response on original findings of your own. Your goal is simply to use other researchers' data and ideas to make a useful contribution to the conversation, to "push it forward, to say something new, something that seems to call for further talk and writing," as Duke University writing professor Joseph Harris puts it (2006, pp. 35–36). You bring your critical thinking skills, the interpretive act of synthesis, your ability to see implications, and your own considered perspective to the conversation of research.

This idea that the purpose of research and the writing based on research is to join in and contribute to a preexisting conversation will shape your research process. Instead of looking for pieces of information that support your view, you will be looking for communities of researchers actively engaged in conversation with one another. In Burke's language, you will conduct research to "listen" in on their conversation, and then "put your oar in" to respond to some researchers in order to contribute to some specific branch of the conversation.

If the Idea of Research Sounds Scary to You, Read On

Many people approach academic research apprehensively or fearfully, thinking that it is complex, difficult, and fraught with danger. If you are one of these people, remember that you do not bear the burden of producing a "Eureka!" discovery in your research. Your job is to notice something unusual or interesting about your topic and contribute to the conversation others are having using reason, evidence drawn from other researchers' work, and your own careful, judicious thinking.

Even though we might not be aware of them, many of us hold anxiety-producing beliefs about research. Many of those beliefs are not founded on fact or experience. And what is worse, many of them work to our disadvantage when we actually try to do academic research. In this section of the chapter, we will debunk some of the more common myths about research, and encourage you to see yourself as well prepared to start and complete your project.

Myth 1: Research is too time-consuming to be done in a first-year writing course.

It is true that some research projects take a long time to develop and complete. But we can design many worthwhile research projects to be completed in a short time. The key to designing a short research project is to define the focus of your research narrowly enough to allow it to be completed in the time allotted, while at the same time doing justice to the topic. Other chapters will help you go through a process of project definition that will enable you to locate a small area of interest to you, and learn enough about it to ask a small set of answerable questions.

Myth 2: I have to have extensive knowledge of a subject to do research.

Actually all you need is the desire to know more about a subject. Using exploratory research techniques, you will quickly learn enough to know what questions need answers. After that, it only takes curiosity, persistence, and a few relatively simple search and reading strategies to pursue the answer.

Myth 3: The experts who conduct research and write research articles are beyond criticism, so what can a newcomer to the field possibly think or write about their findings?

Because most of us think that research is done by experts with advanced degrees and using sophisticated techniques, most of us are reluctant to consider that published professional research might by unreliable, or even simply wrong. But since professional researchers are working to solve complex problems—like Honeybee Colony Collapse Disorder—even experts make mistakes, draw conclusions that their evidence does not support, or produce findings that conflict with other studies. Researchers

While research may seem daunting, as a student researcher, you have plenty of knowledge and experience that will enable you to pose questions and enter the conversation surrounding many topics.

working at all levels—from professional to student—expect their work to be subject to scrutiny. For many topics, student researchers have more than enough knowledge, experience, and perspective to pose questions, extend thoughts, and otherwise respond to the works of professional researchers.

Myth 4: Research always produces big insights and new knowledge.

The vast majority of research being done is small scale. Most researchers aim to add small insights or nuances to existing knowledge. One form of really useful research—synthesis—looks at other researchers' findings and combines them in innovative ways to produce new insights. Other forms of research aim to improve clarity, reduce uncertainty, or justify positions or beliefs. Still others seek to find other uses for ideas or processes, or to reevaluate an issue from a new perspective. For college purposes, research can be what writing specialist Ken Macrorie (1988) calls "I-search," a search for *ideas, insights,* and *information* that enables you to create knowledge and perspectives that are new to you.

Myth 5: Research is super-systematic and analytical; logical, linear thinkers are better at it than intuitive or "messy" thinkers.

It is true that once researchers have a clear idea of the questions they are asking and the data they need, they tend to work systematically, analytically, and in a disciplined manner. However, in order to arrive at those questions, and in order to understand the implications of their findings, researchers must think creatively and be open to new perspectives. Researchers depend as much on associative thinking, serendipity, and other forms of messy-but-productive creative thinking as they do on rigorous systematic thinking.

Myth 6: Research has to be totally fact based and objective; there is no room in my project for my ideas or values.

While researchers do tend to privilege reason over emotion, and try to ensure that their strictly personal beliefs do not unduly influence their work, most of the potential research topics you will encounter will be researchable from a wide range of perspectives. You will need to be open-minded in your research to prevent yourself from introducing bias, but your ideas and values will influence your choice of topic, the set of questions you pursue, your selection of evidence, and your response to the ideas and findings of other researchers.

If you can put these myths aside and embrace the truth about academic research, you can be more confident in your ability to start and complete a research project. Remember Joseph Harris's advice:

> The goal of [academic] writing is not to have the final word on a subject, to bring the discussion to a close, but to push it forward, to say something new, something that seems to call for further talk and writing. . . . A dialogue is not a debate. You don't win a conversation, you add to it, push it ahead, keep it going, "put your oar in," and maybe even sometimes redirect or divert the flow of talk. (2006, pp. 35–36)

When you think of conducting research to join a preexisting conversation, you realize that you are not alone. Other researchers have gone before you and have shared the paths they followed. They have dropped "breadcrumbs" along the way, in the form of sources and ideas for you to follow. As you pick up these breadcrumbs and examine them, you will encounter many surprises and learn something fascinating about yourself and about your world.

At times, making your way through a thick forest of ideas without getting lost, or sidetracked, can be challenging. It can also be frustrating when you struggle to find the right direction or learn you are on a dead-end trail. However, you have your instructor and many other resources—including this text—to help you find your way and show you how to forge ahead again.

IN-CLASS ACTIVITY 1H:
WARMING UP FOR RESEARCH WRITING CONVERSATION

Research writing asks you to respond to someone else's argument. You actually do so every day. For example, when you and your peers discuss a television series, a friend might say, "*Game of Thrones* varies so much from the actual books that it should not bear the same name*," and you might respond, "While admittedly, some plot elements of the series do move away from the original novels, I think the television series remains true to all of the characters." You have made a *counterargument*; you have *talked back with your own contribution*. Research writing merely replicates this same process in a longer format, engaging with several researched arguments on the same topic all at once. Such arguments might do any or all of the following:

- Correct or contradict a position
- Add to a position
- Complicate a position
- Qualify a position
- Agree with a position

PART 1: Changing the One-Sided Dialogue

1. Work <u>individually</u> to complete the following one-sided arguments, which lack a response, by adding your own response.

ARGUMENT/STATEMENT	TYPE OF RESPONSE REQUIRED	YOUR RESPONSE	SIGNAL PHRASE USED
<u>Example:</u> Doctors, in conjunction with the pharmaceutical companies, have caused the opioid epidemic in the United States.	Complicate a position	Yet, I note that doctors and pharmaceutical companies alone cannot account for the problem; they do, after all, try to ease patients' pain. The patients, however, keep requesting that relief.	"Yet, I note" and "however"
Graffiti is not art; it is defacement of privately owned or public property.	Correct or contradict a position		
Standardized testing does little to improve education; it primarily teaches teachers to teach to a test and wastes students' time with testing instead of learning.	Agree with a position OR Qualify a position		

2. Now meet with two to four others to compare and discuss your responses. What different kinds of signal phrases get used for different types of arguments? List them here.

PART 2: Hearing Multiple Responses

1. <u>Individually</u> fill in columns B and C first.
2. Then swap papers three times, and allow your peers to fill in column D ("What others say").

A ISSUE	B WHAT I SAY	C WHAT SOME EXPERTS I KNOW ABOUT SAY	D WHAT 3 OTHERS (MY PEERS) SAY
<u>Example:</u> Fast-food versus home-cooked meals	Home-cooked meals are much healthier than fast–food.	Fast-food offers a preponderance of fats, sugar, and salt, all of which harm our health.	A. Fast-food at places like Panera can offer very healthy food choices that are fresh and fat- and sugar-free B. People can cook a lot of fat-heavy and sugary foods at home too. C. The fast-food industry cares about profit only, so it serves foods full of the sugar, fat, and salt customers enjoy the taste of, so they will keep coming back.
Global Warming			
Self-Driving Cars			
YOUR CHOICE (Any topic that matters to you):			

3. When your paper comes back to you, read what your peers have added. Then write a sentence that argues with at least one other person's response to your claim. You might choose to use the following template, though you may choose to create your own.

While _____ claims that _____,

I contend this view _____

because _____ .

© Rawpixel.com/Shutterstock.com

F.   My Writing Mindset Reflective Letter Model

MODEL "MY WRITING MINDSET REFLECTIVE LETTER" ESSAY

62 Locust Avenue
Mount Kisco, New York 10514

February 6, 2019

Professor Thomas Suiter
SUNY Brockport
350 New Campus Drive
Brockport, New York 14420

Dear Professor Suiter:

I write to you today to share my reflections on my views of myself as writer. Before being asked to write about this topic, I guess I never really thought too much about this part of myself. I suppose I always thought of writing as just one expectation of many in the whole batch of schoolwork requirements, but now that you have forced me to do so, I have singled out that one area of focus and have thought seriously about it. This letter gives you a look at the result of that thinking.

Like many others' assumptions, my thinking about myself has been shaped somewhat by the labels others have given me. For a really long time, I have thought of myself as a good athlete and a mediocre student, especially in writing. Teachers have often told me that I am "too concise," that I "need to expand" my ideas. I have always been interested in just getting the writing done and fulfilling the assignment enough not to fail but to pass with a C. I did not really enjoy writing, but I did not hate it, either. It was just something I had to do, like brushing my teeth or keeping my room clean. And I admit: I never worked very hard at it because I did not actually think I would improve it much. I guess I kind of felt that expending extra effort would not really make much of a difference because I was just a so-so writer, no matter what. Partly, I was just lazy, but partly too I guess I was stuck in what Carol S. Dweck calls "fixed mindset," because I believed, as she says, that my "basic qualities, like [my] intelligence or talent, are simply fixed traits" and that "talent alone creates success." I knew I had talent in athletics, so I worked hard on those skills, whereas I did not think I had talent in writing (or anything else academic), so I did not put too much effort into those assignments. I have pretty much kept these attitudes all the way through school. I kept earning C's, a fact that pretty much cemented the idea in my head that I was just and always would be a C student.

I see now that I have kind of kept myself in a self-perpetuating cycle; because I thought of myself as a C student and writer, I kept performing that way. When I think of what we read by Anne Lamott, I realize I have only ever written what she labels "the shitty first draft," the one in which I "let it all pour out and then let it romp all over the place." Revising several times was never a part of my writing process. Actually, I had no process; I just wrote once and was done. Oh, I always fixed grammar and spelling and made everything look good, but I understand now that I was not really improving the writing much. My reading of Lamott's essay helped me to see that point very clearly.

In addition, when I read Howard Gardner's ideas about multiple intelligences, I discovered that just because one of my strongest abilities is in what he calls "body intelligence," I do not have to believe I have only that one ability. I can actually use what that intelligence gives me and apply it to my writing or really to all of my academics. I would never go a single day without working out my body, so why do I not do the same with my mind?

Now I understand that my mind can grow as much as my muscles, if only I work it out with effort and determination and a belief that I can improve. I came to college and to this writing class thinking I would just keep being a C student, enough to get me into a four-year transfer college where I could get a scholarship to play soccer. Now, however, I am determined to be better than just a C-level student and writer because I believe hard work can actually have an impact. My former teachers were right. I needed to expand, but not just my essay; I needed to expand my whole way of thinking about how to be a successful writer and student.

With gratitude for the new attitude,

Eric Saunders

Eric Saunders

G. Readings on Mindset, Grit, and Intelligence

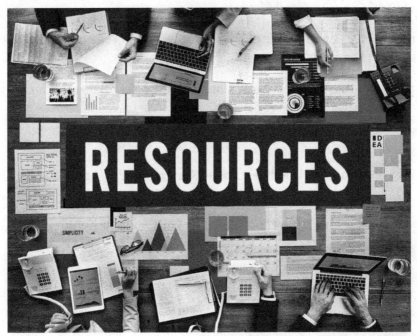

© Rawpixel.com/Shutterstock.com

Read the pages below, from psychologist Carol Dweck's website. These pages will introduce the "mindset" concept.

- "What is Mindset?":

    https://www.mindsetworks.com/science/

    **Be sure to click on the link at the bottom of each section, so you get the full reading.

- "How Does Mindset Affect Success?":

    https://www.mindsetworks.com/science/Impact

- "Test Your Mindset":

    http://blog.mindsetworks.com/what-s-my-mindset?view=quiz

- "Fixed Mindset vs. Growth Mindset: What Characteristics Are Critical to Success?" by S. J. Scott from *Develop Good Habits A Better Life One Habit at a Time*, April 24, 2019:

    https://www.developgoodhabits.com/fixed-mindset-vs-growth-mindset/

- Watch Angela Duckworth's "The Key to Success? Grit":

    http://www.ted.com/talks/angela_lee_duckworth_the_key_to_success_grit?language=en

Duckworth, Angela Lee. "The Key to Success? Grit." *TED Talk Education*. April 2013. Web. 2 January 2015.

- "5 Ways to Develop a Growth Mindset Using Grit and Resilience" by Birgit Ohlin, April 28, 2018, from *Positive Psychology Program:*

    https://positivepsychologyprogram.com/5-ways-develop-grit-resilience/

- "Blue-Collar Brilliance" by Mike Rose, June 1, 2009, *The American Scholar:*

    https://theamericanscholar.org/blue-collar-brilliance/#.XDNbjfx7lN0

- "'Find your passion'? That's bad advice, scientists say" by Tara Bahrampour, July 23, 2018, *Washington Post:*

    https://www.washingtonpost.com/news/inspired-life/wp/2018/07/23/find-your-passion-thats-bad-advice-scientists-say/?noredirect=on&utm_term=.65180

- "Gardner's Theory of Multiple Intelligences" by Kendra Cherry, April 3, 2019, *VERYWELL Mind:*

    https://www.verywellmind.com/gardners-theory-of-multiple-intelligences-2795161

- "Shitty First Drafts" by Ann Lamott presented by University of Kentucky on August 6, 2012 at:

    https://wrd.as.uky.edu/sites/default/files/1-Shitty%20First%20Drafts.pdf

◇◇

ON TRANSITIONS

Just as many writers forget to use topic sentences, so do many writers forget transitions. They forget to put up road signs to show the reader where they're headed. They forget to make the project user-friendly.

There are two kinds of transitions which every writer must pay attention.

- Common transition words and phrases
- Repeated key words and phrases

Common Transition Words and Phrases

The first kind is the familiar word or phrase we plug in between sentences and paragraphs to hook one idea to another:

TRANSITION	TRANSITION	TRANSITION	TRANSITION
Idea A [however]	Idea B [on the other hand]	Idea C [nevertheless]	Idea D [also]

Common transitions fall by function into twelve categories:

To show addition	To show assent	To show contrast
To show details	To show emphasis	To show end
To show examples	To show place	To show purpose
To show results	To show similarity	To show time

When you write a paragraph, try to add as many transitions from the twelve categories as you can, sentence to sentence. You won't need a common transition for every sentence, but for the majority, use these transitions.

Repeated Key Words and Phrases

For the second kind of transition, instead of using familiar transitions like "however" or "on the other hand," here you hook one idea to another by repeating a word or phrase from one sentence to the next.

The repeated word or phrase creates a smooth, neat, unbroken chain of logic that takes the reader from the first sentence of the Introduction to the last sentence of the Conclusion. Two fool-proof strategies will let a writer create this smooth chain:

- Repeat a word or phrase from sentence to sentence.
- Read out loud to make sure you hear words or phrases repeated.

Repeat a Word or Phrase from Sentence to Sentence

Sentence 1	Sentence 2	Sentence 3	Sentence 4
Word A =	Word A		
	Word B =	Word B	
		Word C =	Word C

You don't have to be rigid in the repetitions. For example, you can skip from Sentence to 1 to 3, or use a variation of a word, like love to loving. The possibilities are up to you.

COMMON TRANSITION WORDS AND PHRASES

TO SHOW ADDITION	TO SHOW ASSENT	TO SHOW CONTRAST
again	after all	but/or/nor
also	at any rate	by contrast
and	at least	however
besides	clearly	in contrast
equally important	nevertheless	in spite of this
finally	of course	instead
first, second, etc.	yet	nevertheless
further		notwithstanding
furthermore		on the contrary
just as important		on the one/other hand
moreover		rather
too		still
		whereas

TO SHOW DETAILS	TO SHOW EMPHASIS	TO SHOW END
especially	above all	at last
in particular	certainly	finally
namely	in fact	in conclusion
specifically	in short	in short
that is	in truth	in summary
to enumerate	indeed	on the whole
	most important	overall
	obviously	to sum up
	of course	to summarize
	really	
	surely	

TO SHOW EXAMPLES	TO SHOW PLACE	TO SHOW PURPOSE
for example	beyond	for this/that purpose
for instance	nearby	to do this/that
further	opposite	to this/that end
furthermore	there	with this/that in mind
in addition	to the left	with this/that in view
in the first/second place	to the right	
to illustrate		

TO SHOW RESULTS	TO SHOW SIMILARITY	TO SHOW TIME
accordingly	by the same token	after a while
as a result	equally important	afterward(s)
for that reason	in the same manner	at present
for this reason	in the same way	at the same time
hence	like	directly
otherwise	likewise	during
therefore	similarly	earlier
thus	too	for some time
		in the meantime
		later
		meanwhile
		next
		presently
		recently
		simultaneously
		soon
		then

Observe how the word-and-phrase strategy works in the following:

(1) In Charles Dickens' **Great Expectations**, *after moving to snob-conscious London,* **Pip** *learns painful lessons about* **love** *from* **his** *benefactor* **Magwitch** *that teach him to reconnect with the selfless values of* **his** *rural past. (2) First,* **he** *realizes how shamefully* **he** *has treated* **Magwitch**, *an escaped convict who out of* **love** *makes possible* **Pip's** *dream of becoming a gentleman with "*great expectations." *(3) Second,* **he** *comes to regret being embarrassed by* **his** *poorly educated but* **loving** *brother-in-law, Joe Gargery. (4) Third, he discovers that* **his love** *for* **Estella**, *who belongs to a higher social class, has been a self-serving "reaching for a* **star**."

Chain of repetitions:

Great Expectations *(Sentence 1) goes to "great expectations" (2). Pip (1) goes to Pip's (2). Love (1) goes to love (2) to loving (3) to love (4). Magwitch (1) goes to Magwitch (2). His (1) goes to his (1) to his (3) to his (4). He (2) goes to he (2) to he (3) to he (4). Estella (4) goes to star (4).*

And notice that the first kind of transition, the common word or phrase, shows up in sentences 2, 3, and 4: *First, Second, Third.*

Combined, the two kinds of transitions can hook together any project, providing airtight seams between words, sentences, and paragraphs. For example, you can link Paragraph One to Paragraph Two with either kind of transition:

Common Transition Words and Phrases

Pip discovers that his love for Estella, who belongs to a higher social class, has been a self-serving "reaching for a star."

However, by the final pages of the novel, Dickens seems to contradict …

Repeated Key Words and Phrases

Pip <u>*discovers*</u> *that his love for Estella, who belongs to a higher social class, has been a self-serving "reaching for a star."*

This <u>*discovery*</u> …

Read Out Loud to Make Sure You Hear Words or Phrases Repeated

For many reasons, you should always read what you write out loud. One key reason is to check to hear if the repetitions flow from sentence to sentence, paragraph to paragraph. Good prose sounds like good music—an artful repetition of notes and rhythms. Repeating words will not only hook one sentence to the next, one paragraph to the next; it will also create a repeated rhythm that will unify the whole, leading the reader forward through sound as well as sense.

Use Transitions Like an Expert

Professional writers use transitions in sentence after sentence, paragraph after paragraph. Take any magazine column and highlight the transitions. You may be surprised at the number you'll find.

From "This American Life," by David Remnick (*The New Yorker*, April 25, 2011), on "the making and remaking of Malcolm X":

> *For **nearly twenty years**, Manning Marable, a historian at Columbia, labored on what he hoped would be a definitive scholarly work on Malcolm X. **During this period**, Marable struggled with sarcoidosis, a pulmonary disease, **and** even underwent a double lung transplant. **Recently**, he completed his rigorous and evenhanded biography, Malcolm X: A Life of Reinvention (Viking; $30), **but**, in an echo of his subject's fate, died on the eve of publication. One of his goals was to grapple with Malcolm's autobiography, **and** although he finds much to admire about Malcolm, he makes it clear that the book's drama sometimes comes at the expense of fact.*

From *The Less-Is-More Handbook: A Guide To College Writing, Second Edition* by Larry Edgerton. Copyright © 2017 by Kendall Hunt Publishing Company. Reprinted by permission.

◇◇◇◇◇◇◇◇◇◇◇◇◇◇◇◇◇◇◇◇◇◇◇◇◇◇◇◇◇◇◇◇◇◇◇◇◇◇

H. Grammar Concept: Sentence Structure: Patterns, Combinations, Dangling and Misplaced Modifiers, and Parallelism

You will learn grammar best by applying it within the context of your own writing. Use these rules as a guide. Your teacher will probably help you to target examples from your own writing and your peers' writing to help clarify how these rules work.

◇◇◇◇◇◇◇◇◇◇◇◇◇◇◇◇◇◇◇◇◇◇◇◇◇◇◇◇◇◇◇◇◇◇◇◇◇◇

All Those Rules versus the Four Basic Sentences

If you're like most writers, editing your punctuation can seem pretty intimidating. Where do you start? Every sentence looks different. And what about all those rules? Comma rules are a particular hassle because there are so many. And what's the function of those mysterious punctuation marks—the semicolon, colon, dash, and apostrophe?

Editing punctuation can be an easy job if you approach it from the Big Picture. Instead of coming to every sentence as though it's unique, choosing a punctuation mark because "it sounds right," learn the Big Picture patterns that underlie *all* sentences. Once you learn Four Basic Sentence types, you can apply them to any possible sentence. No sentence is unique. You thus need to memorize the Four Basic Sentences.

Let's begin with the simple sentence. Most writers never have a problem punctuating the simple sentence when it requires just a *final* punctuation mark— an *external* punctuation mark.

- I drove Sandy to soccer practice.
- Will you drive Sandy to soccer practice?
- Please drive Sandy to soccer practice!

The problem comes when we need—or think we need—something in the middle of the sentence, or what is called "*internal* punctuation."

WRONG: I drove Sandy, to soccer practice.

WRONG: Will you please drive Sandy; to soccer practice?

WRONG: Please drive Sandy to: soccer practice!

Along with the apostrophe, internal punctuation causes most of our punctuation problems. Internal punctuation includes the comma, semicolon, colon, dash, parentheses, and brackets.

And that long list probably looks like you have to learn a bunch of rules . . .

But you don't.

The Trick to Mastering Punctuation

There's a trick to mastering punctuation, and especially basic comma rules. If you take all sentences that need internal punctuation and boil them down—reduce them to basic building blocks—you'll end up with just *four* basic sentence types.

So here's the trick: The easy way to master punctuation is to learn what punctuation all four sentence types require. If you do that, then you won't have to check the rules for every sentence you write. You'll know what to do because all sentences, other than the simple ones above, will *always* fall into one of these four types, no matter their infinite number of variations.

All four have a common denominator: *They have two parts* that variously combine the fragment and the sentence. Because all four sentences have two parts, they also share a second common denominator: *internal punctuation*, which is used to separate the two parts. You won't always need internal punctuation with the four sentence types, but when you do, to punctuate properly, you have to be able to tell a fragment from a sentence.

The Fragment

The fragment is a *fragment*—that is, a *part*—of a sentence. By definition, a fragment *doesn't make sense by itself*. To make sense, a <u>fragment</u> needs more information to complete it. That "more information" comes in a short sentence that's part of a bigger sentence, the one that ends with the final period.

Fragment + **Short sentence** = *Bigger Sentence.*

- <u>Because Andrea was sick</u>, **I stayed home.**
- <u>If you come to our place tonight</u>, **we will cook you dinner**.
- <u>After Frank leaves the house</u>, **his dog begins to bark**.

Note that, for each fragment, you can ask a "more information, please" question that the short sentence answers.

- What happened because Andrea was sick? (I stayed home.)
- What will happen if you come to our place tonight? (We will cook you dinner.)
- What happens after Frank leaves the house? (His dog begins to bark.)

Sometimes fragments are exactly what a writer needs, especially fiction writers who use the fragment for a special effect. But academic writers, who try to present their ideas free of distraction, avoid the fragment when it's not user-friendly. A fragment can distract the reader from the flow; he has to pause to figure things out. Look at the next example. Does the <u>fragment</u> belong to the sentence on the left or to the sentence on the right?

- **I tried to get off work.** <u>Because I wanted to go to the concert.</u> **I was upset that my boss said I couldn't leave.**

You can't tell. Writing teachers frown on fragments like this. The reader jerks to a stop. What is the writer trying to say? That ambiguity is one reason why academic writing avoids fragments.

The Dependent Clause

There are two kinds of fragments—the kind that has a <u>subject</u> and a verb and the kind that doesn't. The kind that does is called a *dependent clause*. (It *depends* on more information to make sense; by itself, a dependent clause doesn't make sense because it's a fragment of a complete thought, that is, of a sentence.)

Fragments with a <u>Subject</u> and Verb = Dependent Clauses

- because <u>Andrea</u> **was** sick (what? more information, please)
- if <u>you</u> **come** to our place tonight (what? more information, please)
- after <u>Frank</u> **leaves** the house (what? more information, please)

The Phrase

The kind of fragment that doesn't have a subject and a verb is called a *phrase*. A prepositional phrase is one example of a phrase. (Prepositions are those little words that glue sentence parts together: *in, at, for, by, up, down, with, through, over, out,* etc.). Other kinds of phrases include the infinitive phrase and the participial phrase.

Fragments without a Subject and Verb = Phrases

- **in** the first fifty days
- **at** the last hearing
- **for** each woman

By itself, like the dependent clause, the phrase doesn't make sense. And like the dependent clause, the phrase is a <u>fragment</u>—a fragment of a sentence. To make sense, a phrase needs more information to complete the thought. (Again, that "more information" comes in a short sentence that's part of a bigger sentence, the one that ends with the final period.)

<u>*Fragment*</u> + *Short sentence* = *Bigger Sentence.*

- <u>In the first fifty days</u>, **the new administration accomplished a great deal**.
- <u>At the last hearing</u>, **our witness testified quite effectively**.
- <u>For each woman</u>, **beating her team's archrival was more than just a victory**.

The Sentence (The Independent Clause)

Like a dependent clause, an independent clause has both a <u>subject</u> and a verb. But unlike the dependent clause and the phrase, the independent clause *makes sense by itself*. It doesn't need more words to complete the thought. That's why it's called an *independent clause*. (Independently, by itself, the sentence offers a complete thought. It doesn't depend on other words because it stands on its own.)

Sentences = Independent Clauses.

- Because Andrea was sick, <u>I</u> **stayed** home.
- If you come to our place tonight, <u>we</u> **will cook** you dinner.
- After Frank leaves the house, his <u>dog</u> **begins** to bark.

PUNCTUATION TIP

Sentences belong to a context. Every sentence must somehow connect to the sentence it follows and the sentence it precedes; all together, those sentences belong to a bigger context, which may be the argument you're making in a paragraph. Nevertheless, if you pull a sentence out of its context, no matter how obscure or odd it may sound, it's still a sentence because it's a complete thought.

To test whether you have a fragment or a sentence, read the words out loud. The sentence doesn't automatically require more words to complete it. It's independent. But the fragment does—because it's a fragment of a thought. Now read the following sentences and fragments out loud.

- Go down to the cellar. (*sentence = complete thought*)
- before you go down to the cellar (*dependent clause fragment = incomplete thought*)
- Nobody knew anything. (*sentence = complete thought*)
- because nobody knew anything (*dependent clause fragment = incomplete thought*)
- In the beginning, the seas enveloped the planet. (*sentence = complete thought*)
- in the beginning (*phrase fragment = incomplete thought*)

This test isn't foolproof, but if you read a sentence out loud, it tends to sound finished, complete, whereas a fragment sounds unfinished, left hanging: *Before you go down to the cellar—(?)*

The Four Basic Sentences

Each of the four basic sentence types has two parts. Three of the four combine a fragment (F) and a sentence (S). The fourth combines a sentence (S) and a sentence (S).

The fragment can be either a dependent clause ("because Andrea was sick") or a phrase ("in the first fifty days").

1. Basic Sentence FS = a fragment *plus* a sentence (= *a bigger sentence*)
2. Basic Sentence SF = a sentence *plus* a fragment (= *a bigger sentence*)
3. Basic Sentence S͡FS = a fragment *inside* a sentence (= *a bigger sentence*)

4. Basic Sentence SS = a sentence *plus* another sentence (= *a bigger sentence*)

(The loop above the third type, S͡FS , indicates that you have one sentence cut in half, not two sentences; only the fourth type, SS, has two sentences.)

These four sentences break into eight patterns. Each pattern is punctuated differently.

1. *Basic Sentence FS* Pattern 1 (F,S)	**2.** *Basic Sentence SF* Pattern 2 (SF) Pattern 3 (S,F)
3. *Basic Sentence* S͡FS Pattern 4 (S͡FS) Pattern 5 (S,F͡,S)	**4.** *Basic Sentence SS* Pattern 6 (S, CONJ S) Pattern 7 (S./; S) Pattern 8 (S./; TRANS, S)

1. Basic Sentence FS

Pattern 1 (F,S)

After <u>an introductory fragment</u>, use the comma.

- <u>Because Andrea was sick</u>, I stayed home. (*fragment = dependent clause*)
- <u>In the first fifty days</u>, the new administration accomplished a great deal. (*fragment = phrase*)

PUNCTUATION TIP

When the introductory fragment is no more than three or four short words, some writers and publications leave out the comma. This is a matter of style and preference. To be safe (and correct), you can always use the comma. Using the comma will give your writing clarity and consistency.

---

2. Basic Sentence SF

Pattern 2 (SF)

Don't use the comma before an <u>essential fragment</u>. ("Essential" means that you *can't* get rid of the fragment. It's needed to provide essential information about the rest of the sentence. Without that information, the reader is left hanging: *Why?*)

- **I had to book my hotel online** <u>because I was trying to save money</u>. (*Why* did you have to book your hotel online? The essential fragment gives the reason. *fragment = dependent clause*)
- **I had to book my hotel online** <u>to save money</u>. (*Why* did you have to book your hotel online? The essential fragment gives the reason. *fragment = infinitive phrase*)

Pattern 3 (S,F)

Use the comma before a <u>nonessential fragment</u>. ("Nonessential" means that you *can* get rid of the fragment. It provides nonessential information about the rest of the sentence.)

- **I called my brother**, <u>although I had a lot to do at work</u>. (The sentence doesn't need the nonessential information provided by the fragment. The information is perhaps interesting but in no way essential to explain *why* you called your brother. *fragment = dependent clause*)
- I called my brother. (The sentence is a complete thought that doesn't require more information to complete it.)
- **I called my brother**, <u>with real regret</u>. (*fragment = prepositional phrase*)
- **I called my brother**, <u>to speak of real regret</u>. (*fragment = infinitive phrase*)
- **I called my brother**, <u>having real regret</u>. (*fragment = participial phrase*)
- I called my brother. (The sentence doesn't need nonessential information provided by the fragments.)

   It helps to know the words that start essential and nonessential fragments. Some words start only essential fragments, and some start only nonessential, but some can start both (depending on context).

ESSENTIAL	NONESSENTIAL	BOTH
as . . . as	all of which	after
for	although	as
so . . . that	even though	as if
than	no matter how/what/why	as though
that	none of which/whom	at/by/for/in which
until	some of which/whom	because
	whereas	before
	which	if
		in order that
		unless
		what
		when
		where
		while
		who
		whom
		whose

ALWAYS ESSENTIAL: The girl danced as dramatically as she always had.

ALWAYS NONESSENTIAL: The noisy Cub Scouts sang loudly, which annoyed their scoutmaster.

BOTH: I saw the man who was training for the Olympics. (essential) I saw Kenyon, who was training for the Olympics. (nonessential)

3. Basic Sentence S͡FS

Pattern 4 (S͡FS)

Don't use commas for an <u>essential fragment</u> inside a sentence. (The fragment identifies the subject and thus is essential.)

- **The man** <u>who sells fish</u> **also sells aquariums**.

  (The essential fragment identifies *which* man also sells aquariums–the man <u>who sells fish</u>. Leaving out the fragment will cause confusion: *Which* man do you mean? *fragment = dependent clause*)

- **The woman** <u>wearing the red shirt</u> **also sells aquariums**.

  (The essential fragment identifies *which* woman also sells aquariums–the woman <u>wearing the red shirt</u>. Leaving out the fragment will cause confusion: *Which* woman do you mean? *fragment = participial phrase*)

- **My brother** <u>Bob</u> **also sells aquariums**.

  (The essential fragment identifies *which* brother also sells aquariums. Here we can assume you have more than one brother and need the fragment to distinguish your brother Bob from your brother Tom and your brother Bill. Leaving out the necessary fragment will cause confusion: *Which* brother do you mean? *fragment = appositive, a word or phrase renaming a noun*)

Pattern 5 (S,F,S)

Use commas for a <u>nonessential fragment</u> inside a sentence. (The fragment isn't needed since the subject is already identified.)

- **Mr. Mason**, <u>who sells fish</u>, **also sells aquariums**.

  (The nonessential fragment isn't needed to identify the subject. He's already identified by name: Mr. Mason. Leaving out the fragment won't cause confusion. *fragment = dependent clause*)

- **Frieda Wilson**, <u>wearing the red shirt</u>, **also sells aquariums**.

  (The nonessential fragment isn't needed to identify the subject. She's already identified by name: Frieda Wilson. Leaving out the fragment won't cause confusion. *fragment = participial phrase*)

- **My brother**, <u>Bob</u>, **also sells aquariums**.

  (The nonessential fragment isn't needed to identify the subject. Here we will assume you have only one brother. The fragment isn't needed to distinguish one brother from another since you have only one. *fragment = appositive*)

- **My brother**, <u>however</u>, **also sells aquariums**.

- **My brother**, <u>on the other hand</u>, **also sells aquariums**.

  (The nonessential fragments interrupt the "flow" of each sentence. Like many interrupting transitions, *however* and *on the other hand* can be left out without causing confusion. *fragment = transition, a word or phrase used to connect one part to another*)

4. Basic Sentence SS

Pattern 6 (S, CONJ S)

Use the comma BEFORE the coordinating conjunctions for, and, nor, but, or, yet, so (the FANBOYS) to separate two <u>sentences</u>.

- I <u>went to the store</u>, **for** <u>I needed some bread</u>.
- <u>Bob went to the store</u>, **and** <u>he bought some bread</u>.
- <u>The girl went to the store</u>, **yet** <u>she forgot to buy some bread</u>.

Pattern 7 (S./;S)

Use the period to separate two unrelated <u>sentences</u>; use the period or semicolon to separate two related <u>sentences</u>.

- <u>Marilyn Monroe was a famous movie blonde "bombshell." George W. Bush moved to Texas.</u> (*unrelated sentences = period*)
- <u>Marilyn Monroe was a famous movie blonde "bombshell." The movies' first blonde bombshell was Jean Harlow.</u> (*related sentences = period or semicolon*)
- <u>Marilyn Monroe was a famous movie blonde "bombshell"; the movies' first blonde bombshell was Jean Harlow.</u> (*related sentences = period or semicolon*)

Pattern 8 (S./; TRANS, S)

Use the period or semicolon to separate two related sentences linked with a transition; use the comma after the transition.*
    *Excluding one-syllable transitions: *hence, next, now, then, thus,* etc.

- <u>Marilyn Monroe was a famous movie blonde "bombshell."</u>
  However, <u>the movies' first blonde bombshell was Jean Harlow.</u>
- <u>Marilyn Monroe was a famous movie blonde "bombshell"</u>;
  however, <u>the movies' first blonde bombshell was Jean Harlow.</u>

The period and the semicolon have the same function—to separate sentences. Writers choose the semicolon over the period when they want to emphasize the relation that one sentence has with another.

How Can Just Eight Patterns Punctuate All Possible Sentences?

Easy answer: You can combine each pattern with every other pattern, using as many fragments or sentences as you want. *Any* sentence, as long as it's not just one big fragment, is fine to write as long as you punctuate it properly. If you follow the punctuation required for each pattern, there won't be a problem (though you may end up with some very lengthy, but perfectly punctuated, sentences).

We'll begin with the first pattern: F,S.

To that pattern, we'll add more fragments and sentences, so that we end up with one long (but perfectly punctuated) sentence.

Instead of the two minimum parts (either *a fragment plus a sentence* or *a sentence plus a sentence*), our big sentence will have four parts, each a sentence: $S + S + S + S = S$.

And each S will break into two or three parts:

$S \quad S \quad S \quad S \quad = \quad S.$

$FS + SFF + S + FSF$

PUNCTUATION TIP

It's fine to add parts to each pattern as long as each part is punctuated properly. In other words, you can have have FFFS as long as commas go in where they're supposed to: F,F,F,S.

To prove that long sentences are not run-ons when they're punctuated properly, we'll choose semicolons over periods to separate each sentence. The five fragments are <u>underlined</u>; the four sentences are highlighted.

Sentence 1   Sentence 2
[F,S] <u>After I left town</u>, I walked into the country; [S,FF] my dog went with me, <u>something she likes to do when I go hiking</u>;

Sentence 3   Sentence 4
[S] we kept a good pace; [F,SF] <u>though we stopped a couple of times to rest</u>, we managed to reach home <u>in time for dinner</u>.

PROPERLY PUNCTUATED WITH SEMICOLONS: After I left town, I walked into the country; my dog went with me, something she likes to do when I go hiking; we kept a good pace; though we stopped a couple of times to rest, we managed to reach home in time for dinner.

PROPERLY PUNCTUATED WITH PERIODS: After I left town, I walked into the country. My dog went with me, something she likes to do when I go hiking. We kept a good pace. Though we stopped a couple of times to rest, we managed to reach home in time for dinner.

IMPROPERLY PUNCTUATED WITH COMMAS: After I left town, I walked into the country, my dog went with me, something she likes to do when I go hiking, we kept a good pace, though we stopped a couple of times to rest, we managed to reach home in time for dinner. (*This improperly punctuated sentence is a run-on! Commas instead of semicolons or periods have created the problem.*)

Dangling Modifiers: Driving recklessly, my car went over the cliff.

Definition: A *modifier* is any word or phrase describing another word or phrase somewhere in a sentence. When a modifier *dangles*, it forgets to hook up logically to the word or phrase it's supposed to—that is, that it's supposed to modify (or describe).

> ## GRAMMAR TIP
>
> If a sentence begins with a fragment (usually followed by a comma), look for a dangling modifier.

You can spot a dangling modifier by any of the following signs:

- The fragment starts with a word that ends in *-ing* (*driving, making, using*, etc.)
- The fragment starts with a word that ends in a past tense (*driven, made, used*, etc.)
- The fragment starts with an infinitive: *to + verb* (*to drive, to make, to use*, etc.)
- The fragment starts with a clause word (*if, when, since, because, while*, etc.)

To fix a dangling modifier, give the sentence a subject that logically hooks up to the fragment. Put the subject in the <u>fragment</u> or right after the comma.

> WRONG: <u>Driving recklessly</u>, my car went over the cliff. (How can a car drive recklessly? The <u>fragment</u> needs a logical subject—somebody to drive the car.)
>
> RIGHT: <u>Because I was driving recklessly</u>, my car went over the cliff. (subject in fragment)
>
> ALSO RIGHT: <u>Driving recklessly</u>, I caused my car to go over the cliff. (subject after comma)
>
> WRONG: <u>Driven to alcohol by his problems</u>, vodka brought about his death.
>
> RIGHT: <u>Driven to alcohol by his problems</u>, Jack brought about his death through vodka.
>
> WRONG: <u>To be considered for this special offer</u>, the reply card should be sent.
>
> RIGHT: <u>To be considered for this special offer</u>, you should send the reply card.
>
> WRONG: <u>When at the age of six</u>, my parents moved to Texas.
>
> RIGHT: <u>When I was six</u>, my parents and I moved to Texas.

Misplaced Modifiers: I bought a used Harley from a Hell's Angel with a leak somewhere.

Definition: Like a dangling modifier, a *misplaced modifier* describes another word or phrase somewhere in a sentence. But unlike the dangling modifier, the misplaced modifier has a noun it refers to. The problem is that this modifier has been placed too far from the noun—sometimes with comic results. That's why it's *misplaced*.

> ## GRAMMAR TIP
>
> Place the misplaced modifier as close to its <u>noun</u> as possible.

> WRONG: I bought a used <u>Harley</u> from a Hell's Angel with a leak somewhere.
>
> RIGHT: I bought a used <u>Harley</u> with a leak somewhere from a Hell's Angel.
>
> WRONG: Sandy put the <u>sandwich</u> into the garbage that she had not yet eaten.
>
> RIGHT: Sandy put the <u>sandwich</u> that she had not yet eaten into the garbage.

Sentence Parts That Aren't Parallel: . . . and which?/ which . . . but which?

When coordinating conjunctions connect sentence parts, each item connected must look like every other item. If you connect apple + apple + orange, something has gone wrong.

```
GRAMMAR TIP
Find the key parallel word and use it to set up the rest of the parallel.
```

Key parallel word = running.

            apple   *apple*   *orange*

WRONG: He likes running, rowing, and <u>to swim</u> for exercise.

    running and rowing = **gerunds** (-*ing* verbs used as nouns) = *apples*

    <u>to swim</u> = **infinitive** (to + verb) = *orange*

    swimming = **gerund** = *apple*

To keep the parallel:

          apple   *apple*   *apple*

RIGHT: He likes running, rowing, and swimming for exercise.

           orange orange   *orange*

ALSO RIGHT: He likes <u>to run</u>, <u>to row</u>, and <u>to swim</u> for exercise.

(ALSO RIGHT: He likes to run, row, and swim for exercise.)

Key parallel words = to shape up

             apple   *orange*

WRONG: I was told either to shape up or <u>I would be shipping out</u>.

             apple   *apple*

RIGHT: I was told either to shape up or to ship out.

    to shape up = **infinitive** = *apple*

    <u>I would be shipping out</u> = sentence with **present participle** (<u>shipping out</u>) = *orange*

    to ship out = **infinitive** = *apple*

Key parallel word = important

             apple   *orange*

WRONG: Elections are important and a <u>tradition</u>.

            apple   *apple*

RIGHT: Elections are important and traditional.

    important = **adjective** = *apple*

    a <u>tradition</u> = **noun** = *orange*

    traditional = **adjective** = *apple*

> ## GRAMMAR TIP
>
> Using the **Find** command, search for *that, where, which, who, whom,* and *whose.* Now look for *and* or *but.* Does *and* or *but* precede one of these six words? If so, you may have a problem with parallel sentence parts.

Look for two clauses in a single sentence. Each has to start with *that, where, which, who, whom,* or *whose.* Between them will come *and* or *but.* If you can't find the first clause, fix it with one of the six clause words. The <u>first clause</u> must be parallel with the <u>second clause</u>.

which . . . but which

NOT:

. . . but which

WRONG: In 1867, Dr. David Livingstone found the Lualaba River, mistakenly assumed to be the Nile but <u>which actually flows into the Upper Congo Lake</u>.

RIGHT: In 1867, Dr. David Livingstone found the Lualaba River, <u>which he mistakenly assumed to be the Nile</u> but <u>which actually flows into the Upper Congo Lake</u>.

> ## GRAMMAR TIP
>
> After *no, not,* and *never,* use *nor* to continue a later negative clause that's parallel with an earlier negative clause.

WRONG: I have never appreciated sushi, and I won't ever.

RIGHT: I have never appreciated sushi, nor will I ever appreciate it.

From *The Less-Is-More Handbook: A Guide To College Writing, Second Edition* by Larry Edgerton. Copyright © 2017 by Kendall Hunt Publishing Company. Reprinted by permission.

◇◇

Reference

Burke, K. (1973). *The philosophy of literary form: Studies in symbolic action.* Berkeley, CA: University of California Press.

Galbraith, D. (1999). Writing as a knowledge-constituting process. In M. Torrance & D. Galbraith (Eds.). *Knowing what to write* (pp. 139–160). Amsterdam, NL: Amsterdam University Press.

Harris, J. (2006). *Rewriting: How to do things with texts.* Logan, UT: Utah State University Press.

Jonassen, D. H. (2000). Toward a design theory of problem solving. *Educational Technology: Research & Development, 48*(4), 63–85.

Macrorie, K. (1988). *The I-search paper.* Portsmouth, NH: Heinemann.

Lessons to Use in the Co-Requisite Classroom During This Unit

A co-requisite Writing and Research course has but one absolute rule: no additional assignments outside of class may be assigned; the work of the Writing and Research course *is* the work of the co-requisite course.

Nonetheless, during co-requisite class times, students should engage in activities that address their noncognitive, cognitive, and skills-related areas. The activities I include here encompass all three categories of learning and coordinate with the work of the Writing and Research course. Of course, students' needs regarding whatever occurs in the Writing and Research course on a particular day may at times take precedence in the co-requisite course, and at times the class time may function as a writing workshop, but every class session cannot function in these ways, or the students will not acquire what they need from the course. Individual teachers will of course decide what to use, when to use it, and even what adaptations to apply. Some of the activities, each one designed for a single class session, may actually take longer than a single class because co-requisite courses do not operate on the same schedule on every college campus and different students have different kinds of questions about assignments.

OPENING CLASS REFLECTION

1. I chose to take the co-requisite class option for the following reasons:

2. Especially after attending one Writing and Research class session, my greatest fears about that course include the following:

3. As I think about my previous experiences with writing, I think my greatest strengths include the following:

4. As I think about my previous writing experiences, I think I will need the most help with the following writing elements (CONTENT):

5. As I think about my previous writing experiences, I think I will need the most help with the following GRAMMATICAL and MECHANICAL elements of writing:

6. My experiences with research and research writing include the following:

7. I think I will need some help with the following research/research writing elements:

8. I want to accomplish the following in this extra co-requisite Writing Studio:

9. I have the following questions (about the Writing and Research course of the co-requisite course or anything else on my mind regarding academics right now):

10. CIRCLE ONE: I think of myself as a writer OR I do not think of myself as a writer (not a paid, published writer, just someone who writes), because . . .

FIRST DAY ACTIVITY 2: Breaking the Ice

1. Answer the following questions as quickly as you can, without overthinking your answers. There are no "correct" or "incorrect" answers. In some cases, you should circle an answer choice.

My name is: _____.

I like my first name (Circle one choice):   not at all   a little   very much.

I think my name means _____.

My first language is (Circle one choice):   English   Spanish   French   Farsi
American Sign Language   Mandarin   Chinese   Arabic   Japanese   Korean
Russian   Other: _____.

I can <u>speak</u> fluently in all of the following languages: _____.

I am able to <u>write</u> in all of the following languages: _____.

I am able to <u>read</u> all of the following languages: _____.

I am proficient at text-messaging, with all of its abbreviations, etc.   YES   NO   SORT OF

I consider myself   not very proficient   reasonably proficient   very proficient   in using technology of all kinds to find information, convey information, etc.

I consider myself a writer (someone who uses words to compose blogs, social media posts, text messages, letters, assignments, etc.).   YES   NO   SORT OF

I consider myself a talker (someone who speaks often and comfortably in any situation).
YES   NO   SORT OF

I consider myself a listener (someone who fully hears and processes what others say in any situation).
YES   NO   SORT OF

I like to read.	Not at all	Somewhat	A lot	Depends on what I am reading
I like to write.	Not at all	Somewhat	A lot	Depends on what I am writing
I like to talk.	Not at all	Somewhat	A lot	Depends on the topic and the audience

I learned to read when I was _____ years old, and I found doing so _____
(an adjective [such as "easy," "difficult," "fun," "boring," "frustrating," "natural," etc.] that describes your learning process).

I learned to write when I was _____ years old, and I found doing so _____
(an adjective [such as "easy," "difficult," "fun," "boring," "frustrating," "natural," etc.] that describes your learning process).

I started speaking when I was _____ years old, and my first word(s) was (were) _____.

Write here a few sentences about a memory you have regarding your own reading, writing, speaking, and/or listening.

Write here a few sentences about what you think has affected your attitudes about reading, writing, speaking, and/or listening. You may also write it as a little memory narrative.

If you could remake your literate self (your reading, writing, speaking, listening self), what, if anything would you change and why? If you would change nothing, explain why not.

2. Now, please exchange your sheet with another person. Read each other's answers.
3. Based on what you have read on your peer's paper, please create and record here one question you have for this peer.

4. Now introduce yourselves to each other, and ask your question and allow your peer to answer you. Then swap roles.
5. Now think of a way you can introduce your peer to the rest of the class by using ONE sentence that characterizes your peer in relation to her/his persona as reader/writer/speaker/listener. Write that sentence here.

6. When asked to do so, please introduce your peer. Then return your peer's sheet to him/her.
7. Now answer this question: What reaction did you have to your peer's introduction to you?

VALUES SURVEY ACTIVITY (Noncognitive)

1. See the two lists of values below. Circle the eight to ten you consider the most important in *your* life. Feel free to add one you do not see on these lists but that matters to you.

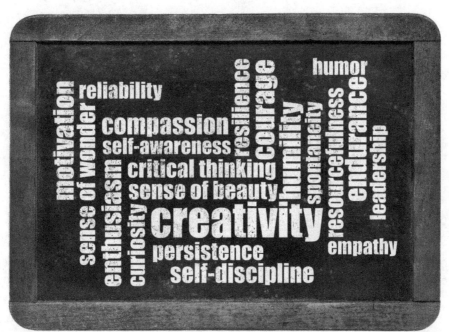

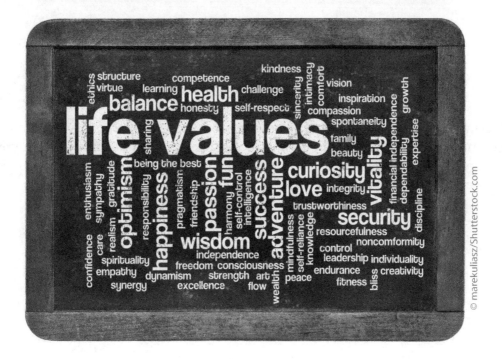

2. Think about those eight to ten values you circled above. Now list, in order of their importance to you, with #1 standing as the most important and #3 standing as the least important, the three *most* important values in *your* life.

3. What key choices have you made in your life because of these three important values?

4. What role, if any, have these three values played in your choice to attend college? What role will they play in the way you proceed at college? Explain.

5. Meet with two to three other students in the class. Together discuss *in general* the impact values can have on our choices in life and in the ways different people might progress through college. (Again, you need NOT share your own answers unless you wish to do so.) Record here any consensus you reach.

HIERARCHY OF NEEDS SURVEY ACTIVITY (Noncognitive)

1. Read the list of Maslow's "Hierarchy of Needs" pyramid.
2. On the right-hand side of the diagram, number each item 1–5, based on *your own* hierarchy, with 1 = most important to you and 5 = least important to you.
3. Within <u>each category</u>'s list of descriptors, circle <u>the one</u> item most important to you.

Self-actualization
desire to become the most that one can be

Esteem
respect, self-esteem, status, recognition, strength, freedom

Love and belonging
friendship, intimacy, family, sense of connection

Safety needs
personal security, employment, resources, health, property

Physiological needs
air, water, food, shelter, sleep, clothing, reproduction

Maslow's hierarchy of needs

© Plateresca/Shutterstock.com

4. Based on your answers to the above questions, now fill in your own personal pyramid. Whatever is at the top represents the most vital element to you.

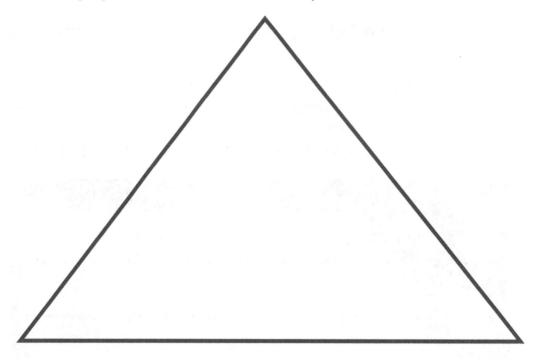

5. As you view your own pyramid, in what ways do you think these needs impact your ability to succeed in college? Explain.

6. Now pair with two other students. You need NOT share your personal pyramid unless you choose to do so. Instead, use what you have learned to discuss the answer to the following question.

> Can a student's hierarchy of needs affect a student's chances for success in college? What needs have the greatest impact on a student's ability to succeed at college? Why? Explain fully. What need do you think must be at the top of the pyramid for a student to be most likely to succeed at college? Be prepared to share your group's consensus with the rest of the class.

ANALYZING A TEXT

© AXpop/Shutterstock.com

Yes, images, ads, etc., are texts, too! In fact, in this era, we are exposed to hundreds of these kinds of texts daily!

1. Examine the above advertisement.
2. Annotate it.

ANNOTATING A TEXT: To complete this part, you must print the reading, so you can follow the recommended steps.

If you follow these steps, you will find that you will improve your comprehension of the text and, as a result, begin the groundwork that will help you to create your claim.

1. **Read the WHOLE text through completely**, just to get an overall sense of it. THEN, reread it, but this time, follow these steps:
2. **Underline, circle, or highlight with a specific color** the items you think represent the most important passages, phrases, ideas, or even contradictions in the text.
3. **Talk back to the text by writing notes, questions, and commentary in the margins** of the text.—SAMPLE:

NOTES IN THE MARGIN	THE PASSAGE
Who exactly is the counterculture? Is this "our" most of us? Is he saying free speech truly FOR ALL?	Those of us in the counterculture saw in the internet an opportunity to topple the storytellers who had dominated our politics, economics, society and religion—in short, our very reality—and to replace their stories with those of our own. (From Rushkoff's *Open Source Democracy*, on Project Guttenberg)

CHAPTER 1

OTHER IDEAS TO HELP YOU ANNOTATE EFFECTIVELY:

1. **NO ONE style of annotation exists.** Do what works best for you. Utilize that which will help you easily review and see the major arguments of the text.

2. **Underline or circle or bracket words not known by you.** Check the context of the sentence for meaning. Record that meaning in the margin of the text. (If you need to look up the word in a dictionary, go ahead!)

3. **Identify the most vital topic sentences by using a consistent code: an asterisk or the use of parentheses or a check mark.**

4. **Do ask questions!** Write those questions in the margins, or if a passage is particularly unclear, write a question mark over it. Later, you can ask your teacher or your peers about that section.

5. **Use any number of helpful, consistent codes:** different colors, sticky notes, paper clips, anything at all that helps you to identify ideas that go together and that are important.

SAMPLE OF AN ANNOTED ESSAY:

The birth of the internet was interpreted by many as a revolution. Those of us in the counterculture saw in the internet an opportunity to topple the storytellers who had dominated our politics, economics, society and religion - in short our very reality - and to replace their stories with those of our own. It was a beautiful and exciting sentiment, but one as based in a particular narrative as any other. Revolutions simply replace one story with another. The capitalist narrative is replaced by that of the communist; the religious fundamentalist's replaced by the gnostic's. The means may be different, but the rewards are the same. So is the exclusivity of their distribution. That's why they're called revolutions - we're just going in a circle. (From Rushkoff's *Open Source Democracy*, on Project Guttenberg)

Annotations (handwritten): What one? — postive? — Contradiction — our own — What rewards? — Examples — So the Internet was not really so good or a revolution? — Means those who doubt existence of God

Source: Patricia Sehulster

Based on your reading and notes, please fill in the following chart.

CATEGORY	NOTATIONS/ COMMENTS/CONCLUSIONS	EXAMPLE (S)	RANKING ON A SCALE OF 1–10 (1 = POOR; 10 = EXCELLENT)
ORGANIZATION—How is this text ordered? What is predominant?			
CLARITY—How clear is the message of the text?			
PROOF/USE OF EXAMPLES—What support does the text offer for its message?			
LANGUAGE AND WORD CHOICE—What words are used and for what purpose? Is the language strong? Does the language convince you?			
STYLE OF PUNTCUATION, SENTENCE STRUCTURE, ETC.			
PURPOSE—What is the text trying to accomplish?			
OVERALL			

Write ONE STATEMENT THAT SUMMARIZES YOUR OVERALL ANALYSIS (a claim/your contribution to the dialogue):

FOR EXAMPLE, you might write something such as the following:

The ad for a _____ _____ (← Choose here a strong verb that

encapsulates what you think the overall effect on the reader is: entices, intrigues, convinces, bores,

angers, etc.) the reader because _____.

1. Now meet with another group to share and then discuss your claims. Reach a consensus about which one is better—AND WHY—and then choose someone from the group to write it on the whiteboard for the rest of the class to see. Be prepared to explain why it succeeds as a claim.

2. As you read the statements on the board, think about the following questions:

   a. Does the statement work as a thesis? Does the statement offer a point to prove that evaluates the ad based NOT on what it says BUT ON HOW it does so?

   b. How well is the statement itself constructed? Do you see any errors? Do you see any areas that could use some improvement?

As you think about what you did in this exercise, what have you learned about analyzing any text—visual or just words? List those lessons here.

Examine any one of the articles we have read during this unit. Apply the same process to that text.

PRACTICING SENTENCE STRUCTURE RULES ACTIVITY

1. Get into groups of three or four students. (We are striving for three even groups, so attendance will determine the number in each group.)

2. Group A will deal with the general rules of sentence structure and combining sentences. Group B will deal with the rules about dangling and misplaced modifiers. Group C will deal with the rules about parallel structure. Each group will become the expert group on that topic and become responsible for teaching the others.

3. Examine the last section of Chapter 1 of our text: "Grammar Concept: Sentence Structure, Misplaced and Dangling Modifiers, and Parallelism." Find the section that applies to your group.

4. As a group, determine what you think are the most important concepts and rules to remember about your topic.

5. Create a single "flash sheet" that outlines those key points. Use bullets, etc., *and* offer some examples. [Each member of your group must create a copy of your flash sheet, so that everyone can bring it to the group they move to next.]

6. Once you have completed your flash sheet, and the teacher asks you to do so, form new groups, with each one having a member from Group A, a member from Group B, and a Member from Group C.

7. Take turns sharing your expert knowledge about your topic with the other members of the group, so everyone gets information about each of the three topics by the time everyone has spoken.

8. When the teacher asks you to do so, take any two paragraphs from anything you have written for the Writing and Research course—a journal entry, an in-class exercise, an essay draft—and examine it carefully for your own sentence structure. Fix any errors you discover.

9. Before you leave class, use the index card the teacher has given you to write down any question(s) you have about sentence structure. Give that card to the teacher as you leave the classroom.

ROUND-ROBIN ACTIVITY WITH OUR "MY WRITING MINDSET REFLECTIVE LETTER" DRAFTS

Directions:

1. Get into groups of THREE.
2. Swap your draft with one other person in the group.
3. Attach this sheet to that draft and record the author's name in the space provided on this sheet.
4. The person who gets the draft will examine it for #1 criteria and sign his/her name on the line adjacent to #1. (See below #1: Progress directions; follow them exactly and completely.)
5. When you have all finished the examination of your peer's essay for #1 criteria, swap the drafts again.
6. This time, the person who gets the draft will examine it for #2 criteria and sign his/her name on the line adjacent to #2. (See below #2: Evidence directions; follow them exactly and completely.)
7. When you have all finished the examination of your peer's essay for #2 criteria, swap the drafts again.
8. This time, the person who gets the draft will examine it for #3 criteria and sign his/her name on the line adjacent to #3. (See below #3: Editing directions; follow them exactly and completely.)
9. When you have finished the examination of your peer's essay for #3 criteria, return each draft to its author.
10. Authors: Read through the comments your peers have made. If you have questions about them, ask your peer.
11. Authors, now complete the answer to the questions about your plan for completion and revision.

#1 _____ for (author) _____

#2 _____

#3 _____

#1: PROGRESS

1. Read through the draft entirely, without doing anything to it; just read it.
2. Read through the draft again. This time, <u>highlight and identify/label</u> what you think is the writer's:
   a. Use of proper letter format
   b. General introduction to the purpose of the letter
   c. Chronological discussion of past and present mindset toward writing
   d. IF you find any or all of these elements are missing or in some way weak, note that point/those points on the draft. If, on the other hand, you find them strong, note that fact on the draft.
3. In looking over the draft, think about how much progress toward the completion of this essay the writer has made. On a scale of 1–10 (1 meaning low and 10 meaning high), how would you rank this writer's progress? _____ EXPLAIN WHY you give it that ranking. _____ _____
4. Do you believe this draft is headed in the direction it needs to go?   YES   NO
5. EXPLAIN WHY. _____

#2: EVIDENCE

1. Read through the draft entirely, without doing anything to it; just read it.
2. Read through the draft again. This time, locate the claim highlighted and labeled in this draft.
3. Now <u>locate, underline, and label</u> supporting evidence for the writer's statements about personal writing mindset. Label the evidence by type: Example (EX), Scholarly Support (SS), Data (D), Refutation of Opposing Point (ORP), Does Not Apply/Illogical Support (DNA), Just a Restatement (HRS). (You might see all of these possibilities or only some of them.)
4. Do you think the writer offers an equal, balanced blend of these types of evidence? YES   NO   EXPLAIN WHY. _____
5. Do you think this writer offers sufficient support or plans for sufficient support for the statements?   YES   NO   EXPLAIN WHY. _____
6. What, if anything, does the writer need to add? _____
7. What, if anything, does the writer need to delete? _____

#3: EDITING

1. Read through the draft entirely, without doing anything to it; just read it.
2. Read through the draft again. This time, circle errors in <u>sentence structure</u>. LABEL the errors, but do not correct them. Note any sentences you do not clearly understand because the prose is muddy. *** Because in this unit, we have studied sentence structure, misplaced and dangling modifiers, and parallelism, pay special attention to those areas. If you notice other kinds of errors, such as those in spelling, pronoun use, subject–verb agreement, etc., please do feel free to circle them too.
3. What does this writer need to pay the most attention to correcting? _____

WRITER'S REFLECTION AND PLAN FOR COMPLETION AND REVISION:

1. Examine what your peers have noted about your draft both on the draft and on the filled-in sections of page 2 (page 80) of this activity.

2. Ask your peers for clarification of anything you do not quite understand about their comments.

3. Make your own notations/reminders on your draft.

4. Record here a step-by-step, concrete plan of the actions you will take in creating your next, FULL draft of this essay. What must you add? What must you delete? What order should you follow or maintain? What else should you revise? Do you need to edit any problem grammar?

WRITING ACROSS THE CURRICULUM/WRITING IN THE DISCIPLINES TIPS AND CONNECTIONS FOR THIS UNIT

1. Bring the discussion of mindset, grit, and multiple intelligences to bear on the particular discipline with which the writing and research class is paired. For example:
   - ▶ Discuss how fixed mindset about X discipline hampers development of understanding of that discipline.
   - ▶ Discuss preconceptions about X discipline.
   - ▶ Point out the cross-disciplinary nature of the very concept of multiple intelligences and discuss whether or not any one of them makes a student more likely to succeed in X discipline.

2. Alter the in-class activities to fit the discipline by making the examples used discipline-related.

3. Discuss and model specific ways of reading and analyzing specific discipline-related texts. What methodology do you wish to impart? What makes texts for X discipline stand out as different from other types of texts? Focus on those particularities.

4. Add a discipline-specific question to each journal entry.

5. Change the "Shitty First Drafts" reading and journal entry to a text about the ways of approaching the study of X discipline. For example, in the sciences, an article about the ways testing a hypothesis may indeed result in a failure that is in itself an answer. Another example might include a text about correcting biases in various studies or about conquering fear of mathematics, etc.

6. Change the *writing* mindset reflective letter to an "X discipline" mindset reflective letter.

7. Discuss the ways research in a particular discipline is written and presented. Clarify the similarities and differences of academic dialogue in varying disciplines.

© Bimbim/Shutterstock.com

CHAPTER 2

Finding a Research Topic and Question

Weeks 4–6

Learning Objectives

Students will:

- Develop and refine a research topic and question.
- Develop a research proposal.
- Demonstrate an understanding of writing as a multistage process.
- Produce texts that present ideas effectively and fluently.
- Think critically.

You have spent the past several weeks warming up to the college environment. You know now that with a frame of mind open to learning through trying, you can and will succeed. You know now some strategies for analyzing college-level reading. And you have already begun practicing ways to participate in and contribute to academic conversations. You now possess the skills to move on to finding a research topic and forming a workable research question.

You might find yourself wondering, "What's the difference between a research topic and a research question?" One does indeed relate to the other, but they do differ. Specificity accounts for that difference, and you have actually already engaged in making this kind of distinction hundreds of times in your life.

Think about the first time you ever used a cell phone, for example. You probably wondered about *the use of that cell phone: a general topic*. And then you asked, "*How do I* turn this cell phone on?" or "*How do I* send a text message?": very *specific questions*. Think about your decision to attend college. You wondered about *the application process: a general topic*. Then you asked, "*What qualifications must I meet?*" and "*How do I apply?*": very *specific questions*.

© Ileezhun/Shutterstock.com

© Peshkova/Shutterstock.com

Academic research mirrors this process, *except* your questions will not necessarily have concrete answers; *the best academic research questions encompass debatable topics, those that will require your analysis of several different answers to the question, so that you can form and contribute your own answer.*

You, your teacher, and your peers may actually decide together what topic to research. Sometimes, the discipline of the course may determine its nature. At other times, you will have a wide-open field of choices. Usually, however, you alone will select your actual research question.

As we discovered in the first chapter, reading can serve as a catalyst for our thinking, and that axiom holds true for choosing a research topic and question too. With this idea in mind, I have included at the end of this chapter a collection of readings that fit into five topic categories: "On the Environment"; "On Technology and Us"; "On Negotiating Cultural, Political, and Other Cultural Differences"; "On College Education"; and "On Food." You, your classmates, and your teacher may decide to sample all of them, or maybe you will choose a focus on just one of them, or perhaps you will decide that none of those general topic categories offers you anything on which you would like to focus. I offer them only as a possible starting place.

© Wowomnom/Shutterstock.com

IN-CLASS ACTIVITY 2A: CHOOSING YOUR TOPIC

TOPIC CHOICE:
(Related to the Environment OR
College Education OR Technology and Us OR
Negotiating Cultural, Political, and Other Differences OR Food):

"Do not go where the path may lead; go instead where there is no path and leave a trail." (Emerson qtd. Stancliff and Goggin 29)

"Research takes you somewhere you haven't been before, in fact, to places you didn't know existed." (Stancliff and Goggin 29)

A. Answer the following questions. Fill the space provided.

1. Read the above quotes. What do they say about the activity of researching? Do you agree with their philosophies? Explain.

2. What issues/topics <u>related to the environment AND/OR college education AND/ OR technology and us AND/OR negotiating cultural, political, and other differences AND/OR food</u> do you discuss most with friends and family? Why?

3. In what issues/topics <u>related to the environment AND/OR college education AND/ OR technology and us AND/OR negotiating cultural, political, and other differences AND/OR food</u> do you feel most emotionally involved? When you discuss them, what issues/topics inspire strong feelings? Identify them and explain why they inspire such feelings.

4. Is there an issue related to the environment AND/OR college education AND/OR technology and us AND/OR negotiating cultural, political, and other differences AND/OR food in your community (family, team, school, workplace, town, state) that is currently having a major impact? Identify and describe that issue and why it matters to you or that community.

5. If you have an intended career or field of interest, what are the major issues related to the environment AND/OR college education AND/OR technology and us AND/OR negotiating cultural, political, and other differences AND/OR food about which members of that field are concerned? Identify them and explain why they are of concern.

6. About what local (town, city, state), national (USA) and/or international (world) issues related to the environment AND/OR college education AND/OR technology and us AND/OR negotiating cultural, political, and other differences AND/OR food are you passionate or concerned? Identify them and explain why they are of concern.

7. Examine your responses to questions 2–6. Do you see any common or recurrent themes there or anything you keep naming that might indicate a solid interest on your part? If so, name that topic here.

Work Cited

Stancliff, Michael and Maureen Daly Goggin. "Research as Creative Practice: Two Metaphors for Teaching and Learning." *English Journal* 105.2 (2015): 27–33. *JSTOR*. https://www.jstor.org/stable/26359352. Accessed 10 May 2019.

A. Searching First

You may think that knowing your interests and narrowing that field will suffice as you choose your topic and try to formulate your question, but you actually need to add another step: testing your idea. Think of yourself as the Goldilocks child from the old fairy tale; you have to find that topic that is just right.

Topics can fit into three categories, and only one of them will succeed for research.

- The Too Broad Topic: a topic so large that you might need a year to research it and a whole book to discuss it
  - ▶ EXAMPLE: The Toxic Waste of the World: What produces it, what types exist, where it is, what effects it produces for humans and the planet, and what we can do to end the problem

- The Too Narrow Topic: a topic so small and narrowly focused that it will not offer sufficient information to discuss in more than a few paragraphs
  - ▶ EXAMPLE: The Components of a Cell Phone That Produce Toxic Waste

- The Just-Right Topic: a topic that has a specific enough focus to avoid including too many elements for consideration but offers enough breadth to provide sufficient and varied information in the time and parameters required
  - ▶ EXAMPLE: What happens to the waste produced by computers, and what corresponding effects result

You must also take note of the parameters and time allowed for a research assignment, for these conditions will play a key role in determining your topic choice. You must ask yourself what you can realistically accomplish in the time allowed and how much you can cover in a specific number of pages and words.

So how do you choose? As you observed in activity 2A, you can start simply with your interests in targeted, broad, and general areas to determine some possible areas to consider. Once you have narrowed that field a little, you can then start testing those ideas with some initial research.

© Golden Sikorka/Shutterstock.com

This phase actually requires you to start with very broad ideas because in searching those, you will soon discover a myriad of possible focal points. For example, if you conducted a general Internet search engine search on "Technology and Us," you might get over a million entries, but their very titles will help you. You might see, for example, "Artificial Intelligence" or "Self-driving Cars," or "Is the Internet making us dumb?" Then if you chose to search any one of those topics, you would narrow your topic still further. For example, "Artificial Intelligence" might bring you to "Robots Replacing Workers," or "Artificial Intelligence in Medicine," or "Artificial Intelligence in Everyday Use." Already, you have singled out very particular areas for consideration, and you can narrow those still further.

B. Forming a Research Question

Once you have selected a viable topic, you need to move to the next step: choosing a research question. Like your topic, the research question needs to avoid the too broad and the too narrow. The strong research question should encompass:

- Something about which several differing opinions exist
- Something about which information is readily available
- Something that matters

A research question to which you can answer "Yes" or "No" or about which only factual answers exist will not suffice.

A strong research question must offer you the opportunity to piece together various strands of the dialogue about the topic to create your own claim or contribution to the conversation. In addition, your research question should remain free of:

- Inherent biases
  - ► EXAMPLE: In what ways can we eliminate the always untrustworthy nature that defines social media?

- Inherent answers or foregone conclusions
  - ► EXAMPLE: What makes America the largest contributor to toxic waste-dumping?

- Inherent lack of depth or breadth
  - ► EXAMPLE: Who determines what Internet sites the Chinese people can view?

- Lastly, though equally important, a strong research question should hold some interest for you; you will want it to engage you throughout the research process.

The following summary regarding research questions should help you to choose.

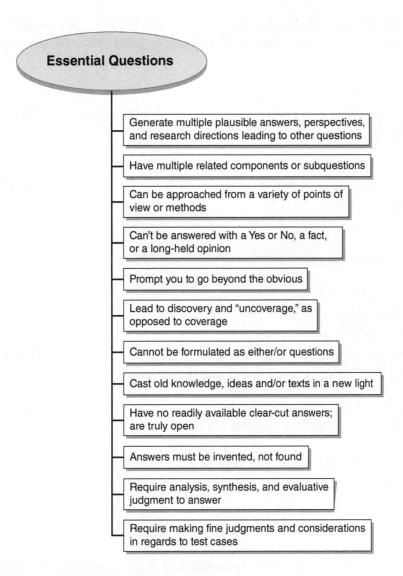

Essential Questions

- Generate multiple plausible answers, perspectives, and research directions leading to other questions
- Have multiple related components or subquestions
- Can be approached from a variety of points of view or methods
- Can't be answered with a Yes or No, a fact, or a long-held opinion
- Prompt you to go beyond the obvious
- Lead to discovery and "uncoverage," as opposed to coverage
- Cannot be formulated as either/or questions
- Cast old knowledge, ideas and/or texts in a new light
- Have no readily available clear-cut answers; are truly open
- Answers must be invented, not found
- Require analysis, synthesis, and evaluative judgment to answer
- Require making fine judgments and considerations in regards to test cases

Formulating essential questions will guide the direction of your research and help keep research focused and within the scope of your project.

IN-CLASS ACTIVITY 2B: CHOOSING YOUR RESEARCH QUESTION

TOPIC CHOICE: (Related to the Environment OR College Education OR Technology and Us OR Negotiating Cultural, Political, and Other Differences OR Food):

A. With the class, watch the following, short videos:

"Narrowing a Research Topic and Question (Picking a Topic *IS* Research)" by NCSU (North Carolina State University) Libraries:

> https://www.youtube.com/embed/Q0B3Gjlu-1o

"Choosing, Narrowing, and Filtering a Research Topic: The D-P-C Method" by David Taylor on October 31, 2010:

> https://www.youtube.com/watch?v=jSHXb83Xtsk

B. Think about the idea that:

- a <u>topic</u> is the general subject in which you have an interest,
- an <u>issue/theme/angle</u> is a situation within that subject that has become the object of discussion and debate, and
- a <u>research question</u> is the very specific focus of your curiosity, confusion, or search for knowledge and understanding about that topic's issue.

WEAK questions take us nowhere, but only demonstrate knowledge/report, offer an already built-in answer or bias, or have too narrow or too broad a focus.

STRONG questions offer us *pathways of inquiry*; they will take digging and discovery to answer and often provide no clear answer but a lot of debate.

EXAMPLES:

WEAK Questions:
How are Twitter and social media reducing and ruining writing? ← A bias/conclusion already there

Why is feminism dead? ← A conclusion already drawn

VERSUS

STRONG Questions:
How are Twitter and other social media affecting writing?

How is feminism practiced today, and why have these practices of feminism changed over time?

C. Now, bearing in mind all you have done and thought about regarding choosing a topic, use the following brainstorming mapping sheets, and start working on choosing your research topic for the term, which will be related to the environment OR attending college OR technology OR cultural, political, and other differences OR food. (You might even decide to combine the categories, for example using food production's impact on the environment or technology's effects on previously disenfranchised cultural groups or college's accessibility for immigrants, etc.)

MAPPING SHEET 1: GENERALIZING YOUR TOPIC

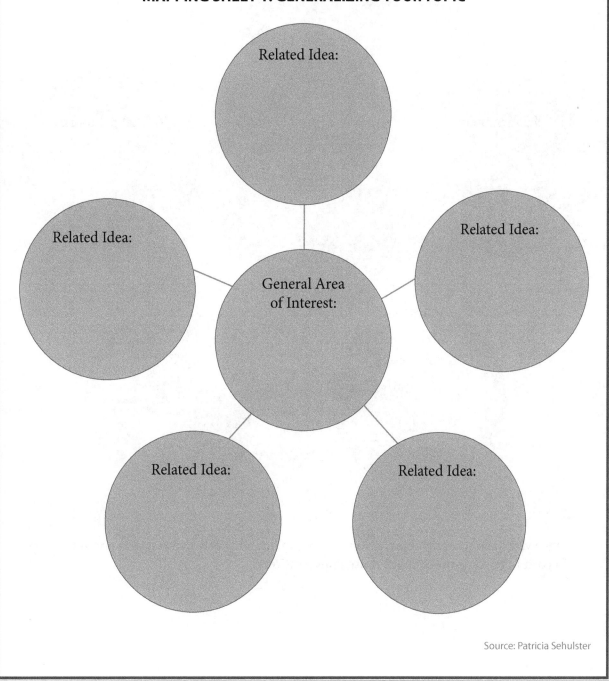

Source: Patricia Sehulster

MAPPING SHEET 2: NARROWING THAT TOPIC

Choose just ONE of the ideas from your first brainstorming map, and brainstorm about it here.

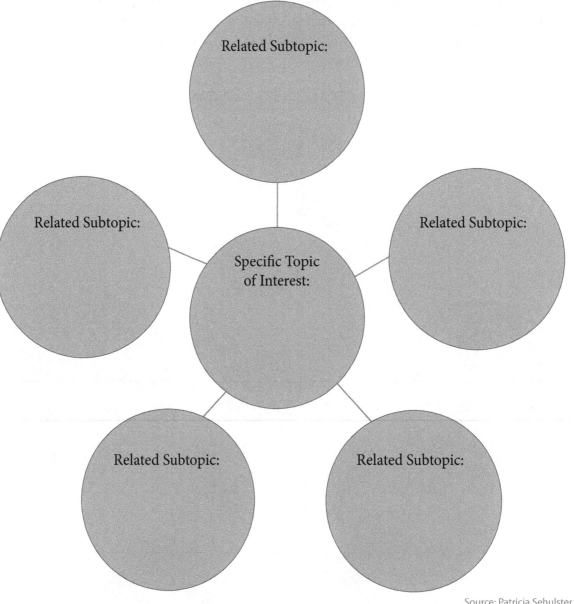

Related Subtopic:

Related Subtopic:

Related Subtopic:

Specific Topic of Interest:

Related Subtopic:

Related Subtopic:

Source: Patricia Sehulster

D. Once you have chosen a topic, go online to find out what others are saying about that topic. Record here some notes about those conversations.

E. Now, based on those ideas, formulate your research question. Write it here.

F. <u>IN-CLASS ONLY</u>: Get into the group of people who have the same circled number on these pages.

[ONLINE STUDENTS: You will post this completed activity sheet and reply to a peer's answer to F using the question [I] below.]

G. Have each person in that group read aloud his/her research topic and question.

H. Dealing with ONE topic and question at a time, have <u>each</u> member of the group make a statement about or ask a question about each person's topic and question. Keep the discussion going to help each other shape each other's questions.

I. Write here your reshaped question.

ACTIVITY 2B

JOURNAL ENTRY 6A: CHOOSING A RESEARCH TOPIC AND QUESTION

Now that you have read the pages about "Essential Research Questions," invent **3+ research topics and questions** you would be interested in writing about this semester. They should relate to something about which we have been reading: the environment OR college education OR technology and us OR food OR negotiating cultural, political, and other differences.

If you still feel a little uncertain about your topic choice, see the following link from the *New York Times*:

"401 Prompts for Argumentative Writing" from The Learning Network of the *New York Times*, March 1, 2017:

https://www.nytimes.com/2017/03/01/learning/lesson-plans/401-prompts-for-argumentative-writing.html

If doing so helps, use the following template:

Developing a Formal Research Question

Use the following sentence templates to develop a formal research question:

- This study asks _____.
- This study seeks to _____.
- In contrast to the conventional wisdom, this study argues _____.
- When _____ is viewed through the lens of _____, X phenomenon appears in a new light.
- In order to support the claim that _____, this study asks _____.

From *Writing College Research Papers, Second Edition* by Eric Drown and Kathy Sole. Copyright © 2013 by Bridgepoint Education Inc. Reprinted by permission.

EXAMPLES:

- "This study asks why we should or should not preserve the national parks."
- "In contrast to conventional beliefs, this study argues that playing video games might actually help people develop essential skills for the future and questions the premise that they make people violent and unrealistic."
- "In order to support the claim that political gridlock results primarily from party partisanship, this study asks why the United States Congress has failed to accomplish in the last ten years even one-tenth of what previous Congresses have."

C. Determining Significance

As we have already considered, a strong research topic and question should matter—and not only to you. It must have significance to some other audience. That audience can come from anywhere; it need not include only elite individuals. For example, if you choose to research public school lunches and their effects on students' health and future eating habits, who might care about that issue? Certainly, some of the students would. But who else might? Perhaps all of the parents of those students eating those school lunches and even the taxpayers helping to pay for those lunches would have an interest. The topic would hold significance for parents because of their interest in their children's well-being and for the taxpayers because of their economic concerns.

How can you determine the significance of your topic and question? Begin by thinking about why it matters to you, and build a backward pyramid from there: from you, the individual to the pertinent group to which you belong, to the even larger category to which that subgroup belongs. If doing so helps, think in terms of classification by profession, position in society, purpose, location, needs, age, etc. No limits exist!

For example, let's build a reverse pyramid based on the topic of the efficacy of using tracking devices on US criminals and parolees.

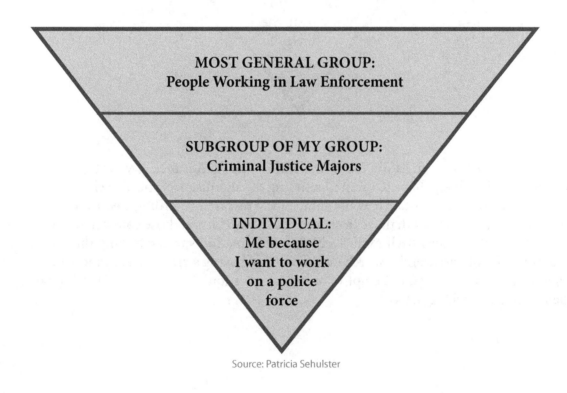

MOST GENERAL GROUP:
People Working in Law Enforcement

SUBGROUP OF MY GROUP:
Criminal Justice Majors

INDIVIDUAL:
Me because
I want to work
on a police
force

Source: Patricia Sehulster

Another way to determine significance stems from thinking about the group on whom your research conclusions might have an effect. Again, you can build from the specific individual to increasingly broad but applicable categories. If you were to imagine that same electronic tracking devices research from a different angle—that of the criminal who wears such technology, for example—you might create a reverse pyramid such as the following:

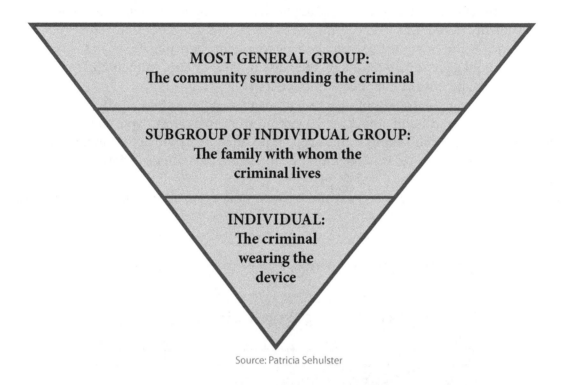

MOST GENERAL GROUP:
The community surrounding the criminal

SUBGROUP OF INDIVIDUAL GROUP:
The family with whom the criminal lives

INDIVIDUAL:
The criminal wearing the device

Source: Patricia Sehulster

You may notice that even as you focus on defining the significance of your topic, you also continue to narrow and finely shape it, for in identifying the significance, you also choose your angle of approach to the topic. For instance, while some of the research regarding electronic monitoring of criminals might pertain to both those in criminal justice work and those connected to the criminal, other research will concern itself exclusively with information specific to only that one angle you choose. You will not find useful research on the value of having a criminal at home versus hundreds of miles away in prison if you attempt to answer a question about how many criminals actually escape from their tracking devices.

IN-CLASS ACTIVITY 2C: DEFINING SIGNIFICANCE

Work in groups of three to four students to answer the following questions.

1. Take out and review your copy of and annotations on the assigned Wallace Stegner's "Wilderness Letter" reading:

   "Wilderness Letter" (1960) by Wallace Stegner from The Wilderness Society, December 28, 2009:

   https://psych.utah.edu/_resources/documents/psych4130/Stenger_W.pdf

2. Let's think about the significance of that letter. Look at to whom he addresses his letter, who has published his letter, and the references he makes in the letter. To whom does the issue he addresses matter?

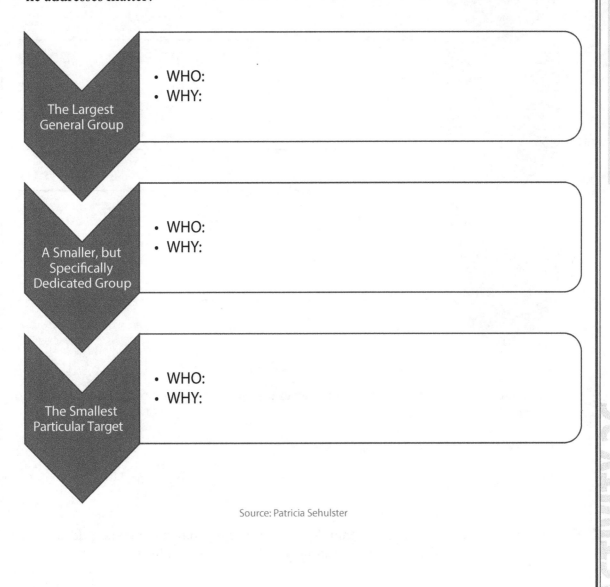

The Largest General Group
- WHO:
- WHY:

A Smaller, but Specifically Dedicated Group
- WHO:
- WHY:

The Smallest Particular Target
- WHO:
- WHY:

Source: Patricia Sehulster

Now work individually.

3. Record your research topic and question here.

4. To whom might your topic and question matter? Fill in the chart below.

• WHO:
• WHY:

The Largest
General Group

• WHO:
• WHY:

A Smaller, but
Specifically
Dedicated Group

• WHO:
• WHY:

Myself

Source: Patricia Sehulster

5. Complete the following statement with several sentences of your own. Base them on the way you filled in the chart.

This topic and question have significance

6. Now convene with your group again. Share and discuss your statements. Add to or help fine-tune your peers' statements by asking questions, commenting, etc.

As you contemplate writing about the significance of your research, you might:

Developing a Significance Section

Use the following sentence templates to create your paper's significance section:

- This project is important to _____ because _____.
- It is hoped that these findings will _____.
- This project brings to light _____.
- People concerned about _____ should better understand _____.
- Professionals charged with _____ can make use of best practices _____.
- Policy makers interested in _____ should conclude _____.

D. Forming a Research Plan

Once you have selected your research topic and question and their significance, you will begin the next phase: planning how you will gather the information you need to learn about and to enter the dialogue about your chosen issue. Having a plan even before you begin your research will enable you to target your efforts, a key strategy for a college student taking more than one class and balancing other responsibilities as well.

To form your plan, you will need to focus on three specific entities:

- What angle/lens you will use
- What words you will use to search
- Where you will search

As we have already discussed, the significance you attach to your research topic and question will in some ways determine the angle or lens you choose. Any given topic offers a plethora of ways to examine it. Researching social media's effects on adolescent self-esteem for its significance to guidance counselors and parents differs considerably from exploring that same topic for its significance to the companies that control social media. With the first angle, you might concentrate your search on what the effects are and how to negotiate their impact, whereas with the second lens, you might focus on the rights of posters, readers, and company controllers. Your search terms will not parallel one another because your angles differ.

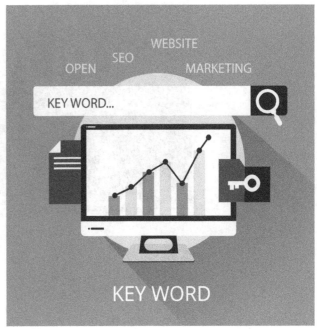

Finding your search terms can actually require some trial-and-error searching to hone them specifically, but you have to start somewhere, and you should plan that strategy before you begin your searching.

One of the easiest ways to do so encompasses what researchers call the use of *key words*. Key words include those single or combination terms most closely related to your topic and question. Starting with several offers you increased probability of finding what you seek. In addition, creating a list of synonyms for these key words doubles your chances for success because every search engine or database complies key words differently; you cannot know in advance which terms will work best in which engine or database. Even in the broad Google search, however, specifying your terms will limit your results.

Your library databases, categorized by type based upon subject matter can also help you to narrow the areas you will search. Information abounds, but you have only so much time. Knowing in advance where you will begin will add efficiency to your search. You will not, for example, find too much information about social media's effects on self-esteem in a database about literature and authors, but you likely will find something about that topic in a psychology or media and communications database. By targeting specific databases for your search, you give yourself an advantage, instead of searching every general database available.

Once you actually begin searching, you can, of course, check a general reference database to get you started and even to find possible other search terms. On a college level, sources such as encyclopedias serve only as jumping-off points: places to find general ideas about your topic and new suggestions for key words, but not actual sources for your research project.

© Gustavo Frazao/Shutterstock.com

IN-CLASS ACTIVITY 2D: FORMING A RESEARCH PLAN

1. Record your research topic, question, and significance area here.

   a. Topic:

   b. Question:

   c. Significant to:

2. As you examine those three entities, reach a conclusion about what general areas might have a connection to them. Circle all that may apply.

General interest	Sciences	Social Sciences	Media	Applied Technology
Education	Business	Health Care	Art	Environmental Studies
History	Philosophy	Government	Ethnicity	
Criminal Justice	Minorities	News	Religion	
Military	Reference	Other: _____		

3. Go to the college's library Home Page. Find the section for "Databases By Subject." It might look something like the following, which comes from the SUNY Westchester Community College's Harold L. Drimmer Library.

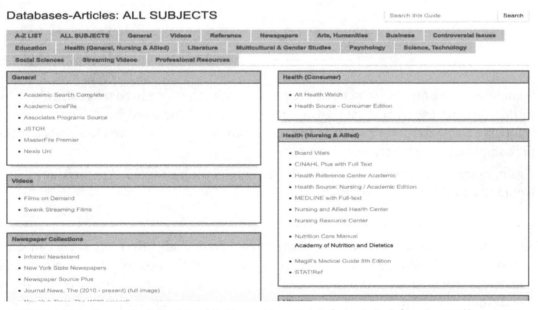

SUNY Westchester Community College's Harold L. Dimmer Library Website by Jessica Tagliaferro. Reprinted by permission.

4. List here some of the databases that might prove helpful given the topic, question, significance to, and general categories you have selected.

5. In Google as well as in library databases and book searches, we can search by key words, subjects, authors, etc. For the purposes of your proposal, let's think just in terms of key words for now. Think about the *terms connected to your topic and your angle or lens*; these words become your key words. Fill in the chart below.

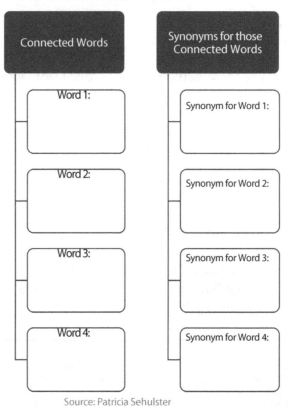

Source: Patricia Sehulster

6. Sometimes, the words we search require pairing with other words, so we get them together. In that case, we use what is called a "Boolean Operator," the word "and." For example, if I wanted to know about computers in the classroom, I might use "computers and education" or "computers and classroom."

   Again, examine your topic choice and the key words you just listed. Are there any you would like to pair for your search?

   _____ and _____

7. Sometimes, we use words that have many forms (nouns, adjectives, etc.). We can use the root of the word followed by an * to help us catch all of the possible combinations in our search. For example, the word "teen" could also spawn the words "teenagers" or "teens." I could simply use "teen*" and get all of those words in my search. Are there any key words you could use in that manner?

   _____ *

E. Making a Research Proposal

In the academic world, before you begin your research project, often you need to propose that project to someone. Sometimes the person reading—and frequently approving—that proposal includes your teacher or the person or group with whom you want to study or with whom you want to conduct an internship or engage in research. Writing that proposal will help you to demonstrate to that audience that your project has merit, but it will also aid you in organizing your own thinking about the project. The proposal, in essence, pulls together for you all of the preliminary strands of your research process—those elements you have focused on in this chapter—by explaining them in a coherent piece of writing.

The research proposal requires seven specific elements:

- Identification of your research topic
  - ▶ In this section, you describe your general topic. The best research proposals lead into the topic with some phrase or hook to pull the reader into the proposal.
- Identification of your research question
  - ▶ Here, you state your research question clearly and succinctly. You will explain what you hope to learn.
- Scope
  - ▶ In this portion of the proposal, you will explain the limitations of your research project. You will clarify what facets of the topic and question you will explore, and which you will not research. You might consider the following:

Setting a Scope

Use the following sentence templates to develop a scope-setting section:

- While most people believe _____, researchers have revealed that _____ more accurately explains _____.
- X's article "_____" represents the conventional wisdom about _____.
- While previous studies have established _____, few have discussed _____.
- This study extends the work of _____, who argued _____.
- This project helps us better understand _____.
- In contrast to most researchers, who argue _____, researcher X argues _____. X's idea better explains _____.
- This study limits its focus to _____ because _____. While this limit enables it to better explain _____, it also means that this study can have little to say about _____.

From *Writing College Research Papers, Second Edition* by Eric Drown and Kathy Sole. Copyright © 2013 by Bridgepoint Education Inc. Reprinted by permission.

- Context and Foregrounding
  - ▶ In this part of the proposal, you will explain
    - What you already know about the topic
    - What *in general* terms others declare about the answer to your question
    - What you imagine you might discover or ultimately conclude

- (Beginning the Academic Dialogue) Identification and Explanation of a Single Guiding Source
  - ▶ This element asks you to:
    - Name a specific, relevant source that has started you thinking about your topic.
    - State where and when that source was published.
    - Summarize the claim and key points of evidence of that source's argument, even using a single, salient quote.
    - Respond to that source, declaring your own view of that premise.
- Significance
  - ▶ Here you will explain why the answer to your question matters to you and
  - ▶ To whom else the answer matters and why.
- Research Plan
  - ▶ In this part, you will explain how you will conduct your research. You will
    - Identify your chosen key words/search terms.
    - Identify probable databases you will use and explain why you have chosen them.
    - Identify possible Internet and other sources.
    - Clarify the tentative deadlines for your work.

Your research proposal will indeed provide you with an organized plan, *but simultaneously, you should remember that all research envelops a process, a journey of discovery* so it may not conform to your plan.

© Pingebat/Shutterstock.com

Not one of you can easily predict the exact pathways the research will follow. In fact, if you could do so, then you would have to ask yourselves if you really are engaging in research or merely reporting on that which you already know.

At times, the research process can make you unsure of yourself; you will think you have jumped into an unknowable space and have become lost. At those times, remember the lessons of our first unit: that growth mindset means experiencing the unfamiliar and eventually finding our way through to new learning.

RESEARCH PROPOSAL ESSAY—700 WORDS (2–2.5 PAGES)

Directions

Compose a 700-word formal document that describes your plan for the Unit 4 Research Essay and Project.

What question do you plan to address, and how will you go about finding an answer?

Your Research Proposal must include the following sections:

TOPIC & QUESTION	DESCRIBE THE TOPIC AND THE SPECIFIC QUESTION YOU HOPE TO ADDRESS.
What I Know, Assume, or Imagine (Context/ Foregrounding/ Background/Scope)	What do you already know about the topic and question? What do others in general think about the topic? What don't you already know about the topic and question? What do you hope to learn?
Source	Identify a published essay on your topic question. (You may use one of the readings in our text.)
	Summarize the essay's argument (identifying the claim and key reasons/evidence). If helpful, use some of the templates we used in doing our class activities on summary and response.
	State your own view, and explain how it compares to the argument presented. If helpful, use some of the templates we used in doing our class activities on summary and response.
Significance	Address the questions, "Why does this topic/question matter to me? Why should it matter to anyone else? To whom does it matter?"
Plan	What kinds of sources could be helpful to answer your question? What will you be looking for in terms of credible and useful sources?

Your audience here is I, your instructor. Persuade me that you have an interesting, but focused and manageable, research plan in mind.

Rubric

CRITERIA	YES [25 POINTS]	NO [0 POINTS]
Topic and Question Author identifies a focused, manageable topic and a specific question.		
What I Know, Assume, or Imagine Author explains what he/she already knows and what he/she does not know about the topic and question as well as what he/she hopes to learn and in general, what others commonly think (scope).		
Source Author identifies a published essay on the topic/question. Author summarizes the essay's argument (identifying the claim and key reasons/evidence). Author states his/her own view, and explains how it compares to the argument presented.		
Significance Author identifies and explains both the personal and larger significance of her/his topic and question.		
Plan Author articulates a detailed plan for accomplishing her/his research project, including the types of sources and databases, etc., to be examined.		
Correctness Author writes clearly and correctly, making few if any errors that confuse the reader. Writer uses MLA formatting correctly.		

Once again, your peers will constitute your first audience for your proposal draft. Open yourself to their feedback and to learning some new ideas from their proposals.

IN-CLASS ACTIVITY 2E:
PEER REVIEW OF DRAFT 1 OF RESEARCH PROPOSAL

Directions Reminder: Research Proposal—700 words (2–2.5 pages)

Compose a 700-word formal document that describes your plan for the Unit 4 Research Essay and Project.

What question do you plan to address, and how will you go about finding an answer?

Your Research Proposal must include the following sections:

TOPIC & QUESTION	Describe the topic and the specific question you hope to address.
WHAT I KNOW, ASSUME, OR IMAGINE (CONTEXT/ FOREGROUNDING/ BACKGROUND)	What do you already know about the topic and question? What do others in general think about the topic? What don't you already know about the topic and question? What do you hope to learn?
SOURCE	• Identify a published essay on your topic question. (You may use one of the readings in our text.) • Summarize the essay's argument (identifying the claim and key reasons/evidence). If helpful, use some of the templates we used in doing our class activities on summary and response. • State your own view, and explain how it compares to the argument presented. If helpful, use some of the templates we used in doing our class activities on summary and response.
SIGNIFICANCE	Address the questions, "Why does this topic/question matter to me? Why should it matter to anyone else? To whom does it matter?"
PLAN	What kinds of sources could be helpful to answer your question? What will you be looking for in terms of credible and useful sources?

Peer Review:

1. Form groups of 3. [ONLINE students will complete this activity as Journal Entry 6B by posting their own drafts and then responding to TWO peers' drafts. ONLINE students will have to upload the peer's draft and then follow these directions, #4 and #5.]

2. Circulate drafts.

3. Assign numbers.

4. Read draft from Writer #1.

   a. ON THE DRAFT ITSELF: Highlight/underline/circle **in blue** the parts of the essay that seem strong.

   b. ON THE DRAFT ITSELF: Highlight/underline/circle **in red** the parts of the essay about which you have questions/concerns or that confuse you.

5. In turn, discuss the essay and your comments with the writer and the rest of your group. [ONLINE students: Add at least five sentences of comments about the draft.]

6. Repeat steps 4 and 5 with next writer, until everyone's draft has been discussed.

** Remember to post journal 7, your reflection on the comments you received regarding your draft.

****Remember to revise your draft and have it ready for peer review 2.

JOURNAL ENTRY 7:
REFLECTION ON PEER REVIEW OF DRAFT 1 OF RESEARCH PROPOSAL

Reflect on what you learned from your peer review session.

1. Explain what you learned from the feedback others gave you on your draft.

2. Explain what you learned from reading your peers' drafts.

Write a three-step plan of action for your revision of your first draft. What three, <u>specific</u> changes—additions, deletions, changes in sequence, etc.—will you make to improve the draft before the next peer review? Why will you make these alterations? What <u>specific</u> effect do you hope they will have?

As you contemplate your revisions for your research proposal, particularly your planning section, you might want to consider the following:

Developing a Methods Section and Defining Essential Concepts

Use the following sentence templates to create a methods section and define essential concepts for your paper:

- This study approaches _____ by _____.
- This study views _____ through the lens of _____.
- Concepts drawn from _____ will be particularly important in analyzing _____.
- By choosing to _____, this study may _____.
- I will draw some data and exhibits from _____.

From *Writing College Research Papers, Second Edition* by Eric Drown and Kathy Sole. Copyright © 2013 by Bridgepoint Education Inc. Reprinted by permission.

In addition, remember: This proposal *belongs to you*. Using "I," a pronoun many of you have come to believe you can never use in your writing, becomes not only appropriate, but also essential. Take ownership of your research question and plan. Yes, you will also refer to what others think, but you will mix those third-person ideas with your own. This proposal, like the activities you practiced in chapter 1, represents another call and response writing, with you ("I") in the leading role.

IN-CLASS ACTIVITY 2F:
PEER REVIEW OF DRAFT 2 OF RESEARCH PROPOSAL

1. Form groups of three. [ONLINE students will complete this activity by posting their own drafts and then responding to TWO peers' drafts. ONLINE students will have to upload the peer's draft and then follow these directions, #4 and #5.]

2. Circulate drafts and fill out the attached sheets for two different drafts.

3. In turn, discuss the essay and your comments with the writer and the rest of your group. [ONLINE students: Add at least five sentences of comments about the draft.]

CHAPTER 2

FIRST ONE: Evaluator: On your peer's actual essay, annotate (use highlighting/bolding/underlining and written replies) the text. <u>Then</u> fill in this sheet. Then return both to the author.

EVALUATOR: _____ AUTHOR: _____

1. Reexamine the directions for the assignment. Does the essay address ALL parts of the directions?

   YES   NO

   If "No," describe what the essay has failed to address. _____

   _____

   _____

   _____

   _____

   _____

   _____

   _____

2. Does the author clearly identify a focused, manageable topic AND ask a clear research question?   YES   NO

   If "No," describe what the essay has failed to address. _____

   _____

   _____

   _____

   _____

   _____

   _____

   _____

3. Does the author identify AND explain BOTH the personal and the larger significance of the topic and question?   YES   NO

   If "No," describe what the essay has failed to address. _____

   _____

   _____

   _____

   _____

   _____

4. Does the author clearly identify and explain the ways in which the topic and question FIT WITHIN A LARGER CONVERSATION?   YES   NO

If "No," describe what the essay has failed to address. _____

_____

_____

_____

_____

5. Has the author articulated a DETAILED plan for accomplishing the research?
YES   NO

If "No," describe what the essay has failed to address. _____

_____

_____

_____

_____

_____

6. Has the author presented sufficient evidence/reasons to support the proposal?
YES   NO

If "No," describe what the essay needs to improve _____

_____

_____

_____

_____

_____

7. Does the title for the essay suit the essay written?   YES   NO

EXPLAIN your rationale for saying so _____

_____

_____

_____

_____

_____

8. Does the author unify the essay with smooth transitions/connections from one point to another and from one paragraph to another?   YES   NO

If "No," describe what the essay needs to improve _____

_____

_____

_____

_____

_____

_____

9. Does the author use strong language (as opposed to an overabundance of weak to be verbs [am, is, are, was, were, be, being, been] and clichés, etc.) and techniques, which compel the reader to read the argument/keep the reader interested?   YES   NO

If "No," describe what the essay needs to improve _____

_____

_____

_____

_____

_____

_____

_____

10. Does the writer adhere to language conventions—proper sentence structure, subject–verb agreement, pronoun–antecedent agreement, tenses, rules of MLA citation and Works Cited, etc.?   YES   NO

If "No," describe what the essay needs to improve _____

_____

_____

_____

_____

_____

_____

_____

11. Do you think this essay should PASS or FAIL?   PASS   FAIL

EXPLAIN why you have chosen this evaluation. _____

_____

_____

_____

_____

_____

_____

Research Proposal Rubric

CRITERIA	YES [25 POINTS] WITH EXPLANATION	NO [0 POINTS] WITH EXPLANATION
Topic and Question Author identifies a focused, manageable topic and a specific question.		
What I Know, Assume, or Imagine Author explains what he/she already knows and what he/she does not know about the topic and question as well as what he/she hopes to learn and, in general, what others commonly know (scope).		
Source Author identifies a published essay on the topic/question. Author summarizes the essay's argument (identifying the claim and key reasons/evidence). Author states his/her own view, and explains how it compares to the argument presented.		
Significance Author identifies and explains both the personal and larger significance of her/his topic and question.		
Plan Author articulates a detailed plan for accomplishing her/his research project, including the types of sources and databases, etc., to be examined.		
Correctness Author writes clearly and correctly, making few if any errors that confuse the reader. Writer uses MLA formatting correctly.		

SECOND ONE: Evaluator: On your peer's actual essay, annotate (use highlighting/ bolding/ underlining and written replies) the text. Then fill in this sheet. Then return both to the author.

Author: You will include this peer evaluation sheet with the final copy of the essay you submit.

EVALUATOR: _____ AUTHOR: _____

1. Reexamine the directions for the assignment. Does the essay address ALL parts of the directions?

   YES   NO

   If "No," describe what the essay has failed to address. _____

   _____

   _____

   _____

   _____

   _____

   _____

2. Does the author clearly identify a focused, manageable topic AND ask a clear research question?   YES   NO

   If "No," describe what the essay has failed to address. _____

   _____

   _____

   _____

   _____

   _____

   _____

3. Does the author identify AND explain BOTH the personal and the larger significance of the topic and question?   YES   NO

   If "No," describe what the essay has failed to address. _____

   _____

   _____

   _____

   _____

   _____

   _____

4. Does the author clearly identify and explain the ways in which the topic and question FIT WITHIN A LARGER CONVERSATION?   YES   NO

   If "No," describe what the essay has failed to address. _____

   _____

   _____

   _____

   _____

5. Has the author articulated a DETAILED plan for accomplishing the research? YES   NO

   If "No," describe what the essay has failed to address. _____

   _____

   _____

   _____

   _____

   _____

   _____

6. Has the author presented sufficient evidence/reasons to support her/his proposal? YES   NO

   If "No," describe what the essay needs to improve _____

   _____

   _____

   _____

   _____

   _____

   _____

7. Does the title for the essay suit the essay written?   YES   NO

   EXPLAIN your rationale for saying so _____

   _____

   _____

   _____

   _____

   _____

8. Does the author unify the essay with smooth transitions/connections from one point to another and from one paragraph to another?   YES   NO

If "No," describe what the essay needs to improve _____

_____

_____

_____

_____

_____

_____

9. Does the author use strong language (as opposed to an overabundance of weak to be verbs [am, is, are, was, were, be, being, been] and clichés, etc.) and techniques, which compel the reader to read the argument/keep the reader interested?   YES   NO

If "No," describe what the essay needs to improve _____

_____

_____

_____

_____

_____

_____

10. Does the writer adhere to language conventions—proper sentence structure, subject–verb agreement, pronoun–antecedent agreement, tenses, rules of MLA citation and Works Cited, etc.?   YES   NO

If "No," describe what the essay needs to improve _____

_____

_____

_____

_____

_____

_____

11. Do you think this essay should PASS or FAIL?   PASS   FAIL

EXPLAIN why you have chosen this evaluation. _____
_____
_____
_____
_____
_____
_____

Research Proposal Rubric

CRITERIA	YES [25 POINTS] WITH EXPLANATION	NO [0 POINTS] WITH EXPLANATION
Topic and Question Author identifies a focused, manageable topic and a specific question.		
What I Know, Assume, or Imagine Author explains what he/she already knows and what he/she does not know about the topic and question as well as what he/she hopes to learn and, in general, what others commonly know (scope).		
Source Author identifies a published essay on the topic/question. Author summarizes the essay's argument (identifying the claim and key reasons/evidence). Author states his/her own view, and explains how it compares to the argument presented.		
Significance Author identifies and explains both the personal and larger significance of her/his topic and question.		
Plan Author articulates a detailed plan for accomplishing her/his research project, including the types of sources and databases, etc., to be examined.		
Correctness Author writes clearly and correctly, making few if any errors that confuse the reader. Writer uses MLA formatting correctly.		

F. Model Research Proposal

MODEL "RESEARCH PROPOSAL" ESSAY

Food Insecurity: Its Causes and Solutions

Today, the issue of food insecurity baffles a great many people. Even the label—"food insecurity"—seems so fancy that it hides the reality of its meaning: that even in this prosperous nation, a great many people do not have enough to eat on a daily basis and go to bed hungry every night. Some believe those who do not have enough food have only themselves to blame because they did not plan their lives well or they spend money on drugs or other objects that do not matter, while others think the amount of food Americans waste in a year could feed all of these people, and the government should step in to control that waste and allocate food resources in a more efficient way than it does. As a future teacher, this topic has become important to me, especially because I know that if students come to school hungry, they cannot learn as well as those who are well-fed. I'd really like to know just two elements of this problem: why so many people in the United States do not have enough to eat and what we as a country can do to solve this problem.

I do know a little something about the problem already. For example, because I volunteer at a food pantry, I understand that a whole lot of working people still do not have enough money to buy food for their families, because food is expensive, but their wages are low. In addition, through listening to news reports, I have learned that the government actually pays farmers not to grow some food, and we also ship some of the food we do grow overseas, to other countries. I know, too, that not having enough food to eat is just one of many symptoms of the problem of poverty. I know that grocery stores and restaurants throw away tons of perfectly good food every year. Lastly, I know that not having food can cause both physical and psychological problems for anyone suffering from that lack of food. Based on this limited knowledge, I have a general theory or hypothesis; I imagine that food insecurity is a societal problem that affects not just the hungry, but also the whole community and nation, and that if we can convince people about these effects, we can get society to commit to ending food insecurity through federal, state, and community programs. Nonetheless, much exists that I do not know or understand fully. Apart from my actual research question, the small sub-issues that encompass my current knowledge gaps include finding out how expansive the problem really is, what kinds of solutions have worked and failed, and what kinds of costs would be involved in addressing the issue fully.

As I consider these knowledge gaps and the direction I need to follow in my research, I have begun with a single article: "America Has A Hunger Problem," written by the *Atlantic* Marketing Team for Food For America and published in *The Atlantic (Original Thinking*

Series) in June 2019. This author's basic claim is that, "America has a hunger problem, and its ripple effects are stronger than [we] think." In essence, these authors postulate that individuals' lack of food actually threatens the whole nation because it harms people's minds and bodies to the point that they cannot function well in school, at work, or anywhere, and as a result they make society as a whole less productive and successful. The authors use a lot of statistics, some concrete examples from real people, and some scientific explanations as the supporting evidence. In addition, they provide a sample of what one community plans to do and an accompanying explanation of how that plan will work. As I contemplate this claim and evidence, my own tentative contention surfaces as the idea that food insecurity is a US societal issue that can and should be addressed with federal, state, and local programs to feed all people because doing so will actually cost society less than addressing the residual problems that occur because of the lack of good nutrition obtained through food.

Regardless of my current premise, I will need to gather additional sources. Gathering these sources and answering my research question matter to me because a great many of the people going hungry daily are children, and as a future educator, I know that having food can affect children's progress in school. I would like to know my future students can think about their schoolwork instead of about the hunger gnawing inside their stomachs and draining away their focus and attention. The topic has significance to a larger audience, too, specifically employers who want educated workers and want employees who can pay attention to their work and work well as well as to all taxpayers in general because they will fund the programs necessary to solve the problem.

To address the importance of the issue by discovering the answers to my research question, I will need to follow a specific plan. I will begin by using the search terms "food insecurity in the USA," "hunger in the USA," "causes of food insecurity in the USA," "ending hunger in the USA," and "programs to alleviate hunger in the USA" in the following databases: *Academic Search Complete*, *New York Times*, *Soc Index*, and *CQ Researcher*. These scholarly resources make the best sense, because the problem is general yet specific to society and something Congress has probably studied. In addition, I will seek books like *Still Hungry in America* by Coles, *All You Can Eat: How Hungry is America?* by Berg, and *Big Hunger: The Unholy Alliance Between Corporate America and Anti-Hunger Groups* by Fisher and Jayaraman, all titles I found in a Google search, and I will examine the Internet for documentaries about the problem and for US Census Bureau data. I might also contemplate conducting a live interview with people who come to the food pantry or find an online interview or documentary with real people or someone from Feed America. I hope to have gathered five to eight sources by October 20th, so that I can get started on my research project's completion by early November.

I look forward to doing this work because I think hunger is an important issue. I still cannot believe how many people in this country cannot eat each day. I hope this project helps me to figure out how to help.

G. Readings to Get You Thinking about 5 Possible Topic Categories

READINGS AND RESOURCES

© Mascha Tace/Shutterstock.com

On The Environment

© Drawii/Shutterstock.com

© Luxxam/Shutterstock.com

Excerpt from *Our Vanishing Wild Life* by William T. Hornaday, Charles Scribner's Sons, 1913.

PART I. EXTERMINATION
CHAPTER I
The Former Abundance of Wild Life

"By my labors my vineyard flourished. But Ahab came. Alas! for Naboth."

In order that the American people may correctly understand and judge the question of the extinction or preservation of our wild life, it is necessary to recall the near past. It is not necessary, however, to go far into the details of history; for a few quick glances at a few high points will be quite sufficient for the purpose in view.

Any man who reads the books which best tell the story of the development of the American colonies of 1712 into the American nation of 1912, and takes due note of the wild-life features of the tale, will say without hesitation that when the American people received this land from the bountiful hand of Nature, it was endowed with a magnificent and all-pervading supply of valuable wild creatures. The pioneers and the early settlers were too busy even to take due note of that fact, or to comment upon it, save in very fragmentary ways.

Nevertheless, the wild-life abundance of early American days survived down to so late a period that it touched the lives of millions of people now living. Any man 55 years of age who when a boy had a taste for "hunting,"—for at that time there were no "sportsmen" in America,—will remember the flocks and herds of wild creatures that he saw and which made upon his mind many indelible impressions.

"Abundance" is the word with which to describe the original animal life that stocked our country, and all North America, only a short half-century ago. Throughout every state, on every shoreline, in all the millions of fresh water lakes, ponds and rivers, on every mountain range, in every forest, *and even on every desert*, the wild flocks and herds held sway. It was impossible to go beyond the settled haunts of civilized man and escape them.

It was a full century after the complete settlement of New England and the Virginia colonies that the wonderful big-game fauna of the great plains and Rocky Mountains was really discovered; but the bison millions, the antelope millions, the mule deer, the mountain sheep and mountain goat were there, all the time. In the early days, the millions of pinnated grouse and quail of the central states attracted no serious attention from the American people-at-large; but they lived and flourished just the same, far down in the seventies, when the greedy market gunners systematically slaughtered them, and barreled them up for "the market," while the foolish farmers calmly permitted them to do it.

We obtain the best of our history of the former abundance of North American wild life first from the pages of Audubon and Wilson; next, from the records left by such pioneers as Lewis and Clark, and last from the testimony of living men. To all this we can, many of us, add observations of our own.

To me the most striking fact that stands forth in the story of American wild life one hundred years ago is the wide extent and thoroughness of its distribution. Wide as our country is, and marvelous as it is in the diversity of its climates, its soils, its topography, its flora, its riches and its poverty, Nature gave to each square mile and to each acre a generous quota of wild creatures, according to its ability to maintain living things. No pioneer ever pushed so far, or into regions so difficult or so remote, that he did not find awaiting him a host of birds and beasts. Sometimes the pioneer was not a good hunter; usually he was a stupid fisherman; but the "game" was there, nevertheless. The time was when every farm had its quota.

The part that the wild life of America played in the settlement and development of this continent was so far-reaching in extent, and so enormous in potential value, that it fairly staggers the imagination. From the landing of the Pilgrims down to the present hour the wild game has been the mainstay and the resource against starvation of the pathfinder, the settler, the prospector, and at times even the railroad-builder. In view of what the bison millions did for the Dakotas, Montana, Wyoming, Kansas and Texas, it is only right and square that those states should now do something for the perpetual preservation of the bison species and all other big game that needs help.

For years and years, the antelope millions of the Montana and Wyoming grass-lands fed the scout and Indian-fighter, freighter, cowboy and surveyor, ranchman *and sheep-herder*; but thus far I have yet to hear of one Western state that has ever spent one penny directly for the preservation of the antelope! And to-day we are in a hand-to-hand fight in Congress, and in Montana, with the Wool-Growers Association, which maintains in Washington a keen lobbyist to keep aloft the tariff on wool, and prevent Congress from taking 15 square miles of grass lands on Snow Creek, Montana, for a National Antelope Preserve. All that the wool-growers want is the entire earth, all to themselves. Mr. McClure, the Secretary of the Association says:

> "The proper place in which to preserve the big game of the West is in city parks, where it can be protected."

To the colonist of the East and pioneer of the West, the white-tailed deer was an ever present help in time of trouble. Without this omnipresent animal, and the supply of good meat that each white flag represented, the commissariat difficulties of the settlers who won the country as far westward as Indiana would have been many times greater than they were. The backwoods Pilgrim's progress was like this:

> Trail, deer; cabin, deer; clearing; bear, corn, deer; hogs, deer; cattle, wheat, independence.

And yet, how many men are there to-day, out of our ninety millions of Americans and pseudo-Americans, who remember with any feeling of gratitude the part played in American history by the white-tailed deer? Very few! How many Americans are there in our land who now preserve that deer for sentimental reasons, and because his forbears were nation-builders? As a matter of fact, are there any?

On every eastern pioneer's monument, the white-tailed deer should figure; and on those of the Great West, the bison and the antelope should be cast in enduring bronze, *"lest we forget!"*

The game birds of America played a different part from that of the deer, antelope and bison. In the early days, shotguns were few, and shot was scarce and dear. The wild turkey and goose were the smallest birds on which a rifleman could afford to expend a bullet and a whole charge of powder. It was for this reason that the deer, bear, bison, and elk disappeared from the eastern United States while the game birds yet remained abundant. With the disappearance of the big game came the fat steer, hog and hominy, the wheat-field, fruit orchard and poultry galore.

The game birds of America, as a class and a mass, have not been swept away to ward off starvation or to rescue the perishing. Even back in the sixties and seventies, very, very few men of the North thought of killing prairie chickens, ducks and quail, snipe and woodcock, in order to keep the hunger wolf from the door. The process was too slow and uncertain; and besides, the really-poor man rarely had the gun and ammunition. Instead of attempting to live on birds, he hustled for the staple food products that the soil of his own farm could produce.

First, last and nearly all the time, the game birds of the United States as a whole, have been sacrificed on the altar of Rank Luxury, to tempt appetites that were tired of fried chicken and other farm delicacies. To-day, even the average poor man hunts birds for the joy of the outing, and the pampered epicures of the hotels and restaurants buy game birds, and eat small portions of them, solely to tempt jaded appetites. If there is such a thing as "class" legislation, it is that which permits a few sordid market-shooters to slaughter the birds of the whole people in order to sell them to a few epicures.

The game of a state belongs to the whole people of the state. The Supreme Court of the United States has so decided. (Geer vs. Connecticut). If it is abundant, it is a valuable asset. The great value of the game birds of America lies not in their meat pounds as they lie upon the table, but in the temptation they annually put before millions of field-weary farmers and desk-weary clerks and merchants to get into their beloved hunting togs, stalk out into the lap of Nature, and say "Begone, dull Care!"

And the man who has had a fine day in the painted woods, on the bright waters of a duck-haunted bay, or in the golden stubble of September, can fill his day and his soul with six good birds just as well as with sixty. The idea that in order to enjoy a fine day in the open a man must kill a wheel-barrow load of birds, is a mistaken idea; and if obstinately adhered to, it becomes vicious! The Outing in the Open is the thing,—not the blood-stained feathers, nasty viscera and Death in the game-bag. One quail on a fence is worth more to the world than ten in a bag.

The farmers of America have, by their own supineness and lack of foresight, permitted the slaughter of a stock of game birds which, had it been properly and wisely conserved, would have furnished a good annual shoot to every farming man and boy of sporting instincts through the past, right down to the present, and far beyond. They have allowed millions of dollars worth of *their* birds to be coolly snatched away from them by the greedy market-shooters.

There is one state in America, and so far as I know *only one*, in which there is at this moment an old-time abundance of game-bird life. That is the state of Louisiana. The reason is not so very far to seek. For the birds that do not migrate,—quail, wild turkeys and doves,—the cover is yet abundant. For the migratory game birds of the Mississippi Valley, Louisiana is a grand central depot, with terminal facilities that are unsurpassed. Her reedy shores, her vast marshes, her long coast line and abundance of food furnish what should be not only a haven but a heaven for ducks and geese. After running the gauntlet of guns all the way from Manitoba and Ontario to the Sunk Lands of Arkansas, the shores of the Gulf must seem like heaven itself.

The great forests of Louisiana shelter deer, turkeys, and fur-bearing animals galore; and rabbits and squirrels abound.

Naturally, this abundance of game has given rise to an extensive industry in shooting for the market. The "big interests" outside the state send their agents into the best game districts, often bringing in their own force of shooters. They comb out the game in enormous quantities, without leaving to the people of Louisiana any decent and fair quid-pro-quo for having despoiled them of their game and shipped a vast annual product outside, to create wealth elsewhere.

At present, however, we are but incidentally interested in the short-sightedness of the people of the Pelican State. As a state of oldtime abundance in killable game, the killing records that were kept in the year 1909-10 possess for us very great interest. They throw a startling searchlight on the subject of this chapter,—the former abundance of wild life.

From the records that with great pains and labor were gathered by the State Game Commission, and which were furnished me for use here by President Frank M. Miller, we set forth this remarkable exhibit of old-fashioned abundance in game, A.D. 1909.

Official Record Of Game Killed In Louisiana During The Season (12 Months) Of 1909–10	
Birds	
Wild Ducks, sea and river	3,176,000
Coots	280,740
Geese and Brant	202,210
Snipe, Sandpiper and Plover	606,635
Quail (Bob-White)	1,140,750
Doves	310,660
Wild Turkeys	2,219

Total number of game birds killed	5,719,214
Mammals	
Deer	5,470
Squirrels and Rabbits	690,270

Total of game mammals	695,740
Fur-bearing mammals	1,971,922

Total of mammals	2,667,662

Grand total of birds and mammals	8,386,876

Of the thousands of slaughtered robins, it would seem that no records exist. It is to be understood that the annual slaughter of wild life in Louisiana never before reached such a pitch as now. Without drastic measures, what will be the inevitable result? Does any man suppose that even the wild millions of Louisiana can long withstand such slaughter as that shown by the official figures given above? It is wildly impossible.

But the darkest hour is just before the dawn. At the session of the Louisiana legislature that was held in the spring of 1912, great improvements were made in the game laws of that state. The most important feature was the suppression of wholesale market hunting, by persons who are not residents of the state. A very limited amount of game may be sold and served as food in public places, but the restrictions placed upon this traffic are so effective that they will vastly reduce the annual slaughter. In other respects, also, the cause of wild life protection gained much; for which great credit is due to Mr. Edward A. McIlhenny.

It is the way of Americans to feel that because game is abundant in a given place at a given time, it always will be abundant, and may therefore be slaughtered without limit. That was the case last winter in California during the awful slaughter of band-tailed pigeons, as will be noted elsewhere.

It is time for all men to be told in the plainest terms that there never has existed, anywhere in historic times, a volume of wild life so great that civilized man could not quickly exterminate it by his methods of destruction. Lift the veil and look at the stories of the bison, the passenger pigeon, the wild ducks, and shore birds of the Atlantic coast, and the fur-seal.

SHALL WE LEAVE ANY ONE OF THEM OPEN?

As reasoning beings, it is our duty to heed the lessons of history, and not rush blindly on until we perpetrate a continent destitute of wild life.

CHAPTER II
Extinct Species of North American Birds

For educated, civilized Man to exterminate a valuable wild species of living things is a crime. It is a crime against his own children, and posterity.

No man has a right, either moral or legal, to destroy or squander an inheritance of his children that he holds for them in trust. And man, the wasteful and greedy spendthrift that he is, has not created even the humblest of the species of birds, mammals and fishes that adorn and enrich this earth. "The earth is THE LORD'S, and the fulness thereof!" With all his wisdom, man has not evolved and placed here so much as a ground-squirrel, a sparrow or a clam. It is true that he has juggled with the wild horse and sheep, the goats and the swine, and produced some hardy breeds that can withstand his abuse without going down before it; but as for species, he has not yet created and placed here even so much as a protozoan.

The wild things of this earth are *not* ours, to do with as we please. They have been given to us *in trust*, and we must account for them to the generations which will come after us and audit our accounts.

But man, the shameless destroyer of Nature's gifts, blithely and persistently exterminates one species after another. Fully ten per cent of the human race consists of people who will lie, steal, throw rubbish in parks, and destroy forests and wild life whenever and wherever they can do so without being stopped by a policemen and a club. These are hard words, but they are absolutely true. From ten per cent (or more) of the human race, the high moral instinct which is honest without compulsion *is absent*. The things that seemingly decent citizens,—men posing as gentlemen,—will do to wild game when they secure great chances to slaughter, are appalling. I could fill a book of this size with cases in point.

From: Hornaday, William T. "Part 1. Extermination Chapter 1 The Formar Abundance of Wild Life." *In Our Vanishing Wild Life,* 1–6. New York: Charles Scribner's Sons, 1913.

https://www.gutenberg.org/files/13249/13249-h/13249-h.htm

◇◇◇

Excerpt from "Wilderness Letter" by Wallace Stegner

Something will have gone out of us as a people if we ever let the remaining wilderness be destroyed; if we permit the last virgin forests to be turned into comic books and plastic cigarette cases; if we drive the few remaining members of the wild species into zoos or to extinction; if we pollute the last clear air and dirty the last clean streams and push our paved roads through the last of the silence, so that never again will Americans be free in their own country from the noise, the exhausts, the stinks of human and automotive waste. And so that never again can we have the chance to see ourselves single, separate, vertical and individual in the world, part of the environment of trees and rocks and soil, brother to the other animals, part of the natural world and competent to belong in it. Without any remaining wilderness we are committed wholly, without chance for even momentary reflection and rest, to a headlong drive into our technological termite-life, the Brave New World of a completely man-controlled environment. We need wilderness preserved—as much of it as is still left, and as many kinds—because it was the challenge against which our character as a people was formed. The reminder and the reassurance that it is still there is good for our spiritual health even if we never once in ten years set foot in it.

From: Stegner, Wallace. "Wilderness Letter (1960)." *The Wilderness Society Newsletter,* December 28, 2009.

https://psych.utah.edu/_resources/documents/psych4130/Stenger_W.pdf

"Your Food Choices Can Have a Big Climate Impact, So Be Picky, New Study Says" by Georgina Gustin, May 31, 2018, in *Inside Climate News:*

https://insideclimatenews.org/news/31052018/environmental-impacts-food-production-climate-change-meat-vegetarian-vegan-diets-global-warming-study

"Food Waste Challenge" by USDA (United States Department of Agriculture) Office of Chief Economist:

https://www.usda.gov/oce/foodwaste/faqs.htm

"The Causes of Climate Change," May 17, 2019, by NASA:

https://climate.nasa.gov/causes/

"Population Control, The Environmental Fix No One Wants to Talk About" by Samantha Dooley on May 16, 2018, in *World Crunch Les Echos:*

https://www.worldcrunch.com/opinion-analysis/population-control-the-environmental-fix-no-one-wants-to-talk-about

"Extreme Weather" by the National Climate Assessment Program, 2014:

https://nca2014.globalchange.gov/highlights/report-findings/extreme-weather

"Landfills" by The Environmental Literacy Council, 2015:

https://enviroliteracy.org/environment-society/waste-management/landfills/

"Health Care Waste" by the World Health Organization, February 8, 2018:

https://www.who.int/news-room/fact-sheets/detail/health-care-waste

"The Link between the Environment and Our Health" by "Earth Talk" in *Scientific American:*

https://www.scientificamerican.com/article/environment-and-our-health/?redirect=1

"Environmental Issues: Green Computing" by Carnegie Melon University, 2019:

http://www.carnegiecyberacademy.com/facultyPages/environment/issues.html

"401 Prompts for Argumentative Writing" from The Learning Network of the *New York Times*, March 1, 2017:

https://www.nytimes.com/2017/03/01/learning/lesson-plans/401-prompts-for-argumentative-writing.html

© HDesert/Shutterstock.com

© Rawpixel.com/Shutterstock.com

CHAPTER 2

Excerpt from *Open Source Democracy: How Online Communication is Changing Offline Politics* by Douglas Rushkoff

CHAPTER 3

The Opportunity for Renaissance

The birth of the internet was interpreted by many as a revolution. Those of us in the counterculture saw in the internet an opportunity to topple the storytellers who had dominated our politics, economics, society and religion—in short our very reality—and to replace their stories with those of our own. It was a beautiful and exciting sentiment, but one as based in a particular narrative as any other. Revolutions simply replace one story with another. The capitalist narrative is replaced by that of the communist; the religious fundamentalist's replaced by the gnostic's. The means may be different, but the rewards are the same. So is the exclusivity of their distribution. That's why they're called revolutions—we're just going in a circle.

This is why it might be more useful to understand the proliferation of interactive media as an opportunity for renaissance: a moment when we have the ability to step out of the story altogether. Renaissances are historical instances of widespread recontextualisation. People in a variety of different arts, philosophies and sciences have the ability to reframe their reality. Renaissance literally means 'rebirth.' It is the rebirth of old ideas in a new context. A renaissance is a dimensional leap, when our perspective shifts so dramatically that our understanding of the oldest, most fundamental elements of existence changes. The stories we have been using no longer work.

Take a look back at what we think of as the original Renaissance; the one we were taught in school. What were the main leaps in perspective? One example is the use of perspective in painting. Artists developed the technique of the vanishing point and with it the ability to paint three-dimensional representations on two-dimensional surfaces. The character of this innovation is subtle but distinct. It is not a technique for working in three dimensions; it is not that artists moved from working on canvas to working with clay. Rather, perspective painting allows an artist to relate between dimensions: representing three-dimensional objects on a two-dimensional plane. . . .

Similarly, the invention of moveable type and the printing press changed the relationship of author and audience to text. The creation of a manuscript was no longer a one-pointed affair. The creation of the first manuscript still was, but now it could be replicated and distributed to everyone. It was still one story, but now was subject to a multiplicity of individual perspectives. This innovation alone changed the landscape of religion in the Western World. Individual interpretation of the Bible led to the collapse of Church authority and the unilateral nature of its decrees. Everyone demanded his or her own relationship to the story.

Our Electronic Renaissance

In all these cases, people experienced a very particular shift in their relationship to, and understanding of, dimensions. Understood this way, a renaissance is a moment of reframing. We step out of the frame as it is currently defined and see the whole picture in a new context. We can then play by new rules.

It is akin to the experience of a computer game player. At first, a gamer will play a video or computer game by the rules. He'll read the manual, if necessary, then move through the various levels of the game. Mastery of the game, at this stage, means getting to the end: making it to the last level, surviving, becoming the most powerful character or, in the case of a simulation game, designing and maintaining a thriving family, city or civilisation. For many gamers, this is as far as it goes.

Some gamers, though—usually after they've mastered this level of play—will venture out onto the internet in search of other fans or user groups. There, they will gather the cheat codes that can be used to acquire special abilities within the game, such as invisibility or an infinite supply of ammunition. When the gamer returns to the game with his secret codes, is he still playing the game or is he cheating? From a renaissance perspective he is still playing the game, albeit a different one. His playing field has grown from the CD on which the game was shipped to the entire universe of computers where these secret codes and abilities can be discussed and shared. He is no longer playing the game, but a meta-game. The inner game world is still fun, but it is distanced by the gamer's new perspective, much in the way we are distanced from the play-within-a-play in one of Shakespeare's comedies or dramas. And the meta-theatrical convention gives us new perspective on the greater story as well. Gaming, as a metaphor but also as a lived experience, invites a renaissance perspective on the world in which we live. Perhaps gamers and their game culture have been as responsible as anyone for the rise in expressly self-similar forms of television like *Beavis and Butthead*, *The Simpsons* and *Southpark*. The joy of such programs is not the relief of reaching the climax of the linear narrative, but rather the momentary thrill of making connections. The satisfaction is in recognising which bits of media are being satirised at any given moment. It is an entirely new perspective on television, where programs exist more in the form of Talmudic commentary: perspectives on perspectives on perspectives. We watch screens within screens, constantly reminded, almost as in a Brecht play, of the artifice of storytelling. It is as if we are looking at a series of proscenium arches, and are being invited as an audience to consider whether we are within a proscenium arch ourselves.

The great Renaissance was a simple leap in perspective. Instead of seeing everything in one dimension, we came to realise there was more than one dimension on which things were occurring.

Even the Elizabethan world picture, with its concentric rings of authority—God, king, man, animals—reflects this newfound way of contending with the simultaneity of action of many dimensions at once. A gamer stepping out onto the internet to find a cheat code certainly reaches this first renaissance's level of awareness and skill.

But what of the gamer who then learns to program new games for himself? He, we might argue, has stepped out of yet another frame into our current renaissance. He has deconstructed the content of the game, demystified the technology of its interface and now feels ready to open the codes and turn the game into a do-it-yourself activity. He has moved from a position of a receiving player to that of a deconstructing user. He has assumed the position of author, himself. This leap to authorship is precisely the character and quality of the dimensional leap associated with today's renaissance.

The evidence of today's renaissance is at least as profound as that of the one that went before. The 16th century saw the successful circumnavigation of the globe via the seas. The 20th century saw the successful circumnavigation of the globe from space. The first pictures of earth from space changed our perspective on this sphere forever. In the same century, our dominance over the planet was confirmed not just through our ability to travel around it, but to destroy it. The atomic bomb (itself the result of a rude dimensional interchange between submolecular particles) gave us the ability to author the globe's very destiny. Now, instead of merely being able to comprehend 'God's creation,' we could actively control it. This is a new perspective.

We also have our equivalent of perspective painting, in the invention of the holograph. The holograph allows us to represent not just three, but four dimensions on a two-dimensional plate. When the viewer walks past a holograph she can observe the three-dimensional object over a course of time. A bird can flap its wings in a single picture. But, more importantly for our renaissance's purposes, the holographic plate itself embodies a new renaissance principle. When the plate is smashed into hundreds of pieces, we do not find that one piece contains the bird's wing, and another piece the bird's beak. Each piece of the plate contains a faint image of the entire subject. When the pieces are put together, the image achieves greater resolution. But each piece contains a representation of the totality. This leap in dimensional understanding is now informing disciplines as diverse as brain anatomy and computer programming. . . .

Finally, our renaissance's answer to the printing press is the computer and its ability to network. Just as the printing press gave everyone access to readership, the computer and internet give everyone access to authorship. The first Renaissance took us from the position of passive recipient to active interpreter. Our current renaissance brings us from the role of interpreter to the role of author. We are the creators.

As game programmers instead of game players, the creators of testimony rather than the believers in testament, we begin to become aware of just how much of our reality is open source and up for discussion. So much of what seemed like impenetrable hardware is actually software and ripe for reprogramming. The stories we use to understand the world seem less like explanations and more like collaborations. They are rule sets, only as good as their ability to explain the patterns of history or predict those of the future. . . .

What Gets Reborn

The renaissance experience of moving beyond the frame allows everything old to look new again. We are liberated from the maps we have been using to navigate our world and free to create new ones based on our own observations. This invariably leads to a whole new era of competition. Renaissance may be a rebirth of old ideas in a new context, but which ideas get to be reborn?

The first to recognise the new renaissance will compete to have their ideologies be the ones that are rebirthed in this new context. This is why, with the emergence of the internet, we saw the attempted rebirth (and occasional stillbirth) of everything from paganism to libertarianism, and communism to psychedelia. Predictably, the financial markets and consumer capitalism, the dominant narratives of our era, were the first to successfully commandeer the renaissance. But they squandered their story on a pyramid scheme (indeed, the accelerating force of computers and networks tends to force any story to its logical conclusion) and now the interactive renaissance is once again up for grabs. . . .

From: Rushkoff, Douglas. "Chapter 3 The opportunity for renaissance." In *Open Source Democracy How online communication is changing offline politics,* N.P. Guttenburg EBook through Demos Open Access, 2003.

> http://www.gutenberg.org/cache/epub/10753/pg10753-images.html

◇◇

"The Future of Truth and Misinformation Online" by Janna Anderson and Lee Rainie on October 19, 2017, for The Pew Research Center:

> https://www.pewinternet.org/2017/10/19/the-future-of-truth-and-misinformation-online/

"How the Internet is Changing Our Brains" by Academic Earth (a video with written summary):

> https://academicearth.org/electives/internet-changing-your-brain/

"Pros and Cons of Online Dating" by Jeremy Nicholson, April 30, 2014, in *Psychology Today:*

> https://www.psychologytoday.com/us/blog/the-attraction-doctor/201404/pros-and-cons-online-dating

"Social Media and Adolescents' and Young Adults' Mental Health" by Elina Mir and Caroline Novas for the National Center for Health Research:

> http://www.center4research.org/social-media-affects-mental-health/

"Big Fail: The internet hasn't helped democracy" by Bryan Keogh, October 15, 2019, on *The Conversation:*

> https://theconversation.com/big-fail-the-internet-hasnt-helped-democracy-104817

© Lightspring/Shutterstock.com

Excerpt From *Imported Americans* by Broughton Brandenburg

The story of the experiences of a disguised American and his wife studying the immigration question

CHAPTER I
THE IMPETUS AND THE METHOD

That there was a tremendous increase in immigration in prospect was announced by the agents of the great immigrant-carrying lines of steamships as early as January of 1903. All Europe seemed stirred with that tide of unrest. It was to be a great year for the departure from the Continental hives of the new swarms, and an authoritative foreign journal prophesied that the sum total would be 1,500,000 for the twelve months.

In America the cry was redoubled that the doors of the United States should be altogether closed or rendered still more difficult to pass. The Shattuc bill was about to find favor in the House of Representatives, the Lodge bill was cooking in Boston, and in every newspaper or periodical of the land articles and editorials were appearing that attacked or defended various phases, conditions or proposed remedies of immigration. Even in the German and Italian papers, which speak for Germany, Austria and Italy, the most fertile immigrant-producing grounds, there was but the barest trifle printed that was *from the point of view of the immigrant himself*. In the American papers there was absolutely nothing.

One day I was in the Grand Central station in New York, ready to take a train for New Haven, and as I came up to the gate I saw, passing through before me, a group of more than twenty newly arrived Italians, following the leadership of one short, black, thick-set prosperous-seeming man who spoke Italian to the left and broken English to the right. They were tagged for Boston and other New England towns, and, bearing their heavy burdens of luggage and bundles, with faces drawn with weariness, eyes dull with too much gazing at the wonders of a new land, with scarce a smile among them except on the faces of the unreasoning children, they were herded together, counted off as they passed through the gate and taken aboard the train, much as if they had been some sort of animals worth more than ordinary care, instead of rational human beings. Here they were in charge of the conductor, who grouped them in seats according to the towns to which they were destined.

When I was seated and had unfolded my paper the first thing that caught my eye was an article in which a noted sociologist was liberally quoted recommending the total suspension of immigration for three years and *then* new laws admitting only those who would come with their families and were trained in some work demanding skill. The arguments were specious, but as I looked over the top of the paper at the poor creatures huddled in the car seats about, very thinly dressed for so cold a January day, it occurred to me that the true light, the revelation of the natural remedies and the only real understanding of the immigrant situation lay in seeing from the underside, in getting the immigrants' point of view to compare with the public-spirited American one.

That was the leaven and it grew. The idea ramified into a plan, and this plan was laid before Mr. Ellery Sedgwick, the editor of *Leslie's Monthly*, and very soon it was decided that I was to go seeking the immigrants' point of view and was to take my wife with me.

All of the intricacies of how, where and just what, evolved slowly, but this in brief was our general plan: First of all we must choose the ground for our investigation. Since Italy sends not only three times more immigrants than any other country, but a larger proportion of the sort that are objected to in America, it was plain that our work lay among the Italians. We must know the language well enough to ask questions and understand answers; we must know the conditions of Italian life in America in order to know what good and what evil things to trace to their sources. To understand the people properly, we must live with them and be of them, and, to get the fullest grasp on the process of their transmutation we must become immigrants ourselves and re-enter our own country as strangers and aliens.

Therefore we must take up our abode in the Italian quarter, and, when duly prepared and informed, voyage to the home land with some of the returning Italians and, having learned the actual conditions there, come back in the steerage and pass through Ellis Island, bringing with us some typical immigrant family whose exact circumstances we had fully learned in their native community. Using them as a central strand we would weave a story of small things that should be worthy of being taken into reckoning by thinking minds, as a new and important fund of information.

Though we knew full well the hardships which we must endure for many long months, the difficulties which would arise like forbidding barriers, I am free to say that the things on which we had counted and against which we had armed ourselves did not come to pass for the most part; while a multitude of things happened that were as unexpected as gold in breakfast food.

Work began at once, by the book, on the language, and while in the wilds of Yucatan in February we were studying Italian. In March we landed in New York late one night from the Ward liner *Monterey*, and the very next day went into the Italian quarter seeking a place to live. When we had been in the reeking streets, amid the tumult of innumerable children, and had entered a few of the tenements, my wife turned pale and sick and said:

"Don't think I am faltering at the threshold; but, please, if we must go through all this, let us have a week of comfort and preparation. Then we will take the plunge."

Thus I knew how much harder it was for her, with all her love of comfort and her accustomed-ness to it, to forsake it for any purpose, however important or worth while, than it was for me, who, manlike, enjoy "the fare of the field, and the habit of the strange land." And thereafter, particularly when we were in the steerage of the *Prinzessin Irene* and were bound home, actually counting the half-hours of the twelve-day voyage amid utter wretchedness, never did I hear one complaint from her lips or did she give other sign of failing.

At the very outset we had difficulty in gaining admission to any all-Italian house. In the tene-ments where several rooms were to be had, the Italian real-estate agents eyed us with suspicion and averred solemnly that they were all full, even to the roof. This they asserted, notwithstanding empty apartments to be seen from the street and "Rooms to Let" signs without number. In the boarding houses we were met with a very cold reception even before it was known what we wanted. In the Italian hotels it was the same way with the exception of one south of Washington Square, and there the proprietor kindly offered to let us in at twice the ordinary price, according to the rates tacked on the room doors. At last, however, we came to the domicile of the Chevalier Celestin Tonella. Here we found our haven.

It was some time after we were settled before we learned that we were under the roof of a noble-man. If we had been familiar with the nice distinctions of Italian caste, however, we should have known it instantly. The three houses Nos. 141, 145, 147 West Houston Street, entered by the door of No. 147, seemed to us very little different from many of the other tenements in which we had been, and indeed they were not. The difference all lay in the master not in the mansion. If I had known before paying my rent in advance that my landlord had a title, I should have demurred, thinking that in his house there would be life a little too high in grade for the real Italian quarter; but before I knew the Chevalier's station, I had learned that we were in the proper element and surrounded by the very atmosphere we sought, though the same at meal times would have almost killed a strong man in his prime.

Just before we gained admittance to the desired quarters we were in the office of a real-estate man who has an exclusively Italian custom in the lower West Side quarter, renting to people of his own race and tongue houses owned by wealthy people up-town. When he had refused to give us an opportunity at anything on his lists I said to him:

"See here. We have been hunting rooms all day. We have been frustrated from Mulberry Street to Fifteenth. I have got money and can give references, but nobody seems to care about either. What is the matter? Why can we not get into an Italian house?"

"Scoose me, mister, bot wye youse want to?"

"We want to live with Italians in order to learn to speak Italian properly."

"Yes, all ri—ght. I don' know wye." A shrug of the shoulders and a side glance with dropped eyes. "Mebbe Eyetayun peoples sink-a youse try to fin' a out somesings, mebbe don' a want some-bodys fin' youse. Youse knows deys-a only dirty dagoes."

This last was said with a bitterness which showed clearly how well the Italians understand the tolerant, semi-contemptuous regard of Americans towards them and how keenly they resent it. I understood at once how and why they suspected us because we, who were obviously "Americans proper" as they nicely express the difference between the native and imported American, desired to come and make our home among them. Only a knowledge that the persons are still living and a wholesome respect for the libel law prevent me from telling how well founded were the suspicions among the Italians of the "Americans proper" who lived about us later.

Thus, to begin with we were met by the barrier of suspicion and misunderstanding raised against us by all our neighbors. We had to overcome it carefully or do our work in spite of it.

From: Brandenburg, Broughton. "Chapter 1 The Impetus and the Method." In *Imported Americans the story of the experiences of a disguised American and his wife studying the immigration question,* 1–6. New York: Frederick A. Stokes Company Publishers, 1904.

https://www.gutenberg.org/files/57517/57517-h/57517-h.htm

◇◇

"What Makes a Good Interaction Between Divided Groups?" By Zaid Jilani, May 14, 2019, for *The Greater Good Magazine:*

https://greatergood.berkeley.edu/article/item/what_makes_a_good_interaction_between_divided_groups

"Is Diversity Good for the Bottom Line?" by Zaid Jilani, January 7, 2019, for *The Greater Good Magazine:*

https://greatergood.berkeley.edu/article/item/is_diversity_good_for_the_bottom_line

"These Kids Are Learning How To Have Bipartisan Conversations" by Elizabeth Svoboda, December 4, 2018, for *The Greater Good Magazine:*

https://greatergood.berkeley.edu/article/item/these_kids_are_learning_how_to_have_bipartisan_conversations

"How Good People Can Fight Bias" by Jill Suttie, December 7, 2018, for *The Greater Good Magazine:*

https://greatergood.berkeley.edu/article/item/how_good_people_can_fight_bias

"Bridging America's Divide: Can the Internet Help?" by John Gable, April 23, 2017, for *The Huffington Post:*

https://www.huffpost.com/entry/bridging-americas-divide_b_9752176

"Bridging Cultural Gaps: 3 Ways to Speak English" by Jamila Lyiscott, a TED Talk

https://www.ted.com/talks/jamila_lyiscott_3_ways_to_speak_english?referrer=playlist-bridging_cultural_differences

© Matrioshka/Shutterstock.com

Excerpts from *The School and Society* by John Dewey

I
THE SCHOOL AND SOCIAL PROGRESS

We are apt to look at the school from an individualistic standpoint, as something between teacher and pupil, or between teacher and parent. That which interests us most is naturally the progress made by the individual child of our acquaintance, his normal physical development, his advance in ability to read, write, and figure, his growth in the knowledge of geography and history, improvement in manners, habits of promptness, order, and industry—it is from such standards as these that we judge the work of the school. And rightly so. Yet the range of the outlook needs to be enlarged. What the best and wisest parent wants for his own child, that must the community want for all of its children. Any other ideal for our schools is narrow and unlovely; acted upon, it destroys our democracy. All that society has accomplished for itself is put, through the agency of the school, at the disposal of its future members. All its better thoughts of itself it hopes to realize through the new possibilities thus opened to its future self. Here individualism and socialism are at one. Only by being true to the full growth of all the individuals who make it up, can society by any chance be true to itself. And in the self-direction thus given, nothing counts as much as the school, for, as Horace Mann said, "Where anything is growing, one former is worth a thousand re-formers."

Whenever we have in mind the discussion of a new movement in education, it is especially necessary to take the broader, or social view. Otherwise, changes in the school institution and tradition will be looked at as the arbitrary inventions of particular teachers; at the worst transitory fads, and at the best merely improvements in certain details—and this is the plane upon which it is too customary to consider school changes. It is as rational to conceive of the locomotive or the telegraph as personal devices. The modification going on in the method and curriculum of education is as much a product of the changed social situation, and as much an effort to meet the needs of the new society that is forming, as are changes in modes of industry and commerce.

It is to this, then, that I especially ask your attention: the effort to conceive what roughly may be termed the "New Education" in the light of larger changes in society. Can we connect this "New Education" with the general march of events? If we can, it will lose its isolated character, and will cease to be an affair which proceeds only from the over-ingenious minds of pedagogues dealing with particular pupils. It will appear as part and parcel of the whole social evolution, and, in its more general features at least, as inevitable. Let us then ask after the main aspects of the social movement; and afterwards turn to the school to find what witness it gives of effort to put itself in line. And since it is quite impossible to cover the whole ground, I shall for the most part confine myself to one typical thing in the modern school movement—that which passes under the name of manual training, hoping if the relation of that to changed social conditions appears, we shall be ready to concede the point as well regarding other educational innovations.

I make no apology for not dwelling at length upon the social changes in question. Those I shall mention are writ so large that he who runs may read. The change that comes first to mind, the one that overshadows and even controls all others, is the industrial one—the application of science resulting in the great inventions that have utilized the forces of nature on a vast and inexpensive scale: the growth of a world-wide market as the object of production, of vast manufacturing centers to supply this market, of cheap and rapid means of communication and distribution between all its parts. Even as to its feebler beginnings, this change is not much more than a century old; in many of its most important aspects it falls within the short span of those now living. One can hardly believe there has been a revolution in all history so rapid, so extensive, so complete. Through it the face of the earth is making over, even as to its physical forms; political boundaries are wiped out and moved about, as if they were indeed only lines on a paper map; population is hurriedly gathered into cities from the ends of the earth; habits of living are altered with startling abruptness and thoroughness; the search for the truths of nature is infinitely stimulated and facilitated and their application to life made not only practicable, but commercially necessary. Even our moral and religious ideas and interests, the most conservative because the deepest-lying things in our nature, are profoundly affected. That this revolution should not affect education in other than formal and superficial fashion is inconceivable. . . .

But why should I make this labored presentation? The obvious fact is that our social life has undergone a thorough and radical change. If our education is to have any meaning for life, it must pass through an equally complete transformation. This transformation is not something to appear suddenly, to be executed in a day by conscious purpose. It is already in progress. Those modifications of our school system which often appear (even to those most actively concerned with them, to say nothing of their spectators) to be mere changes of detail, mere improvement within the school mechanism, are in reality signs and evidences of evolution. The introduction of active occupations, of nature study, of elementary science, of art, of history; the relegation of the merely symbolic and formal to a secondary position; the change in the moral school atmosphere, in the relation of pupils and teachers—of discipline; the introduction of more active, expressive, and self-directing factors—all these are not mere accidents, they are necessities of the larger social evolution. It remains but to organize all these factors, to appreciate them in their fullness of meaning, and to put the ideas and ideals involved into complete, uncompromising possession of our school system. To do this means to make each one of our schools an embryonic community life, active with types of occupations that reflect the life of the larger society, and permeated throughout with the spirit of art, history, and science. When the school introduces and trains each child of society into membership within such a little community, saturating him with the spirit of service, and providing him with the instruments of effective self-direction, we shall have the deepest and best guarantee of a larger society which is worthy, lovely, and harmonious.

From: Dewey, John. "I: The School and Social Progress." In *The School and Society*, 19–46. Illinois: The University of Chicago Press, 1900.

> https://www.gutenberg.org/files/53910/53910-h/53910-h.htm

"How much is too much to pay for college?" by Jeffrey J. Selingo, February 24, 2018, *Washington Post Online:*

> https://www.washingtonpost.com/news/grade-point/wp/2018/02/24/how-much-is-too-much-to-pay-for-college/?noredirect=on&utm_term=.cadf2dfbab1f

"College is more expensive than it's ever been, and the 5 reasons why suggest it's only going to get worse" by Hillary Hoffower, July 8, 2018, *Business Insider:*

> https://www.businessinsider.com/why-is-college-so-expensive-2018-4

"Is College Education Worth It?" by ProCon.org, 20 May 2019:

> https://college-education.procon.org/

"The Value of GE or the Answer to 'Why do I Need to Take This Class?'" by Beth Smith, September 2012, from Rostrum, by the Academic Senate for California Community Colleges:

> https://www.asccc.org/content/value-ge-or-answer-why-do-i-need-take-class

"A Comparison of Online and Face-To-Face Instruction in an Undergraduate Foundations of American Education Course" by Barbara Slater Stern, 2016, *Contemporary Issues in Technology And Teacher Education (CITE) Journal:*

> https://www.citejournal.org/volume-4/issue-2-04/general/a-comparison-of-online-and-face-to-face-instruction-in-an-undergraduate-foundations-of-american-education-course/

"Does everyone need a college degree? Maybe not, says Harvard study" by Amanda Paulson, February 2, 2011, *Christian Science Monitor:*

> https://www.csmonitor.com/USA/Education/2011/0202/
> Does-everyone-need-a-college-degree-Maybe-not-says-Harvard-study

On Food

© Igor Bukhlin/Shutterstock.com

Excerpts from "The Logic of Vegetarianism" in *Essays and Dialogues* by Henry S. Salt

THE MORALIST AT THE SHAMBLES.

Where slaughter'd beasts lie quivering, pile on pile,
And bare-armed fleshers, bathed in bloody dew,
Ply hard their ghastly trade, and hack and hew,
And mock sweet Mercy's name, yet loathe the while
The lot that chains them to this service vile,
Their hands in hideous carnage to imbrue:
Lo, there!—the preacher of the Good and True,
The Moral Man, with sanctimonious smile!
"Thrice happy beasts," he murmurs, "'tis our love,
Our thoughtful love that sends ye to the knife
(Nay, doubt not, as ye welter in your gore!);
For thus alone ye earned the boon of life,
And thus alone the Moralist may prove
His sympathetic soul—by eating more."

Why "Vegetarian"?

The term "vegetarian," as applied to those who abstain from all flesh food, but not necessarily from such animal products as eggs, milk, and cheese, appears to have come into existence over fifty years ago, at the time of the founding of the Vegetarian Society in 1847. Until that date no special name had been appropriated for the reformed diet system, which was usually known as the "Pythagorean" or "vegetable diet," as may be seen by a reference to the writings of that period. Presumably, it was felt that when the movement grew in volume, and was about to enter on a new phase, with an organised propaganda, it was advisable to coin for it an original and distinctive title. Whether, from this point of view, the name "vegetarian" was wisely or unwisely chosen is a question on which there has been some difference of opinion among food reformers themselves, and it is possible that adverse criticism would have been still more strongly expressed but for the fact that no better title has been forthcoming.

. . . .

The *Raison d'être* of Vegetarianism

Behind the mere name of the reformed diet, whatever name be employed (and, as we have seen, "vegetarian" at present holds the field), lies the far more important reality. What is the *raison d'être*, the real purport of vegetarianism? Certainly not any *a priori* assumption that all animal substances, as such, are unfit for human food; for though it is quite probable that the movement will ultimately lead us to the disuse of animal products, vegetarianism is not primarily based on any such hard-and-fast formula, but on the conviction, suggested in the first place by instinctive feeling, but confirmed by reason and experience, that there are certain grave evils inseparable from the practice of flesh-eating. The aversion to flesh food is not chemical, but moral, social, hygienic. Believing as we do that the grosser forms of diet not only cause a vast amount of unnecessary suffering to the animals, but also react most injuriously on the health and morals of mankind, we advocate their gradual discontinuance; and so long as this protest is successfully launched, the mere name by which it is called is a matter of minor concern. But here on this practical issue, as before on the nominal issue, we come into conflict with the superior person who, with a smile of supercilious compassion, cannot see *why* we poor ascetics should thus afflict ourselves without cause.

. . . We conclude, then, that the cause which vegetarians have at heart is the outcome, not of some barren academic formula, but of a practical reasoned conviction that flesh food, especially butchers' meat, is a harmful and barbarous diet. Into the details of this belief we need not at present enter; it has been sufficient here to show that such belief exists, and that the good people who can see in vegetarianism nothing but a whimsical "fad" have altogether failed to grasp its true purport and significance. The *raison d'être* of vegetarianism is the growing sense that flesh-eating is a cruel, disgusting, unwholesome, and wasteful practice, and that it behoves humane and rational persons, disregarding the common cant about "consistency" and "all-or-nothing," to reform their diet to what extent and with what speed they can.

But, it may be said, before entering on a consideration of this reformed diet, for which such great merits are claimed by its exponents, the practical man is justified in asking for certain solid assurances, since busy people cannot be expected to give their time to speculations which, however beautiful in themselves, may prove at the end to be in conflict with the hard facts of life. And the first of these questions is, What is the historic basis of vegetarianism? In what sense is it an old movement, and in what sense a new one? Has it a past which may serve in some measure to explain its present and guarantee its future?

Such questions have been dealt with fully from time to time in vegetarian literature.[1] I can here do no more than epitomise the answers. Vegetarianism, regarded simply as a practice and without relation to any principle, is of immemorial date; it was, in fact, as physiology shows us, the original diet of mankind, while, as history shows us, it has always been the diet of the many, as flesh food has been the diet of the few, and even to this day it is the main support of the greater part of the world's inhabitants. Numberless instances might be quoted in proof of these assertions; it is sufficient to refer to the people of India, China, and Japan, the Egyptian fellah, the Bedouin Arab, the peasantry of Russia and Turkey, the labourers and miners of Chili and other South American States; and, to come nearer home, the great bulk of the country folk in Western Europe and Great Britain. The peasant, here and all the world over, has been, and still is, in the main a vegetarian, and must for the most part continue so; and the fact that this diet has been the result, not of choice, but of necessity, does not lessen the significance of its perfect sufficiency to maintain those who do the hard work of the world. Side by side with the tendency of the wealthier classes to indulge more and more in flesh food has been the undisputed admission that for the workers such luxuries were unneeded.

During the last half-century, however, as we all know, the unhealthy and crowded civilisation of great industrial centres has produced among the urban populations of Europe a craving for flesh food, which has resulted in their being fed largely on cheap butchers' meat and offal; while there has grown up a corresponding belief that we must look almost entirely to a flesh diet for bodily and mental vigour. It is in protest against this comparatively new demand for flesh as a necessity of life that vegetarianism, as a modern organised movement, has arisen.

Secondly, if we look back for examples of deliberate abstinence from flesh—that is, of vegetarianism practised as a *principle* before it was denoted by a name—we find no lack of them in the history of religious and moral systems and individual lives. Such abstinence was an essential feature in the teaching of Buddha and Pythagoras and is still practised in the East on religious and ceremonial grounds by Brahmins and Buddhists. It was inculcated in the humanitarian writings of great "pagan" philosophers, such as Plutarch and Porphyry, whose ethical precepts, as far as the treatment of the lower animals is concerned, are still far in advance of modern Christian sentiment. Again, in the prescribed regimen of certain religious Orders, such as Benedictines, Trappists, and Carthusians, we have further unquestionable evidence of the disuse of flesh food, though in such cases the reason for the abstinence is ascetic rather than humane. When we turn to the biographies of individuals, we learn that there have been numerous examples of what is now called "vegetarianism"—not always consistent, indeed, or continuous in practice, yet sufficiently so to prove the entire possibility of the diet, and to remove it from the category of generous aspiration into that of accomplished fact.[2]

NOTES

1. As in "The Perfect Way in Diet," by Dr. Anna Kingsford; and "Strength and Diet," by the Hon. R. Russell.
2. See the list of names cited in Mr. Howard Williams's "Ethics of Diet," a biographical history of the literature of humane dietetics from the earliest period to the present day.

From: Salt, Henry S. "Why Vegetarian?" In *The Logic of Vegetarianism Essays and Dialogues*, 4–13. London: George Bell and Sons, 1906.

http://www.gutenberg.org/files/49949/49949-h/49949-h.htm.

"Where GMO's Hide in Your Food" by *Consumer Reports*, October 2014:

https://www.consumerreports.org/cro/2014/10/where-gmos-hide-in-your-food/index.htm

"How to Force Ethics on the Food Industry" by Michael Mudd, March 16, 2013, in *New York Times Sunday Review:*

https://www.nytimes.com/2013/03/17/opinion/sunday/how-to-force-ethics-on-the-food-industry.html

"Sugar is Definitely Toxic, a New Study Says" by Alice Park, October 29, 2015, in *Time Magazine:*

http://time.com/4087775/sugar-is-definitely-toxic-a-new-study-says/

"The disturbing ways that fast food chains disproportionally target black kids" by Roberto A. Ferdman, November 12, 2014, *Washington Post:*

https://www.washingtonpost.com/news/wonk/wp/2014/11/12/the-disturbing-ways-that-fast-food-chains-disproportionately-target-black-kids/?noredirect=on&utm_term=.95af5a6bd144

"The Extraordinary Science of Addictive Junk Food" by Michael Moss, February 20, 2013, *The New York Times Magazine:*

https://www.nytimes.com/2013/02/24/magazine/the-extraordinary-science-of-junk-food.html

"Is Your Meat Safe?—Antibiotic Debate Overview" by PBS

https://www.pbs.org/wgbh/pages/frontline/shows/meat/safe/overview.html

"America Has A Hunger Problem" in *The Atlantic* (Think Original Series) *by Atlantic's* Marketing Team for Feed America

https://www.theatlantic.com/sponsored/hunger-2019/america-has-a-hunger-problem/3067/?sr_source=pocket&sr_lift=true&utm_source=pocket&utm_medium=CPC&utm_campaign=simplereach&utm_source=PK_SR_P_3067

H. Grammar Concept: Subject–Verb Agreement

You will learn grammar best by applying it within the context of your own writing. Use these rules as a guide. Your teacher will probably help you to target examples from your own writing and your peers' writing to help clarify how these rules work.

Tricky Subject-Verb Agreement

> **WARNING!**
>
> **In English, an -s ending makes a <u>noun</u> plural but a verb singular.**
>
> <u>dog</u> = singular   <u>dogs</u> = plural
>
> runs = singular   run = plural
>
> The <u>dog</u> runs. (singular noun + singular verb)
>
> The <u>dogs</u> run. (plural noun + plural verb)

> **GRAMMAR TIP**
>
> When a subject and verb are in *agreement*, they agree in number: A singular subject takes a singular verb; a plural subject takes a plural verb.

Look out for problems showing up with:

- Subject-Verb Split: *I, among all my friends, (am/is/are) leaving.*
- Collective Subject + Singular Verb: *Two-thirds of the pie (was/were) eaten.*
- Subject before a *To Be* Verb + Noun: *What mattered (was/were) the rules.*
- *A* or *The* + Subject + Verb: *A number of voters (was/were) delayed.*
- Compound Subjects with *Either/Or*: *Either my aunt or my uncles (is/are) retired.*
- Verb before Subject: *(What's/what're) the priorities?*
- *There* + Verb + Plural or Compound Subject: *(There's/there're) some cops here.*
- *Each* or *Every* before a Compound Subject: *Each boy and each girl (is/are) voting.*
- *Each* after a Compound Subject: *The dog and cat each (is/are) eating snacks.*
- *Plural Noun* + *Who* or *That*: *Sara is one of the bicyclists who (wants/want) to quit.*
- *None* or *Some* + Verb: *None of the lumber (was/were) sold; none of the trees (was/were) cut down.*

Subject-Verb Split: *I, among all my friends, (am/is/are) leaving.*

> ## GRAMMAR TIP
> Underline the subject and highlight the verb. *Do words split them up? That's* often the sign of a subject-verb agreement error. When a *fragment* separates the subject from its verb, don't let the fragment's last word determine the verb.

<u>I</u>, *among all my friends*, (**am/is/are**) leaving. (am)

The lone <u>Republican</u>, *as well as the Democrats*, (**wants/want**) to reconsider a filibuster. (wants)

<u>Dr. Foxways</u>, *along with the hospital's other staff physicians*, (**is/are**) planning to leave. (is)

Marcy's <u>sales</u>, *despite competition from that other yard sale*, (**promises/promise**) many bargains. (promise)

Collective Subject + Singular Verb: *Two-thirds of the pie (was/were) eaten.*

> ## GRAMMAR TIP
> Underline the subject. Is it a word like *jury, team, congress, senate, series, band, orchestra, a million dollars*? Or a word ending in *-s* like *statistics, athletics, economics, politics, physics, news, mumps*, or *measles*? In other words, is it a <u>collective</u>? *When the subject is a collective, usually use a singular verb.*

<u>Two-thirds</u> of the pie (was/were) eaten. (was)

The <u>jury</u> (is/are) filing into the courtroom. (is)

The newspaper reported that a <u>million dollars</u> (was/were) missing from the bank. (was)

<u>Statistics</u> (is/are) my favorite class. (is)

<u>Politics</u> (is/are) one of my interests. (is)

<u>Ice cream and cake</u> (is/are) a favorite dessert. (is)

Sometimes you may need a plural when the collective isn't entirely united, like a jury debating a verdict.

The <u>jury</u> (is/are) arguing among themselves. (are)

Or something is considered separately instead of as a unit.

A <u>million dollars</u> (was/were) counted out on the table. (were)

The <u>statistics</u> (shows/show) him to be right. (show)

Their <u>politics</u> (is/are) difficult to understand. (are)

The <u>ice cream and</u> the <u>cake</u> (is/are) sold out. (are)

Subject before a *To Be* Verb + Noun: *What mattered (was/were) the rules.*

> ## GRAMMAR TIP
>
> Underline the subject. Is it a group of words acting as a unit—as one subject? Does it come before a to be verb (*is, are, was, were,* etc.)? *When <u>what as a subject</u> comes before a to be verb and a noun comes after, the verb agrees with the noun, not the subject.*

<u>What mattered</u> (was/were) the rules. (were)

(The rules were what mattered.)

<u>What she really wanted to buy</u> (was/were) both DVDs. (were)

(Both DVDs were what she really wanted to buy.)

The logic becomes clear when you consider:

<u>What the telescope reveals</u> is the man.

(The man is what the telescope reveals.)

<u>What the telescope reveals</u> are the men.

(The men are what the telescope reveals.)

A or *The* + Subject + Verb: *A number of voters (was/were) delayed.*

> ## GRAMMAR TIP
>
> Underline the subject. Is it a collective noun? Does *the* or *a* come before the subject? *When* the *comes before, the verb is usually singular; when* a *comes before, the verb is usually plural.*

The <u>number</u> of voters (was/were) unexpected. (was)

A <u>number</u> of voters (was/were) delayed. (were)

Compound Subjects with *Either/Or*: *Either my aunt or my uncles (is/are) retired.*

A compound subject has more than one subject, like *my aunt and my uncles, neither my aunt nor my uncles,* or *neither my uncles nor my aunt.*

> ## GRAMMAR TIP
>
> Underline the subject. Is it a compound? *With* either/or *and* neither/nor, *the <u>subject</u> next to the verb controls the verb.*

1. My <u>aunt and my uncles</u> (is/are) retired. (are)
2. My <u>uncles and my aunt</u> (is/are) retired. (are)
3. **Either** my aunt or my <u>uncles</u> (is/are) retired. (are)
4. **Neither** my uncles nor my <u>aunt</u> (is/are) retired. (is)
5. **Neither** Bob nor <u>I</u> (am/is/are) going to take care of that issue. (am)

    1. aunt and uncles = plural = **are**
    2. uncles and aunt = plural = **are**
    3. uncles = plural = **are**
    4. aunt = singular = **is**
    5. I = singular = **am**

Verb before Subject: (*What's/what're*) *the priorities?*

GRAMMAR TIP

Underline the subject and highlight the verb. Usually the subject comes before the verb. *But when the verb comes before the <u>subject</u>, make sure they still agree—singular subject with singular verb; plural subject with plural verb.*

(What's/what're) the <u>priorities</u>? (what're = what are)
    (The priorities we're supposed to follow are what?)
In this databank (is/are) many reliable <u>sources</u>. (are)
    (Many reliable sources are in this databank.)
Beyond the orchard (was/were) the storm <u>cave</u> and the <u>shed</u>. (were)
    (The storm cave and the shed were beyond the orchard.)

There + Verb + Plural or Compound Subject: (*There's/there're*) *some cops here.*

GRAMMAR TIP

Using the *Find* command, search for *there*. When a plural or compound <u>subject</u> follows there *and the verb, use a plural verb.*

---

1. (There's/there're) some <u>cops</u> here. (there're = there are)
2. (There was/there were) a tool <u>chest</u> and some old garden <u>tools</u> in the garage. (were)
    1. cops = plural = **are**
    2. chest and tools = compound = **were**

Each or *Every* before a Compound Subject: *Each boy and each girl (is/are) voting.*

> ## GRAMMAR TIP
>
> Using the *Find* command, search for *each* and *every*. Does a <u>subject</u> follow? Is the subject compound? *When each or every comes before a compound subject, use a singular verb.*

Each <u>boy</u> and each <u>girl</u> (is/are) voting. (is)

Every <u>mentor</u> and every <u>mentee</u> (was/were) instructed to meet in Bascom Hall. (was)

Each after a Compound Subject: *The dog and cat each (is/are) eating snacks.*

> ## GRAMMAR TIP
>
> Using the *Find* command, search for *each*. Does a <u>subject</u> come before it? Is the subject compound? *When each comes after a plural subject, use a plural verb.*

The <u>dog</u> and <u>cat</u> each (is/are) eating snacks. (are)

The <u>animals</u> each (is/are) eating their food. (are)

Plural Noun + *Who* or *That*: *Sara is one of the bicyclists who (wants/want) to quit.*

> ## GRAMMAR TIP
>
> Using the *Find* command, search for *who* and *that*. Does a plural <u>noun</u> come before it? *When you have a <u>plural noun</u> + who or that, proceed with caution: You may need a singular or plural verb.*

1. **Sara is one of the <u>bicyclists</u> who (wants/want) to quit. (want)**
2. **Sammy is one of the <u>volunteers</u> who (comes/come) to visit. (come)**
3. **Ignacio is the only one of the <u>volunteers</u> who (comes/come) to visit. (comes)**
4. **Chicken pox is among those <u>diseases</u> that (is/are) curable. (are)**
5. **Jack is the only one of the <u>bicyclists</u> who (wants/want) to quit. (wants)**
6. **_Monopoly_ is just one of the <u>games</u> that (was/were) invented in during the 1930s. (were)**

Here's the logic of this common and difficult error:

1. MANY bicyclists want to quit. Sara is ONE of them.
2. MANY of the volunteers come to visit. Sammy is just ONE of them.
3. No volunteer comes to visit except Ignacio: He's the ONLY one.
4. MANY diseases are curable. Chicken pox is ONE of them.
5. No bicyclist wants to quit except Jack. He's the ONLY one.
6. MANY games were invented in the 1930s. *Monopoly* is just ONE of them.

None or *Some* + Verb: *None of the lumber (was/were) sold; none of the trees (was/were) cut down.*

GRAMMAR TIP

Unlike the personal pronoun, the *indefinite pronoun* doesn't refer to specific people or things. Using the *Find* command, find these indefinite pronouns: *none, some, all, any, more,* and *most.*

Some indefinite pronouns can be <u>singular</u> or plural, depending on the words they refer to.

None of the <u>lumber</u> (was/were) sold; none of the <u>trees</u> (was/were) cut down.

    (lumber = singular = <u>was</u>; trees = plural = <u>were</u>)

Some of the <u>vegetables</u> (has/have) spoiled; some of the <u>food</u> (has/have) spoiled.

    (vegetables = plural = <u>have</u>; <u>food</u> = singular = <u>has</u>)

Most of the university's original <u>buildings</u> (was/were) built before 1900. (were)

Lessons to Use in the Co-Requisite Classroom During This Unit

A co-requisite Writing and Research course has but one absolute rule: no additional assignments outside of class may be assigned; the work of the Writing and Research course *is* the work of the co-requisite course.

Nonetheless, during co-requisite class times, students should engage in activities that address their noncognitive, cognitive, and skills-related areas. The activities I include here encompass all three categories of learning and coordinate with the work of the Writing and Research course. Of course, students' needs regarding whatever occurs in the Writing and Research course on a particular day may at times take precedence in the co-requisite course, and at times, the class time may function as a writing workshop, but every class session cannot function in these ways, or the students will not acquire what they need from the course. Individual teachers will of course decide what to use, when to use it, and even what adaptations to apply. Some of the activities, each one designed for a single class session, may actually take longer than a single class because co-requisite courses do not operate on the same schedule on every college campus and different students have different kinds of questions about assignments.

TOPIC AND QUESTION EVALUATION EXERCISE

Work in pairs to complete this exercise.

A good research question requires complexity, depth and breadth, and originality. It offers the possibility of research and an argument or conversation positioned within that research. As David Taylor notes in his video, "It is debatable, plausible, and consequential."

Read the sample questions below. Using the above criteria, grade them Pass or Fail, and explain why.

1. What effect is modern technology having on young people? They were born into it, but do cell phones give them cancer? Are laptops in class making them poor readers and writers? Are social media sites terrorizing them and actually making them less social? I am researching technology use and its effects on adolescents.

2. I am looking into waste and the environment. How much waste do we United States people create every day and then dump into the environment around us or around other people?

3. Here I am at college. I am working three part-time jobs to pay for it. I'm giving up pretty much all of my free time for it. I am learning a lot about various subjects, about myself, and about life in general. But, my question is, "Is this college education worth the expense and sacrifice? Compared to hands-on work experience, will it really be valuable?"

CHAPTER 2

4. Probably about a million students a day eat school lunches. Some pay for that lunch, while others have lunch through the federal government's free lunch program. The government regulates what can be served in school cafeterias all across the United States. So who started this federally-regulated program and why? What is its history? Have lunch requirements changed over time, and in its current form, is it healthy for children, or is it contributing to the obesity epidemic in this country?

5. When people hear the terms, "deaf culture," they often either ask if such an entity exists or dismiss it as a ridiculous notion. Yet, the terms and the culture do actually exist. I want to know why—other than the commonality of not possessing the ability to hear—such a culture does exist, and how it functions as an actual "culture" of its own.

RESEARCH PLANS AND SIGNIFICANCE REVIEW

1. Work in teams of two. Match Column A with Column B.
2. When you have finished, meet with another pair and compare your answers. See if there is any answer you might change.
3. Then, on your own, write your own sentences for your research plan OR your research question's significance.

COLUMN A

1. Research Topic

2. Research Question

3. Research Plan

4. Significance of Research Topic and Question

5. Lead/Hook

6. Foregrounding/Background/ Context

COLUMN B

_____ Who among us has not ever looked at our cell phones during a class, or while someone is speaking to us, or while we are driving?

_____ The ubiquitous use of cell phones has become an interest of mine.

_____ The US Census Bureau tells us that pretty much everyone has a cell phone, so all of those people certainly would have an interest in knowing the answer to this question.

_____ Everyone from six-year-olds to great grandmothers has a cell phone these days, and most carry it everywhere they go. Cell phone companies and plans abound because so many people use cell phones and need carriers to provide that service, no matter where they go.

_____ Logically, I would use the search terms, "cell phone use, effects of" and "cell phone addiction," probably in the *Applied Technology* database. But I will also want to check the *PsychInfo* databases and do some Google searching for interviews with experts in the field or documentaries about the subject.

_____ But I wonder if all of this cell phone usage has actually spawned an addiction to our cell phones. Do we actually develop a need for them the way a drug addict needs a fix?

IDENTIFYING AND COMBATTING OBSTACLES TO OUR SUCCESS ACTIVITY (Noncognitive)

1. Below you see a drawing of two staircases. On the left side, insert on the steps the names of obstacles you have already overcome to get to college. Note briefly how you did so. On the right side, insert on the steps the names of current obstacles you need to overcome to succeed now that you are in college. You do not have to use every step.

© Ollyy/Shutterstock.com

2. Now pass your paper to the person behind/to the right of/to the left of you.

3. Read the left-side stairway labels on the paper you possess. Mentally note any new-to-you strategies for overcoming certain obstacles.

4. Now read the right-side stairway labels. Choose one or two of those obstacles and write a suggestion for overcoming them.

5. Now pass the paper to another person. Repeat the process in steps 3 and 4.

6. Now pass the paper to yet another person. Once again, repeat the process in steps 3 and 4.

7. Now make certain to get the paper back to its creator.

8. Examine the ideas your peers have offered you.

9. Do you think any of these solutions might help you overcome any of the current obstacles you have named? Explain how you might follow through with the suggestion.

OUR SUPPORT STRUCTURES ACTIVITY (Noncognitive)

1. Most psychologists have concluded that several areas of our lives require attention if we are to have full wellness: the ability to live a healthy, fulfilling life that is free of illness, stress, emotional turmoil, etc. These same psychologists usually agree that having support networks in each of those areas helps us to achieve that wellness.

   Do you have support networks? Fill in each of the categories with the identities of the support person in your life who helps with that category.

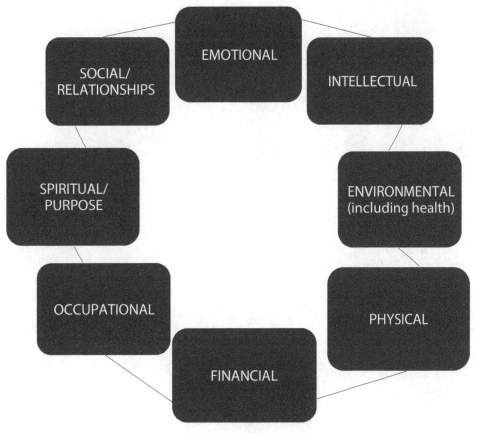

Source: Patricia Sehulster

2. As you look at the way you filled in the above chart, can you draw any conclusions about your support network? For example, do you rely heavily on the same support for many categories? Do you not have support in some categories? Do you not have support in some categories because you do not think much about that category or because you do not know who could serve to support you in that regard? Do you prefer not to use support networks, or are you comfortable asking for help at times?

CHAPTER 2

3. Look again at the intellectual, financial, occupational, and emotional categories. Do you include there any of the College's offerings of support systems? Use your phone, laptop, tablet, etc., to go to the College's website. Search for the support systems it offers in these categories, and add the contact information for each of them to your list above. [** HINT: You may need to use search terms such as "career services" or "personal counseling" or "academic support" or "tutoring centers," etc., to find what you need.]

4. What difference do you think having support systems can make to your academic success? Explain.

Name_____ Date_____

TIME-MANAGEMENT ACTIVITY (Noncognitive)

1. Fill in the diagram below.

Source: Patricia Sehulster

2. Categorize the items you have listed in "Must do TODAY." Do they constitute predominantly family duties, academic duties, work duties, sustenance/survival duties, etc., or do you have six different categories for the six activities?

3. Again, categorize your "Must do TOMORROW" items. And again, figure out what category (categories) dominate. Also, comment on why you must put them off until another day.

4. One last time, categorize your "NEVER do" items. Do you see a pattern or theme in this realm? Why do you choose never to do these activities?

5. Do you view your time management as choices you make, or as something else? Explain.

6. Review your lists above, and think of them as a hierarchy of priorities in your life. Where do academics fit into that hierarchy? Do you think that placement will lead to successful academic work? Why/why not?

7. What <u>deliberate</u> strategies do you use to manage your time? List them here. If you do not use any deliberate strategies, explain how you get everything on your to-do list done then.

8. Meet with one peer. Share your ideas for time-management strategies and setting priorities. Can either of you find a way to add at least one "NEVER do" item to your "TODAY" list?

9. As a result of this activity, what will you change about your time management?

BRAINSTORMING YOUR RESEARCH PROPOSAL

1. What is your general topic of study?

2. What is your research question? (What do you want to find out?)

3. As you think about this topic and question, what do you already know about it and the way people feel about it?

4. Why does this topic matter to YOU?

5. Why does this topic matter—or should it matter—to OTHERS? List specifically who those OTHERS are. Explain WHY those others care about the topic.

6. Make a list of what you need to do to get your research moving forward. Where will you start? Why?

   a. What will you do next?

   b. For what kinds of research will you look, and where will you find that type of research (specific databases, Internet sites, interviews with experts, etc.)?

   Using the information from your answer to #3, write a one- to two-sentence lead/hook/beginning of the proposal.

A POSSIBLE RESEARCH PROPOSAL TEMPLATE

REMINDER: What Are the Components of a Research Proposal?

- Topic and Question: In this section, you should identify your topic and question, demonstrate a general understanding of the topic, and articulate your goals for the research essay and project.
- What I Know, Assume, or Imagine: In this section, you'll discuss what you already know about the topic and question and what you do not know, as well as what you hope to learn and what, in general, others think.
- Source: In this section, you will identify a published source on your topic, summarize that essay's claim, and state your own view.
- Significance: In this section, you should address the questions, "Why does this topic/question matter to me? Why should it matter to anyone else?"
- Plan: This section should include not only a specific timeline of when you will accomplish your goals, but also a detailed description of how you will find out what you want to find out. Which sorts of sources, databases, Internet sites, and publications will be most helpful to you and why?

Today, the topic/issue/idea/concept/problem (← Choose one) of _____

concerns/interests/intrigues/worries/registers (← Choose one) many people. Some believe

_____

_____, while others think _____

_____.

As a _____, this topic has become ever present in my mind too, especially

because _____. I'd really like to know _____.

I do know a little something about the topic already. For example, I understand

_____

because I _____. In addition, through _____, I have

comprehended that _____. In fact, I even have a general

theory or hypothesis; I imagine that _____.

Nonetheless, much exists that I do not know or understand fully. Apart from my actual

research question, the small sub-issues that encompass my current knowledge gaps include

_____.

As I consider these knowledge gaps and the direction I need to follow in my research, I have

begun with a single article: "_____," written by _____

and published in _____ on _____. This

author's basic claim is that, "_____" ( ). In essence, he postulates

that _____ because _____

_____, and uses _____
_____ as the supporting evidence. As I contemplate this claim and evidence, my own contention surfaces as _____
because _____.

Regardless of my current premise, I will need to gather additional sources. Gathering these sources and answering my research question matter to me because _____
_____. The topic itself has significance to a larger audience, specifically _____, because _____.

To address the importance of the issue by discovering the answers to my research question, I will need to follow a specific plan. I will begin by using the search terms "_____
_____" in the following databases: _____
_____. These scholarly resources make the best sense because _____
_____.

In addition, I will seek books like _____ and examine the Internet for
_____. I might also contemplate conducting a live interview with _____ or finding an online interview or documentary about/with _____. I hope to have gathered _____ sources by _____(Date)_____, so that I can get started on my research project's completion by _____ (Date)_____.

ROUND-ROBIN ACTIVITY WITH OUR "RESEARCH PROPOSAL" DRAFTS

Directions:

1. Get into groups of THREE.
2. Swap your draft with one other person in the group.
3. Attach this sheet to that draft and record the author's name in the space provided on this sheet.
4. The person who gets the draft will examine it for #1 criteria and sign his/her name on the line adjacent to #1. (See below #1: Elements directions, and follow them exactly and completely.)
5. When you have all finished the examination of your peer's essay for #1 criteria, swap the drafts again.
6. This time, the person who gets the draft will examine it for #2 criteria and sign his/her name on the line adjacent to #2. (See below #2: Source Explanation directions, and follow them exactly and completely.)
7. When you have all finished the examination of your peer's essay for #2 criteria, swap the drafts again.
8. This time, the person who gets the draft will examine it for #3 criteria and sign his/her name on the line adjacent to #3. (See below #3: Editing directions, and follow them exactly and completely.)
9. When you have finished the examination of your peer's essay for #3 criteria, then return each draft to its author.
10. Authors: Read through the comments your peers have made. If you have questions about them, ask your peer.
11. Authors, now complete the answers to the questions about your plan for completion and revision.

#1 _____ for (author) _____

#2 _____

#3 _____

#1: ELEMENTS

1. Read through the draft entirely, without doing anything to it; just read it.

2. Read through the draft again. This time, highlight and identify/label what you think is the writer's:

   a. Research Topic
   b. Research Question
   c. Context/Foregrounding and What the Author Knows
   d. Reference to a Source
   e. Explanation of Significance to Self and Others
   f. Plan for Research [including search terms, databases, and Internet possibilities]
   g. IF you find any or all of these elements missing or in some way weak, note that point/those points on the draft. If, on the other hand, you find them strong, note that fact on the draft.

3. In looking over the draft, think about how much progress toward the completion of this essay the writer has made. On a scale of 1–10 (1 meaning low and 10 meaning high), how would you rank this writer's progress? _____ EXPLAIN WHY you give it that ranking.

   _____

4. Do you believe this draft is headed in the direction it needs to go?   YES   NO

   EXPLAIN WHY. _____

   _____

#2: SOURCE EXPLANATION

1. Read through the draft entirely, without doing anything to it; just read it.

2. Read through the draft again. This time, locate in the draft the section that discusses the source the writer has already discovered.

3. Now locate, underline, and label the name, author, and publication information about that source.

4. Now locate, circle, and label the sentence that identifies the article's claim.

5. Now locate, highlight, and label the part that explains what evidence the article uses to support that claim.

6. Now locate, draw a rectangle around, and label the writer's response to that article's claim and evidence.

7. Do you think the writer offers a thorough explanation of this source?   YES   NO

8. EXPLAIN WHY. _____

9. What, if anything, does the writer need to add? _____

10. What, if anything, does the writer need to delete? _____

#3: EDITING

1. Read through the draft entirely, without doing anything to it; just read it.

2. Read through the draft again. This time, circle errors in <u>subject–verb agreement</u>. LABEL the errors, but do not correct them. Note any sentences you do not clearly understand because the prose is muddy. *** Because in this unit, we have studied subject–verb agreement, pay special attention to those areas. If you notice other kinds of errors, such as those in sentence structure, spelling, pronoun use, etc., please do feel free to circle them too.

3. What does this writer need to pay the most attention to correcting? _____

_____

WRITER'S REFLECTION AND PLAN FOR COMPLETION AND REVISION:

1. Examine what your peers have noted about your draft, both on the draft and on the filled-in sections of this activity.

2. Ask your peers for clarification of anything you do not quite understand about their comments.

3. Make your own notations/reminders on your draft.

4. Record here a step-by-step, concrete plan of the actions you will take in creating your next FULL draft of this essay. What must you add? What must you delete? What order should you follow or maintain? What else should you revise? Do you need to edit any problem grammar?

USE OR ABUSE
A SUBJECT–VERB AGREEMENT MATCHING GAME

1. You will work in two teams.
2. You should keep the pages about subject–verb agreement rules in front of you, and you may use them during the game.
3. You may confer with one another before ONE of you gives the answer.
4. You will have two minutes to respond.

- In each of the following boxes, you will see sentences that come from your own writing.
- Find the <u>subject and verb</u> in each one.
- Decide whether or not they are correct—"Use"—or incorrect—"Abuse"—and state the rule that is used or abused to defend your answer.

My experiences with writing were not positive in the least.	To my frustration, the group of assignments in those classes always use writing.	Neither the writing assignments nor the teacher were my favorite.
If growth mindset, along with the various intelligences, really are true, then anyone can excel, right?	But Lamott's essay about shitty first drafts and her claim that all writing means revising gives me hope.	If "Follow your passion" is bad advice, then what plans make sense?
Rose's essay reminds me of my mom and dad, each of whom work at a restaurant.	Little victories in writing, not earning all A's all the time means progress.	When I write, my paper and my writing is a mess at first.
I like the idea of shitty first drafts because that means there's many chances to improve.	Which one of us students start as perfect writers?	I learned that really, neither professionals nor novices start without that first, terrible draft.

WRITING ACROSS THE CURRICULUM/WRITING IN THE DISCIPLINES TIPS AND CONNECTIONS FOR THIS UNIT

1. Explore with your class topics most related to your discipline. Change In-Class Activity 2A's optional categories to a single category or several categories related to your discipline.

2. Instead of using the two videos in In-class Activity 2B, find (or create) and use a video that demonstrates the same principles for researching a topic in your discipline.

3. To get students thinking about broad, unanswerable questions, you might want to show Chris Anderson's TED Talk "Questions No one Knows the Answer to":

   http://www.ted.com/talks/questions_no_one_knows_the_answers_to

4. Explore with the class the library's databases most applicable to your discipline. Make certain students know which ones deal with the field, where to locate them, and how the key words search command works in them.

5. Explore with the class the best and most commonly used Internet sources of reliable information in your discipline.

6. Adapt/Revise the Research Proposal directions to fit the kind of proposal done in your discipline. For example, a science-related field will include a more expansive plan section that details methodology (procedure, group studied, etc.). Show a model or two of that type.

7. Select other readings or only one category in the reading selections to fit your discipline.

CHAPTER 3

Finding and Assessing Academic Dialogues

Weeks 7–9

Learning Objectives

Students will:

- Evaluate the credibility and reliability of sources.
- Identify and evaluate arguments in sources.
- Document where information and ideas come from in the style appropriate for the discipline.
- Compose an annotated bibliography.
- Demonstrate an understanding of writing as a multistage process.
- Produce texts that present ideas effectively and fluently.
- Think critically.

You have now chosen your research topic, refined your research question, and decided what approaches and search terms will best suit finding the answer to your question. You are now ready to begin the actual work of discovering what various sources have to say in the conversation about your topic and question. This phase of the process will engage you not only in finding sources or those contributing voices to the dialogue, but also in summarizing, evaluating, and compiling them. Then you will assess what the overall conversation concludes—including opposition viewpoints—and then begin to decide what your own contribution to that dialogue will say.

© Venimo/Shutterstock.com

A. Using Databases versus Using Internet Search Engines

A great many of you have spent hours using the Internet's available search engines. These searches have become ubiquitous, so much so that we have turned some of the engines' names into commonly used verbs. For example, we "*google* it" when we want to know something quickly. Most of you, however, have probably spent considerably less time using subscription databases to conduct your searches for information. You might wonder in what ways these approaches differ or how much you can trust one method versus another or what kinds of information you will find using one type of search versus another or if they actually differ that much at all.

These two tools for finding information do, in fact, diverge in several key ways. The following chart demonstrates those differences.

INTERNET SOURCES *Free with Paid Internet Service Provider Subscription *Some Links on Pay-For-Information System	DATABASE SOURCES *Paid for through Library's Paid Subscriptions (Your tuition or public taxes)
SAMPLE NAMES OF	
Google	*Academic Search Complete*
Bing	*JSTOR*
Yahoo	*Literature Resource Center*
Ask.com	*National Newspaper Premier*
AOL.com	*.CINAHL Plus With Full Text*
DuckDuckGo	*Business Insights Essentials*
HotBot	*PsychArticles*
Lycos	*SocIndex*
HOW THE SOURCES CONDUCT THE SEARCH	
Indexes billions of pages by following links	Uses records organized by field or discipline
Results based on criteria such as: • the page's rank (how often it is viewed), • the number of times the search words appear in the link, • how often the search words appear in the URL or in the title, and • your previous search history of similar topics	Offers a range of options: • by key word, • by subject, • by title, • by author, • by date, • by type of article (peer-reviewed, newspaper, periodical, etc.)
Crawls through the billions of pages to find any matches at all	Searches based on relevance

KINDS OF INFORMATION TO BE FOUND	
Some free scholarly articles and books	Scholarly journal articles
Culturally Popular Web sites	Reference Books, Articles, and Directories
Commercial Web sites [.com, .net]	Chapters from and Whole Books
Web sites By and For Organizations [.org] and ASP's (Applications)	Popular Magazines and Specialized Magazines
Web sites Sponsored by the Government (local, state, and federal) [.gov]	Newspapers (International, National, Local)
Educational Web sites [.edu]	Government Publications (including *Congressional Quarterly*, various studies, educational references, etc.)
Data and Statistics	
PROCESS USED TO REVIEW CONTENT FOR CREDIBILITY	
Anybody can publish and post	Texts written by journalists or professionals in the discipline/field
No evaluation process: *No one* checks for accuracy, bias, thoroughness, or timeliness.	Evaluated and reviewed for accuracy, credibility, and thoroughness by experts in the field and/or publishers and fact-checkers—Always dated
References and author biography or credentials *not* required	Evaluated and updated frequently
BEST USES FOR	
Personal information needs	College-level (or higher-level) research
Entertainment	When you need to find reliable information expediently
When you have enough time to check and cross-reference them with other known, credible sources (from databases)	
When it is a college-level .edu source or a .gov source	
Digitized Archives of Original Documents	
Documentaries and live interviews with experts in the field	

As you can see by examining this chart carefully, in many ways, *the purpose* of your research can determine which search tool will give you the most useful and trustworthy information. The type of information you need also plays a role in the choice you make.

In conducting any research, *you* will assume the crucial roles of finder, evaluator, and keeper or rejecter. When you want to find the most reliable additions to a college-level research project or essay in the most expedient way, you will most likely find yourself increasingly relying upon database discoveries. This fact does not mean you will not ever find anything useful on Internet search engines; rather, it means that predominantly, you should seek the consistently vetted sources of the databases, even at times to confirm what you may have found on an Internet search engine. As scholars in the sciences and social sciences continue to offer increasing amounts of verified information for free on the Internet, you may see that in those disciplines, you may uncover some quite worthwhile sources, but always use some caution about the reliability of a source.

IN-CLASS ACTIVITY 3A: INTERNET SOURCES VERSUS DATABASE SOURCES

1. Let's begin with a quick review of some of the key differences between what source types offer.

INTERNET SOURCES	DATABASE SOURCES
KINDS OF INFORMATION TO BE FOUND	
Some free scholarly articles and books	Scholarly journal articles
Culturally Popular Web sites	Reference Books, Articles, and Directories
Commercial Web sites [.com, .net]	Chapters from and Whole Books
Web sites By and For Organizations [.org] and ASP's (Applications)	Popular Magazines and Specialized Magazines
Web sites Sponsored by the Government (local, state, and federal) [.gov]	Newspapers (International, National, Local)
Educational Web sites [.edu]	Government Publications (including *Congressional Quarterly*, various studies, educational references, etc.)
Data and Statistics	
BEST USES FOR	
Personal information needs	College-level (or higher-level) research
Entertainment	When you need to find reliable information expediently
When you have enough time to check and cross-reference them with other known, credible sources (from databases)	
When it is a college-level .edu source or a .gov source	
Digitized Archives of Original Documents	

2. Let's watch the following two quick videos:

   "Google vs. Databases" by Penfield Library, February 3, 2014:

   https://www.youtube.com/watch?v=lMYZiUv47x8

   "What Are Databases and Why You Need Them" by Yavapai College Library, September 29, 2011:

   https://www.youtube.com/watch?v=Q2GMtluaNzU

3. Get into groups of three or four.

4. Examine the scenarios below.

5. Decide what kind of search—Internet, Database, Both, or Neither—you should use <u>and why.</u> (Feel free to conduct the searches, if you like.)

6. Be prepared to argue your conclusions in a whole class Call and Response circle activity.

A. Your history professor has asked you to find current opinion pieces about gun control laws, so you can draw a conclusion about the general mood of the nation about this issue.

CHOICE:

WHY:

B. Your sociology professor wants the most current demographic data regarding farm workers versus farm owners in California.

CHOICE:

WHY:

C. For a criminal justice class, you need to find out about the rules regarding the history of, and the effects of the use of, solitary confinement for inmates.

CHOICE:

WHY:

D. For a literature class, you need to find and bring to class another novel written by John Irving.

CHOICE:

WHY:

E. For your Anatomy and Physiology class, you need information about the biological reasons the American Red Cross will not accept blood donations from people who lived in the United Kingdom for more than six months during 1980–96.

CHOICE:

WHY:

CHAPTER 3

ACTIVITY 3A

B. Summarizing and Evaluating Sources

No matter where you find your sources, two key steps will help you to ascertain whether or not you should use these texts: summarizing and evaluating.

We have already practiced summarizing some of our assigned readings, and that process remains the same when you apply it to a source. To summarize effectively, after you read the source, you will:

- Concisely state the writer's primary claim/point/main idea.
  - ▶ EXAMPLE: Lewitsky's premise contends that no standard treatment for depression exists. He claims that treatment remains a very individualized endeavor.
- Concisely and *in general*, clarify any explanatory key details or evidence.
  - ▶ EXAMPLE: Lewitsky bases this claim on a study of over 1,000 patients undergoing treatment with 50 different psychiatrists. He maintains that the variations even within specific doctors' practices demonstrate that no prescriptive one way to treat depressed patients can succeed.

In a summary, you will *avoid* offering your own response, using anything but your own words, and using too many details or specifics from the source. Think of a summary as the one-to-two-minute recap you would give a friend about a movie. You would say, "It's about X, when Y does Z." You would not offer every plot twist or character analysis. You would keep it brief and to the point.

© Fabrik Bilder/Shutterstock.com

You may have noticed that many scholarly articles are preceded by something labeled an "abstract." These abstracts are simply the summaries the authors have written about their own articles. They offer you clear examples of what summaries do.

IN-CLASS ACTIVITY 3B: EFFECTIVE SUMMARIES

A SUMMARY IS:	A SUMMARY IS NOT:
• A concise recap of the main idea	• A blow-by-blow of the details
• Written in our own words	• A word-for-word restatement
• Focused on the key points only	• Ever as long as or longer than the original
• A general overview	• Bogged down in full explanations
• Always brief	• An explanation of your interpretation

1. On your phone, laptop, tablet, or station computer, see ONE of the following videos. Take notes on the index card given to you.

   "How to Write a Summary" by Smrt English, November 15, 2012:

   > https://www.youtube.com/watch?v=eGWO1ldEhtQ

   OR

   "How to Write an Effective Academic Summary Paragraph" by Maritez Apigo, December 5, 2015:

   > https://www.youtube.com/watch?v=WZFI6dvgOzU

   OR the following handout:

   "Summarizing: Five Keys To Writing Effective Summaries" by SIU Writing Center:

   > https://write.siu.edu/_common/documents/handouts/summarizing.pdf

2. Watch three to five minutes of the following video, and JUDGE its summary: Good? Bad? Too much? Too little? We'll vote on and briefly discuss your conclusions.

   "Before you see *Godzilla King of The Monsters*, Here's Your 5-Minute Recap" by Dread Central Media, 2019:

   > https://www.dreadcentral.com/news/294848/before-you-see-king-of-the-monsters-heres-your-5-minute-recap-of-godzilla-2014-kong-skull-island/

   Your ranking on a scale of 1 (poor) to 10 (excellent): _____

   WHY you gave it that score:

3. Turn to your neighbor and discuss your evaluation. Can you reach a consensus?

4. A TEXTUAL EXAMPLE FROM THE READINGS IN CHAPTER 2

Highlight/underline those sections that summarize.

◇◇

Excerpt from *Open Source Democracy: How Online Communication is Changing Offline Politics* by Douglas Rushkoff

CHAPTER 3
The Opportunity for Renaissance

The birth of the internet was interpreted by many as a revolution. Those of us in the counter-culture saw in the internet an opportunity to topple the storytellers who had dominated our politics, economics, society and religion—in short our very reality—and to replace their stories with those of our own. It was a beautiful and exciting sentiment, but one as based in a particular narrative as any other. Revolutions simply replace one story with another. The capitalist narrative is replaced by that of the communist; the religious fundamentalist's replaced by the gnostic's. The means may be different, but the rewards are the same. So is the exclusivity of their distribution. That's why they're called revolutions—we're just going in a circle.

This is why it might be more useful to understand the proliferation of interactive media as an opportunity for renaissance: a moment when we have the ability to step out of the story altogether. Renaissances are historical instances of widespread recontextualisation. People in a variety of different arts, philosophies and sciences have the ability to reframe their reality. Renaissance literally means 'rebirth.' It is the rebirth of old ideas in a new context. A renaissance is a dimensional leap, when our perspective shifts so dramatically that our understanding of the oldest, most fundamental elements of existence changes. The stories we have been using no longer work.

Take a look back at what we think of as the original Renaissance; the one we were taught in school. What were the main leaps in perspective? One example is the use of perspective in painting. Artists developed the technique of the vanishing point and with it the ability to paint three-dimensional representations on two-dimensional surfaces. The character of this innovation is subtle but distinct. It is not a technique for working in three dimensions; it is not that artists moved from working on canvas to working with clay. Rather, perspective painting allows an artist to relate between dimensions: representing three-dimensional objects on a two-dimensional plane. . . .

Similarly, the invention of moveable type and the printing press changed the relationship of author and audience to text. The creation of a manuscript was no longer a one-pointed affair. The creation of the first manuscript still was, but now it could be replicated and distributed to everyone. It was still one story, but now was subject to a multiplicity of individual perspectives. This innovation alone changed the landscape of religion in the Western World. Individual interpretation of the Bible led to the collapse of Church authority and the unilateral nature of its decrees. Everyone demanded his or her own relationship to the story.

Our Electronic Renaissance

In all these cases, people experienced a very particular shift in their relationship to, and understanding of, dimensions. Understood this way, a renaissance is a moment of reframing. We step out of the frame as it is currently defined and see the whole picture in a new context. We can then play by new rules.

It is akin to the experience of a computer game player. At first, a gamer will play a video or computer game by the rules. He'll read the manual, if necessary, then move through the various levels of the game. Mastery of the game, at this stage, means getting to the end: making it to the last level, surviving, becoming the most powerful character or, in the case of a simulation game, designing and maintaining a thriving family, city or civilisation. For many gamers, this is as far as it goes.

Some gamers, though—usually after they've mastered this level of play—will venture out onto the internet in search of other fans or user groups. There, they will gather the cheat codes that can be used to acquire special abilities within the game, such as invisibility or an infinite supply of ammunition. When the gamer returns to the game with his secret codes, is he still playing the game or is he cheating? From a renaissance perspective he is still playing the game, albeit a different one. His playing field has grown from the CD on which the game was shipped to the entire universe of computers where these secret codes and abilities can be discussed and shared. He is no longer playing the game, but a meta-game. The inner game world is still fun, but it is distanced by the gamer's new perspective, much in the way we are distanced from the play-within-a-play in one of Shakespeare's comedies or dramas. And the meta-theatrical convention gives us new perspective on the greater story as well. Gaming, as a metaphor but also as a lived experience, invites a renaissance perspective on the world in which we live. Perhaps gamers and their game culture have been as responsible as anyone for the rise in expressly self-similar forms of television like *Beavis and Butt-head*, *The Simpsons* and *Southpark*. The joy of such programs is not the relief of reaching the climax of the linear narrative, but rather the momentary thrill of making connections. The satisfaction is in recognising which bits of media are being satirised at any given moment. It is an entirely new perspective on television, where programs exist more in the form of Talmudic commentary: perspectives on perspectives on perspectives. We watch screens within screens, constantly reminded, almost as in a Brecht play, of the artifice of storytelling. It is as if we are looking at a series of proscenium arches, and are being invited as an audience to consider whether we are within a proscenium arch ourselves.

The great Renaissance was a simple leap in perspective. Instead of seeing everything in one dimension, we came to realise there was more than one dimension on which things were occurring. Even the Elizabethan world picture, with its concentric rings of authority—God, king, man, animals—reflects this newfound way of contending with the simultaneity of action of many dimensions at once. A gamer stepping out onto the internet to find a cheat code certainly reaches this first renaissance's level of awareness and skill.

But what of the gamer who then learns to program new games for himself? He, we might argue, has stepped out of yet another frame into our current renaissance. He has deconstructed the content of the game, demystified the technology of its interface and now feels ready to open the codes and turn the game into a do-it-yourself activity. He has moved from a position of a receiving player to that of a deconstructing user. He has assumed the position of author, himself. This leap to authorship is precisely the character and quality of the dimensional leap associated with today's renaissance.

The evidence of today's renaissance is at least as profound as that of the one that went before. The 16th century saw the successful circumnavigation of the globe via the seas. The 20th century saw the successful circumnavigation of the globe from space. The first pictures of earth from space changed our perspective on this sphere forever. In the same century, our dominance over the planet was confirmed not just through our ability to travel around it, but to destroy it. The atomic bomb (itself the result of a rude dimensional interchange between submolecular particles) gave us the ability to author the globe's very destiny. Now, instead of merely being able to comprehend 'God's creation,' we could actively control it. This is a new perspective.

We also have our equivalent of perspective painting, in the invention of the holograph. The holograph allows us to represent not just three, but four dimensions on a two-dimensional plate. When the viewer walks past a holograph she can observe the three-dimensional object over a course of time. A bird can flap its wings in a single picture. But, more importantly for our renaissance's purposes, the holographic plate itself embodies a new renaissance principle. When the plate is smashed into hundreds of pieces, we do not find that one piece contains the bird's wing, and another piece the bird's beak. Each piece of the plate contains a faint image of the entire subject. When the pieces are put together, the image achieves greater resolution. But each piece contains a representation of the totality. This leap in dimensional understanding is now informing disciplines as diverse as brain anatomy and computer programming. . . .

Finally, our renaissance's answer to the printing press is the computer and its ability to network. Just as the printing press gave everyone access to readership, the computer and internet give everyone access to authorship. The first Renaissance took us from the position of passive recipient to active interpreter. Our current renaissance brings us from the role of interpreter to the role of author. We are the creators.

As game programmers instead of game players, the creators of testimony rather than the believers in testament, we begin to become aware of just how much of our reality is open source and up for discussion. So much of what seemed like impenetrable hardware is actually software and ripe for reprogramming. The stories we use to understand the world seem less like explanations and more like collaborations. They are rule sets, only as good as their ability to explain the patterns of history or predict those of the future. . . .

What Gets Reborn

The renaissance experience of moving beyond the frame allows everything old to look new again. We are liberated from the maps we have been using to navigate our world and free to create new ones based on our own observations. This invariably leads to a whole new era of competition. Renaissance may be a rebirth of old ideas in a new context, but which ideas get to be reborn?

The first to recognise the new renaissance will compete to have their ideologies be the ones that are rebirthed in this new context. This is why, with the emergence of the internet, we saw the attempted rebirth (and occasional stillbirth) of everything from paganism to libertarianism, and communism to psychedelia. Predictably, the financial markets and consumer capitalism, the dominant narratives of our era, were the first to successfully commandeer the renaissance. But they squandered their story on a pyramid scheme (indeed, the accelerating force of computers and networks tends to force any story to its logical conclusion) and now the interactive renaissance is once again up for grabs. . . .

From: Rushkoff, Douglas. "Chapter 3 The opportunity for renaissance." In *Open Source Democracy How online communication is changing offline politics,* N.P. Guttenburg EBook through Demos Open Access, 2003.

http://www.gutenberg.org/cache/epub/10753/pg10753-images.html

◇◇◇◇◇◇◇◇◇◇◇◇◇◇◇◇◇◇◇◇◇◇◇◇◇◇◇◇◇◇◇◇◇◇◇◇◇

Activity A—Groups—Summarize the full chapter from Douglas Rushkoff.

Work in groups of three to four students to complete the following exercise. [ONLINE students: You will complete and post the activities A and B and then reply to one peer's post, first commenting on the summary your peer wrote for activity 1 and then following the directions for activity B.]

In your summary, make certain to:

- Identify the claim.
- Identify the key reasons and evidence, <u>but not</u> all of the major details.
- Write an actual three-to-six-sentence paragraph that SUMMARIZES.

You might like to use any of the following patterns:

- X tells us that _____.
- X posits the premise that _____.
- X argues that _____.
- X laments that _____.
- X clarifies that _____.
- X emphasizes that _____.

YOUR GROUP'S SUMMARY:

Activity B—Groups—Rewrite Summary

Continue to work in the same group of three to four students to complete the following exercise. [ONLINE students: You will complete the activity B part by replying to the same peer's post, rewriting that peer's summary twice, as directed below. Identify whose post you are rewriting.]

Our summaries often must assess the point of view held by the writer in relation to the argument we hope to make. In doing so, the summaries might choose a different set of introductory patterns.

For example:

- believes that _____.
- counters the opposition by claiming _____.
- demonstrates his leaning toward _____ by arguing that _____.
- clings to his firm point that _____.
- maintains the position that _____.

Rewrite your summary twice.

1. For an essay that claims "[T]he internet [emerged as] an opportunity to topple the story-tellers who had dominated our politics, economics, society and religion—in short our very reality—and to replace their stories with those of our own."

2. For an essay that claims "[The internet renaissance is actually] a moment when we have the ability to step out of the story altogether."

3. Now explain how these summaries differ and why they differ. What has such an exercise taught you about the art and skill of summarizing? How might you apply the lesson to your own academic writing?

Once you have summarized a source and therefore know precisely and concisely what it says, you can move to the next vital step: evaluating the source. Just because you have found a source does not mean you will necessarily ultimately use that source. You must decide whether or not it meets specific criteria. That criteria include all of the following, a list that librarian Sarah Blakeslee at Meriam Library at California State University in Chico calls "the CRAAP Test."

- **C**urrency
  - ► How timely is the information?
    - When was the source published?
    - From what dates do the sources used in the text come?
    - How current does the particular topic require the source to be?
    - If the source comes from the Internet, do its posted links still work?
      - EXAMPLE 1: You are researching a nineteenth-century novel. You find an archived book review from 1880. It is old, but so is the literature you are studying, so in this case, the source passes the currency test; it is timely, given the period.
      - EXAMPLE 2: You are researching the use of social media to bully people. You find an article written in 2018 that uses sources from 2002–10. You decide it is not truly current because social media change monthly, so information from so many years ago is not timely.

- **R**elevance
  - ► How well does this information relate to your topic and your question?
  - ► Does the information make sense to you? Was the piece targeting an audience appropriate for you?
  - ► Does the source provide an opposition position against which you can argue? (This condition too makes it relevant; it does not have to agree with your ideas or the ideas of others.)
    - EXAMPLE: For an essay about mandatory drug sentencing, you find an article on the algorithms used to analyze prison populations. While it is tangentially related, its focus does not truly fit your own because it is too broad. In addition, you are not a math or computer science major, so the algorithm formulas are difficult to understand. You decide this source is not relevant for you and your research topic and question.

- **A**uthority
  - ► How credible/trustworthy/believable is the source? How do you know so?
    - Who is the author, and what credentials does that author possess?
    - Do the author's credentials apply to this topic?
    - In what publication did you find the source? Is it a known and valued publication? Can you actually contact that publication's editors?
    - If you found the source on the Internet, what extension (.com, .net, .org, .edu, .gov, .asp) does it have?
    - If you found the source on the Internet, does it provide information regarding the Web designer or sponsor? Can you contact that designer or sponsor?
      - EXAMPLE: You find a source about overcrowded prisons written by a person with a PhD in British literature. You reject this article because the scholar has no expertise in this discipline.

- <u>A</u>ccuracy
  - ▶ How reliable, truthful, and correct is this source?
    - What sources does this article use? Do they come from varied and reliable experts?
    - What kinds of evidence does the argument use?
    - Does the article come from a peer-reviewed or fact-checked source?
    - Does the essay have an obvious bias or slant?
    - Does the article demonstrate correct use of language conventions and spelling?
      - EXAMPLE: You find an essay about gun control. In examining its sources, you find many are blogs from gun-control lobbyists. You reject the source as biased and unreliable.
- <u>P</u>urpose
  - ▶ What does the source strive to accomplish: inform, persuade, advertise, entertain, etc.?
    - Does the source use facts, opinions, or emotional appeals?
    - Does the article clearly state or demonstrate its purpose?
    - Does the essay seem objective?
      - EXAMPLE: You find an article in *The Christian Science Monitor* that analyzes senators' voting records on euthanasia. You choose to use the source because even though it appears in a Christian-biased publication, it uses hard data to inform readers about senators' positions based on their voting records.

© thodonal88/Shutterstock.com

Evaluating your sources objectively by using these criteria will help you to decide which research you will rely upon to form your own conclusions. Sometimes, you will reject a source simply because it does not relate to what you hope to address in *your* research project or essay. Sometimes you will choose not to use a source because you deem it unreliable. Finding and evaluating such sources serve as part of the process. You have still learned something in evaluating and rejecting a source; you have made a clear decision about what dialogues you want to include in your own conversation about the topic and the answer to your question.

IN-CLASS ACTIVITY 3C: EVALUATING SOURCES

1. Review the CRAAP Test criteria which comes from librarian Sarah Blakeslee at California State University in Chico. She has granted "Creative Commons Attribution" use of this formula.

When you search for information, you're going to find lots of it . . . but is it good information? You will have to determine that for yourself, and the **CRAAP Test** can help. The **CRAAP Test** is a list of questions to help you evaluate the information you find. Different criteria will be more or less important depending on your situation or need.

Key: ■ indicates criteria is for Web

CURRENCY
- When was the information published or posted?
- Has the information been revised or updated?
- Does your topic require current information, or will older sources work as well?
- ■ Are the links functional?

RELEVANCE: *The importance of the information for your needs.*
- Does the information relate to your topic or answer your question?
- Who is the intended audience?
- Is the information at an appropriate level (i.e. ,not too elementary or advanced)
- Have you looked at a variety of sources before determining this is one you will use?
- Would you be comfortable citing this source in your research paper?

AUTHORITY: *The source of the information.*
- Who is the author/publisher/source/sponsor?
- What are the author's credentials or organizational affiliations?
- Is the author qualified to write on the topic?
- Is there contact information, such as a publisher or email address?
- ■ Does the URL reveal anything about the author or source?
  examples: **.com .edu .gov .org .net**

ACCURACY: *The reliability, truthfulness and correctness of the content.*
- Where does the information come from?
- Is the information supported by evidence?
- Has the information been reviewed or refereed?
- Can you verify any of the information in another souce or from personal knowledge?
- Does the language or tone seem unbiased and free of emotion?
- Are there spelling, grammar, or typographical errors?

PURPOSE: *The reason the information exists.*
- What is the purpose of the information? Is it to inform, teach, sell, entertain or persuade?
- Do the authors/sponsors make their intentions or purpose clear?
- Is the information fact, opinion, or propaganda?
- Does the point of view appear objective and impartial?
- Are there political, ideological, cultural, religious, institutional, or personal biases?

Source: Sarah Blakeslee. Reprinted by permission.

2. Let's now reread one of the assignments from Chapter 2. Annotate it, paying special attention to and locating: its claim, its evidence, and its adherence to the CRAAP Test elements.

◇◇◇

Excerpts From "The Logic of Vegetarianism" in *Essays and Dialogues* by Henry S. Salt

THE MORALIST AT THE SHAMBLES.

Where slaughter'd beasts lie quivering, pile on pile,
And bare-armed fleshers, bathed in bloody dew,
Ply hard their ghastly trade, and hack and hew,
And mock sweet Mercy's name, yet loathe the while
The lot that chains them to this service vile,
Their hands in hideous carnage to imbrue:
Lo, there!—the preacher of the Good and True,
The Moral Man, with sanctimonious smile!
"Thrice happy beasts," he murmurs, "'tis our love,
Our thoughtful love that sends ye to the knife
(Nay, doubt not, as ye welter in your gore!);
For thus alone ye earned the boon of life,
And thus alone the Moralist may prove
His sympathetic soul—by eating more."

Why "Vegetarian"?

The term "vegetarian," as applied to those who abstain from all flesh food, but not necessarily from such animal products as eggs, milk, and cheese, appears to have come into existence over fifty years ago, at the time of the founding of the Vegetarian Society in 1847. Until that date no special name had been appropriated for the reformed diet system, which was usually known as the "Pythagorean" or "vegetable diet," as may be seen by a reference to the writings of that period. Presumably, it was felt that when the movement grew in volume, and was about to enter on a new phase, with an organised propaganda, it was advisable to coin for it an original and distinctive title. Whether, from this point of view, the name "vegetarian" was wisely or unwisely chosen is a question on which there has been some difference of opinion among food reformers themselves, and it is possible that adverse criticism would have been still more strongly expressed but for the fact that no better title has been forthcoming.

. . . .

The *Raison d'être* of Vegetarianism

Behind the mere name of the reformed diet, whatever name be employed (and, as we have seen, "vegetarian" at present holds the field), lies the far more important reality. What is the *raison d'être*, the real purport of vegetarianism? Certainly not any *a priori* assumption that all animal substances, as such, are unfit for human food; for though it is quite probable that the movement will ultimately lead us to the disuse of animal products, vegetarianism is not primarily based on any such hard-and-fast formula, but on the conviction, suggested in the first place by instinctive feeling, but confirmed by reason and experience, that there are certain grave evils inseparable from the practice of flesh-eating. The aversion to flesh food is not chemical, but moral, social, hygienic. Believing as we do that the grosser forms of diet not only cause a vast amount of unnecessary suffering to the animals, but also react most injuriously on the health and morals of mankind, we advocate their gradual discontinuance; and so long as this protest is successfully launched, the mere name by which it is called is a matter of minor concern. But here on this practical issue, as before on the nominal issue, we come into conflict with the superior person who, with a smile of supercilious compassion, cannot see *why* we poor ascetics should thus afflict ourselves without cause.

. . . We conclude, then, that the cause which vegetarians have at heart is the outcome, not of some barren academic formula, but of a practical reasoned conviction that flesh food, especially butchers' meat, is a harmful and barbarous diet. Into the details of this belief we need not at present enter; it has been sufficient here to show that such belief exists, and that the good people who can see in vegetarianism nothing but a whimsical "fad" have altogether failed to grasp its true purport and significance. The *raison d'être* of vegetarianism is the growing sense that flesh-eating is a cruel, disgusting, unwholesome, and wasteful practice, and that it behoves humane and rational persons, disregarding the common cant about "consistency" and "all-or-nothing," to reform their diet to what extent and with what speed they can.

But, it may be said, before entering on a consideration of this reformed diet, for which such great merits are claimed by its exponents, the practical man is justified in asking for certain solid assurances, since busy people cannot be expected to give their time to speculations which, however beautiful in themselves, may prove at the end to be in conflict with the hard facts of life. And the first of these questions is, What is the historic basis of vegetarianism? In what sense is it an old movement, and in what sense a new one? Has it a past which may serve in some measure to explain its present and guarantee its future?

Such questions have been dealt with fully from time to time in vegetarian literature.[1] I can here do no more than epitomise the answers. Vegetarianism, regarded simply as a practice and without relation to any principle, is of immemorial date; it was, in fact, as physiology shows us, the original diet of mankind, while, as history shows us, it has always been the diet of the many, as flesh food has been the diet of the few, and even to this day it is the main support of the greater part of the world's inhabitants. Numberless instances might be quoted in proof of these assertions; it is sufficient to refer to the people of India, China, and Japan, the Egyptian fellah, the Bedouin Arab, the peasantry of Russia and Turkey, the labourers and miners of Chili and other South American States; and, to come nearer home, the great bulk of the country folk in Western Europe and Great Britain. The peasant, here and all the world over, has been, and still is, in the main a vegetarian, and must for the most part continue so; and the fact that this diet has been the result, not of choice, but of necessity, does not lessen the significance of its perfect sufficiency to maintain those who do the hard work of the world. Side by side with the tendency of the wealthier classes to indulge more and more in flesh food has been the undisputed admission that for the workers such luxuries were unneeded.

During the last half-century, however, as we all know, the unhealthy and crowded civilisation of great industrial centres has produced among the urban populations of Europe a craving for flesh food, which has resulted in their being fed largely on cheap butchers' meat and offal; while there has grown up a corresponding belief that we must look almost entirely to a flesh diet for bodily and mental vigour. It is in protest against this comparatively new demand for flesh as a necessity of life that vegetarianism, as a modern organised movement, has arisen.

Secondly, if we look back for examples of deliberate abstinence from flesh—that is, of vegetarianism practised as a *principle* before it was denoted by a name—we find no lack of them in the history of religious and moral systems and individual lives. Such abstinence was an essential feature in the teaching of Buddha and Pythagoras and is still practised in the East on religious and ceremonial grounds by Brahmins and Buddhists. It was inculcated in the humanitarian writings of great "pagan" philosophers, such as Plutarch and Porphyry, whose ethical precepts, as far as the treatment of the lower animals is concerned, are still far in advance of modern Christian sentiment. Again, in the prescribed regimen of certain religious Orders, such as Benedictines, Trappists, and Carthusians, we have further unquestionable evidence of the disuse of flesh food, though in such cases the reason for the abstinence is ascetic rather than humane. When we turn to the biographies of individuals, we learn that there have been numerous examples of what is now called "vegetarianism"—not always consistent, indeed, or continuous in practice, yet sufficiently so to prove the entire possibility of the diet, and to remove it from the category of generous aspiration into that of accomplished fact.[2]

NOTES

1. As in "The Perfect Way in Diet," by Dr. Anna Kingsford; and "Strength and Diet," by the Hon. R. Russell.

2. See the list of names cited in Mr. Howard Williams's "Ethics of Diet," a biographical history of the literature of humane dietetics from the earliest period to the present day.

From: Salt, Henry S. "Why Vegetarian?" In *The Logic of Vegetarianism Essays and Dialogues,* 4–13. London: George Bell and Sons, 1906.

http://www.gutenberg.org/files/49949/49949-h/49949-h.htm

3. When we write about our evaluation of a source, we use what is called an "Annotated Bibliography." It includes the components listed here.

- List each of your sources in MLA format and, below EVERY source, write one to two paragraphs in which you:
  - Using terms from CRAAP Test, explain why this is a relevant and reliable source.

- Summarize the basic claim of the source. What did this author (these authors) say? (Recall our Summary and Response Activities from Chapter 1 and Activity 3B on summary.)
- Respond to the source. What do "you" say? You might agree, disagree, raise questions, etc. (Recall our Summary and Response Activities from Chapter 1.)
- Explain how you will use this source in your research article. Be specific.
- Synthesize. Explain the way this work fits with—or challenges—other information you have about the topic.

Read the following Annotated Bibliography entry about Salt's article, and decide whether or not it passes the CRAAP test.

Salt, Henry S. "Why Vegetarian?" In *The Logic of Vegetarianism Essays and Dialogues,* 4–13. London: George Bell and Sons, 1906. http://www.gutenberg.org/files/49949/49949-h/49949-h.htm. Accessed 8 February 2019.

Although written way back in 1906, this essay by Henry S. Salt makes basically the same arguments made today about why everyone should be a vegetarian: that meat-eating is "a harmful and barbarous diet." He starts with a poem about the immorality of meat-eating. He claims it is a social class issue, with the wealthy making meat the most important food group. He explains why being vegetarian is a more viable diet for everyone, rich or poor.

CATEGORY	PASS AND WHY	FAIL AND WHY
Currency		
Relevance		
Authority		
Accuracy		
Purpose		
Works Cited		

OVERALL: PASS OR FAIL
WHY?

NOW, write an annotated bibliography entry for one of your sources.

FACE-TO-FACE Classes Only: SWAP your annotated bibliography entry with a peer. Evaluate each other's entry according to the table below. Discuss your conclusions with each other. Make suggestions for improvement. Reflect on how this advice applies to the other entries you wrote in journal 8.

ONLINE Class Only: SELECT one of your own annotated bibliography entries. Evaluate that entry according to the table below. Think about your conclusions. Think about what you need to do to improve the entry. Reflect on how this advice applies to your other entries in journal 8.

CATEGORY	PASS AND WHY	FAIL AND WHY
Currency		
Relevance		
Authority		
Accuracy		
Purpose		
Works Cited		

OVERALL: PASS OR FAIL
WHY?

ACTIVITY 3C

JOURNAL ENTRY 8

Review the reading and activities about using the CRAAP Test to evaluate sources.
By now, you have found at least three sources for your research project/essay.
Write THREE paragraphs, <u>one for each</u> of your THREE sources, in which you do the following:

- Name the source, its author(s), its publication date, and its place of publication.
- Summarize the source (claim + general evidence). Use no more than three sentences.
- Evaluate each source's:
  - ▶ Currency
  - ▶ Relevance
  - ▶ Authority
  - ▶ Accuracy
  - ▶ Purpose

You may wish to use the following template, but you do not have to do so.

I found the source, "_____," written by _____ and published in

_____ on _____ in the _____ database, using the

search terms "_____." Basically, this entire article supports the idea

that _____.

This author utilizes _____ and _____ to substantiate the claim, and

this evidence _____ [←Verb] the reader. The source absolutely possesses

reliability and credibility, for its author _____,

and the piece draws from _____ sources, all of them from _____ - _____, and

all of them from scholarly publications. The vocabulary does _____,

for it is _____. Because I contend that _____

_____, this source will _____

_____ with my claim, though it will contradict

_____. In general,

it will _____

my other research.

C. Assessing the Overall Dialogue

Once you have summarized and evaluated all of your individual sources, you should take some time to think about what you have actually learned from them. When you think about what they have to say *in total*:

- What general conclusions do these sources reach?
- On what do most of these dialogues agree?
- On what do they disagree?
- *In general*, do they focus on some particular idea?
- *In general*, do they all exclude a particular idea?

As you ponder your answers to these questions, you can, in essence, create a summary of the overall conversation about your topic. Only then can you begin thinking about where your ideas fit into that dialogue and about what additions you will contribute.

© Alexander Limbach/Shutterstock.com

D. Addressing the Opposition Positions

You cannot consider the whole of any academic conversation without addressing the opposition's position. If you recall any successful discussion you have ever had with anyone—a parent, a sibling, a friend—you will probably remember that to convince your listener to understand and agree with your point, you had to anticipate that individual's position and counter it. In defeating that person's objections, you bolstered your own claim enough to change your listener's mind.

A research argument does not differ in this regard. In fact, because of the very reality that the opposition position, like your own, very probably comes clothed in research, your counterargument can truly lend power to your own position. Acknowledging an opposing viewpoint actually strengthens your own argument because:

- It demonstrates your awareness that not everyone will agree with you.
- It gives your argument increased credibility because you take on the opposition.
- It anticipates objections so you can counter them.
- It requires you to use logic to reiterate your claim.

Typically, opposing an argument requires:

- Introducing and clarifying that opposing viewpoint
  ▶ Summarize the claim and main points
  ▶ Use patterns such as
    - According to X _____
    - X has argued that _____
    - Opponents of this idea claim _____
- Acknowledging the parts of the opposition that are valid.
  ▶ State that some part of the opposition's claim makes sense
  ▶ Use patterns such as
    - I/We/One cannot deny that _____
    - Admittedly, _____
    - Of course, some truth lies in the idea that _____
- Countering the opposing viewpoint.
  ▶ Explain what your position is, relative to the opposition's point; show that viewpoint as incorrect, inconsequential, or weak. Discredit it.
  ▶ Use patterns such as
    - . . . deny that _____, but _____
    - However, _____
    - Nonetheless, _____
    - To the contrary, _____
- Concluding the refutation/counterargument
  ▶ Summarize why the opposition viewpoint is insufficient, but your claim is correct. Do so without getting redundant.
  ▶ Use patterns such as
    - As such, _____
    - Therefore, _____
    - As a consequence/result, _____
    - In essence, then, _____

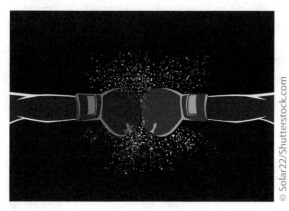

IN-CLASS ACTIVITY 3D: ASSESSING THE OVERALL DIALOGUE AND ADDRESSING OPPOSITION POSITIONS

1. INDIVIDUALLY, using the assigned readings about a college education, fill in the following chart.

CATEGORY	Amanda Paulson's "Does everyone need a college degree? Maybe not, a Harvard study finds"	*Pro Con.org's* "Is College Education Worth It?"	Jeffrey J. Selingo's "How much is too much to pay for college?"	John Dewey's "Excerpts from *The School and Society*"
CLAIM				
GENERAL EVIDENCE				
OPPOSITION POSITION TO THE CLAIM				
YOUR RESPONSE TO THE CLAIM AND ARGUMENT				

2. Now move into a group of three to four students.

3. Discuss and compare your answers.

4. Create ONE to THREE sentences that make your group's claim about <u>the overall arguments concerning the need—or lack of need—to attend college</u>. Write that sentence/those sentences here.

5. Now reform your groups, including one member from each of the other groups in your new group.

6. Discuss and compare the statements your separate groups created.

7. Based on that discussion, create a revised statement about <u>the overall arguments concerning the need—or lack of need—to attend college</u>. Write that statement here.

8. Create and write below a three-to-five-step process to use to create a statement that assesses an overall academic argument about a particular topic. (What process did you follow as you designed your statements? What did you consider? What did you ignore? What needed doing first and last?) Post that process to the Padlet link sent to you (or to the Blackboard, if your professor prefers), so we can all see it.

9. Now let's all watch the following video.

"Addressing Opposing Viewpoints" by Brigham Young University Idaho, 2019:

   http://www.byui.edu/academic-support-centers/writing/video-lessons-and-handouts/addressing-opposing-viewpoints

10. INDIVIDUALLY review your answers on the chart we completed in the beginning of the class.

11. Choose any ONE of the claims about any ONE of the essays. Record it here in one of the patterns of expression we have learned:

   - X posits the premise that _____.
   - X tells us that _____.
   - X argues that _____.
   - X laments that _____.
   - X clarifies that _____.
   - X emphasizes that _____.
   - According to X, _____.

   CLAIM:

12. Now, use one of the following patterns to make a counterargument about that claim.

   - X claims _____; however, _____.
   - X argues that _____, but _____.
   - While X asserts _____, I contend _____.
   - Although X contends _____, X fails to consider _____.
   - Though others tell us _____, X posits the premise that _____.

13. Now, find others in the class who have chosen the same essay you have. Meet with them to discuss and compare your claims and counterclaim statements.

14. Create and write below a three- to five-step process to use to create a counterargument about a particular topic. (What process did you follow as you designed your statements? What did you consider? What did you ignore? What needed doing first and last?) Post that process to the Padlet link sent to you (or to the Blackboard, if your professor prefers), so we can all see it.

E. Creating and Annotating a Bibliography

Now that you have gathered and evaluated all of your sources, you can create what academia calls an *annotated bibliography* (or in some institutions, a literature [as in the sources available] review). The annotated bibliography serves two purposes:

1. It brings together all of your sources.
2. It enables you—and future researchers—to understand and assess what a particular list of sources offers regarding a specific research topic and question.

Some annotated bibliographies merely describe the sources, while others evaluate them. Those that evaluate provide useful information that identifies key elements of each source and assists the researcher in determining if the source merits a full reading. For the researcher who composes the annotations, the evaluative annotated bibliography allows for an opportunity to consider the entire scope of the conversation that researcher has discovered, so that before writing the actual essay or completing the culminating project, that researcher has assimilated it in a way that will facilitate choosing and making a specific argument.

An evaluative annotated bibliography consists of two parts: the overview and the annotations.

The overview does exactly what you might guess, based on its title: it provides a general and concise summary of the research conducted. It:

- Begins with a statement of research topic and question.
- Briefly summarizes upon what points the bulk of the research agrees. (It may include a direct quote or two here.)
- Briefly notes upon what points the research disagrees. (It may use a direct quote or two here.)
- Succinctly states the researcher's (your) tentative claim based on the research.
- Briefly comments on any additional research the researcher (you) might still need to complete.

A Possible Overview Template

Today, the topic/issue/idea/concept/problem (←Choose one) of _____

concerns/interests/intrigues/worries/registers (←Choose one) many people. Some believe _____

_____, while others think _____

_____.

At present, I contend that _____

because _____.

I have reached this tentative claim based upon the research I have completed so far. As I have researched this topic, I have discovered that scholars have actually drawn different conclusions. While some of them, particularly _____ (←Names of scholars/writers of the articles) contend that, "_____

_____" ( ), a few others such as _____ propose the premise that "_____" ( ). The bulk of the research on this topic seems to lean in favor of _____, and I agree with those ideas/but I cannot fully concur with such positions because _____.

I also recognize that I may need to find additional research about _____

_____.

The second and primary part of the evaluative annotated bibliography, *the annotations*, must include all of the following <u>for each source</u>:

- The properly formatted information about the source
- A statement about how and where the researcher (you) found the source
- A summary of the claim of the source
- A summary of the evidence used in the source (It may include a direct quote).

- An evaluation of the source's currency, authority, and accuracy
- A statement regarding the source's relevance to the researcher's (your) claim
- A statement regarding where the source fits among the other sources.

A Possible Template for Each Annotation

I found this source in the database _____, using the search terms "_____." Basically, this entire article supports the idea that _____ and strongly suggests that, "_____ ( ). This author utilizes _____ and _____ to substantiate the claim, and this evidence _____ [←Verb] the reader. The source absolutely possesses reliability and credibility, for its author _____, and the piece draws from _____ sources, all of them from _____- _____, and all of them from scholarly publications. The vocabulary does_____, for it is_____. Because I contend that _____ _____, this source will _____ with my claim, though it will contradict _____. In general, it will _____ my other research.

Ultimately, the evaluative annotated bibliography will help you to compose your draft of the research essay or project because it begins for you the process of synthesizing all of the material you have gathered over the course of several weeks.

IN-CLASS ACTIVITY 3E: CREATING AN ANNOTATION

1. Watch the following two-part video.

   "APA-MLA Annotated Bibliography: Complete Guide To Writing Annotated Bibliography Part 1" by David Taylor, July 16, 2016:

   https://www.youtube.com/watch?v=iW4eXLAtOhk

   Part 2: https://www.youtube.com/watch?v=w3A_wEMvnFA

2. Let's review one of your assigned readings together. (Take notes.)

   "How the Internet is Changing Our Brains" by Academic Earth (a video with written summary):

   https://academicearth.org/electives/internet-changing-your-brain/

---

3. Fill in the following chart regarding that [video] text. Use catchphrases, etc.

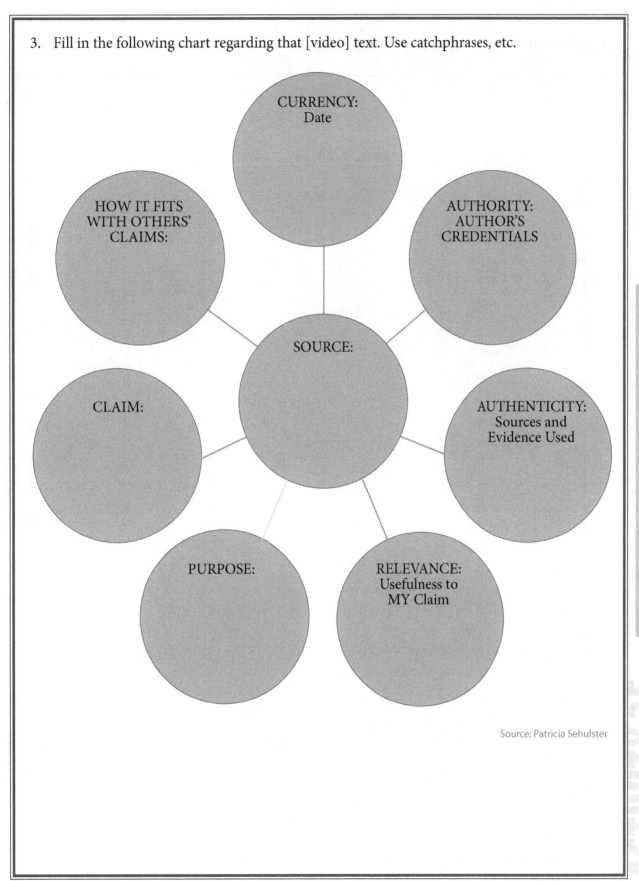

CURRENCY:
Date

AUTHORITY:
AUTHOR'S
CREDENTIALS

HOW IT FITS
WITH OTHERS'
CLAIMS:

SOURCE:

AUTHENTICITY:
Sources and
Evidence Used

CLAIM:

PURPOSE:

RELEVANCE:
Usefulness to
MY Claim

Source: Patricia Sehulster

4. Now compose a paragraph that utilizes all of that information to create an annotation for the source.

JOURNAL ENTRY 9

1. Fill out the following pyramid chart in catchphrases.

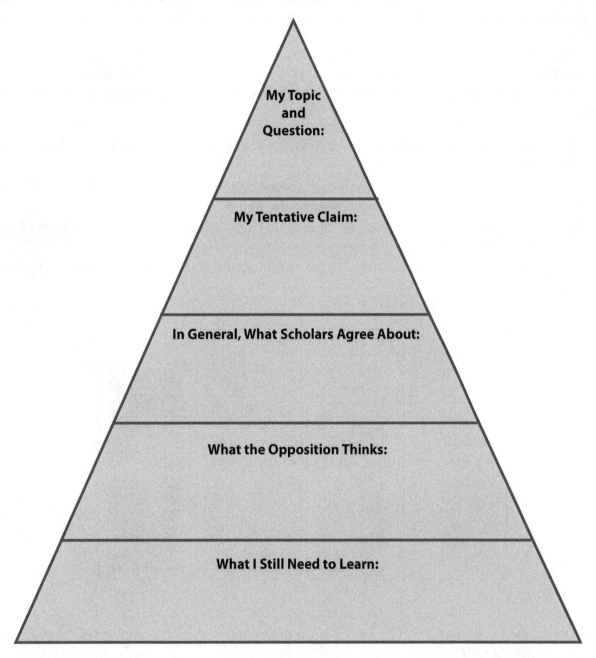

My Topic
and
Question:

My Tentative Claim:

In General, What Scholars Agree About:

What the Opposition Thinks:

What I Still Need to Learn:

© Kendall Hunt Publishing Company

2. Using the above information, construct the draft of your overview paragraph for the annotated bibliography.

F. Documenting Your Sources

Annotations and research essays and projects do not exist without an acknowledgment of the academic conversations that have come before them and to which you now contribute. As ethical scholars, you must credit that research by using a list of the sources and, within the text of the research essay or project, citing those sources.

Specific formats used all over the world exist for giving that credit, and their components vary slightly, though the basic procedure remains parallel. As such, if you have learned how to use one system, you will quickly apply those skills to the other systems. The four most commonly used formats include:

- MLA—created by the Modern Language Association and generally used for work done within the Humanities discipline
- APA—created by the American Psychological Association and generally used for work done within the Psychology, Education, and Science disciplines
- Chicago—created by the University of Chicago and generally used for work done in the Business, History, and Fine Arts disciplines
- Turabian—created by Kate Turabian and generally used for work done in the Business, History, and Fine Arts disciplines

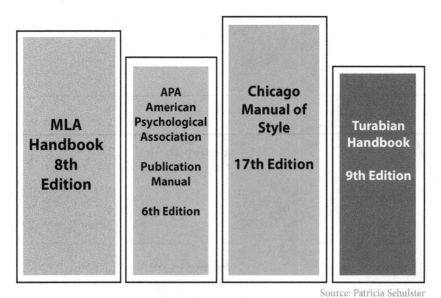

Source: Patricia Sehulster

The titles of the list of sources differ, but each list incorporates similar key information about the sources, though the order of those elements and the punctuation surrounding them do diverge. MLA formatting labels the list, "Works Cited," APA formatting uses "References," and Chicago and Turabian use "Bibliography" or "Reference List." No matter the title, all of them contain in some sequence:

- Author's (s') name(s)
- Title of the source

- Title of the journal, magazine, newspaper, book, or Web site in which the article exists
- Volume and issue numbers (if they exist)
- Date of publication
- Page numbers
- URL (for both databases and online sources)
- *In some cases*, the access date

Different types of sources—books, journal articles, Web sites, media, etc.—use a unique sequence of these elements. *Very few people memorize these combinations; rather, they utilize the handbooks* about how to compose the source information, or, conveniently, *in some databases, they use the citation feature* to see exactly how that source's entry should look in a particular format. For example, depending upon the particular database, if you examine the right-hand side menu, you will see the word "Cite" or "Citation" or something similar. If you click on that category, the database will take you to a list of citation formats for the particular source you have discovered. You will scroll until you find the correct format. Then you can simply copy and paste the correctly formatted entry.

Your source/article → the "Cite/Citation" Link → the list of correctly formatted citations for your required source list

Source: Patricia Sehulster

In the Appendices of this book, you will find the full set of rules governing MLA and APA source list (and in-text citation) formatting. (In Chapter 4, you will learn about the in-text citations.) Each of your annotations must begin with the properly formatted entry.

ANNOTATED BIBLIOGRAPHY ESSAY DIRECTIONS

Context. You have spent the last few weeks thinking and researching. Your annotated bibliography gives you an opportunity to take stock of your sources so that you see what sources you have, whether or not they are reliable and relevant, how you might use them in your research essay and project, and what sources you still need to find.

What is an Annotated Bibliography? There are many different types of annotated bibliographies and professors use the term in a variety of ways. Essentially, though, an annotated bibliography is a document that lists sources on a particular topic/question and offers a brief discussion of each source, summarizing that source and discussing how it connects to the other sources and to the researcher's own thinking-in-progress, including the researcher's working thesis.

Why Write an Annotated Bibliography? Creating an annotated bibliography gives structure and purpose to the (otherwise messy) research process. Writing an annotated bibliography requires you, the researcher, to read, think about, and analyze each of your sources, so that you are clear about how you will use them. Often while working on an annotated bibliography, a researcher realizes a source cannot be used or additional or different sources are needed. This kind of setback can be frustrating, but necessary as you, the researcher, figure out what you really want to know—and argue.

What are the components of an Annotated Bibliography?

- <u>An Overview</u>: This paragraph or two will:
  - ▶ Explain your topic, question, and claim or working thesis (what your thesis would be if you were to write the paper right now. It's called "working" because it might change.). *[Often, you can use a part of your already written proposal to create this section.]
  - ▶ Summarize what you have found out so far from your sources and what you still want/need to find out.

- Then, <u>list each of your sources in MLA format</u> and, below EVERY source, write one to two <u>paragraphs in which you</u>:
  - ▶ Using terms from the CRAAP Test, explain why this is a relevant and reliable source (You will not include sources that are not relevant or reliable).
  - ▶ Summarize the basic claim of the source. What did the author(s) say? Use the call and response and summary patterns we have studied.
  - ▶ Respond to the source. What do "you" say? Use the call and response and summary patterns we have studied. You might agree, disagree, raise questions, etc.
  - ▶ Explain how you will use this source in your research essay. Be specific.
  - ▶ Synthesize. Explain the way this work fits with—or challenges—other information you have about the topic.

Use MLA Citation in the Appendix of your text (or actually written in your sources or found in the database citation tools). Citations are important because they help researchers organize and share information about sources in a standardized way. There are many online resources that will help you create citations for your sources, including a thorough guide at the Purdue Online Writing Lab.

How many sources do I need? You need enough sources to address your research question from a variety of perspectives; **six is the minimum.**

Annotated Bibliography Rubric

CRITERIA	A—EXCELLENT	B—VERY GOOD	C—AVERAGE	F—UNACCEPTABLE
Selection of Sources	Sources discussed are numerous and varied. Together, they are more than sufficient to address the writer's question.	Sources discussed are numerous and/or varied. Together, they are sufficient to address the writer's question.	Sources discussed are sufficient to address the writer's question.	Author includes too few sources, or sources that are not varied. These sources are insufficient to address the writer's question.
Overview	Overview articulates a clear and focused topic and question, and describes in-depth how the sources gathered address that question.	Overview articulates a clear and focused topic and question, and describes how the sources gathered address that question.	Overview articulates a topic and question, and describes how the sources gathered address that question.	Overview does not articulate a clear and focused topic and question—or the overview is not included at all.
Source Evaluation	Author persuasively argues that all sources are reliable and relevant to her/his topic.	Author argues that sources are reliable and relevant to her/his topic.	Author discusses whether sources are reliable and relevant.	Author does not discuss whether sources are reliable and/or reputable.
Source Summary	Author presents a summary of each source that is clear, thorough, accurate, and unbiased.	Author presents a summary of most sources that is clear, thorough, accurate, and unbiased.	Summaries are sometimes clear, thorough, accurate, and unbiased.	Summaries are not clear, through, accurate, or unbiased—or are not present at all.
Response to Sources	Author consistently articulates a response to the sources' claims that is nuanced and in-depth.	Author articulates a response to the sources' claims that is nuanced and in-depth.	Author articulates a response to the sources' claims.	Author does not offer a response to the sources' claims.
Source Synthesis	Author identifies complex interrelationships among sources, often probing sources down to the assumption-level, in order to identify points of convergence and divergence.	Author identifies complex interrelationships among sources.	Author identifies interrelationships among sources.	Author does not identify interrelationships among sources.
MLA Style	Author consistently follows MLA format.	Author follows MLA format.	Author mostly follows MLA format.	Author rarely or does not follow MLA format.
Correctness	No errors that confuse or distract. Author uses word choice, punctuation, and sentence structure effectively.	Only a few errors that confuse or distract. Author uses word choice, punctuation, and sentence structure effectively.	Many errors that confuse or distract. Words, punctuation, and sentence structure are ineffective or inappropriate to the writing task.	Many errors that confuse or distract.

Now that you have composed your initial draft of the evaluative annotated bibliography, you will turn again to your peers to learn how they read your work and to discover how they have completed the same assignment.

IN-CLASS ACTIVITY 3F:
PEER REVIEW 1 FOR ANNOTATED BIBLIOGRAPHY DRAFT 1

What are the components of an Annotated Bibliography?

- An Overview: This paragraph or two will:
  ▶ Explain your topic, question, and claim or working thesis (what your thesis would be if you were to write the paper right now. It's called "working" because it might change.). *[Often, you can use a part of your already written proposal to create this section.]
  ▶ Summarize what you have found out so far from your sources and what you still want/need to find out.

- Then, list each of your sources in MLA format and, below EVERY source, write one to two paragraphs in which you:
  ▶ Using terms from the CRAAP Test, explain why this is a relevant and reliable source (You will not include sources that are not relevant or reliable).
  ▶ Summarize the basic claim of the source. What did the author(s) say? Use the call and response and summary patterns we have studied.
  ▶ Respond to the source. What do "you" say? Use the call and response and summary patterns we have studied. You might agree, disagree, raise questions, etc.
  ▶ Explain how you will use this source in your research essay. Be specific.
  ▶ Synthesize. Explain the way this work fits with—or challenges—other information you have about the topic.

Peer Review:

1. Form groups of three. [ONLINE students will complete this activity by posting their own drafts and then responding to TWO peers' drafts. ONLINE students will have to upload the peer's draft and then follow these directions, #4 and #5.]

2. Circulate drafts.

3. Assign numbers.

4. Read draft from Writer #1.
   a. ON THE DRAFT ITSELF: Highlight/underline/circle in blue the parts of the essay that seem strong.
   b. ON THE DRAFT ITSELF: Highlight/underline/circle in red the parts of the essay about which you have questions/concerns or that confuse you.

5. In turn, discuss the essay and your comments with the writer and the rest of your group. [ONLINE students: Add at least five sentences of comments about the draft.]

6. Repeat steps 4 and 5 with next writer, until everyone's draft has been discussed.

** Remember to post journal 10, your reflection on the comments you received regarding your draft.

****Remember to revise your draft and have it ready for peer review 2.

JOURNAL ENTRY 10
REFLECTION ON PEER REVIEW OF DRAFT 1 OF ANNOTATED BIBLIOGRAPHY

Reflect on what you learned from your peer review session.

1. Explain what you learned from the feedback others gave you on your draft.

2. Explain what you learned from reading your peers' drafts.

Write a three-step plan of action for your revision of your first draft. What three specific changes—additions, deletions, changes in sequence, etc.—will you make to improve the draft before the next peer review? Why will you make these alterations? What specific effect do you hope they will have?

G. Making Our Claim: Our Contribution to the Dialogue

As you have contemplated both the sources that agree and those that do not, you have learned how the majority answers some or part of your research question. Now you must decide what *you* think: you must create your own original claim.

Your *claim* may do any one of the following, or even a combination of the following, in order to *maintain originality and make an actual contribution to the existing dialogue*:

- Agree with most scholars, but with a qualifier to their position (s)
  - ▶ EXAMPLE: Most scholars contend _____, but they must also consider _____. I argue that _____.
- Disagree with most scholars
  - ▶ EXAMPLE: While most researchers maintain _____, I disagree with them because _____.
- Expand on the claims of others
  - ▶ EXAMPLE: While the experts who conclude _____ have valid arguments, I would add _____.

- Invent an entirely new claim that comes as a result of the research but goes in an entirely new direction not previously contemplated

  ▶ EXAMPLE: Scholars have long argued _____ or _____, but none has ever considered _____. I postulate _____.

No matter which direction you choose to bring your claim, you will ultimately have to prove it with reasons, evidence, and explanation, so you must make certain that your claim does relate to what you can argue convincingly. Sometimes the claim you create for your annotated bibliography remains unchanged as you complete your research essay or project, but at other times, it may shift as you finish writing. Like every other part of the research endeavor, claim-creation involves process too. You should not grow concerned if, as you compose your project, you see a need to alter your claim. Changing your claim to fit with what you actually write makes a lot more sense than attempting to force your research to fit a claim with which it does not truly coincide.

H. Model Annotated Bibliograpy

A MODEL "ANNOTATED BIBLIOGRAPHY" ESSAY

Food Insecurity: Its Causes and Solutions

Today, the issue of food insecurity baffles a great many people. Even the label—"food insecurity"—seems so fancy that it hides the reality of its meaning: that even in this prosperous nation, a great many people do not have enough to eat on a daily basis and go to bed hungry every night. Some believe those who do not have enough food have only themselves to blame because they did not plan their lives well or they spend money on drugs or other objects that do not matter, while others think the amount of food Americans waste in a year could feed all of these people, and the government should step in to control that waste and allocate food resources in a more efficient way than it does. As a future teacher, this topic has become important to me, especially because I know that if students come to school hungry, they cannot learn as well as those who are well-fed. I really wanted to understand just two elements of this problem: why so many people in the United States do not have enough to eat and what we as a country can do to solve this problem. At present, I contend that so many Americans face hunger because they have to live on too little money that forces them to make impossible choices and because the government and society have not thought about their right to eat as a human right simply because they fear doing so would mean they would have to spend money they do not want to spend. Additionally, I assert that we can solve this problem by allocating resources more efficiently than we do now.

I have reached this tentative claim based upon the research I have completed so far. As I have researched this topic, I have discovered that scholars have actually drawn different conclusions. While some of them, particularly activist Joel Berg and systems ecologist Molly D. Anderson contend that "The right to food is widely accepted by nations, with the notable exception of the United States (US) and four other countries. The US government deals with

---

CHAPTER 3

domestic food insecurity through an array of needs-based food assistance programs instead of rights-based approaches" (Anderson 113), a few others such as sociologists Craig Gunderson and James P. Ziliak propose the premise that "drug use [. . . and] household head's marital status" play key roles in food insecurity and must be addressed (6). The bulk of the research on this topic seems to lean in favor of extending government assistance, and I agree with those ideas because the right to eat is tantamount to the right to breathe. I also recognize that I may need to find additional research about how to manage the cost of additional assistance programs, but I will probably not include anything on food waste because that issue could create an essay all by itself. I also need to find at least one truly opposing viewpoint, as I have not really found any clear dissent yet.

So far, my sources include the following. They number more than the minimum required, but I might decide not to use all of them, and some offer only a little bit that I can use.

Anderson, Molly D. "Beyond Food Security to Realizing Food Rights in the US." *Journal of Rural Studies*, vol. 29, January 2013, pp. 113–22. https://doi.org/10.1016/j.jrurstud.2012.09.004.

I found this source in the *Science Direct* database using the search terms, "food insecurity in USA, causes of." Basically, this entire article supports the idea that the United States could and would be doing more for hungry people if it embraced the idea that having enough food to eat is a human right and strongly suggests that "this right cannot be achieved in full without coordinated efforts" (119) that include not just government NGO's, but also other help. To substantiate her claim, this author uses a lot of data from the United States, but also compares it to many examples of what other countries around the world are doing and offers a concrete plan for how the United States could replicate such efforts, and in doing so, she not only convinces the reader, but also kind of shames the United States. The source absolutely possesses reliability and credibility, for its author holds a PhD in Systems Ecology, is a professor at Middlebury College, has led many food program initiatives, and has published widely. The essay draws from thirty-three sources, all of them from between 2014 and 2018, and all of them from scholarly publications. The vocabulary does not put the reader off, for it is scholarly, but not difficult. Because I contend that the US government could do more to help the hungry, this source will concur with my claim, though it will contradict some of my other sources that claim SNAP suffices. In general, it will go along with most of my other research.

Atlantic Marketing Team For Food For America. "America Has A Hunger Problem." *The Atlantic Online (Original Thinking Series)*, June, 2019, https://www.theatlantic.com/sponsored/hunger-2019/america-has-a-hunger-problem/3067/?sr_source=pocket&sr_lift=true&utm_source=pocket&utm_medium=CPC&utm_campaign=simplereach&utm_source=PK_SR_P_3067. Accessed 10 June 2019.

I found this source without searching because it was one of our assigned readings for the course. Basically, this entire PowerPoint presentation supports the idea that there is a huge hunger problem in America and strongly suggests that "hunger threatens our minds, our bodies, and our communities" and we had better address the issue. This group uses a lot of scientific evidence and data as well as examples of people's real lives to substantiate the claim, and this evidence does affect the reader emotionally. The source somewhat possesses reliability and credibility for the Food For America group's sole purpose is research on hunger, but the presentation quotes information without using a reference list of any scholarly publications, and it is done kind of like an ad. The vocabulary is easy to understand and kind of loaded toward an emotional guilt response. Because I claim that the government and society need to do more to help the hungry, this source offers supporting evidence, though it does contradict some of the statistics I have. In general, it will help me to make my argument.

Berg, Joel. *All You Can Eat: How Hungry Is America?* Seven Stories Press, 2008.

I found this source in my public library after searching for its actual title because I had first found the book announced in a Google search of "books about hunger in America." This entire book basically supports the claim that hunger is a big problem all across America and strongly suggests that "only government has the size, scope, resources—and yes, the legitimacy—to take the lead in actually solving the problem. And make no mistake: Government can solve the problem" (1). This author uses a lot of history, data, comparisons to bread line days, and experience to prove his claim, and he does make us agree with him. He is a reliable and credible source because he worked as the Secretary of Agriculture under President Clinton and is currently the director of the New York City Coalition Against Hunger. He also used over six pages of sources from the 1900s through 2007. In that way, the book is a little outdated. (However, surprisingly, there are not many other whole and researched-based books about the problem after 2008). It is easy to read, though it is a little sarcastic at times. It agrees with my contention that the government can and should help solve the hunger problem, and because it offers some concrete steps to do so, I will be able to build from it. In general, it supports most of my other research.

Bridges, Jeff. *A Place at the Table*. Ed. Peter Pringle. Public Affairs, 2013.

I also found this book in my public library after searching for its actual title because I had first found the book announced in a Google search of "books about hunger in America." This book is actually written by twelve people with one editor, Peter Pringle, and one leader of the project, actor Jeff Bridges, and it is the book that goes along with the documentary film of the same name. Even though all twelve writers add different stories, they all support one overarching premise: that we actually have the means to end hunger for the millions suffering from it. These authors, a mix of actors, producers, and directors of various food and nutrition organizations, all of them people who have worked at food pantries, etc., use some data, but mostly they use experiences to support their claim. These experiences provide examples of successful programs and of the great need for food in the US. This source and these authors are not as credentialed as other texts, but the hands-on experience does offer some reliability. It is very easy to read with no difficult vocabulary. It agrees with my claim because it supports the idea that the hunger problem can be solved, though it, like the Anderson essay, shows that more than government help is needed.

Duke Sanford World Food Policy Center. "Food Insecurity," 20 September 2018, *World Food Policy Center at Duke,* https://wfpc.sanford.duke.edu/media/food-insecurity. Accessed 2 February 2019.

I found this source with a Google search of "Food insecurity in America, experts and documentaries about." This group's whole purpose is to study food insecurity in the US and the world. It offers videos, data charts, podcasts, reports, links, and brief summaries. Its primary claim is that there is a "web of poverty, racism, and sexism surrounding food insecurity." The group is affiliated with Duke University and a lot of scholars in the field, and every piece offers references, so it is a trustworthy, reliable source. It is updated regularly, so it is timely too, and it is written for average people to grasp the problem. Because I contend partly that food insecurity can affect anyone, this source will add to my explanation of causes but contradict my belief about anyone being affected because it targets the links between going hungry and being poor, black, and female. It will add to my other sources about the causes of food insecurity.

Gundersen, Craig and James P. Ziliak. "Childhood Food Insecurity in the U.S.: Trends, Causes, and Policy Options." *Future of Children,* Oct. 2014, pp. 1–19. *EBSCOhost,* search. ebscohost.com/login.aspx?direct=true&db=sih&AN=98472473&site=ehost-live.

I found this source in the *SocIndex* database by using the search terms "food insecurity in the USA, causes of." The overarching claim of this piece is that there are many reasons food insecurity continues to rise, and "One is that we don't fully understand what causes food insecurity or how food assistance and other programs can help alleviate it" (1). This article discusses the whys and hows, with particular focus on children and the effects of this food insecurity on their health, their school performance, and their general psychology. It then attempts to make some policy recommendations. To verify their claims, these authors use a lot of data, graphs, and studies. Both professors in sociology and micro-economics and experts with hands-on experience in their fields, these authors possess extreme credibility. They use fifty sources, all ranging from 1990–2014, so they are thorough and mostly current. Sometimes they use incomprehensible jargon, but mostly they write so general audiences can understand them. Their claims fit with mine because they discuss ways government programs might change for improved effectiveness. Their work also complements that of other sources I have because they add to information on causes and ways to address the issue.

Laterman, Kaya. "Hunger on Campus: Pay Tuition Or Eat [Metropolitan Desk]." *New York Times,* May 05, 2019. *ProQuest,* http://libproxy.sunywcc.edu/login?url=https://search. proquest.com/docview/2219855076?accountid=14174.

I found this source in the *New York Times* database because I wanted a newspaper source. I used the search terms, "hunger in America." Its basic claim is that college students at public universities and community colleges need increased financial aid because "over 50% of them are going hungry every day" (Laterman MB1). It uses references to studies, quotes from students, and information from experts in the field, but no reference list. Nonetheless, because it is from the *New York Times*, I assume it is a vetted source, and it certainly is very current and easy to read. I can use this source to add to my information about the kinds of people who go hungry—not always those we expect. It enhances other information I have about how many the hunger problem affects.

> Nord, Mark, USDA. "Household Food Security And SNAP in the Wake of the 2007–2009 Recession." United States Department of Agriculture, Economic Research Service Report, 14 February 2014, https://www.ers.usda.gov/webdocs/publications/ 45655/. Accessed 10 March 2019.

I found this source with a Google search of "Food insecurity in America, experts and documentaries about." This report from an expert at the United States Department of Agriculture Economic Research division actually makes no claim, except maybe that food insecurity is on the rise since the recession of 2007–09, though that statement is a fact, not a claim. The entire report consists of graphs and charts based on its research/data collection, all of it relative to SNAP recipients. That it does not cover the food insecure not receiving SNAP is a limitation of the information, and that it goes up to 2012 only is another limitation. Still, its breakdown by region of the country, age, and household income is helpful. This source will help to support my claim about the need for government help, and it supports the other types of data I have found.

> Price, Tom. "Hunger in America." *CQ Researcher*, vol. 27, no. 24, 7 July 2017, pp. 557–80, www.cqresearcher.com.

I found this source in the *Congressional Quarterly* database by using "hunger" as my search term. This source too offers no actual claim, but is a comprehensive study of hunger in America. It covers thirty-three pages of history, needs, causes, effects, and programs that address the problem, and ways to look ahead regarding the problem. Created by researchers for Congress and using fourteen sources and seventy-three references, many of them as recent as 2017, this source is reliable and geared primarily to provide information about the whole of the problem because that is its intended purpose: to inform so as to help Congressional leaders and federal judges make decisions. It includes lots of data, graphics, studies, etc., all laid out in an easy-to-read format. This source will help me to defend every part of my claim because it is so thorough. Because it is mostly facts, it will not really address any of the other research claims, but it will add information to what I already have.

Swindle, Taren M., Linda Whiteside-Mansell, and Lorraine McKelvey. "Food Insecurity: Validation of a Two-Item Screen Using Convergent Risks." *Journal of Child & Family Studies*, vol. 22, no. 7, Oct. 2013, pp. 932–41. *EBSCOhost*, https://doi.org/10.1007/s10826-012-9652-7.

I found this source in the *SocIndex* database by using the search terms "food insecurity in the USA." This article claims that "With an efficient screen, these front-line service providers can be a valuable resource to identify and combat FI and its deleterious effects on children" (932). It names those front-line providers and identifies the two screens it suggests. In essence, it is a study of the use of those two screens, and ultimately concludes those two screens are effective and can make a difference in preventing and stopping food insecurity. It also discusses why doing so matters by examining the consequences of food insecurity on children. The authors of the study and the article are three MDs and PhDs, who direct the Medical Prevention Center at University of Alabama, so they are reliable, credible experts. They also use about forty-seven sources, all of them from 2010–13, though 2013 is now six years removed from us, so currency could be better. This source does not address my claim directly; rather, it offers an alternative methodology for finding the hungry, an idea that might then fit into the possible solutions I discuss. In this way, it differs from all of my other sources too because they speak of what is done and why.

US Department of Health and Human Services. "Food Insecurity The Healthy People 2020," *HealthyPeople.gov*, 2019, https://www.healthypeople.gov/2020/topics-objectives/topic/social-determinants-health/interventions-resources/food-insecurity. Accessed 3 March 2019.

I found this source with a Google search of "Food insecurity in America, experts and documentaries about." Although this source comes from a government department, it is geared primarily toward economic and health issues surrounding the food insecurity problem. It is basically a list of information from thirty-four end-noted sources. It makes no claim, and though it does cover causes, it is mostly about the effects of food insecurity. Its sources are from 2001–17, and some of them are other government department references or references to other sources I have already found. I may not use this source at all because it pretty much echoes material I have found in other sources.

CHAPTER 3

I. Readings and Resources

© Mascha Tace/Shutterstock.com

"Google vs. Databases" by Penfield Library, February 3, 2014:

https://www.youtube.com/watch?v=IMYZiUv47x8

"What Are Databases and Why You Need Them" by Yavapai College Library, September 29, 2011:

https://www.youtube.com/watch?v=Q2GMtluaNzU

"Summarizing: Five Keys To Writing Effective Summaries" by SIU Writing Center:

https://write.siu.edu/_common/documents/handouts/summarizing.pdf

"How to Write a Summary" by Smrt English, November 15, 2012:

https://www.youtube.com/watch?v=eGWO1ldEhtQ

"How to Write an Effective Academic Summary Paragraph" by Maritez Apigo, December 5, 2015:

https://www.youtube.com/watch?v=WZFI6dvgOzU

"Addressing Opposing Viewpoints" by Brigham Young University Idaho, 2019:

http://www.byui.edu/academic-support-centers/writing/video-lessons-and-handouts/
addressing-opposing-viewpoints

"APA-MLA Annotated Bibliography: Complete Guide To Writing Annotated Bibliography" by David Taylor, July 16, 2016:

Part 1: https://www.youtube.com/watch?v=iW4eXLAtOhk

Part 2: https://www.youtube.com/watch?v=w3A_wEMvnFA

"Making a Claim" by Caroline Johmann on October 4, 2014:

https://www.youtube.com/watch?v=5-tOeh8n8yQ

J. Grammar Concept: Pronouns

You will learn grammar best by applying it within the context of your own writing. Use these rules as a guide. Your teacher will probably help you to target examples from your own writing and your peers' writing to help clarify how these rules work.

◇◇◇◇◇◇◇◇◇◇◇◇◇◇◇◇◇◇◇◇◇◇◇◇◇◇◇◇◇◇◇◇◇◇◇◇◇◇◇

Pronouns—Big Picture Plan of Attack

Step 1. Highlight the verb.

Step 2. Highlight the pronoun. (See **Personal Pronouns Box below.**)

A pronoun takes the place of the noun. Instead of *computer* or *computers*, we say *it* or *they/them*. We'll look at four kinds of personal pronouns: subjective (used for a sentence subject), objective (used for an object), possessive (used for possession), and reflexive (used for emphasis).

PERSONAL PRONOUNS			
SUBJECTIVE	**OBJECTIVE**	**POSSESSIVE**	**REFLEXIVE**
I	me	my, mine	myself
you	you	your, yours	yourself(ves)
he	him	his	himself
she	her	her, hers	herself
it	it	its	itself
we	us	our, ours	ourselves
they	them	their, theirs	themselves
who*, whoever	whom, whomever	whose	(no word)

*Though *who* and its forms are relative pronouns, they're treated here like personal pronouns. In sentences, <u>subjective</u> pronouns usually come *before* the verb; objective pronouns come *after*.

<u>SUBJECTIVE</u> **PRONOUN**	**VERB**	**OBJECTIVE PRONOUN**
I	TOLD	him.
You	VISITED	whom?
He	INVITED	us.
She	MAILED	it.
It	DELIGHTED	me.
We	TEASED	them.
They	SAW	you.
Who	CALLED	her?

Errors take place when a writer puts an objective pronoun *before* the verb instead of *after*. Or puts a subjective pronoun *after* the verb instead of *before*.

GRAMMAR TIP

Use the *Find* command to find the pronouns in your project (all are listed **above** in the **Personal Pronouns** box).

Does the pronoun come *before* or *after* the verb?

Tommy and him WENT to the movies.

(WRONG: him = objective pronoun)

(Tommy and <u>he</u> WENT to the movies.)

WARNING!

Nervous about their grammar, many speakers and writers automatically reject *me* and choose *I*, ending up with errors like *between you* and *I*. *I* has its place in a sentence, but so does *me*, as in the grammatically correct *between you and me*.

Troubleshooting Pronoun Trouble Spots

Pronoun problems show up in eleven classic trouble spots.

1. **Subjective or Objective Pronoun as Subject?** *Bob and (I/me) saw the Grand Canyon.*
2. **Subjective or Objective Pronoun in a Comparison?** *He's taller than (I/me).*
3. **Subjective or Objective Pronoun after a Verb?** *Dan told (we/us) workers the truth.*
4. **Subjective or Objective Pronoun after a *To Be* Verb?** *Yes, this is (he/him).*
5. **Subjective or Objective Pronoun after a Preposition?** *She gave money to Jim and (I/me).*
6. **Subjective *Who* or Objective *Whom*?** *The boy (who/whom) is tall is here.*
7. **Noun + *That, Which,* or *Who/Whom*?** *The corporation (that/which/who/whom) we contacted needs workers.*
8. **Singular or Plural Possessive Pronoun Agreement?** *A writer needs to write (his/her/their) own essays.*
9. **Singular or Plural Indefinite Pronoun?** *Everyone completed (his or her/their) assignment.*
10. **Reflexive, Subjective, or Objective Pronoun?** *Tom and (I/myself) will pay the bill.*
11. **Possessive or Objective Pronoun before a Gerund?** *(His/him) singing is terrible.*

1. **Subjective or Objective Pronoun as Subject? Bob and (I/me) saw the Grand Canyon.**

Definitions: A *subjective* pronoun is used as the <u>subject</u> of a verb: <u>*I*</u> *saw him.* An *objective* pronoun is used as the <u>object</u> of the verb: He saw <u>me</u>.

> ## GRAMMAR TIP
>
> (1) Highlight the VERB. Does the pronoun come *before* or *after* the verb? Usually, before = subjective; after = objective. (2) With a compound subject like Bob and (*I/me*), delete everything but the pronoun. Say the sentence: (*I/me*) *saw the Grand Canyon*. Which pronoun sounds more natural?

Bob and (I/me) SAW the Grand Canyon. (I)
  (<u>I</u> saw the Grand Canyon.)
Clarise and (she/her) ARE MAILING the report. (she)
  (<u>She</u> is mailing the report.)
I believe that Samantha and (he/him) WILL PLAY cards tomorrow. (he)
  (I believe that <u>he</u> will play cards tomorrow.)
Hannah suggested that Dell and (he/him) SHOULD COME for supper. (he)
  (Hannah suggested that <u>he</u> should come for supper.)
(I/me) and (she/her) HOPE to take the train to New Orleans.
  (always put the *I* last: <u>She</u> and <u>I</u> hope to take the train to New Orleans.)
Nevertheless, despite being broke, Alicia and (they/them) TOOK the trip. (they)
  (Nevertheless, despite being broke, <u>they</u> took the trip.)
MAY LaKiesha and (I/me) LEAVE early? (I)
  (May <u>I</u> leave early?)

2. **Subjective or Objective Pronoun in a Comparison? He's taller than (I/me).**

> ## GRAMMAR TIP
>
> In a comparison, try putting a verb like *am* or *do* after the comparison. If the sentence sounds natural, use the <u>subjective</u> pronoun. If the sentence reads ambiguously, you may need an <u>objective</u> pronoun.

He's taller than (I/me). (I)
  (He is taller than <u>I</u> [am].)

Cynthia plays violin better than (he/him). (he)

(Cynthia plays violin better than <u>he</u> [does].)

The historian admires Richard Nixon more than (we/us). (we)

(The historian admires Richard Nixon more than <u>we</u> [do].)

But: The historian admires Richard Nixon more than [the historian admires] <u>us</u>.

(The sentence reads ambiguously: *more than <u>we</u> admire Richard Nixon* or *more than the historian admires <u>us</u>?*)

3. Subjective or Objective Pronoun after a Verb? Dan told (we/us) workers the truth.

GRAMMAR TIP

Other than in a question, normal sentence order is <u>Subject</u>-Verb-<u>Object</u> (*I like baseball*). Question order is Verb-<u>Subject</u>-<u>Object</u> (*Do <u>you</u> like baseball*?) In normal sentence order, use an objective pronoun after a verb unless it's a *to be* verb (see 4, **next**).

Highlight the verb. (1) Does the pronoun come before or after? (2) Leave out words before or after the pronoun to hear what sounds natural.

Dan **TOLD** (we/us) workers the truth. (us)

(Dan told <u>us</u> the truth.)

They **MAILED** Amber and (I/me) a present. (me)

(They mailed <u>me</u> a present.)

Bette **WILL LEAD** Brian and (I/me) to the office. (me)

(Bette will lead <u>me</u> to the office.)

4. Subjective or Objective Pronoun after a To Be Verb? Yes, this is (he/him).

GRAMMAR TIP

Though an objective pronoun usually comes *after* the verb, *to be* verbs cause the exception. After a *to be* verb, use the <u>subjective</u> pronoun. If it sounds too odd or formal, in everyday conversation use the <u>objective</u>, like *me*, instead of *I*. But remember: Academic writing prefers a <u>subjective</u> pronoun. (And you always have the option of revising the sentence to get rid of the formal pronoun.)

Hello? Yes, this *is* (he/him). (he)

(<u>He</u> *is* here not <u>Him</u> *is* here.

Are we all of the volunteers? Yes, all the volunteers *are* (we/us). (we)

(<u>We</u> are all of the volunteers.)

The mysterious caller *had been* (she/her). (she)

(<u>She</u> *had been* the mysterious caller.)

5. Subjective or Objective Pronoun after a Preposition? She gave money to Jim and (I/me).

> ### GRAMMAR TIP
>
> (1) Using the *Find* command, find the preposition. (See page 154, under **Prepositions**, the **Prepositions** box.) (2) Use the <u>objective</u> pronoun after a <u>preposition</u>. (3) Leave out words between the preposition and the pronoun to hear what sounds natural.

She gave money <u>to</u> Jim and (I/me). (me)

(She gave money to <u>me</u>.)

Deciding what protocol to follow was <u>for</u> (we/us) women to decide. (us)

(Deciding what protocol to follow was for <u>us</u> women to decide.)

Just <u>between</u> you and (I/me), her theory is pure nonsense. (me)

([To] <u>me</u>, her theory is pure nonsense.)

<u>Except for</u> Sandra, Keith, and (he/him), we have no reliable workers. (him)

(Except for <u>him</u>, we have no reliable workers.)

6. Subjective Who or Objective Whom? The boy (who/whom) is tall is here.

> ### GRAMMAR TIP
>
> Use a simple trick to choose *who* and *whom* correctly: Since *who* needs a verb and *whom* doesn't, match up every VERB with a <u>subject</u>. If there's a word left over, the word left has to be *whom* (since it doesn't need a verb). That word is an <u>object</u>.

An infinitive (*to* + *verb*) can't have a subject; thus don't try to match it with a subject.

1. The boy (who/whom) IS tall IS here. (who)
2. The boy (who/whom) he SAW IS here. (whom)
3. Willie TOLD Brenda (who/whom) to hire. (whom)
4. DO you REMEMBER (who/whom) WON the U.S. Open in 1997? (who)
5. You HAVE a pizza delivery for (who/whom)? (whom)
6. You HAVE a pizza delivery for (whoever/whomever) LIVES upstairs? (whoever)
7. You HAVE a pizza delivery for (whoever/whomever) they WANT to give it to? (whomever)
8. (Who/whom) DOES she RECOMMEND? (whom)
9. (Who/whom) DO you THINK WILL BE GOING tomorrow? (who)

   1. <u>Boy</u> matches with first IS. Second IS needs a subject = <u>who</u>.
   2. <u>He</u> matches with SAW. <u>Boy</u> matches with IS. Word left over = <u>whom</u>.
   3. <u>Willie</u> matches with TOLD. *To hire* is an infinitive and can't have subject. Leftover word = <u>whom</u>.
   4. <u>You</u> matches with DO REMEMBER. WON needs a subject = <u>who</u>.
   5. <u>You</u> matches with HAVE. Word left over (with preposition) = <u>whom</u>.
   6. <u>You</u> matches with HAVE. LIVES needs a subject = <u>whoever</u>. (Though the preposition for needs *whomever*, the verb LIVES has more power and matches with whoever.)
   7. <u>You</u> matches with HAVE. <u>They</u> matches with WANT. *To give* = infinitive = no subject. Leftover word = <u>whomever</u>.
   8. <u>She</u> matches with DOES RECOMMEND. Leftover word = <u>whom</u>.
   9. <u>You</u> matches with DO THINK. WILL BE GOING needs a subject = <u>who</u>.

7. Noun + That, Which, or Who/Whom? The corporation (that/which/who/whom) we contacted needs workers.

GRAMMAR TIP

(1) *That* refers to animals, things, and types or classes of people.
(2) *Which* refers to animals, things, and groups of people.
(3) *Who/whom* refer to individual people, groups of people, and animals with names.

That, which, and *who* all refer to groups. But remember this distinction:

- When a group is an <u>*it*</u>, referring to the collective unit, use *that* for essential fragments and *which* for nonessential (the <u>company</u> *that* we've audited; <u>Sims & Pierce</u>, *which* we've audited)
- When a group is a <u>*they*</u>, referring to the people who make it up, use *who/whom* (the <u>managers</u> of Sims & Pierce, *whom* we've interviewed)

The <u>corporation</u> (that/which/who/whom) we contracted needs workers.

    (corporation = it = *that*)

The <u>executives</u> at Smythe, Chadwick, and Co., (that/which/who/whom) received large bonuses, have been criticized for their salaries.

    (executives = they = *who*)

Lilia is the <u>kind of painter</u> (that/which/who/whom) will win fame and money.

    (kind of painter = a type of something = *that*)

Have you seen the <u>cat</u> (that/which/who/whom) got stuck in the tree?

    (cat = unnamed animal = *that*)

Have you seen <u>Tiger</u>, (that/which/who/whom) got stuck in the tree?

    (Tiger = named animal = *who*)

GRAMMAR TIP

When *that* follows another *that* somewhere in the sentence, change the second *that* to *which*: *That* is a movie (that/which) I wish I'd seen. (which)

---

8. Singular or Plural Possessive Pronoun Agreement? A writer needs to write (his/her/their) own essays.

Definition: A *possessive* pronoun shows possession: *my* car, *his* apartment, *their* house. A <u>singular</u> noun matches with a <u>singular</u> possessive pronoun (*writer = his* or *her*); a <u>plural</u> noun matches with a <u>plural</u> possessive pronoun (*writers = their*).

    A <u>writer</u> needs to write (his/her/their) own essays. (his or her)

    Is that the <u>firefighter</u> who had (his/her/their) picture in the paper? (his or her)

    We found the <u>dog</u> that ran away from (its/his/her/their) home. (its, his, or her)

    How well did that <u>nun</u> do on (her/their) driving test? (her)

    We knew a <u>priest</u> from Rome who had (his/their) novel published. (his)

Because a collective noun like *jury, team*, and *committee* is usually singular, use a singular pronoun.

    The <u>jury</u> has come to (its/their) decision. (its)

    The <u>team</u> is playing (its/their) best. (its)

    The <u>committee</u> will submit (its/their) final report. (its)

But if members of the collective are acting independently and not as a unit, use a plural pronoun.

    The <u>jury</u> have argued (its/their) individual positions for the last three hours. (their)

GRAMMAR TIP

To avoid sexism and the awkwardness of *his/her*, try several strategies:

1. **Change the gender-biased noun or pronoun to *you*:**
   Each *man* will be responsible for *his* leave reports.
   = You are responsible for your leave reports.

2. **Change gender-biased words to neutral words:**
   Each *man* will be responsible for *his* leave reports.
   = Each will be responsible for leave reports.

3. **Use plural nouns and pronouns:**
   Each *man* will be responsible for *his* leave reports.
   = All workers are responsible for their leave reports.

4. **Use job titles:**
   Each *man* will be responsible for *his* leave reports.
   = All firefighters are responsible for their leave reports.

5. **Use *the*, *a*, and *an* instead of pronouns:**
   Each *man* will be responsible for *his* leave reports.
   = Each worker will be responsible for the leave reports.

6. **Alternate pronouns: One time use *he* or *him*; the next, *she* or *her*.**

7. **Choose a singular pronoun and use it consistently through a text. Some writers add a prefatory note that says the consistent use of *he* or *she* does not intend sexism.**

WARNING!

In conversation, many people make this grammar error: *A writer needs to write their own essays.* **Academic writing, however, still expects a singular noun to match with a singular pronoun, a plural noun to match with a plural pronoun:** *A writer needs to write his (or her) own essays.*

9. **Singular or Plural Indefinite Pronoun? Everyone completed (his or her/their) assignment.**

Definition: Unlike the personal pronoun, the *indefinite* pronoun doesn't refer to specific people or things. Instead of listing the states by specific name (Alabama, Alaska, etc.), we say *each* state, *some* states, or *all* states.

GRAMMAR TIP

Use the box **below** to identify indefinite pronouns.

INDEFINITE PRONOUNS		
ALWAYS SINGULAR	SOMETIMES SINGULAR, SOMETIMES PLURAL	ALWAYS PLURAL
another	all	both
anybody	any	few
anyone	more	many
anything	most	several
each	none	
either (see **Note***)	some	
everybody		
everyone		
everything		
much neither*		
no one		
nobody		
nothing		
one		
somebody		
someone		
something		

*Although *either* and *neither* usually require singular possessive pronouns, they may require a plural pronoun with a compound subject (like *the singers or the actor*). If *either/neither* is the subject, it controls the verb. Otherwise, the <u>subject</u> next to the verb controls the possessive pronoun.

Either the singers or the <u>actor</u> left (her/their) shoes. (her)

Either the actor or the <u>singers</u> left (her/their) shoes. (their)

But here *neither* becomes the <u>subject</u>:

<u>Neither</u> of the cashiers was in (her/their) checkout lane. (her)

(*of the cashiers* = a prepositional phrase, not the subject)

Always <u>singular</u>:

<u>Everyone</u> completed (his or her/their) assignment. (his or her)

<u>Every one</u> of the clan practiced (his/her/their) hunting skills. (his or her)

<u>One horse</u> left (its/their) oats untouched. (its)

No one else on the men's team has mounted (his/their) bike. (his)

Each member of the women's team ran (her/their) personal best. (her)

Each violinist tuned (his/her/their) instrument. (his or her)

Anybody can plan (his/her/their) own vacation. (his or her)

Sometimes <u>singular</u>, sometimes plural:

All of the employees acted as if (his or her/their) jobs were in danger. (their)

All of the <u>juice</u> has lost (its/their) flavor. (its)

Do you know if <u>any rose</u> has sent out (its/their) first bud? (its)

Do you know if any roses have sent out (its/their) first buds? (their)

Always plural:

Few of the geese have (his or her/their) nests built. (their)

Several of the girls, including Maggie, have finished (her/their) chores. (their)

10. Reflexive, Subjective, or Objective Pronoun? Tom and (I/myself) will pay the bill.

Definition: Within a sentence, a *reflexive* pronoun reflects an earlier noun or pronoun like a mirror reflects an image:

The *woman* saw *herself* on TV. (woman = herself)

He cut *himself* shaving. (he = himself)

The reflexive *emphasizes* the noun or pronoun. Like subjective, objective, and possessive pronouns, the reflexive is a personal pronoun. It also shares *-self* endings with the *intensive* pronoun, which, like the reflexive, is used to emphasize (see **below, Intensive Pronoun**).

> # GRAMMAR TIP
>
> Find pronouns ending in *-self* or *-selves*: *myself, yourself, your-selves, himself, herself, itself, ourselves*. Look for misspellings: *hisself, theirself,* and *theirselves*.

Two rules govern the use of the reflexive pronoun:

- SUBJECT: Don't use it unless the sentence has a subjective **noun** or **pronoun** that the reflexive reflects. (The **woman** saw *herself* on TV; **he** cut *himself shaving*.)
- OBJECT: Don't substitute it for the <u>objective pronoun</u>. (*Give it to Bob or <u>me</u>*, not *Give it to Bob or myself*.)

We can use *herself* because we've already used *woman*; we can use *himself* because we've already used *he*. Both *woman* and *he* are *antecedents*—the nouns or pronouns used *before* the reflexive can be used (*ante* = before).

Failing to remember this basic rule leads to grammar errors:

SUBJECT ERROR: Tom and myself will pay the bill. (I)

(The antecedent *I* hasn't been set up, so *myself* can't be used.)

SUBJECT-VERB ERROR: Hey, how're you? Fine, how's *yourself*? (are you)

(No antecedent, so the subjective pronoun must follow a plural *to be* verb.)

OBJECT ERROR: The plan was discussed by Ralph and *himself*. (him)

OBJECT ERROR: The estate was split between the Pattersons and *ourselves*. (us)

OBJECT ERROR: Give it to Bob or *myself*. (me)

WARNING!

In an imperative sentence—a sentence that commands somebody to do something—the subject <u>you</u> serves as the antecedent. Since <u>you</u> in an imperative is *understood* (that is, not present in the sentence), the reflexive pronoun is correct (see below).

- Please present *yourselves* to the Queen.
  (The plural subject/antecedent *you* is understood: *[You] please present yourselves to the Queen.*)

- Go over the budget yourself.
  (The singular subject/antecedent *you* is understood: *[You] go over the budget yourself.*)

Intensive pronoun:

Definition: The *intensive* pronoun, a personal pronoun, uses *-self* to *intensify* a noun or pronoun—that is, to *emphasize* it.

- I *myself* will take care of planning the party.
- Mrs. Steinberg wanted to speak with the supervisors *themselves*.
- The President *himself* will speak to the press.

GRAMMAR TIP

Never use commas with an *intensive* pronoun. Because it's an *essential* appositive emphasizing a noun or pronoun, commas aren't necessary.

WRONG: I, *myself*, will take care of planning the party.

(I myself will)

WRONG: Mrs. Steinberg wanted to speak with the supervisors, *themselves*. (supervisors themselves)

WRONG: The President, *himself*, will speak to the press.

(The President himself)

11. Possessive or Objective Pronoun before a Gerund? (His/him) singing is terrible.

Definitions: A *possessive pronoun* shows who owns something: *my house* or *the house is mine, your/yours, his, her/hers, its, our/ours, their/theirs*. A *gerund* is a word that comes from a verb, ends in -*ing*, and functions as a noun—either as a subject (*Dancing is fun*) or as an object (*I like dancing*). A **present participle** also comes from a verb and ends in -*ing*, but unlike the gerund, it functions as a verb (*I am singing*).

GRAMMAR TIP

Use a possessive pronoun before a gerund but not before a present participle. Likewise, show possession by using a noun + apostrophe in front of a gerund.

(His/him) singing is terrible. (His)

   (gerund = subject)

I hate (his/him) singing. (his)

   (gerund = object)

BUT ALSO RIGHT: I hate him <u>singing</u>.

   (singing = a present participle: I hate him [when he is] singing.)

(You/your) working so many hours will see a bigger paycheck. (<u>your</u>)

   (gerund = subject)

BUT ALSO RIGHT: You, <u>working</u> so many hours, will see a bigger paycheck.

   (working = a present participle: You [who are] working so many hours . . .)

(Jill/Jill's) studying will make a difference on the test. (Jill's)

   (gerund = subject)

Lessons to Use in the Co-Requisite Classroom During This Unit

A co-requisite Writing and Research course has but one absolute rule: no additional assignments outside of class may be assigned; the work of the Writing and Research course *is* the work of the co-requisite course.

Nonetheless, during co-requisite class times, students should engage in activities that address their noncognitive, cognitive, and skills-related areas. The activities I include here encompass all three categories of learning and coordinate with the work of the Writing and Research course. Of course, students' needs regarding whatever occurs in the Writing and Research course on a particular day may at times take precedence in the co-requisite course, and at times, the class time may function as a writing workshop, but every class session cannot function in these ways, or the students will not acquire what they need from the course. Individual teachers will of course decide what to use, when to use it, and even what adaptations to apply. Some of the activities, each one designed for a single class session, may actually take longer than a single class because co-requisite courses do not operate on the same schedule on every college campus and different students have different kinds of questions about assignments.

WRITING SUMMARIES PRACTICE

A GOOD SUMMARY:

- has a BIG or MAIN idea,
- has two to three general explanations <u>without a lot of detail,</u>
- does NOT have opinions or judgments,
- does NOT offer a blow-by-blow list,
- is shorter than the source,
- repeats the ideas of the source in different phrases and sentences, and
- demonstrates **conciseness**, **clarity**, **completeness**, **unity**, and **coherence**.

**A good summary of course requires your interpretation and analysis of the text's meaning.

CHECK OUT THESE SUMMARIES. How well do they fit the standards?

"What is Snapchat?" by Webwise, 2018:

https://www.webwise.ie/parents/explainer-what-is-snapchat-2/

RANKING: (1 = poor; 10 = Excellent): _____

WHY? _____

"Speed Reading" by Mind Tools, no date:

https://www.mindtools.com/speedrd.html

RANKING: (1 = poor; 10 = Excellent): _____

WHY? _____

WRITE the summary for the following ad. Use no more than five sentences.

"Pokemon Go Coins Hack" by Karolina Malecka on September 18, 2016:

https://www.youtube.com/watch?v=wtRXMxzR2pw

Swap your summary with a peer, and discuss your evaluations of each other's summaries.

CHAPTER 3

JUDGING THE VALIDITY OF AN INTERNET SITE

1. **Examine the letters which follow ".":**

   ---> .edu ---> from an educational institution (university or college, NOT high school or elementary school), usually valid

   ---> .gov ---> from a government agency, usually valid

   ---> .com ---> from a commercial company (one that makes profit): BEWARE!

   ---> .net ---> from a commercial company (one that makes profit): BEWARE!

   ---> .org ---> from some type of organization, sometimes for profit and sometimes not for profit: USE CAUTION!

   ---> .asp ---> active server pages or application service provider—commercial and may or may not be valid; often biased: BEWARE!

2. **Note the date on the site.**
   a. Does it even have a "last updated" notation (sometimes at the very end, sometimes at the beginning)? If it does not, then you have no idea how old or recent the information is.
   b. If it does provide a date, is that date within the last three to four years? If it isn't, then the site does not offer the most recent data.

3. **Note the site's sponsor and/or web contact.**
   a. Does the site name a sponsor (American Council of Pediatricians, American Association of Psychiatry, etc.) and/or provide a Web contact?
      1. If it does, is that organization valid and well-known?
      2. If there is no Web contact, then what level of trust can you assume you should give the site?
      3. Does the sponsoring group have a particular bias? (For example, the ACLU site has lots of researched, valid information, but the majority of it comes from one viewpoint, and you should know that fact as you examine the information.)

4. **Note the use of citations within the information presented.**
   a. Does the text presented provide a list of references?
      1. How recent are those references?
      2. Do the references consist of scholarly journals and books, or of only chat rooms, blogs, and other Internet sites?

5. **Examine the level of language use.**
   a. Does the site contain a fair number of spelling, syntax, sentence structure, etc., errors?
   b. Does the level of vocabulary suit a five-year-old or an adult?
   c. Is the language inflammatory, biased, etc.?

CHAPTER 3

6. NOW, examine the following Web sites as they are displayed to you. Record here your evaluation of each site and the criteria upon which you base that judgment.

Whitehouse.org VERSUS www.whitehouse.gov

http://www.malepregnancy.com

http://www.aclu.org

WRITING AN ANNOTATED BIBLIOGRAPHY

1. USING proper MLA 8 formatting, list your source. Then below that entry, write one to two paragraphs in which you:

   - Explain why this is a relevant and reliable source (Credibility, reliability, relevance: EVALUATION of the source).
   - Summarize the basic claim of the source. What did the author(s) say?
   - Respond to the source. What do "you" say? You might agree, disagree, raise questions, etc.
   - Explain how you will use this source in your research article. Be specific.
   - Synthesize. Explain the way this work fits with—or challenges—other information you have about the topic.

2. **Watch the following video about the CRAAP method of evaluating sources:**

   https://www.youtube.com/watch?v=EyMT08mD7Ds .

3. **Using that CRAAP method + the directions for an annotated bibliography entry, evaluate the following annotations. Rate them with the rubric that follows them.**

CHAPTER 3

SAMPLE 1:

Sam Borden The New York Times Sepp Blatter decides to resign as president

Sam explains in his article that Sepp stepping down in soccer is a step in the right direction and soccer says they feel the same as well. With Sepp stepping down, soccer will try to have an election as soon as possible, but something of that magnitude is not easy especially since in the new election, Sepp could be elected again in spite of everything that happened. So even though everything seems to be running smoothly in soccer, it will take some time for everything to be running legitimately and honorably.

CATEGORY	YES/PASS (+10)	IN BETWEEN (HAS SOME BUT MISSING OTHER PARTS OR WEAKLY DONE – +5)	NO/FAIL
Correctly done Work Cited Entry (MLA format)			
Summary that includes primary claim of article and at least one quote			
Evaluation: Currency (timeliness/date)			
Evaluation: Relevance (connection to topic, details, thoroughness)			
Evaluation: Authority (credentials, peer-reviewed, etc.)			
Evaluation: Accuracy (verified in other sources, has variety and many references, etc.)			
Evaluation: Purpose (objective or biased, etc.)			
Synthesis (how it fits with other research)			
Response (what student says)			
Plan (how one will use the source)			

TOTAL: _____ OVERALL PASS (70 or above) or FAIL (69 or below): _____

SAMPLE 2:

Carr, Nicholas. "Is Google Making Us Stupid?" *The Journal of Technology Online*, vol. 12, no. 6, 2008, https://www.theatlantic.com/magazine/archive/2008/07/is-google-making-us-stupid/306868/. Accessed 20 March 2019.

Nicholas Carr, a technology expert who writes for publications such as *Wired* and *New York Times*, facts that make him quite credible on the subject, claims that our use of technology has changed the way we think. He explains that our use of the Internet, for example, is "ubiquitous," and "it promises to have far-reaching effects on cognition." I contend that he is correct in his assumptions, particularly those about reading. Though this article is ten years old, it still seems valid because his claims still hold true. Given the article's claim, this article can mostly serve as an opposing viewpoint to my own, or at least not a supporting viewpoint of my claim that technology harms our thinking. Though this author provides no Works Cited, he does quote from some experts in the field by using their books and articles. However, here too we see a small problem in that the date of some of these references is as old as 1976.

CATEGORY	YES/PASS (+10)	IN BETWEEN (HAS SOME BUT MISSING OTHER PARTS OR WEAKLY DONE − +5)	NO/FAIL
Correctly done Work Cited Entry (MLA format)			
Summary that includes primary claim of article and at least one quote			
Evaluation: Currency (timeliness/date)			
Evaluation: Relevance (connection to topic, details, thoroughness)			
Evaluation: Authority (credentials, peer-reviewed, etc.)			
Evaluation: Accuracy (verified in other sources, has variety and many references, etc.)			
Evaluation: Purpose (objective or biased, etc.)			
Synthesis (how it fits with other research)			
Response (what student says)			
Plan (how one will use the source)			

TOTAL: _____ OVERALL PASS (70 or above) or FAIL (69 or below): _____

Name _____ Date _____

"DO I ACT ON IMPULSE?" ACTIVITY (Noncognitive)

Fill in the following chart by checking the column that applies best. Don't overthink; just answer truthfully. (This information is for only you; no one else will see it.). Please do not look at the next page/side of this page until directed to do so.

STATEMENT	ALWAYS	SOMETIMES	NEVER
Self-control is important to me.			
Self-control is within my grasp.			
I express my opinion freely without necessarily thinking about my words first.			
If I am doing schoolwork or something around the house, but I am offered the chance for a fun activity, I go.			
I often buy something on impulse, regardless of what is on my shopping list.			
I delay gratification if I have another goal in mind.			
If I get insulted, I quickly respond in a harsh or verbally or physically aggressive manner.			
When I was a child, I "ran away from home" often if my parents upset me.			
When I get emotional, I say or do things I regret later.			
I am patient and good at waiting.			
I get upset quickly over little things.			
I work at long-term goals.			
I require—and I give—instant feedback.			
I get tasks done quickly just to get them out of the way in a hurry.			
Did you flip to the back side of this sheet before asked to do so?	YES	NO	xxxxxxxxxxxxxxxx

1. Now, look over your list. Impulsivity is defined by Webster's Dictionary as, "acting suddenly and quickly, based on feeling and often involuntarily or without willful thought or deliberation or regardless of forethought regarding consequences." Based on your answers on the chart above, do you consider yourself an impulsive person?

2. Let's look at the following video: "The Marshmallow Test": https://www.youtube.com/watch?v=QX_oy9614HQ .

   This video is a clip of a test done on 509 toddlers. These toddlers were followed into their forties to see if the results of this test could predict anything about their future lives. What do you think those results might have shown? Record your answer here.

3. In what ways do you think impulsivity might affect people's lives in general and people's academic lives in particular? Is impulsivity necessarily always negative or positive? Explain your responses by offering some concrete examples.

4. What do you think people can do to curb their impulsivity? Make a list of three strategies.

5. Now meet with a group of two to three peers, and discuss your various answers. See if you can reach any consensus. Be ready to share your ideas with the whole class.

FEAR OF FAILURE ACTIVITY (Noncognitive)

1. Many students experience a lot of fears about various kinds of failure when they begin college. In this game, you'll see if you and your teammates can match some of the fears with some possible consequences, solutions, and lessons.

2. Form a team of three to four students. Using the peel-and-stick labels you have, see if you can figure out what answers belong in which spaces. If the labels do not fit with decisions your group chooses, please feel free to create your own. You may even decide some labels can fit in more than one place.

Labels include the following.

CONSEQUENCE/ IMPACT LABELS	DAMAGE LEVEL ARROWS	HOW TO MOVE FORWARD LABELS	WHAT I MIGHT LEARN LABELS
I will be challenged to change my mind.	↑	Try again with some support structures in place.	How to do something differently the next time.
I will have to overcome shyness and possibly listen to critique.	↑	Make another appointment, bring a less shy friend with me.	Worry less about what others think and value my own ideas.
I will have to repeat the course, take an F on the assignment, or have to repeat a whole semester at great cost.	↑	Practice and try again.	Improve at speaking to others; maybe gain a friend.
I will be embarrassed.	↑	Think about my own progress instead of worrying about what others might think of me.	Professors are there to help us.
I will feel insecure.	↑	Set a goal to say 1 thing. Write it down. Then read it.	No one laughs at me; my fear was unfounded.
I will have to fumble and struggle to figure it out.	↑	Listen with an open mind.	Learn something I did not know and learn how to get help.
I will have to admit I do not know.	↑	Take on a role in the group— the scribe or the one who goes to the board, etc.	How to work effectively with others to accomplish one goal.
I will have to contribute ideas to the whole.	↑	Outside of class, make a list of what I have accomplished to remind myself I am capable.	Gain confidence.
I will have to risk expressing my opinion.	↑	Face the fear/accept that I just have to do it.	A new way to think about something.

CHAPTER 3

THE GAME BOARD

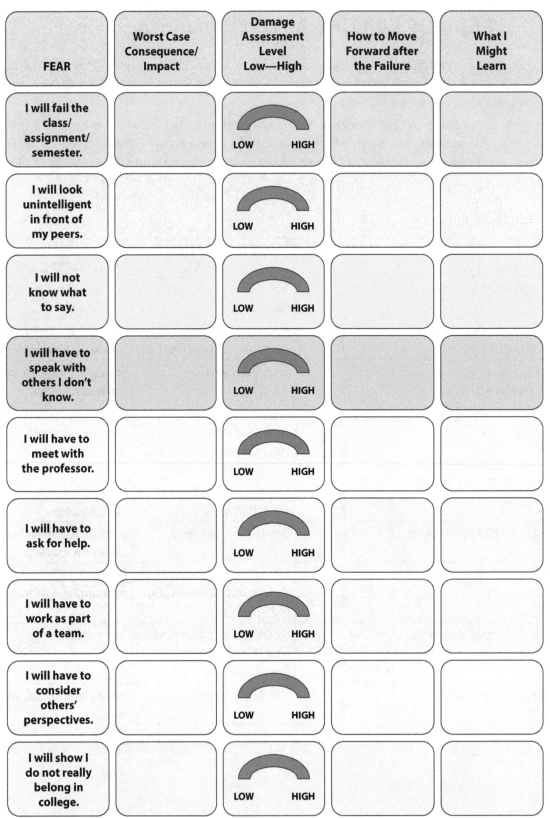

FEAR	Worst Case Consequence/ Impact	Damage Assessment Level Low—High	How to Move Forward after the Failure	What I Might Learn
I will fail the class/ assignment/ semester.		LOW HIGH		
I will look unintelligent in front of my peers.		LOW HIGH		
I will not know what to say.		LOW HIGH		
I will have to speak with others I don't know.		LOW HIGH		
I will have to meet with the professor.		LOW HIGH		
I will have to ask for help.		LOW HIGH		
I will have to work as part of a team.		LOW HIGH		
I will have to consider others' perspectives.		LOW HIGH		
I will show I do not really belong in college.		LOW HIGH		

Source: Patricia Sehulster

3. As you look at your game board, can you draw any conclusions about handling academic fears and about what impact failure can actually have?

4. Watch the following video, "Get Comfortable being Uncomfortable," a TED Talk from 2007 by Luvvie Ajayi:

   https://www.ted.com/talks/luvvie_ajayi_get_comfortable_with_being_uncomfortable/
   transcript?language=en

5. <u>INDIVIDUALLY</u>, think about the exercise you did as a team member, the message of the video, and the two images below. Then write a brief reflection on what you now think about fears of failure and failure itself.

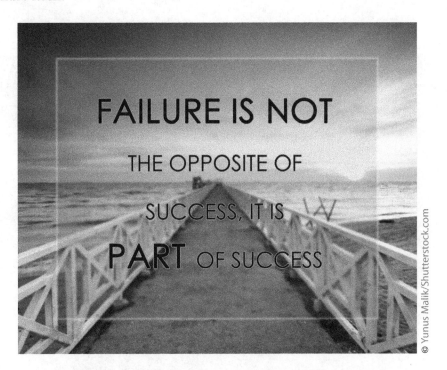

STRESS ASSESSMENT ACTIVITY (Noncognitive)

1. Each of you has a bunch of small peel-and-stick labels. Some of them have words already written on them (*job, family issues, illness/health, finances, deadlines for school, deadlines for work, food insecurity, where I live, prejudice about my race/ethnicity, prejudice about my gender or gender identity, transportation needs, upcoming exams, physical appearance*). Some of them are blank. You get to fill those in as you see fit. All of these labels represent the <u>causes of stress</u> in your life.

2. On three different desks, you will see a large sheet of paper that contains a drawing of a big pressure gauge.

© Schmidt/Shutterstock.com

The green section represents "low-level pressure or stress," while the red section indicates "high-level and even dangerous-level pressure or stress."

3. Go to any one of the drawings, and stick your labels where you think they belong on the pressure spectrum. It's okay if you find another label of the same or different word in the same general area.

4. After all of you have finished adhering your labels to the drawings of the gauges, now spend about ten minutes traveling to the various drawings and looking at/reading what has been placed where. Respond to some of these labels by adding in pen or pencil some handwritten comments alongside of them. You might agree or disagree, explain, or note that you never knew such an entity could cause stress, etc. NO comment is "wrong"; just react to the labels and their placement.

5. Let's discuss as a large group what conclusions we can reach about the causes of stress in our lives. Are there some that stand out as in common to all? Are there some that are unique? Which cause the greatest stress?

CHAPTER 3

6. In what ways does stress impact our ability to succeed as students?

7. Examine the chart below. It consists of recommendations for ways to manage stress. <u>Individually</u> circle the methods YOU already use.

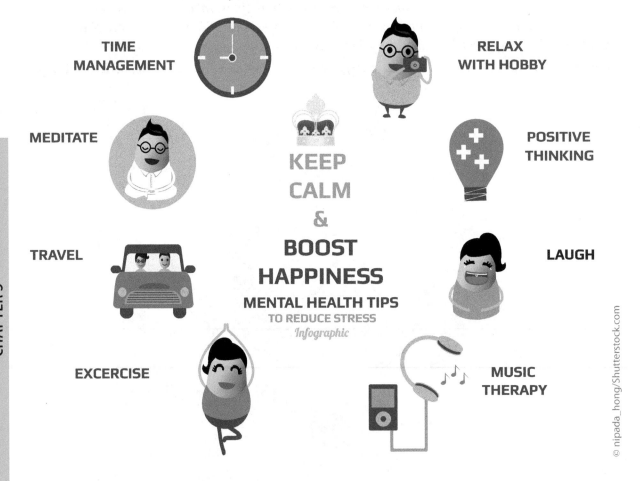

TIME MANAGEMENT

RELAX WITH HOBBY

MEDITATE

KEEP CALM & BOOST HAPPINESS

MENTAL HEALTH TIPS

TO REDUCE STRESS

Infographic

POSITIVE THINKING

TRAVEL

LAUGH

EXCERCISE

MUSIC THERAPY

© nipada_hong/Shutterstock.com

8. List any methods you would add to the list.

9. As you examine the list, do you think any of the recommendations are more useful than others? Why or why not?

10. Do you see one you might try that you have not previously used?

REFUTATION, COUNTERARGUMENT, AND OPPOSING A VIEWPOINT EXERCISE

REMINDERS:
Acknowledging an opposing viewpoint strengthens your own argument.

- It demonstrates your awareness that not everyone will agree with you.
- It gives your argument increased credibility because you take on the opposition.
- It anticipates objections so you can counter them.
- It requires you to use logic to reiterate your claim.

Typically, opposing an argument requires:

- Introducing and clarifying that opposing viewpoint.
  - ▶ Summarize the claim and main points
  - ▶ Use patterns such as
    - According to X _____
    - X has argued that _____
    - Opponents of this idea claim _____
- Acknowledging the parts of the opposition that are valid.
  - ▶ State that some part of the opposition's claim makes sense
  - ▶ Use patterns such as
    - I/We/One cannot deny that _____
    - Admittedly, _____
    - Of course, some truth lies in the idea that _____
- Countering the opposing viewpoint.
  - ▶ Explain what your position is, relative to the opposition's point; show that viewpoint as incorrect, inconsequential, or weak. Discredit it.
  - ▶ Use patterns such as
    - . . . deny that _____, but _____
    - However, _____
    - Nonetheless, _____
    - To the contrary, _____
- Concluding the refutation/counterargument.
  - ▶ Summarize why the opposition viewpoint is insufficient, but your claim is correct. Do so without getting redundant.
  - ▶ Use patterns such as
    - As such, _____
    - Therefore, _____
    - As a consequence/result, _____
    - In essence, then, _____

Let's look at the following excerpt from your assigned readings.

EXCERPT FROM IMPORTED AMERICANS

The story of the experiences of a disguised American and his wife studying the immigration question—
By Broughton Brandenburg

[. . .] In America the cry was redoubled that the doors of the United States should be altogether closed or rendered still more difficult to pass. The Shattuc bill was about to find favor in the House of Representatives, the Lodge bill was cooking in Boston, and in every newspaper or periodical of the land articles and editorials were appearing that attacked or defended various phases, conditions or proposed remedies of immigration. Even in the German and Italian papers, which speak for Germany, Austria and Italy, the most fertile immigrant-producing grounds, there was but the barest trifle printed that was *from the point of view of the immigrant himself.* In the American papers there was absolutely nothing. [. . .]. When I was seated and had unfolded my paper the first thing that caught my eye was an article in which a noted sociologist was liberally quoted recommending the total suspension of immigration for three years and *then* new laws admitting only those who would come with their families and were trained in some work demanding skill. The arguments were specious, but as I looked over the top of the paper at the poor creatures huddled in the car seats about, very thinly dressed for so cold a January day, it occurred to me that the true light, the revelation of the natural remedies and the only real understanding of the immigrant situation lay in seeing from the underside, in getting the immigrants' point of view to compare with the public-spirited American one. [. . .]

State the claim of the above passage: _____

_____.

State what could be a counterargument to that claim. _____

_____

List any ONE point of the claim that cannot be argued against/that makes sense. _____

_____

List three points that make the counterargument true. _____,

_____

Now, following the formula on the first page, write a paragraph that refutes the excerpt's claim.

Exchange paragraph, and evaluate one another's paragraphs. Use the checklist on the first page as your criteria.

A POSSIBLE ANNOTATED BIBLIOGRAPHY TEMPLATE

Today, the topic/issue/idea/concept/problem (←Choose one) of _____

concerns/interests/intrigues/worries/registers (←Choose one) many people. Some believe

_____,

while others think _____.

As a _____, this topic has become ever present in my mind too, especially

because _____.

I'd really like to know _____.

At present, I contend that _____.

because _____.

I have reached this tentative claim based upon the research I have completed so far. As I have researched

this topic, I have discovered that scholars have actually drawn different conclusions. While some of

them, particularly _____(←Names of scholars/writers of the articles)

contend that, "_____" ( ), a few others such

as _____ propose the premise that "_____" ( ). The bulk

of the research on this topic seems to lean in favor of _____, and I

agree with those ideas/but I cannot fully concur with such positions because _____

I also recognize that I may need to find additional research about _____.

    So far, my sources include the following.

_____.

CHAPTER 3

I found this source in the database _____, using the search terms "_____." Basically, this entire article supports the idea that _____ and strongly suggests that, "_____" ( ). This author utilizes _____ and _____ to substantiate the claim, and this evidence _____ [←Verb] the reader. The source absolutely possesses reliability and credibility, for its author _____, and the piece draws from _____ sources, all of them from _____-_____, and all of them from scholarly publications. The vocabulary does _____, for it is _____. Because I contend that _____ _____, this source will _____ with my claim, though it will contradict _____. In general, it will _____ my other research.

I found this source in the database _____, using the search terms "_____." Basically, this entire article supports the idea that _____ and strongly suggests that, "_____ ( ). This author utilizes _____ and _____ to substantiate the claim, and this evidence _____ [←Verb] the reader. The source absolutely possesses reliability and credibility, for its author _____, and the piece draws from _____ sources, all of them from _____-_____, and all of them from scholarly publications. The vocabulary does _____, for it is _____. Because I contend that _____ _____, this source will _____ with my claim, though it will contradict _____. In general, it will _____ my other research.

I found this source in the database _____, using the search terms "_____." Basically, this entire article supports the idea that _____ and strongly suggests that, "_____ ( ). This author utilizes _____ and _____ to substantiate the claim, and this evidence _____ [←Verb] the reader. The source absolutely possesses reliability and credibility, for its author _____, and the piece draws from _____ sources, all of them from _____-_____, and all of them from scholarly publications. The vocabulary does _____, for it is _____. Because I contend that _____ _____, this source will _____ with my claim, though it will contradict _____. In general, it will _____ my other research.

I found this source in the database _____, using the search terms "_____." Basically, this entire article supports the idea that _____ and strongly suggests that, "_____ ( ). This author utilizes _____ and _____ to substantiate the claim, and this evidence _____ [←Verb] the reader. The source absolutely possesses reliability and credibility, for its author _____, and the piece draws from _____ sources, all of them from _____-_____, and all of them from scholarly publications. The vocabulary does _____, for it is _____. Because I contend that _____ _____, this source will _____ with my claim, though it will contradict _____. In general, it will _____ my other research.

I found this source in the database _____, using the search terms
"_____." Basically, this entire article supports the idea
that _____ and strongly suggests that, "_____ ( ).
This author utilizes _____ and _____
to substantiate the claim, and this evidence _____ [←Verb] the reader.
The source absolutely possesses reliability and credibility, for its author _____, and
the piece draws from _____ sources, all of them from _____-_____,
and all of them from scholarly publications. The vocabulary does _____, for it is
_____. Because I contend that _____
_____, this source will _____ with
my claim, though it will contradict _____. In general, it will
_____ my other research.

I found this source in the database _____, using the search terms
"_____." Basically, this entire article supports the idea
that _____ and strongly suggests that, "_____ ( ).
This author utilizes _____ and _____
to substantiate the claim, and this evidence _____ [←Verb] the reader.
The source absolutely possesses reliability and credibility, for its author _____, and
the piece draws from _____ sources, all of them from _____-_____,
and all of them from scholarly publications. The vocabulary does _____, for it is
_____. Because I contend that _____
_____, this source will _____ with
my claim, though it will contradict _____. In general, it will
_____ my other research.

MID-TERM ATTITUDE ASSESSMENT CO-REQUISITE COURSE

Using the Likert scale, please answer the following questions by checking the column you feel appropriate.

QUESTION	3 – DEFINITELY	2 – SOMEWHAT	1 – NOT AT ALL
1. I am getting the help that I need to complete this course and the 3-credit Writing and Research companion course.			
2. I know where to go for specific help.			
3. This course is providing a variety of ways to learn the content.			
4. I am kept abreast of my progress so I can get help when I need it.			
5. I take advantage of the academic supports on campus.			
6. I am making good progress so far.			
7. This course is enabling me to pass the 3-credit Writing and Research course.			
8. This course is a necessary tool for me to understand what is going on in my Writing and Research course.			

Please write in the answers you feel appropriate.

QUESTION	YOUR ANSWER
9. Additional comments I would make include . . .	

CHAPTER 3

PRONOUN ROULETTE

1. Keep your text's pages about pronoun use in front of you during this exercise. Feel free to use it as a reference.
2. Work in teams of two.
3. Examine the sentence cards the teacher gave you.
4. Find and circle or underline the pronouns used in each one. Some sentences use more than one.
5. Determine what roulette wheel rule applies, and place that card on the appropriate wheel section. You may place more than one card on a single wheel section.
6. When the teacher tells you to stop, move to another group's wheel and by cross-referencing the rules about pronouns, check their answers. If there are disputes, the teacher will settle them.
7. Tally the number of points your team has earned, and we'll see who has won.

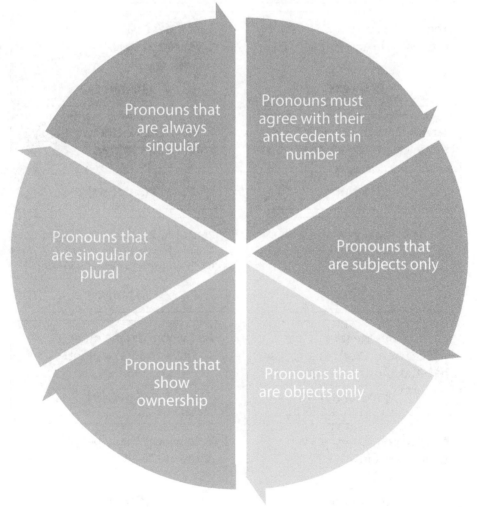

Pronouns that are always singular

Pronouns must agree with their antecedents in number

Pronouns that are singular or plural

Pronouns that are subjects only

Pronouns that show ownership

Pronouns that are objects only

Source: Patricia Sehulster

CHAPTER 3

Sentence Cards

None of those resources uses its references very effectively.

[10 points]

Its Works Cited list is extensive and current.

[5 points]

Those authors have sufficient credentials for their work to be considered reliable.

[5 points]

All of these sources agree with the claim.

[5 points]

If anyone recognizes any validity in this claim, she will need proof.

[10 points]

It is we who bear the burden of using concrete evidence.

[10 points]

The scholars whom we trust are not always in agreement.

[5 points]

That is data with which no person can argue.

[10 points]

Jared's claim is also mine, though our reasons differ.

[5 points]

Some of the research definitely contradicts this idea.

[5 points]

There is virtually no one in the field like him for such outlandish claims.

[10 points]

Butterfield contends that mankind cannot change its ways without motivation from catastrophic events.

[5 points]

Books about the subject are scarce because everyone focuses her studies on other elements.

[10 points]

And whom did the other scholars dismiss outright?

[5 points]

My own premise agrees with theirs except in one regard.

[5 points]

With which should people agree positively?

[5 points]

Source: Patricia Sehulster

WRITING ACROSS THE CURRICULUM/WRITING IN THE DISCIPLINES TIPS AND CONNECTIONS FOR THIS UNIT

1. With In-Class Activity 3A, use Internet and database sources specific to your discipline.

2. For In-Class Activities 3B, 3C, and 3D, use articles related to your discipline. View and discuss examples of abstracts from articles in your field of study. Emphasize the jargon and conventions.

3. Clarify which of the style formats your field uses, and spend some time reviewing those specific pages in the text's Appendices or online.

4. Show students a few of the online annotated bibliographies done for your field of study.

CHAPTER 3

CHAPTER 4

Formalizing Our Contribution to the Dialogue

Weeks 10–14

Learning Objectives

Students will:

- Compose a research essay.
- Compose an outreach project.
- Use a clear focus.
- Support ideas with reasoning and evidence.
- Summarize others' ideas clearly, accurately, thoroughly, and concisely.
- Integrate their own ideas with those of others.
- Organize ideas to clarify and support the controlling idea or question and to best suit a targeted audience.
- Document where information and ideas come from in the style appropriate for the discipline.
- Demonstrate an understanding of writing as a multistage process.
- Produce texts that present ideas effectively and fluently.
- Think critically in a way that considers a multiplicity of perspectives.

You now begin the final stages of your research process: composing a project or essay that clarifies and defends your own contribution to the dialogue about your topic in the context of the whole conversation about that topic.

Up to this point, you have engaged in a great deal of reading about your topic. As readers, you looked for, summarized, analyzed, and evaluated the tools other research writers have used. Now, as writers, you will actually use those tools yourselves.

A. Types of Evidence and Argument Structures

As you have gathered your research, you may have noticed that you discovered two distinct, general types of research: *primary sources and secondary sources.*

Primary sources encompass what you might label "firsthand material"; these sources are original and created at the time to which they connect. They offer on-the-scene experience, if you will. They include such entities as:

- Original historical documents, including official government implements and policies and court proceedings, as well as original correspondence, diaries, journals, etc.
- Original artifacts, including photos, manuscripts, audio and visual recordings, speeches, scrapbooks, oral histories, clothing, furniture, etc.
- Original research data, including scientific studies, ethnographies, opinion polls, etc.
- Original newspapers, magazines, etc., from the historical period.

Secondary sources envelop exactly what you might guess: secondhand reporting, interpretation, and analysis of such primary sources after-the-fact. In other words, no matter how erudite these scholars may be, they have not, themselves, lived through the period or experience, conducted the studies, or written the documents they discuss.

You might wonder if one type of source offers better information than another. No clear answer to this question exists. If, for example, I study a historical concept, examining some original correspondence from the period certainly will assist me and lend authenticity to my study, but analyzing an expert scholar's interpretation of that document can also aid me in understanding the topic. Interviewing actual participants in an event, for example, offers us valuable information, but processing secondhand coverage of the event provides us with something important too. As a final example, looking at the actual, original text of a piece of legislation matters, but so too does reading a scholar's study of the effects of that legislation. If you can find—or even create through experimentation, surveys, interviews, etc.—primary sources and balance them with secondary sources, you will have a solid set of research with which to understand fully and then contribute to the conversation about any topic.

As you examine your research before you begin the actual writing of your research project or essay, what types of evidence do you see? You may recall from our work in Chapter 1 some of the types of evidence research writers use. Now that you have completed your research, you can add others to that list.

CHAPTER 4

TYPE OF SUPPORTING EVIDENCE	DEFINITION	EXAMPLE
Testimonials/Scholarly Support	Quotations from people in authority/ experts/ researchers (e.g., criminologist, scientists, Census Bureau, etc.)	According to psychologist David Smith, " . . . " (22).
Data/Statistics	Data/numbers/charts that identify concrete results and tell how much, how many, how often, etc.	"40 million Americans need food assistance every day" (Food for America).
Facts	Irrefutable statements of truth	Tesla makes hybrid cars.
Examples	Specific samples or instances that help to illustrate the point	For example, Westchester County Jail gets paid to house prisoners from other states with overcrowded jails.
Reasons	Explanations of any of the above types of evidence	This number means that . . .
Analogies	Comparisons that demonstrate similarities between what you discuss and something you think your readers will readily identify	This kind of treatment is like . . .
Refutation of Opposing Viewpoint	Counterargument	While X says y, X misses z.
Restatements of Clarification	Using other words to state a point again to make it clear and to emphasize it	In essence, then, . . .
Concrete Imagery	Detailed descriptions that paint a mental and identifiable picture	Often with distended bellies and haunted eyes, these people line up for food.
Personal Experience or Connection (your own, experiential knowledge)	Your own experience or observations as a result of your experience	As a food pantry volunteer, I have seen the number we serve climb weekly.

You may have gathered all of these types of evidence or only some of them. All of them will help you offer support and credibility to your claim. As you construct your research project or essay—your argument—you will need to decide what combinations and sequences of these types of evidence you will use.

Traditionally, constructing a solid argument in which you attempt to persuade your audience to agree with your answer to your research question approaches the task using what the Greek Aristotle called a combination of *ethos* (appeal to credibility), *logos* (appeal to logic and reason), and *pathos* (appeal to emotions). An argument may emphasize one of these approaches more than another, or it may use them in equal measure. Largely, your purpose, audience, and available evidence will dictate which approaches you use.

Many of you have probably grown very accustomed to writing "the five-paragraph essay": an introduction containing the thesis, three body paragraphs, and a conclusion (that often merely restates your claim). On a college level, you should strive to compose beyond that model. You will expand, include subclaims and refutations, and maybe even explore a bit. Your conclusion will probably even make suggestions regarding what else those involved in the dialogue ought to consider next. In a research argument, you will in many ways actually reconstruct your discovery process to

CHAPTER 4

demonstrate the validity of your conclusions. You will place yourself in the middle of an argument—the dialogue or conversation about your topic—and fight for your ascertains with the evidence you have found, your interpretation and explanations of that evidence, your counterarguments, and your look forward. Your argument will be unique to you because your process has been unique to you.

Maybe your claim will appear in the very first paragraph, or maybe you will build your argument and save your final overarching claim until the very end or insert it somewhere in the middle. You will have an organizational plan, but it may not conform to that five-paragraph essay model. Think about the ways some of the arguments you have read in your research have been constructed. Not all of them followed exactly the same organizational structure; did they?

B. Using the Research: Plagiarism, Quoting, Paraphrasing, and Summarizing

You may have noticed that all of the scholars you have read have posited original ideas, but like you, they examined the dialogues of others first. In each instance in which they used some of that material, they avoided *plagiarism*. So must you.

Plagiarism amounts to theft of intellectual property; it means stealing someone else's ideas and claiming them as your own. Doing so breaks every rule of ethical research. Plagiarism comes in several forms, some more obvious than others, but all equally incorrect and unacceptable. Let's examine these forms of plagiarism by using the following excerpt from Janna Anderson and Leo Rainie's "The Future of Truth and Misinformation Online" as our base.

> "A Pew Research Center study just after the 2016 election found 64% of adults believe fake news stories cause a great deal of confusion and 23% said they had shared fabricated political stories themselves—sometimes by mistake and sometimes intentionally."

- **The Full-On Theft**: Using someone's exact words without quoting them or crediting them to their source.

  The Plagiarism:

  Sixty-four percent of adults believe fake news stories cause a great deal of confusion, and twenty-three percent have shared fabricated political stories.

- **The Changed-Some Theft**: Changing and rearranging some of someone else's words somewhat and not quoting them or crediting them to their source.

  The Plagiarism:

  Many—64% of—adults think fake news stories confuse people, yet 23% have shared these made-up stories.

- **The Medley Theft**: Mixing various pieces of someone else's work with your own without quoting or giving credit to the source.

  The Plagiarism:

  After 2016, fake news postings on the Internet escalated, and 64% of people found it confusing. However, amid that confusion, still 23% of people reposted those fake stories somewhere else.

- **The Summary Theft**: Summarizing the work of someone else without giving credit to the source

  The Plagiarism:

  More than 50% of people think that made-up, untruthful news stories baffle everyone. Nonetheless, slightly less than half that number of people will knowingly or unknowingly spread those falsehoods.

- **The Copy Theft**: Copying some or all of someone else's original research project or essay and submitting it as your own. (Sometimes, students use previous students' work, or sometimes, they copy and paste from models on the Internet.)
- **The Pay-for-a-Paper Theft**: Buying some or all of a research project or essay done by someone else and submitting it as your own.

All forms of plagiarism are wrong, and all colleges, universities, and publishing houses have policies against it.

IN-CLASS ACTIVITY 4A: MAKING PLAGIARISM PERSONAL

1. Use the index card to answer the following question: "What's good about attending your college?" Sign your statement.

2. Exchange statements. [30 seconds]

3. Imagine you write ad copy to lure new students to your college.

4. Write that copy.

5. Include some words from the writer of the index card you now hold.

6. Now let's hear some of those ads.

7. Let's discuss how you felt when you heard your words read. Did getting credit for your own words matter to you? How many of you did not ascribe credit?

8. Does your ad copy look something like the following? It should have.

   At X College, teachers "really get to know [their] students and help them to shape their lives" (Gaffney).

   OR

   As Liz Gaffney says, at X College, teachers "really get to know [their] students and help them to shape their lives."

   OR

   As Liz Gaffney explains, students get personal attention from professors.

9. Watch the following videos and take notes on the key points.

   "What is Plagiarism?" by mjmfoodie, November 28, 2016:

   https://www.youtube.com/watch?v=zPqKXJbzRP4

   "What is Plagiarism and How to Avoid It" by Brock University Library, September 2, 2014:

   https://www.youtube.com/watch?v=Pmab92ghG0M

10. List three ways to avoid plagiarizing.

11. Compare your list with a peer's.

How, then, can you avoid plagiarizing, but still use the supporting evidence you need to contextualize and bolster your argument? You can correctly use *quotations, paraphrases, and summaries, all* of them *cited*.

Sometimes, you will find a quotation so salient or remarkable that you will want to use it exactly as it is because putting it into your own words would dilute its power and meaning. Sometimes, you will need to use specific data, dates, or other numbers. In these instances, you will use *direct quotations*. You should choose to do so judiciously and sparingly, so that your entire essay does not merely offer quote after quote from someone else.

When you do quote, you may use one of two different options. Let's use the following excerpt from Oren Gazal-Ayal's "A Global Perspective on Sentencing Reforms" to see the differences.

> "No nation outside of the United States has more people in prison. Other nations use different sentencing to reform criminals and manage drug crimes instead of warehousing them in jails. Rehabilitation is seen as both more effective and more humane, and it costs far less than jailing these criminals." (76)

- **Direct Quote Method 1:** Use a short part of the quotation integrated smoothly within your own text through a blending of the quotation with your own text.

    Example:

    The United States seems to prefer punishment for drug-related crimes, whereas "[o]ther nations use different sentencing to reform criminals [. . .] instead of warehousing them in jails" (Gazal-Aval 76).

    - Note the way the quoted material fits into the student's text.
    - Note the choice to use only part of the quote.
    - Note the choice to use brackets and ellipsis to alter the capital letter and to leave out a section not germane to the emphasis desired. The use of brackets tells the reader that the student changed the text.
    - Note the use of quotation marks and the citation at the end.

- **Direct Quote Method 2:** Use a long quotation of longer than four lines (or forty words) as a block citation, indented ten spaces on the left and eliminating the quotation marks.

    Example:

    The United States compares unfavorably to most of the rest of the world. In fact, according to studies,

    > No nation outside of the United States has more people in prison. Other nations use different sentencing to reform criminals and manage drug crimes instead of warehousing them in jails. Rehabilitation is seen as both more effective and more humane, and it costs far less than jailing these criminals. (76)

    In other words, America has a penchant for punishment and no true desire to reform drug-law offenders.

• Note the use of the layer-cake framework:

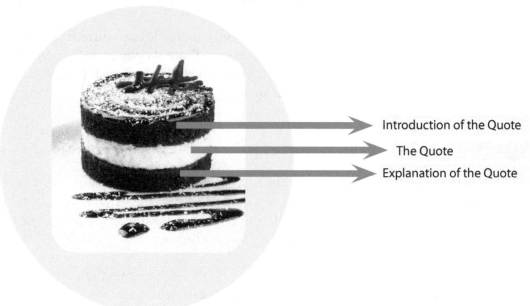

Introduction of the Quote

The Quote

Explanation of the Quote

© image: Lana_M/Shutterstock.com. Adapted by Kendall Hunt Publishing Company.

The quote is introduced: In fact, according to studies . . .
The quote appears.
The quote is explained: In other words . . .

• Note the lack of the need for quotation marks.
• Note the use of the follow-up sentence, so no paragraph ends in a block citation (with someone else's words).

When you use only part of a quote, beware altering it so much or deleting so much that you actually change its meaning. Stay true to its message.

HOW SHOULD YOU INTEGRATE QUOTATIONS INTO YOUR TEXT?

• **Directly quote only sparingly**; be sure that you have a good reason to include a direct quotation when you decide to do so.

• Often, a short quotation works well when integrated into a sentence by blending its words with your own. Use ellipses [. . .] and brackets [] when you eliminate or alter words.

• Long quotations (more than four lines long) can stand alone as block citations.

• Use the layer cake framework:

  ▶ Introduce the quote.
  ▶ Insert the quote.
  ▶ Explain the quote thoroughly. (What does it mean? How is it relevant to your point? How does it engage with your argument?)

• Never alter a quote so much or remove so much of its context that you change its meaning.

Patterns You Can Use When You Use Direct Quotations:

INTRODUCING QUOTATIONS	EXPLAINING QUOTATIONS
According to _____, a sociologist, "_____."	In essence, _____ maintains that _____.
_____ contends that, "_____."	In this case, then, _____ emphasizes the idea that _____.
_____ maintains that "_____."	This statement basically says _____.
_____ contradicts this theory in saying that, "_____."	_____'s point tells us that _____.
_____ adds to this complexity by concluding "_____."	This statement simply means _____.
Tackling this issue in her *Science Journal* article, _____ claims "_____."	In making this comment, _____ argues that _____.
_____'s viewpoint embraces the idea that "_____"	In other words, _____ claims that _____.
_____ concurs with this idea when she states, "_____."	
_____ argues that "_____."	
In his book, _____ complains that "_____."	

Using quotations only sparingly means that at other times you will want to *paraphrase*—but still cite—sources instead.

To paraphrase something means to put a passage in your own words. You will want to parallel—but not copy—the basic structure and length of the passage, but use language of your own instead of the words used by the source. You will choose this method when you know something a source says matters considerably, but the source does not state the content in a manner worthy of quoting word-for-word. In completing a paraphrase, you will not merely substitute synonyms or delete a few words from the passage; rather, you will make the passage your own, but maintain its original point.

CHAPTER 4

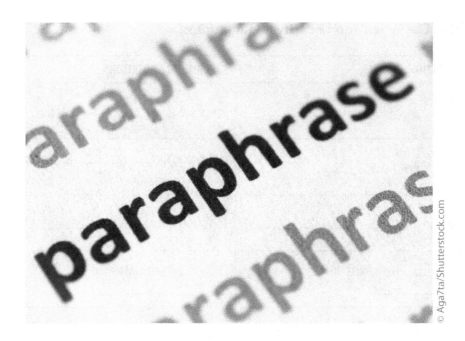

Let's use the following example from Bryan Keogh's "Big Fail: The internet hasn't helped democracy" to demonstrate a well-composed paraphrase.

> "[M]ore and more of our public conversation is unfolding within a dwindling coterie of sites that are controlled by a small few, largely unregulated and geared primarily to profit rather than public interest."

The Paraphrase:

According to a writer for *The Conversation*, a public watchdog group, increasing amounts of Internet content rest in the hands of a tiny group of companies that care mostly about making money and have no government or other oversight (Keogh). This observation means that a select few companies determine what the public reads online, and these decisions are driven mostly by desire for profit, not by desire for truth or anything else.

- Note that this paraphrase mirrors ideas and length, but not word choices or exact sentence structure.
- Note that the paraphrase does get cited.
- Note that the paraphrase too follows the layer-cake framework: introduction (According to . . .), the paraphrase, and the explanation (This observation . . .).
- Note that a paraphrase does not use quotation marks.

When you want to use evidence from several paragraphs or even a full page or two, then you will want to *summarize*. As you have learned and practiced in Chapter 3, when you summarize, you use only your own words and sentence structure to condense a source to its essence or main idea. You leave out details and strive for conciseness. Nonetheless, because these ideas do not originate with you, you still must cite your summaries.

Patterns to Use to Summarize:

SUMMARIZING
_____ contends that _____.
_____ argues that _____.
_____'s premise is that _____.
_____ acknowledges that _____.
In _____'s view, _____.
_____ complains that _____.

**See Chapter 3 for additional patterns to use for summarizing.

A Comparative Chart of the 3 Ways to Avoid Plagiarism:

CATEGORY	DEFINITION	BEST TO USE WHEN YOU . . .	TIPS
QUOTATION	That which you take word-for-word, exactly as it is written in the original source.	. . . use dates, data, statistics . . . use an especially striking phrase or passage . . . cannot say it better yourself	*Use sparingly and judiciously. *Use quotation marks. *Use only the part of the quote that is relevant.
PARAPHRASE	That which you put into your own words, paralleling—but NOT copying—the phrasing and length of the original source.	. . . know the point of the original matters, but it is not stated in any special way worth preserving.	*Use your own words; do not merely plug in synonyms or delete a few words. Make it your own.
SUMMARY	That which you condense, using your own words and sentence structure, to offer the main ideas of the original source.	. . . can get to the essence of a point without using so many words.	*Leave out the details. *Use only your own words. *Be concise.

IN-CLASS ACTIVITY 4B: QUOTING, PARAPHRASING, AND SUMMARIZING

WHY should you quote from, paraphrase, or summarize your sources?
****<u>ALL </u>REQUIRE CITING!****

Quotations, paraphrases, and summaries serve many <u>purposes.</u> You might use them to:

- **Provide support** for claims and **add credibility** to your writing.

- **Offer context by referring to work** that leads up to the work you are now doing.

- **Give examples** of several points of view on a topic.

- **Call attention** to a position with which you agree or disagree.

- **Emphasize an especially salient or remarkable phrase, sentence, or passage or include particular dates or data** by quoting the original.

- **Distance yourself from the original** by quoting it to clarify for the readers that the words are not your own.

- **Expand the breadth or depth** of your writing.

How should you integrate quotations into your text?

- **Directly quote only sparingly**; be sure that you have a good reason to include a direct quotation when you decide to do so.

- Often, a <u>short quotation</u> works well when <u>integrated into a sentence by blending its words with your own.</u> Use ellipses [. . .] and brackets [] when you eliminate or alter words.

- Long quotations (more than four lines long) can stand alone as block citations.

- Use the layer cake framework:

    ▶ Introduce the quote.
    ▶ Insert the quote.
    ▶ Explain the quote thoroughly. (What does it mean? How is it relevant to your point? How does it engage with your argument?)

- Never alter a quote so much or remove so much of its context that you change its meaning.

What's the difference?

CATEGORY	DEFINITION	BEST TO USE WHEN YOU . . .	TIPS
QUOTATION	That which you take word-for-word, exactly as it is written in the original source	. . . use dates, data, statistics . . . use an especially striking phrase or passage . . . cannot say it better yourself	*Use sparingly and judiciously. *Use quotation marks. *Use only the part of the quote that is relevant.
PARAPHRASE	That which you put into your own words, paralleling—but NOT copying—the phrasing and length of the original source	. . . know the point of the original matters, but it is not stated in any special way worth preserving	*Use your own words; do not merely plug in synonyms or delete a few words. Make it your own.
SUMMARY	That which you condense, using your own words and sentence structure, to offer the main ideas of the original source	. . . can get to the essence of a point without using so many words	*Leave out the details. *Use only your own words. *Be concise.

Part 1: View and take notes on the following video:

"How to Integrate Quotations In Writing Essays—APA or MLA" by David Taylor, November 7, 2010: https://www.youtube.com/watch?v=_M0F1rOnFUY

Patterns You Can Use in Your Research Dialogue:

INTRODUCING QUOTATIONS	EXPLAINING QUOTATIONS	SUMMARIZING
According to _____, a sociologist, "_____."	In essence, _____ maintains that _____.	_____ contends that _____.
_____ contends that, "_____."	In this case, then, _____ emphasizes the idea that _____.	_____ argues that _____.
_____ maintains that "_____."	This statement basically says _____.	_____'s premise is that _____.
_____ contradicts this theory in saying that, "_____."	_____'s point tells us that _____.	_____ acknowledges that _____.
_____ adds to this complexity by concluding "_____."	This statement simply means _____.	In _____'s view, _____.
Tackling this issue in her *Science Journal* article, _____ claims "_____."	In making this comment, _____ argues that _____.	_____ complains that _____.
_____'s viewpoint embraces the idea that "_____."	In other words, _____ claims that _____.	
_____ concurs with this idea when she states, "_____."		
_____ argues that "_____."		
In his book, _____ complains that "_____."		

Part 2: Reread the following excerpt, assigned in our Chapter 2 readings.

Excerpts from The School and Society by John Dewey

I

THE SCHOOL AND SOCIAL PROGRESS

We are apt to look at the school from an individualistic standpoint, as something between teacher and pupil, or between teacher and parent. That which interests us most is naturally the progress made by the individual child of our acquaintance, his normal physical development, his advance in ability to read, write, and figure, his growth in the knowledge of geography and history, improvement in manners, habits of promptness, order, and industry—it is from such standards as these that we judge the work of the school. And rightly so. Yet the range of the outlook needs to be enlarged. What the best and wisest parent wants for his own child, that must the community want for all of its children. Any other ideal for our schools is narrow and unlovely; acted upon, it destroys our democracy. All that society has accomplished for itself is put, through the agency of the school, at the disposal of its future members. All its better thoughts of itself it hopes to realize through the new possibilities thus opened to its future self. Here individualism and socialism are at one. Only by being true to the full growth of all the individuals who make it up, can society by any chance be true to itself. And in the self-direction thus given, nothing counts as much as the school, for, as Horace Mann said, "Where anything is growing, one former is worth a thousand re-formers."

Whenever we have in mind the discussion of a new movement in education, it is especially necessary to take the broader, or social view. Otherwise, changes in the school institution and tradition will be looked at as the arbitrary inventions of particular teachers; at the worst transitory fads, and at the best merely improvements in certain details—and this is the plane upon which it is too customary to consider school changes. It is as rational to conceive of the locomotive or the telegraph as personal devices. The modification going on in the method and curriculum of education is as much a product of the changed social situation, and as much an effort to meet the needs of the new society that is forming, as are changes in modes of industry and commerce.

It is to this, then, that I especially ask your attention: the effort to conceive what roughly may be termed the "New Education" in the light of larger changes in society. Can we connect this "New Education" with the general march of events? If we can, it will lose its isolated character, and will cease to be an affair which proceeds only from the over-ingenious minds of pedagogues dealing with particular pupils. It will appear as part and parcel of the whole social evolution, and, in its more general features at least, as inevitable. Let us then ask after the main aspects of the social movement; and afterwards turn to the school to find what witness it gives of effort to put itself in line. And since it is quite impossible to cover the whole ground, I shall for the most part confine myself to one typical thing in the modern school movement—that which passes under the name of manual training, hoping if the relation of that to changed social conditions appears, we shall be ready to concede the point as well regarding other educational innovations.

I make no apology for not dwelling at length upon the social changes in question. Those I shall mention are writ so large that he who runs may read. The change that comes first to mind, the one that overshadows and even controls all others, is the industrial one—the application of science resulting in the great inventions that have utilized the forces of nature on a vast and inexpensive scale: the growth of a world-wide market as the object of production, of vast manufacturing centers to supply this market, of cheap and rapid means of communication and distribution between all its parts. Even as to its feebler beginnings, this change is not much more than a century old; in many of its most important aspects it falls within the short span of those now living. One can hardly believe there has been a revolution in all history so rapid, so extensive, so complete. Through it the face of the earth is making over, even as to its physical forms; political boundaries are wiped out and moved about, as if they were indeed only lines on a paper map; population is hurriedly gathered into cities from the ends of the earth; habits of living are altered with startling abruptness and thoroughness; the search for the truths of nature is infinitely stimulated and facilitated and their application to life made not only practicable, but commercially necessary. Even our moral and religious ideas and interests, the most conservative because the deepest-lying things in our nature, are profoundly affected. That this revolution should not affect education in other than formal and superficial fashion is inconceivable. . . .

But why should I make this labored presentation? The obvious fact is that our social life has undergone a thorough and radical change. If our education is to have any meaning for life, it must pass through an equally complete transformation. This transformation is not something to appear suddenly, to be executed in a day by conscious purpose. It is already in progress. Those modifications of our school system which often appear (even to those most actively concerned with them, to say nothing of their spectators) to be mere changes of detail, mere improvement within the school mechanism, are in reality signs and evidences of evolution. The introduction of active occupations, of nature study, of elementary science, of art, of history; the relegation of the merely symbolic and formal to a secondary position; the change in the moral school atmosphere, in the relation of pupils and teachers—of discipline; the introduction of more active, expressive, and self-directing factors—all these are not mere accidents, they are necessities of the larger social evolution. It remains but to organize all these factors, to appreciate them in their fullness of meaning, and to put the ideas and ideals involved into complete, uncompromising possession of our school system. To do this means to make each one of our schools an embryonic community life, active with types of occupations that reflect the life of the larger society, and permeated throughout with the spirit of art, history, and science. When the school introduces and trains each child of society into membership within such a little community, saturating him with the spirit of service, and providing him with the instruments of effective self-direction, we shall have the deepest and best guarantee of a larger society which is worthy, lovely, and harmonious.

From: Dewey, John. "I The School and Social Progress." In *The School and Society,* 19–46. Illinois: The University of Chicago Press, 1900.

https://www.gutenberg.org/files/53910/53910-h/53910-h.htm

Part 3: Group Activity: Quoting, Paraphrasing, and Summarizing Team Game

1. Form a group of three to four people.

2. Imagine that you must write an essay that contends that "Educational reform must make its primary concern all of society's needs and shifts not just individuals' needs," and you must use Dewey's essay to support that point.

3. Using the five index cards the teacher gave you, craft one of each of the following, but do NOT label or identify which is which. DO insert your group members' names on the back of the cards.

    a. A summary of Dewey's total argument (claim and general evidence/reasons)
    b. A paraphrase of any one of Dewey's points
    c. A direct quote of any one of Dewey's points
    d. An explanation of that quote
    e. Your own original sentence(s) and idea(s) about the topic. [No more than three]

4. Pass your whole set of index cards to another group.

5. Examine the index cards the neighboring group just gave you.

6. Use the chart on the last page to place the index cards in their appropriate category. ** You may determine that one or several cards do not fit any of the categories because they are done incorrectly.

7. When the teacher directs you to do so, go examine the chart of another group, but not the group to whom you gave your group's index cards.

8. Remove any cards that are in the wrong category. The wrong category determination includes any of the following:

    a. The card does not belong in the category in which it was placed.
    b. The card actually does not correctly execute the parameters of that category, though it seems to do so.

9. Tally the total points for that team. Report that total to the teacher.

10. Return to the group that created them all of its index cards. Note any corrections you think need to be made.

11. Using your index cards, create a paragraph that puts all of them together. Make certain to use a layer cake framework and to use some of the patterns we have already examined.

Part 3—Done Individually

1. Examine your Writing Mindset Letter, Research Proposal, or Annotated Bibliography (or something else you wrote recently and that you have access to in either hard copy or online right now).

2. Respond to the questions below.

Did you include any quotations?	
Choose one. How did you integrate that quotation?	
Did you introduce the quotation?	
Did you explain what the quotation means to you, and how it relates to your claim and topic?	

3. Identify a section in which you could have used a quotation but did not.

4. Revise that section, using one of the patterns in the chart we have already studied.

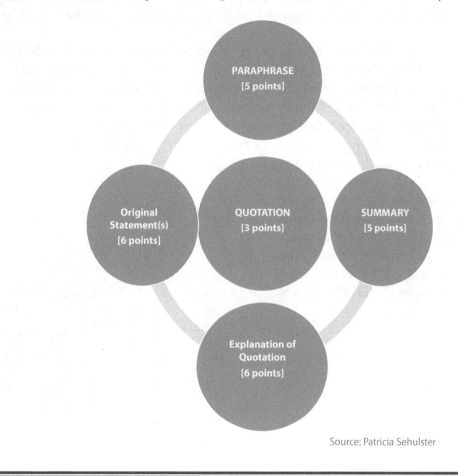

Source: Patricia Sehulster

CHAPTER 4

C. Synthesis

As you consider your use of quotations, paraphrases, and summaries, you need to engage in a process called *synthesis*. You actually synthesize on a daily basis. Often, when you converse with your friends about a topic you have discussed with others—maybe cafeteria food or a movie or a news report—and you pull into that conversation various people's opinions, you are synthesizing. Synthesizing effectively means connecting the different pieces of a dialogue together to integrate them into your own contribution to a conversation. Without making those connections—those clearly identified relationships between one piece of information and another and between that information and your own topic and claim—you have merely a list of disjointed bits of information.

Let's go back to that conversation with friends. If you were to state the following, who would understand your point?

> "Well, Dominica said the new mall is just so full of high-end stores that she thinks she will not shop there. Carlos told me you even have to pay to park at that mall, so he thinks it's discouraging anybody not upper class. Andrew shouted that he actually went inside a store, and they followed him around and wouldn't let him try on a $350 coat. I haven't been there yet."

This use of others' statements lacks any synthesis; the speaker has not related the remarks to each other or made any point that connects them. Without that synthesis, the listener cannot fully understand the speaker's meaning. A synthesized version might look something like the following:

> "Though I have not visited the new mall yet, based on remarks other friends have made, I do not think I'll ever bother going there. Dominica and Carlos made me think the place is outrageously expensive, Dominica complaining about high-end stores and Carlos complaining about parking fees. If those comments were not enough to convince me, when Andrew told me about his experience of being followed around and not being allowed to try on a $350.00 coat, I decided that mall is not for me or maybe anybody not of the upper class."

In this synthesis, the speaker has connected the various conversations to create one that makes sense and makes a point. Instead of only listing what others have said—Dominca said X, Carlos said Y, and Andrew said W—the speaker relates each strand of the dialogue to the other and to her own claim.

© Giuseppe_R/Shutterstock.com

The strategies for effective synthesis, then, include the following:

1. You must first identify the main idea of each source/each piece of the dialogue.
2. You must connect or relate each of these main ideas to the other main ideas by:
    a. Using key phrases to introduce the ideas of others and self
    b. Identifying the sources
    c. Repeating some phrases or synonyms of phrases
    d. Relating the sources as points of opposition, similarity, or expansion.
3. You must integrate the ideas of others into your own understanding of the topic.
4. You must avoid mere reporting or listing of others' ideas.

IN-CLASS ACTIVITY 4C: SYNTHESIS

Your Objective: *The author effectively synthesizes information from a variety of sources.*

WARM-UP:

1. [5 minutes] Use your first index card to write the answer to the following question: "In *your own experience*, what is the best, most affordable cell phone plan/carrier that offers quality phones with the service?"
2. [5 minutes] Meet with any peer, and discuss your two answers. What points of comparison—similarities and differences—do they have? Use your second index card to write a few notes about what you have discovered, and what your peer said. (Make sure you record your peer's name.)
3. [5 minutes] Meet with a different peer, and discuss your two answers. What points of comparison—similarities and differences—do they have? Use your third index card to write a few notes about what you have discovered, and what your peer said. (Make sure you record your peer's name.)
4. [5 minutes] Meet with a third peer, and again discuss your two answers. What points of comparison—similarities and differences—do they have? Use your fourth index card to write a few notes about what you have discovered, and what your peer said. (Make sure you record your peer's name.)
5. [5 minutes] Now go to the back side of your original index card. Based upon the three discussions you just had plus your own ideas, write a new analysis that answers the question, "What is the best, most affordable cell phone plan/carrier that offers quality phones with the service?"

WHAT IS SYNTHESIS?

See the following video with the rest of the class, and take a few notes on what you learn.

"Synthesizing Information" by GCF Learn Free, August 6, 2012:

https://www.youtube.com/watch?v=7dEGoJdb6O0

Synthesis includes all of the following actions taken by the writer:

1. Author demonstrates ability to identify the main idea of each source.
2. Author then <u>relates</u> that main idea to the main ideas of other sources and <u>evaluates it in relation</u> to the topic. [**CONNECTIONS**]
3. Author effectively <u>integrates</u> the ideas of others into her/his own evolving understanding of a research topic.
4. Author smoothly incorporates these other texts into his/her own writing with an <u>appropriate balance</u>.
5. Author <u>avoids a mere reporting</u>/listing/cataloguing of others' ideas.

Watch this second video, and again, take a few notes on what you learn.

"Strategies for Synthesis" by Mary Lourdes Silva, June 12, 2013:

https://www.youtube.com/watch?v=c7HtCHtQ9w0

Synthesis Exercises (In several parts, over several class periods, perhaps)

Let's now, together, examine a successful example of synthesis and analyze why it succeeds.

But maybe at least a small part of the reason the hunger problem continues in such large numbers and totally unabated in the United States stems from the very labels we give the problem—everything from the euphemistic "food insecurity" to the only partially realistic "food poor." According to systems ecologist Molly D. Anderson, PhD, the United States could and would be doing more for hungry people if it embraced the idea that having enough food to eat is a human right and that "this right cannot be achieved in full without coordinated efforts" (119) that include not just government NGO's, but also other help. She would therefore change the labels to reflect the human rights angle—maybe something like *denial of the right to food* or something similar. On the other hand, a group like the Duke Sanford World Food Policy Center does not think labels bear much weight; its conclusions lean more toward blaming the "web of poverty, racism, and sexism surrounding food insecurity." Clearly, these two points are not actually unrelated, yet, the fact that these researchers offer divergent explanations instead of making connections between the two research projects cannot help to address the problem.

SUCCESSFUL BECAUSE:

- The writer uses key phrases to introduce the ideas of others and herself.
- The writer clearly identifies who those researchers are.
- The writer connects ideas by repeating certain phrases or words.
- The writer connects these two very different ideas by relating them both in opposition ["On the other hand"] and reaching a conclusion about them [yet].
- The writer inserts her own thinking where necessary [the lead, the supposition about a new label, the closing sentence] to bring unity to the whole paragraph.
- At no point does this writer merely report "X said Y" and "Z said W"; rather, she connects the two to each other *and* relates both to where her essay claim goes.

EXERCISE 1

1. <u>Individually</u> look at the two examples below. <u>Label</u> each sentence according to the actions 1–5 that a good synthesis should contain. (You may discover you cannot use all of the labels in each example.)

2. Then <u>turn to your neighbor and compare</u> your evaluations.

3. <u>Discuss</u>: Did both of these samples synthesize effectively? Why or why not?

4. <u>Record</u> the three key lessons about synthesis you gained by completing this exercise. Be ready to share with the entire class both your responses and your rationale for those responses.

SAMPLE 1:

Even if we do not agree that enacting the sentencing laws demonstrates an unequal, prejudiced justice system, what effects of these sentencing laws should we consider? I contend that two, primary effects of these laws should command our attention: the economic impacts of the laws and the toll on families that these laws take. According to a study conducted by *Economist* in 2015, taking these half-million people out of our workforce and out of our consumer population costs our economy billions of dollars each year ("Jailhouse Nation" 12). Even if we consider that maybe only half of those half-million people might be working and spending in our country, that number of non-working, non-spending people is considerable. And that loss just gets compounded every year they spend in jail and every year that we add people to the prison population. Some would contend that these people probably were not productive workers anyway, that they were just drug dealers, but I would argue that many drug dealers hold other jobs as well, and even if they did not, drug dealers earn money so they can spend money, and spending money keeps our economy going. If we add to this loss to our economy the costs of incarcerating this many people, we see another problem. Depending on the year, keeping these people in prison "costs between 63 and 75 billion dollars each year" (Valdez and Shank), all money that taxpayers send to the government and cannot keep and spend themselves. In addition, there are other costs because of whom we incarcerate. Every time we put a mother or father in jail for a long sentence, something has to be done with their children. Some go into state or foster care, while others go to family members, but in either case, the government then spends money for their care either in foster care payments, welfare checks, or orphan home costs (Frandino). Some say these costs actually save the children by pulling them out of a drug culture family, but I contend that putting children in some of these situations does not always save them and may, in fact, have quite detrimental effects on them. If we are a country that claims to regard family values highly, these drug sentences contradict that concept because by imprisoning all of these mothers and fathers, we are destroying families and family bonds. And if families are the basic unit of any society, by destroying all of these families, what are we doing to our society as a whole?

SAMPLE 2:

Documented criminal cases related to babies harmed by the mother's drug abuse during pregnancy go back as far as the late 1980s. "Since 1986, at least fifty women across the country have been charged or prosecuted for distributing illegal drugs or alcohol through the umbilical cord" (Grabar 23). At one point, Medicaid insurance even stepped in to keep records of women whose babies were born with fetal alcohol syndrome and addicted to narcotics. Medicaid started tracking the women who delivered these babies (Chavkin et al. 117). Illegal substance use among expectant mothers does affect the growing life inside of them. "Cocaine easily passes the placenta and the blood brain barrier" (Lewis and Bendersky 22). Physically, "'before the umbilical cord is cut, it is really only something arbitrary delivering drugs to that baby, just like a straw or a hypodermic needle'" (Deen qtd. Grabar 23). In the United States, "approximately 375,000 infants are born each year to women who abuse narcotic drugs" (Watson 1). How do such narcotics affect the child after birth, and what are the results of the differing approaches to the women who abuse substances during pregnancy?

EXERCISE 2

EXCERPT 1:

> From: "The Future of Truth and Misinformation Online" by Janna Anderson and Lee Rainie on October 19, 2017, for The Pew Research Center:
>
> https://www.pewinternet.org/2017/10/19/the-future-of-truth-and-misinformation-online/

"A 2016 study that analyzed 376 million Facebook users' interactions with over 900 news outlets found that people tend to seek information that aligns with their views.

This makes many vulnerable to accepting and acting on misinformation.

> [. . .] Americans worry about that: A Pew Research Center study conducted just after the 2016 election found 64% of adults believe fake news stories cause a great deal of confusion and 23% said they had shared fabricated political stories themselves—sometimes by mistake and sometimes intentionally.

The question arises, then: What will happen to the online information environment in the coming decade?"

EXCERPT 2:

> From: "Big Fail: The internet hasn't helped democracy" Bby Bryan Keogh, October 15, 2019, on *The Conversation*:
>
> https://theconversation.com/big-fail-the-internet-hasnt-helped-democracy-104817

"We have yet to come to terms with the staggering degree of control the major platforms exercise over political speech and what it means for democracy.

A new book on the economics of attention online urges us to do so. It shows that more and more of our public conversation is unfolding within a dwindling coterie of sites that are controlled by a small few, largely unregulated and geared primarily to profit rather than public interest.

[. . . P]rofessor Matthew Hindman suggests that as we enter the web's third decade, market forces drive the vast majority of traffic and profit to an exceedingly small group of sites, with no change on the horizon."

EXCERPT 3:

From: *Open Source Democracy How online communication is changing offline politics* by Douglas Rushkoff:

http://www.gutenberg.org/cache/epub/10753/pg10753-images.html

"Finally, our renaissance's answer to the printing press is the computer and its ability to network. Just as the printing press gave everyone access to readership, the computer and internet give everyone access to authorship. The first Renaissance took us from the position of passive recipient to active interpreter. Our current renaissance brings us from the role of interpreter to the role of author. We are the creators."

YOUR TASKS:

1. Read the above material actively.
2. Underline/highlight the main ideas of each excerpt.
3. Imagine your research question is, "Does the Internet enhance democracy through free speech?"
4. Imagine your claim is "The Internet enhances democracy through free speech available to everyone." (IF you choose, you may go in the opposite direction.) In the above articles, circle the particular passages that will bolster your argument.
5. In the above articles, bracket [ ] the passages that oppose your claim and refute the passages you circled for #4.
6. Now, pair with one or two others in the class and discuss the answers to #'s 2–5. Compare your responses and try to determine what answers work best.
7. Now, considering your understanding of the above excerpts, write a summary/overview sentence by filling in the blanks below. (You may complete this part individually or as a pair/group.)

While some scholars, including _____ posit the premise

that the Internet _____

_____, others, including _____

and _____ argue that _____

_____.

8. Now, write a sentence that relates/connects these viewpoints. _____
    _____
    _____

9. Now, write a sentence that expresses your own position/perspective on these points.
    _____

10. Now, flesh out the paragraph(s) of explanation and support. Avoid listing/reporting.
    Make your argument. Use a combination of your own ideas and explanations, para-
    phrase, summary, and direct quotes. Cite as necessary.

D. Balance

As you prepare to quote, paraphrase, summarize, and synthesize, try to remember that this part of the research contribution *belongs to you*. While you will want to use others' research to provide context, to explain how you have reached your own conclusions, and to offer counterarguments, you will want to *maintain your own voice*. You will want to strive for *balance* between what you contribute to the dialogue and what others have contributed to the conversation.

© Niroworld/Shutterstock.com

You can achieve that kind of balance by utilizing a few techniques.

- Your own claim must drive the entire project or essay through repeated emphasis (though not repeated word choice).
- Always relate others' conversations on the topic to that claim.
- Use summaries and paraphrases more often than you use direct quotations.
- Avoid using block citations whenever you can.
- In your use of the layer-cake framework, make the bottom layer—your own explanation—the biggest layer.

- Trust in your own words, your own expressions, and your own ideas. Your own interpretations, after all, have created your claim and have come only after you have immersed yourself in—and become an expert on—your topic.
- Blend your own thinking and expression with that of others, making others' ideas fit your way of writing them. Use the ellipsis and bracket to integrate smoothly.

Striking a balance enables you to create an original project or essay instead of writing a report that merely lists what others have said.

E. Citing Sources

To use any of your sources through quoting, paraphrasing, or summarizing, as you have already learned, to avoid plagiarizing, you must cite them properly. As you discovered in Chapter 3, several formats for listing the particulars of a source exist. Those same formats remain for citing within your project's or essay's text. *Only listing the sources at the end of the project or essay does not suffice; you must also cite particular material* acquired from sources and used within the body of the project or essay.

Just as formatting differences occur in creating your list of sources, so too do they exist in in-text citations. In this book, for example, you have seen three different formats used: MLA in-text citation for almost all included examples and models, APA in-text citations for one of the traditional research essay models at the end of this chapter, and Chicago Manual of Style in-text citations (actually footnotes) in the introduction to this book. In general, MLA and APA use parenthetical in-text citations and employ footnotes or endnotes only when explaining something additional about a cited passage or when referring to additional sources on the topic of the cited information. Chicago Manual of Style, however, uses footnotes for all three types.

Regardless of these slight differences, *all* in-text citations follow some general rules.

1. Borrowed material of a specified number of lines (four in MLA) or words (forty in APA; one hundred in Chicago) will remain in the regular text of the project or essay.

2. Borrowed material beyond that specified number of lines or words will use a block citation: indenting the passage ten spaces on the left side and eliminating quotation marks unless using a quote within a quote.

3. The citation follows the information from the source.

4. The citation is in parentheses (MLA and APA) or in a superscript (raised) number (Chicago).

5. The citation uses whatever appears first in the source list for that source (usually the author's last name, or, if no author exists, the title of the article).

6. The specific page number(s) from which the information comes is included, if the source has page numbers.

7. Each specific format uses its own sequence of inclusions and its own style of punctuation, so always see the rules of MLA or APA in the Appendices of this book, or a Chicago Manual of Style book to make certain you follow those rules.

Once you have applied the basic rules for any one of these formats, you will possess the knowledge necessary to use any other format by simply shifting the sequences and punctuation. Your project or essay pages will look something like the following example. (See the full essay models at the end of this chapter for additional examples.)

If we did so, then we might change our solution to the problem from a punishment approach to a rehabilitation approach. Some, like prosecutor John Stalwart claim that "Trying to rehabilitate drug addicts and pushers is a losing, expensive proposition" (qtd. Valdez and Shank 82), but others, like psychiatrist Dr. James Bertrandt contend that when rehabilitation is individualized by patient and drug, even if the patient requires more than one attempt, that treatment saves money compared to jail time costs (Gazal-Ayal 83). While in the most recent year, Congress and the President have addressed decreasing minimum sentences and releasing some prisoners who have already served more than ten years for drug crimes, so far, no one has really discussed eliminating the sentences entirely and replacing them with mandatory drug rehabilitation instead. Yet, no fewer than eight other industrialized nations use such an approach successfully. All across Europe, for example, instead of building and filling new prisons with non-violent drug abusers who sell drugs to sustain their own habits, these nations mandate treatment in government-run drug rehabilitation facilities.

> Their success rate is approximately 80%. [In these nations, the cost of drug rehabilitation], even for those who have to repeat treatment twice, over a 2–3 year period, is 60% lower than the cost of incarcerating them, and they come out productive, whole citizens ready to contribute to the country. (Gazal-Ayal 84)

Is the United States so different from these countries that such an effort would not succeed here, too? I propose that we at least try this approach before we keep forcing judges to impose mandatory prison sentences. ETC.

This citation cites another speaker, so it uses "qtd." and the source. It is 4 or fewer lines long, so it stays in the regular text of the essay.

This citation paraphrases a scholar. It is 4 or fewer lines long, so it stays in the regular text of the essay.

This citation is a block citation because it uses more than 4 lines of cited text.

CHAPTER 4

F. Targeting a Purpose and an Audience

Deciding what exactly to write and how to approach that writing hinges on two key concepts: *purpose* and *audience*. While all of you write to fulfill a class assignment for your professor, you also actually can and should decide upon a specific purpose and targeted audience that suits your particular research topic and question.

Your *purpose* answers the questions, "Why do I write this project/essay? What do I hope to accomplish with it?" Answers to those questions might include:

- To inform my reader
- To persuade others to agree with my point or to take a specific action
- To explain something to my reader
- To explore an idea and its nuances
- To report on or record something
- To entertain my reader
- To express my thoughts and emotions
- To demonstrate my knowledge.

Often, writers combine these purposes; they do not always remain exclusive. Yet, every writer, including you, should focus on one primary purpose, and organize the project or essay in the most effective way possible to attain that goal.

© Gustavo Frazao/Shutterstock.com

The purpose of a project or essay will to some extent determine its emphasis, its inclusions and exclusions, its sequence, and its angle or approach.

For example, if you wanted to compose a research project or essay about antibiotics in our food, you might decide you want to educate or inform the public. In this case, you would emphasize how the antibiotics get into our food and what effects they have on the food and on us. But suppose instead, you wanted to advocate against their use? Then you might emphasize their impact on the treatment of our own diseases and on the resulting cost to health care. If, however, you chose primarily to entertain, you might complete a comparative study of former, scrawny food of the 1980s to the plump and robust food available today, and you might use a great many graphics. As you can see, purpose makes a great deal of difference to your writing choices.

Equally important, you must consider *audience*. Whom do you wish to address or at whom do you aim your project or essay? This choice, too, will direct your writing.

When you ponder your audience, you should consider several factors.

- What specific age, race, ethnicity, gender, socioeconomic class, ability, etc., does your target audience have?
- What specific interests does your target audience share?
- What kind of educational or experiential background does your audience have?
- What particular attitudes, biases, or opinions about political matters does your audience possess?
- What kind of language (formal, jargon-filled, etc.) and language level would most appeal to and be understood by your audience?
- What expectations will your chosen audience have?

Just as purpose will influence your project's or essay's emphasis and approach, so too will your audience. For example, if you were to create a discussion of mandatory sentencing for an audience of teenagers living in a drug-saturated environment, your approach would vary considerably from one on the same topic for a group of legislators considering amending those sentencing laws.

G. Acknowledging What Remains to Discover

In any given academic dialogue, gaps always exist. Sometimes, you will discover the missing research relates exactly to the very question you have attempted to answer. At other times, you will find the need for additional research concerns topics tangential to your claim. And sometimes, your own research will uncover a whole new realm of research scholars should address.

Whichever of these situations applies to you and your topic, the conclusion of your research project or essay should discuss it. You will identify the gap and explain why you think additional research in that area matters. No predictable pattern for this discussion stands out; it may require a full paragraph or only a few sentences. Think of this part of your project or essay as a recommendation for where the conversation should go next. Like everything else in your project or essay, this recommendation will stem logically from the evidence you have already gathered.

H. Choosing a Delivery Genre, Part A: I-Search Essay or Traditional Research Essay

The delivery of your research and conclusions about that research can utilize several research genre formats, all depending upon what your course requires. The three most commonly used research genres include:

- The I-Search Essay, designed by Ken Macrorie: a documented essay using narrative form to tell the story of your research journey and the conclusions you reach (the argument you make based on that journey)
- The Traditional Research Essay: a formal documented essay that presents research as an argument, exploration, or informative piece
- The Multimedia Project: a piece that can take many forms but uses media to convey a documented argument, exploration, or informative report (PowerPoint, poster, social media, web site, advertisement, etc.)

Not one of these research genres has greater value than the other; rather, each one merely takes a different approach to presenting the research and conclusions. All require the same diligence regarding claims, evidence, documentation, synthesis, focus, and organization. Sometimes, you will choose which genre to use, but most often, the course professor or venue (conference, scholarly publication, class presentation, etc.) will select for you.

A COMPARATIVE CHART OF THE THREE PRIMARY RESEARCH GENRES			
CATEGORY	**I-SEARCH ESSAY**	**TRADITIONAL RESEARCH ESSAY**	**MULTIMEDIA PRESENTATION**
Definition	A documented essay using narrative form to tell the story of your research journey and the conclusions you reach (the argument you make based on that journey)	A formal, documented essay that presents research as an argument, exploration, or informative piece	A piece that can take many forms but uses media to convey a documented argument, exploration, or informative report
Inclusions/ Elements	• Title • Introduction of the topic and research question and their personal and other significance • Description of what you knew, assumed, or imagined before your research • Discussion of what you discovered [context of other dialogues] • Reflection on what you found/conclusions/claim • Discussion of what remains to be discovered	• Title • Introduction with research topic, question, and personal and other significance as well as your claim • Discussion of other research context and your responses to it • Conclusion • Discussion of what remains to be researched	• Title • Graphics • Claim • Support for claim
Documentation	• In-text citations • Works Cited/References/ Bibliography	• In-text citations • Works Cited/References/ Bibliography	*In-text citations *Works Cited/References/ Bibliography including for the graphics
Style	Personal and reflective; formal but less formal than the traditional essay	Very formal, but still uses first-person pronouns • Specific disciplines require specific formats (e.g., Science requires sections and subtitles for Purpose, Method, Procedure, Conclusion, etc.)	Varied by medium—includes PowerPoint, web page, poster, video, radio address, social media post, advertisement, etc.

THE I-SEARCH RESEARCH ESSAY

1,750 words (5–6 pages)

In a formal, fully-documented MLA 8-style essay, tell the story of your research project. Describe what you found, and how your perspective evolved.

Write your essay in narrative form, recording the steps of the discovery process. Do not feel obligated to tell everything, but highlight the findings and happenings that were crucial to your hunt and contributed to your understanding of the topic. Organize your essay into the following sections:

1. **What I Knew, Assumed, or Imagined.** Describe your prior knowledge and understanding of the topic and question, before you began the project. Yes, you may adapt this section from your Proposal.

2. **What I Discovered.** Describe the information and ideas you gathered. Organize this section as a chronological narrative (like a story) recording the steps of the discovery process. Don't share every detail; instead, highlight key findings and happenings, the ones that really impacted your perspective. Feel free to include missteps and mistakes you may have made along the way.

3. **Reflections**. Reflect on what you found and draw some conclusions. Compare what you thought you knew, assumed, or imagined with what you actually discovered. Discuss what you still hope to learn about this topic/question, and reflect on how you might further share or act on what you have learned.

While your essay should be personal and reflective, it should be crafted for readers both real (me, your instructor) and imagined (others interested in your topic, but who may lack your newfound expertise—your targeted audience.). This consideration means you'll need to write clearly and engagingly, explain ideas and information thoroughly, and of course document everything.

Rubric

When evaluating your essay, I will ask the following questions.

Focus	Does the writer remain focused on a specific topic and question?
Summary	Does the writer summarize sources clearly, accurately, and thoroughly?
Evaluation	Does the writer present evaluations of source credibility and reliability?
Synthesis	Does the writer discuss connections and disconnections among multiple sources?
Organization	Does the writer organize ideas effectively? Does the writer use paragraphing, topic sentences, transitions?
Reflection	Does the writer show how her thinking has evolved, explaining how she thought at the beginning of the project, and how that thinking changed as they researched and wrote?
Documentation	Does the writer use correct MLA signal phrases, in-text citations, and Works Cited page?
Correctness	Does the writer avoid errors that confuse or distract?

This prompt was adapted from Olson, Carol Booth. "A Sample Prompt, Scoring Guide, and Model Paper for the I-Search." *Practical Ideas for Teaching Writing as a Process.* Diane Publishing, 1996.

OR TRADITIONAL RESEARCH ARTICLE ESSAY DIRECTIONS

1,750 words (5–6 pages)

Context: You have engaged in a process of exploration and discovery of your research topic. You began with a proposal in which you posed a question that was meaningful to you. Your annotated bibliography discussed various ideas from an array of sources and opinions. You are now ready for the "culminating event," to write an article in which you will discuss your research, draw conclusions, and offer a persuasive argument.

What is a Research Article? A research article discusses the results of original research and contributes something new to the body of knowledge in a given area. Your goal in writing a research article is to express an informed argument or thesis and to try to persuade the reader to care about your findings and to accept your conclusions about your original question.

(How) and Why Write a Research Article? Craft this persuasive article for a general audience, an audience who might be interested in this particular topic, but lacks your expertise. In other words, pitch the article to someone like me, or like your classmates.

Your role as a researcher is to deepen others' understanding of an issue, problem, or question, while also offering your own original perspective. Present yourself as an expert who can educate your audience on this topic. After all, you have been researching and writing about this topic for many weeks now, so you are a legitimate local expert.

What are the Components of a Research Article? In terms of its format, your article should include:

- a title
- a body in which you present your research and conclusions:
  - ► an original claim supported by reasoning and evidence
  - ► discussions of how your claim responds to the research you have done
  - ► some reflection on what remains to be researched relative to this question
- a Works Cited page in MLA style (or, if you prefer, some other formal documentation style)

CHAPTER 4

Rubric for Either Version

CRITERIA	EXCEEDS STANDARDS (A TO B+)	MEETS STANDARDS (B TO C)	APPROACHES STANDARDS (D)	DOES NOT MEET STANDARDS (F)
Focus Writer identifies a focused and manageable topic and research question or problem. Writer has a clear, thoughtful, and substantive claim in response to the research question or problem. Writer places the claim and its significance within the context of the broader conversation going on about the topic.				
Organization of Argument and Evidence Writer builds a logical and clearly organized argument in support of the claim. Topic sentences unify paragraphs. Transitions clearly indicate relationships between ideas. Evidence, including quotations, is effectively introduced, explained, and contextualized.				

CRITERIA	EXCEEDS STANDARDS (A TO B+)	MEETS STANDARDS (B TO C)	APPROACHES STANDARDS (D)	DOES NOT MEET STANDARDS (F)
Analysis of Research Writer gathers numerous, varied, and reliable sources to develop evidence in support of a claim. Writer applies source information that advances the claim. Writer effectively summarizes, paraphrases, and quotes from research materials. Writer effectively acknowledges multiple perspectives on a claim, including potential objections to the claim. Writer shows awareness of interrelationships among sources.				
Documentation Writer attributes evidence to sources using MLA documentation style, including in-text citations and a Works Cited list.				
Revision Writer's work demonstrates revision for clarity, organization, and depth of thought.* (*When based on comparison of rubric scores for final version vs. initial draft)				
Editing Writer effectively edits the essay; the writing does not confuse or distract.				

I.   Outlining the Research Essay

By now, you have read all of your sources and have decided what you want to use from each one. You have created your claim. Perhaps at this point, you are wondering what to do with all of this information.

You can start by organizing it. You will defend your claim by making various subclaims and using the information that applies to those subtopics, so creating a *tentative outline* will help you. This outline, like all other writing, may ultimately change as you complete the actual writing process, but starting with something concrete that can be altered still offers advantages.

- An outline aids you in assessing and thinking about or rethinking all the information you have gathered.
- An outline allows you to give some kind of order to all of your information without committing you to whole paragraphs you might later delete.
- An outline allows you to see clearly and easily what you might decide not to use or might choose to move around because it does not fit well.
- An outline helps you to see easily if you have enough evidence to support your claim.
- An outline gives you something to start with before you confront the blank page.

*Some students actually create two outlines, one before they start researching, so they have a guide regarding what they seek, and one after they have discovered what information they could actually find.

© iQoncept/Shutterstock.com

Think of your outline as your plan of attack. You have a clear claim, so now ask yourself:

1. How will I defend that claim?
   a. What evidence must I use?
   b. What context must I provide?
   c. What explanations must I offer?
   d. What essential opposing positions must I address?
2. What order or sequence will best suit my argument?
   a. What pieces build on other pieces, so must come after or before something else?
   b. What will make logical sense for readers unfamiliar with my topic?
3. Do my topic and claim most easily lend themselves to a particular organizational strategy or approach? To answer this question, think about your purpose and evidence. You might use any one of the following strategies.
   a. Chronological or Reverse Chronological Style: Use a time-ordered sequence, either from oldest to newest or newest to oldest.
   b. Refutation Style: Argue your position against a standard and widely accepted opposing position.
   c. Difference/Comparison and Contrast Style: Argue in comparison or contrast to others' claims.
   d. Process Style: Argue with a step-by-step process. (Common in scientific papers)
   e. Cycle Style: Argue by starting in one place you ultimately intend to circle back to by the end of the essay or project.
   f. Classification Style: Argue by placing like groups of ideas or subjects together.
   g. Deductive Reasoning Style: Argue by building point A, which leads to point B, which leads to point C, etc.
4. Do I have information in which I have interest but does not truly fit with my claim?

Once you have answered all of these questions, you can begin constructing your outline.

Some people believe every outline must follow a very even pattern: for every A, a B must exist, etc. Often, however, that paradigm does not work for every topic. Rather, you should simply develop each category as appropriate for your topic.

An outline may use single words, short phrases, or full sentences, but not full paragraphs. It consists of headings and subheadings, and each of the subheadings may include additional headings for the kind of details you will include. Often, each of these categories may represent what will become a specific, fully developed paragraph in your essay or project. Sometimes, assignment directions even determine the basic structure of your outline because they dictate the content sections you must include in the essay or project.

Your research outline will generally note what information from sources you might use, but it generally will not include your explanations of that information, though some students do include a notation such as, "Explanation here" to remind themselves to include that content.

Every outline will begin with an Introduction section. Even in this section, you must make some decisions.

- Do you want a one-paragraph or two-paragraph introduction?
- Do you want your claim stated immediately?

- How much context, and what specific context, do you want to include in the opening?
- What kind of lead or hook do you want to use to pull your reader immediately into your project or essay: a question, a startling statistic, an anecdote, something else?

Once you have outlined your introduction, you will continue to outline what will become the body of the project or essay. No required number of sections exists, as each project or essay is unique. You will bear in mind your answers to those initial four questions you asked yourself at the beginning of this section about outlining your research essay, and you'll keep in mind the length requirements of the assignment. Then you will create your headings, subheadings, and sequence accordingly. Every outline of a research essay or project will end with a conclusion heading and the Works Cited/References/Bibliography heading.

An outline serves as a guide, not as a monument. It may shift as you write because in the process of writing, you may discover slight alterations in sequence or additions or deletions to content become necessary. No outline is ever final until the project or essay is complete.

MODEL OUTLINE FOR TRADITIONAL RESEARCH ESSAY

I. Introduction

    A. Hook: Two Questions

        1. Who among us has not spent an afternoon or evening—and a lot of money—at the mall?

        2. Who among us has not needed at least once in awhile to see and examine what we buy instead of just shopping online?

    B. Foregrounding/Positioning Statement:

        1. Number of malls and acreage—See Turco page 344.

        2. When mall arrived and why—See Lenox page 2.

    C. Thesis Statement/Claim:

        1. Question: Is the mall, like society, stratified according to socioeconomic class, race, ethnicity, etc.?

        2. Answer: I contend that malls do indeed represent a microcosm of society: most are built for rich and mostly white people.

II. General Reason 1: **Placement of Malls**

    A. Supporting Evidence

        1. Detail of Evidence—Kind of Neighborhoods built in—See Turco page 340.

        2. My explanation

        3. Detail of Evidence—Examples of places where biggest malls are—Jetison statistics and graphs

        4. My explanation

III. General Reason 2: **Types of Stores in Malls**

    A.   Supporting Evidence

        1.   Detail of Evidence—Costs of products in malls—See Turco page 339

        2.   My explanation

        3.   Detail of Evidence—Signature store types—See Jetison

        4.   My explanation

IV. General Reason 3: **Reach/Access to Malls**

    A.   Supporting Evidence

        1.   Detail of Evidence—Necessity of car ownership and malls—See Salinger pages 34–36

        2.   My explanation

        3.   Detail of Evidence—How to get to the large acreage, where exits are, etc.—See Turco and Salinger

        4.   My explanation

V. General Reason 4: **Clothing and the Models/Window Displays**

    A.   Supporting Evidence

        1.   Detail of Evidence—Types of models used by percentage—See Jetison page 67

        2.   My explanation

        3.   Detail of Evidence—Clothing styles and chic couture—See Turco page 330

        4.   My explanation

VI. Opposing Arguments

    A.   What the opposition says: Free access to all—See Falcon page 33

    B.   Counterargument: Preventative costs, locations, and styles

VII. Conclusion

    A.   Concluding statements: Reiteration of claim points

    B.   What research remains to be done:

        1.   Can malls succeed in other kinds of places?

        2.   How to create equality in shopping opportunities

VIII. Works Cited

Sample Outline Template for I-Search Essay

I. Introduction

    A. Hook:

    B. Foregrounding/Positioning Statement:

    C. Claim:

II. What I Knew, Assumed, or Imagined:

    A. Idea 1: _____

        1. Detail of Evidence:

        2. My Explanation/Comments:

        3. Detail of Evidence:

        4. My Explanation/Comments:

    B. Idea 2: _____

        1. Detail of Evidence:

        2. My Explanation/Comments:

        3. Detail of Evidence:

        4. My Explanation/Comments:

    C. Idea 3: _____

        1. Detail of Evidence:

        2. My Explanation/Comments:

        3. Detail of Evidence:

        4. My Explanation/Comments:

III. What I discovered

    A. Idea 1 (Perhaps from source 1): _____

        1. Detail of Evidence:

        2. Detail of Evidence:

        3. Explanation and My Reaction:

      B.   Idea 2 (Perhaps from source 2): _____

          1.   Detail of Evidence:

          2.   Detail of Evidence:

          3.   Explanation and My Reaction:

      C.   Idea 3 (Perhaps from source 3): _____

          1.   Detail of Evidence:

          2.   Detail of Evidence:

          3.   Explanation and My Reaction:

      D.   Idea 4 (Perhaps from source 4): _____

          1.   Detail of Evidence:

          2.   Detail of Evidence:

          3.   Explanation and My Reaction:

      E.   Idea 5 (Perhaps from source 5): _____

          1.   Detail of Evidence:

          2.   Detail of Evidence:

          3.   Explanation and My Reaction:

      F.   Idea 6 (Perhaps from source 6 and perhaps an opposing argument): _____

          1.   Detail of Evidence:

          2.   Detail of Evidence—Counterargument:

          3.   Explanation and My Reaction:

IV.   Reflections (Or What I Learned and What Conclusions I Have Drawn):

      A.   Idea 1: _____

          1.   Detail of Evidence:

          2.   Detail of Evidence:

      B.   Idea 2: _____

          1.   Detail of Evidence:

          2.   My Explanation/Comments:

            3.   Detail of Evidence:

            4.   My Explanation/Comments:

      C.   Idea 3: _____

            1.   Detail of Evidence:

            2.   My Explanation/Comments:

            3.   Detail of Evidence:

            4.   My Explanation/Comments:

      D.   What Future Researchers Still Need To Do
            1.

            2.

V.   Works Cited

Once you have made your outline, you can:

1.   Go back to your notes, or to the highlighting you have done on your printed electronic sources.

2.   Label each note card or highlighted area according to your outline. (Assign a number and/or letter.). Where does this information belong? In what section of your outline will it fit best?

3.   If you have used note cards, start laying them out in the order you will use them, based on the labels you just gave them. If you have highlighted sections of printed pages, then cut them into squares or rectangles, and start laying them out in the order you will use them based on the labels you just gave them. (Do not hesitate to exclude some.)

4.   If you have not already done so in your reading and note-taking process, start writing "Idea Notes," in which you will write your own ideas and explanations to go with your notes or highlighted sections.

5.   Insert these idea notes in the appropriate places among the other notes you have laid out.

In using this process, you are actually creating a kind of very rough draft.

J. Drafting the Research Essay

© Houbaczech/Shutterstock.com

Now that you have decided upon your claim, your purpose, your audience, and your format, and you have created an outline into which you have fed your notes and ideas, you are ready to begin writing your first draft of the project or essay.

Remember what you learned in Chapter 1: a draft will never be perfect; rather, it serves as your initial attempt at composing your project or essay. Just write, without censoring yourself.

Start by reexamining the parameters of the assignment. Does it direct you to include any specific elements? Does it require a predetermined number of words or pages? Does it require a specific format for citations and your list of sources?

Because research projects and essays tend to include more pages than class essays, some students like to write the piece in parts, in any order, and then later put those parts together. Other students find working straight down their outlines useful. Still other students like to write all of their own thinking parts first and then insert their research afterward.

Because in this course you have completed scaffolded assignments, you should feel free to use some of the writing you have already created. For example, your proposal and overview for the annotated bibliography already contain some words regarding your topic and research question, context, and significance, so why not use some of them in your draft? Your annotated bibliography already discusses the contributions of some scholars engaged in the dialogue and some points of your agreement and disagreement, so why not include some of those words in your draft too?

Once you have composed that draft, you will benefit from peer feedback.

IN-CLASS ACTIVITY 4D: PEER REVIEW 1 I-SEARCH ESSAY/TRADITIONAL RESEARCH ESSAY—ROUND-ROBIN

Directions:

1. Get into groups of THREE.

2. Do **not** allow anyone into your group who does not have A HARD COPY of the research essay draft.

3. Swap your draft/essay beginning material with one other person in the group.

4. Attach this sheet to that draft, and record the author's name in the space provided on this sheet.

5. The person who gets the draft will examine it for #1 criteria and sign his/her name on the line adjacent to #1. (See below #1: Progress directions, and follow them exactly and completely.)

6. When you have all finished the examination of your peer's essay for #1 criteria, swap the drafts again.

7. This time, the person who gets the draft will examine it for #2 criteria and sign his/her name on the line adjacent to #2. (See below #2: Evidence directions, and follow them exactly and completely.)

8. When you have all finished the examination of your peer's essay for #2 criteria, swap the drafts again.

9. This time, the person who gets the draft will examine it for #3 criteria and sign his/her name on the line adjacent to #3. (See below #3: Editing directions, and follow them exactly and completely.)

10. When you have finished the examination of your peer's essay for #3 criteria, then return each draft to its author.

11. Authors: Read through the comments your peers have made. If you have questions about them, ask your peer.

12. Authors, now complete the answers to the questions about your plan for completion and revision.

#1 _____ for (author) _____

#2 _____

#3 _____

[ONLINE STUDENTS: You have a choice; you may do all three evaluations on one student's essay, or you may do each of the three evaluations on three different students' essays—as long as that particular evaluation type has not yet been done on that student's essay.]

#1: PROGRESS

1. Read through the draft entirely, without doing anything to it; just read it.
2. Read through the draft again. This time, <u>highlight and identify/label</u> what you think is the writer's:
   a. Hook
   b. Claim
   c. Follow-up statement/what will be discussed in the rest of the essay.
   d. IF you find any or all of these elements missing or in some way weak, note that point/those points on the partial draft. If, on the other hand, you find them strong, note that fact on the draft.
3. In looking over the partial draft, think about how much progress toward the completion of this five-to-six-page essay the writer has made. On a scale of 1–10 (1 meaning low and 10 meaning high), how would you rank this writer's progress? _____ EXPLAIN WHY you give it that ranking. _____

   _____

4. Does the writer position him/herself within a scholarly conversation as a contributor with his/her own idea?   YES   NO   EXPLAIN your response. _____

   _____

   _____

5. Do you believe this draft sets a reasonable and thorough plan in motion?
   YES   NO

   EXPLAIN WHY _____

   _____

#2: EVIDENCE

1. Read through the draft entirely, without doing anything to it; just read it.
2. Read through the draft again. This time, locate the claim highlighted and labeled in this draft.
3. Now <u>locate, underline, and label</u> supporting evidence for this claim. Label the evidence by type: Example (EX), Scholarly Support (SS), Data (D), Refutation of Opposing Point (ORP), Does Not Apply/Illogical Support (DNA), Just a Restatement (HRS). (You might see all of these possibilities or only some of them.)
4. Do you think the writer offers an equal, balanced blend of these types of evidence?   YES   NO   EXPLAIN WHY. _____

   _____

5. Do you think this writer offers sufficient support for the claim, including addressing the opposition?   YES   NO   EXPLAIN WHY. _____

   _____

6. What, if anything, does the writer need to add? _____

   _____

#3: EDITING

1. Read through the draft entirely, without doing anything to it; just read it.

2. Read through the draft again. This time, circle errors in <u>sentence structure, word choice, subject–verb agreement, pronoun use, MLA citations</u>, etc. LABEL the errors, but do not correct them. Note any sentences you do not clearly understand because the prose is muddy.

3. What does this writer need to pay the most attention to correcting? _____
   _____
   _____

WRITER'S REFLECTION AND PLAN FOR COMPLETION AND REVISION:

1. Examine what your peers have noted about your draft both on the draft and on the filled-in sections of page 2 of this activity.

2. Ask your peers for clarification of anything you do not quite understand about their comments.

3. Make your own notations/reminders on your draft.

4. Record here a step-by-step, concrete plan of the actions you will take in creating your FULLY REVISED, FINAL draft of this essay. What must you add? What must you delete? What order should you follow or maintain? What else should you revise? Do you need to attend to any editing? [You may use what you write here for part of journal entry 11.]

JOURNAL ENTRY 11

Reflection on Peer Review of Draft 1 of I-Search Essay/Traditional Research Essay
Reflect on what you learned from your peer review session.

1. Explain what you learned from the feedback others gave you on your draft.
2. Explain what you learned from reading your peers' drafts.

Write a three-step plan of action for your revision of your first draft. What three <u>specific</u> changes—additions, deletions, changes in sequence, etc.—will you make to improve the draft before the next peer review? Why will you make these alterations? What <u>specific</u> effect do you hope they will have?

K. Revising the Research Essay

Your research project or essay has many parts, so revising it will require a directed approach. Of course, you should bear in mind the feedback your peers offered; your revisions serve as your way of talking back to that peer dialogue.

In revising, you should pay attention to seven key areas. Systematically review them by asking questions of yourself and making necessary changes based on your answers.

- ▶ Step 1: Review your essay's *organization*.
  - Have I chosen a clear organizational plan, and is that choice evident and consistent in the essay?
  - Does my claim appear in a place that makes logical sense and fits with the organization method I have chosen?
  - Do the ideas I have included have a logical sequence that helps the reader make sense of my points?
  - Does each paragraph contain some type of topic sentence or main idea that serves as an umbrella for the paragraph that follows?
  - Do I include enough details to support what I say in each paragraph?
  - Do I have a clear introduction?
  - Do I have a clear conclusion?

- ▶ Step 2: Review your essay's *unity*.
  - Does each of my paragraphs relate to my overall topic and claim? Do I make that connection clear and explicit?
  - Have I synthesized my research smoothly by employing the layer-cake framework effectively?
  - Do I avoid using the same research to make a different point?
  - Have I used effective transitions into new paragraphs and ideas?
  - Do my conclusions fit with the arguments of the rest of the essay?

- ▶ Step 3: Review your essay's *balance*.
  - Does my own claim drive every aspect of the essay?
  - Have I used an equal amount or more of my own thinking compared to the amount of research I have used?

- ▶ Step 4: Review your essay's *word choices*.
  - Have I used any vague, imprecise terms I should avoid?
  - Have I used strong verbs instead of a preponderance of weak to be verbs (am, is, are, was, were, be, being, been) or linking verbs (seem, appear)?
  - Have I avoided the use of any loaded words that demonstrate clear bias?
  - Have I avoided the use of gender and other bias in my word choices?
  - Have I avoided using repetitive words, phrases, and introductions to source materials?
  - Have I avoided using slang, colloquialisms, and clichés?
  - Have I explained unclear terms related to a discipline or organization?

- ▶ Step 5: Review your essay's *style, tone, and voice*.
  - Do I use a variety of sentence structures and lengths?
  - Do I avoid wordiness and awkward structures?
  - Have I remained consistent in my choice of persona?
  - Have I used clear, straight-forward language?
  - Have I maintained a balanced and unbiased approach?

- ▶ Step 6: Review your essay's *documentation*.
  - Have I used ONE documentation format (MLA or APA or Chicago Manual of Style or other), or have I used a mixture of formats?
  - Have I included a complete Works Cited/References/Bibliography?
  - Have I cited every piece of information taken from an outside source?
  - Does every in-text citation have a corresponding entry in my Works Cited/References/Bibliography list?
  - Does every in-text citation (or footnote) include the required information?
  - Have I used any block citations, and if so, have I done them correctly?
  - Does my source list indent the second and subsequent line of each entry?
  - Have I organized my source list alphabetically?
  - Have I followed every rule of the chosen formatting precisely?

- ▶ Step 7: *Editing*: Review your essay's *grammar and mechanics*.
  - Does my essay have any errors in spelling or punctuation?
  - Does my essay have any errors in sentence structure, subject–verb agreement, or pronoun–antecedent agreement?

Now that you have completed your revision of your project or essay draft, once again, you can turn to your peers to get their feedback.

IN-CLASS ACTIVITY 4E:
PEER REVIEW OF DRAFT 2 I-SEARCH/TRADITIONAL RESEARCH ESSAY

FIRST READ AND Annotate (use highlighting/bolding/underlining and written comments) the ENTIRE text.

<u>Then</u> fill in this sheet. As you answer EACH question, go through the draft to look specifically for each item discussed; don't merely dash off an answer without actually rereading the essay for the specific element the question addresses.

1. FIRST: Highlight ALL material (quoted, paraphrased, summarized) that is <u>cited</u>.

   What percentage of the argument is cited? _____

   What percentage is the writer's own commentary? _____

   Do you see a BALANCE?   YES   NO

   If "No," what do you see that must change? Explain. _____

   _____

2. Does the essay make an actual argument: support/argue for <u>a very specific claim</u>/thesis/ premise?   YES   NO

   If "No," what do you see that must change? Explain. _____

   _____

3. Does the essay USE the research as part of the supporting argument instead of just reporting on/listing the research?   YES   NO

   If "No," what do you see that must change? Explain. _____

   _____

4. When the writer uses the research, does he/she start by telling us what others say, AND does he/she remind the reader about what others say at various points throughout the text?   YES   NO

   If "No," describe what the essay has failed to address. _____

   _____

   _____

5. In discussing what others say/using the research, does the writer use a *combination* of summary, paraphrase, and direct quotations?   YES   NO

   If "No," describe what the essay has failed to address. _____

   _____

   _____

6. Does the writer document this information correctly in the text <u>and</u> in the Works Cited? YES   NO

    If "No," describe what the essay has failed to address. _____

    _____

    _____

7. Has the writer presented <u>**sufficient**</u> evidence/reasons to support the argument?   YES   NO

    If "No," describe what the essay needs to improve. _____

    _____

    _____

8. Does the writer present a voice and so distinguish what HE/SHE says from what others say/the research?   YES   NO

9. Does the writer segue smoothly from the research to his/her own view?   YES   NO

    If "No," describe what the essay needs to improve. _____

    _____

    _____

10. Has the writer acknowledged likely objections to the argument and responded to them persuasively (refutation)?   YES   NO

    If "No," describe what the essay has failed to address. _____

    _____

    _____

11. Does the writer use comments to clarify/give explanations of the quoted material? YES   NO

    If "No," describe what the essay has failed to address. _____

    _____

    _____

12. Does the title for the essay suit the essay written?   YES   NO

    EXPLAIN the rationale for saying so. _____

    _____

    _____

13. Does the writer unify the essay with smooth transitions/connections from one point to another and from one paragraph to another?   YES   NO

If "No," describe what the essay needs to improve. _____

_____

_____

14. Does the writer use strong language (as opposed to an overabundance of weak to be verbs [am, is, are, was, were, be, being, been] and clichés, etc.) and techniques, which compel the reader to read the argument/keep the reader interested?   YES   NO

If "No," describe what the essay needs to improve. _____

_____

_____

15. Does the writer adhere to language conventions—proper sentence structure, subject–verb agreement, pronoun–antecedent agreement, tenses, rules of MLA citation, and Works Cited, etc.?   YES   NO

If "No," list the areas in which the author needs to improve. _____

_____

_____

16. Fill in this evaluation rubric WITH explanations for each of the columns you have checked. Then return these sheets to the author.

CRITERIA	EXCEEDS STANDARDS (A TO B+)	MEETS STANDARDS (B TO C)	APPROACHES STANDARDS (D)	DOES NOT MEET STANDARDS (F)
Focus Writer identifies a focused and manageable topic and research question or problem. Writer has a clear, thoughtful, and substantive claim in response to the research question or problem. Writer places the claim and its significance within the context of the broader conversation going on about the topic.				

CRITERIA	EXCEEDS STANDARDS (A TO B+)	MEETS STANDARDS (B TO C)	APPROACHES STANDARDS (D)	DOES NOT MEET STANDARDS (F)
Organization of Argument and Evidence Writer builds a logical and clearly organized argument in support of the claim. Topic sentences unify paragraphs. Transitions clearly indicate relationships between ideas. Evidence, including quotations, is effectively introduced, explained, and contextualized.				
Analysis of Research Writer gathers numerous, varied, and reliable sources to develop evidence in support of a claim. Writer applies source information that advances the claim. Writer effectively summarizes, paraphrases, and quotes from research materials. Writer effectively acknowledges multiple perspectives on a claim, including potential objections to the claim. Writer shows awareness of interrelationships among sources.				
Documentation Writer attributes evidence to sources using MLA documentation style, including in-text citations and a Works Cited list.				

L. Choosing a Delivery Genre, Part B: Outreach Project: Pamphlets, Letters to Editors, Speeches, Social Media Posts, etc.

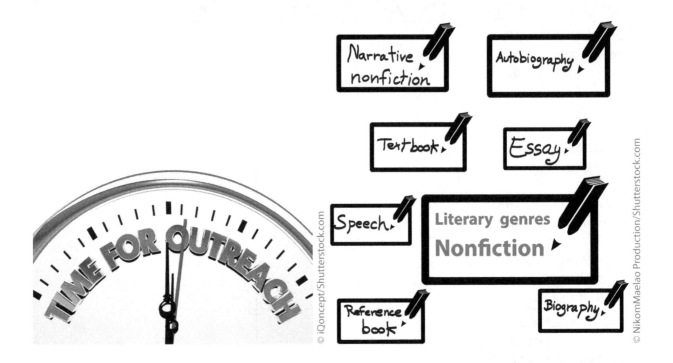

In academia, perhaps the most common use of research does indeed embrace some kind of research essay, but outside the world of academia, research can be used in other nonfiction genres too. Now that you have completed your academic research project or essay, you can share it with others outside that academic community. Do you remember the targeted purpose and audience you chose for the project/essay? Now think about them again; even change them if you want to do so for this use of your research. Maybe you want to think about those to whom you said your topic held significance.

For this use of your research, you will select from among several different genres other than the academic research essay. You will still have to add to the conversation surrounding your claim, but this time you will use a different delivery tool. You have familiarity with all of these tools—genres—though you may not even realize you do. On a daily basis, you have exposure to these kinds of texts, the most common among them the following.

COMMON NONFICTION GENRES

- Biography—the [factual] story of a person's life or part of a person's life [if told by the self about the self = an autobiography]

- [Nonacademic] Essay (including letters to the editor and blogs and letters to businesses and government officials)—brief composition that makes an argument about the writer's point of view and usually uses some examples and evidence

- Manuals (Owner's Manual, Instruction Manual, User's Guide, Repair Manual, etc.)—a pamphlet, book, or booklet that outlines how to use, operate, repair, etc., an object purchased from a company

- Lab Report—a report on the hypothesis, method, procedure, and results of a controlled experiment

- Memoir—a sub-genre of autobiography; the [factual] narrative of all or part of a person's own life, focused on a particular theme, relationship, series of events, etc.

- News Article—a report of current events or events about to happen

- Personal Narrative—a sub-genre of autobiography, but shorter than the autobiography or memoir; a first-person, factual account of a particular event in an individual's life

- Pamphlet (including brochures and leaflets)—a concise, small, unbound (often folded or tri-fold) booklet that conveys information on one narrow subject and sometimes advocates a particular position or the purchase of a particular product

- Reference Book—a text designed to summarize specific information; includes such books as an almanac, atlas, encyclopedia, dictionary, etc.

- Self-Help Book—an instructional text on how to solve a particular personal problem or on how to succeed at doing a particular activity

- Speech—an oral presentation/talk done in front of a specific audience for a particular purpose

- Textbook—a discipline-specific book designed to explain knowledge in a particular field to an audience of learners in the field

***Social Media may use all of the above genres in electronic format, though the veracity of social media content frequently requires checking.

CHAPTER 4

Composing a piece for each of these various genres still requires your forethought regarding purpose and audience, and these genres demand your attention to one additional element: *venue*.

Venue means the place for which or in which you will publish or distribute your piece. The world holds many, varied venues, everything from newspapers to online forums and blogs to public spaces such as town halls and libraries to political spaces such as government offices to businesses and hobbyists' gathering places. The venue you choose will depend in part on your choice of genre, your designed purpose, and the audience you want to reach.

COMMON NONFICTION GENRES FROM WHICH YOU WILL MOST LIKELY CHOOSE: THEIR DEFINITIONS, THEIR COMMON VENUES, AND POSSIBLE PURPOSES AND AUDIENCES				
TYPE	**DEFINITION**	**VENUE**	**POSSIBLE PURPOSE**	**POSSIBLE AUDIENCE**
Nonacademic Essay	(Including letters to the editor and blogs and letters to businesses and government officials)—brief composition that makes an argument about the writer's point of view and usually uses some examples and evidence	Paper and online newspapers and newsletters Customer service or management offices Offices of elected officials	To convince others to agree with me To get others to act or to change something	General public Specific community Specific government official Specific company
News Article	A report of current events or events about to happen	Paper and online newspapers and newsletters Online newsfeeds and subject-specific sites	To convey information about an existing or future issue or event	General public Specific community
Pamphlet or Brochure or Flyer or Leaflet	A concise, small, unbound (often folded or tri-fold) booklet that conveys information on one narrow subject and sometimes advocates a particular position or the purchase of a particular product	Town halls Libraries Public spaces Offices Hobbyists' gathering places Malls	To convey information To advocate for something and convince others of its value	Specific, affected community People you want to become involved with or have an awareness of the issue

Social Media Post	A blog or vlog (like a letter to the editor); GoFund Me page, etc. (like a brochure or flyer to advocate for something or to inform)	Online forums	Any or all of those listed above	Any or all of those listed above
Web Page	Can replicate a letter, news article, or brochure or flyer with links to other key sources	Online	Any or all of those listed above	Any or all of those listed above
Political Cartoon	Satirizes someone or something to argue a point	Paper and online newspapers and newsletters Online newsfeeds and subject-specific sites	To criticize someone or something To make people aware of those faults	General public A specific community

Thinking about and recording these choices before you begin to compose your outreach project will help you considerably.

OUTREACH PIECE—700 WORDS (2–2.5 PAGES)

Compose a written piece that draws on your academic research but "reaches out" to a wider public audience. Your document should . . .

- target a specific public audience
- share your research
- connect that research to a specific public issue or problem
- present an argument, persuading readers to take a certain action or adopt a certain way of thinking

You will decide which genre to write in, but it must be a public genre (not an academic essay). Possibilities include:

- letter to the editor (for the school newspaper or local newspaper)
- social media post (blog, vlog, GoFundMe, etc.)
- brochure or flyer
- web site
- political cartoon

No matter what genre you choose, your piece must make an argument. Argument, in this context, means . . .

- making an overall **claim** (a big, debatable idea you want readers to consider)
- supporting that claim with **reasons** (smaller ideas that explain the big idea)
- providing **evidence** for those reasons (specifics that firm up those smaller ideas)
- offering **counterarguments** that acknowledge and respond to contrasting perspectives

Sample Pre-Writing

Research question: Why do so many people in the United States not have enough to eat, and what can we as a country do to solve this problem?

Possibilities:

AUDIENCE	GENRE	VENUE/PUBLICATION	CLAIM
Local Voters	Letter to the editor	Lifestyle section of my local newspaper, *LoHud Gannett*	Voters need to understand the food needs of the community and the reason to approve the new food closet as part of the town's public services.
Youth at Various Local High Schools and Colleges	Pamphlet	To hand out to students at the schools	Students need to understand the food needs of the community and volunteer for service at the new food closet.
Local Businesses	Open letter	Through regular mail and on social media platform	Local businesses need to understand the food needs of their community and donate funds or food.

Grading

When evaluating your piece, I will ask the following questions. Does the writer:

- Craft the piece for a specific audience or audiences?
- Follow genre conventions?
- Present a clear and debatable claim?
- Support the claim with reasons and evidence?
- Draw support (info and ideas) from credible research sources?
- Summarize, paraphrase, and/or quote sources effectively?
- Offer counterarguments?
- Document where information and ideas come from using an appropriate method (for the chosen genre)?

Rubric

CATEGORY	EXCEEDS STANDARDS	MEETS STANDARDS	APPROACHES STANDARDS	DOES NOT MEET STANDARDS
Crafts the piece for a specific audience or audiences clearly identifiable				
Follows genre conventions				
Presents a clear and debatable claim				
Supports the claim with reasons and evidence; Draws that support (info and ideas) from credible research sources				
Summarizes, paraphrases, and/or quotes sources effectively; Offers counterarguments				
Documents where information and ideas come from using an appropriate method (for the chosen genre)				

Like all other writing, your outreach piece draft will benefit from peer review.

IN-CLASS ACTIVITY 4F: GENRE AND OUTREACH PIECE PEER REVIEW

COMMON NONFICTION GENRES FROM WHICH YOU WILL MOST LIKELY CHOOSE, THEIR DEFINITIONS, AND THEIR COMMON VENUES

TYPE	DEFINITION	VENUE
Nonacademic Essay	(Including letters to the editor and blogs and letters to businesses and government officials)—brief composition that makes an argument about the writer's point of view and usually uses some examples and evidence	Paper and online newspapers and newsletters Customer service or management offices Offices of elected officials
News Article	A report of current events or events about to happen	Paper and online newspapers and newsletters Online newsfeeds and subject-specific sites
Pamphlet or Brochure or Flyer or Leaflet	A concise, small, unbound (often folded or tri-fold) booklet that conveys information on one narrow subject and sometimes advocates a particular position or the purchase of a particular product	Town halls Libraries Public spaces Offices Hobbyists' gathering places Malls
Social Media Post	A blog or vlog (like a letter to the editor); GoFund Me page, etc. (like a brochure or flyer to advocate for something or to inform)	Online forums
Web Page	Can replicate a letter, news article, or brochure or flyer with links to other key sources	Online
Political Cartoon	Satirizes someone or something to argue a point	Paper and online newspapers and newsletters Online newsfeeds and subject-specific sites

See the following videos:

"Purpose and Genre" by BYU Idaho, 2019:

http://www.byui.edu/academic-support-centers/writing/video-lessons-and-handouts/purpose-and-genre

"Audience, Purpose, and Genre" by Caitlin Foley, January 26, 2016:

https://www.youtube.com/watch?v=bXO8jEVQssA

PEER REVIEW 1 OF OUTREACH ESSAY

The Assignment:

Outreach Piece—700 words (2–2.5 pages)

Compose a written piece that draws on your academic research but "reaches out" to a wider public audience. Your document should . . .

- target a specific public audience
- share your research (from Unit 3)
- connect that research to a specific public issue or problem
- present an argument, persuading readers to take a certain action or adopt a certain way of thinking

You will decide which genre to write in, but it must be a public genre (not an academic essay). Possibilities include:

- letter to the editor (for the school newspaper or local newspaper)
- social media post (blog, vlog, GoFundMe, etc.)
- brochure or flyer
- Web site
- Political cartoon

Your piece must make an argument, no matter what genre you write in. Argument, in this context, means . . .

- making an overall **claim** (a big, debatable idea/position you want readers to consider)
- supporting that claim with **reasons** (smaller ideas that explain the big idea)
- providing **evidence** for those reasons (specifics that firm up those smaller ideas)
- offering **counterarguments** that acknowledge and respond to contrasting perspectives

Sample Pre-Writing

Research question: Why do so many people in the United States not have enough to eat, and what can we as a country do to solve this problem?

Possibilities:

AUDIENCE	GENRE	VENUE/PUBLICATION	CLAIM
Local Voters	Letter to the editor	Lifestyle section of my local newspaper, *LoHud Gannett*	Voters need to understand the food needs of the community and the reason to approve the new food closet as part of the town's public services.
Youth at Various Local High Schools and Colleges	Pamphlet	To hand out to students at the schools	Students need to understand the food needs of the community and volunteer for service at the new food closet.
Local Businesses	Open letter	Through regular mail and on social media platform	Local businesses need to understand the food needs of their community and donate funds or food.

Peer Review Directions

1. Form groups of three. [ONLINE students will complete this activity by posting their own drafts and then responding to TWO peers' drafts. ONLINE students will have to upload the peers' drafts and then follow these directions, #4 and #5.]

2. Circulate drafts.

3. Assign numbers.

4. Read the draft from Writer #1.

   a. Fill in the chart below, based on what you discover in the draft. What do you, the reader, think this writer's piece does?

AUDIENCE	GENRE	VENUE/PUBLICATION	CLAIM

   b. ON THE DRAFT ITSELF: Highlight/underline/circle **in blue** the parts of the essay that seem strong.

   c. ON THE DRAFT ITSELF: Highlight/underline/circle **in red** the parts of the essay about which you have questions/concerns or that confuse you.

5. In turn, discuss the essay and your comments with the writer and the rest of your group. [ONLINE students: Add at least five sentences of comments about the draft.]

6. Read draft from Writer #2.

   a. Fill in the chart below, based on what you discover in the draft. What do you, the reader, think this writer's piece does?

AUDIENCE	GENRE	VENUE/PUBLICATION	CLAIM

b. ON THE DRAFT ITSELF: Highlight/underline/circle **in blue** the parts of the essay that seem strong.

c. ON THE DRAFT ITSELF: Highlight/underline/circle **in red** the parts of the essay about which you have questions/concerns or that confuse you.

7. In turn, discuss the essay and your comments with the writer and the rest of your group. [ONLINE students: Add at least five sentences of comments about the draft.]

** Remember to post journal 12, your reflection on the comments you received regarding your draft.

****Remember to revise your draft and have it ready for peer review 2.

JOURNAL ENTRY 12
REFLECTION ON PEER REVIEW OF DRAFT 1
OF OUTREACH PROJECT ESSAY

Reflect on what you learned from your peer review session.

1. Explain what you learned from the feedback others gave you on your draft.

2. Explain what you learned from reading your peers' drafts.

Write a three-step plan of action for your revision of your first draft. What three <u>specific</u> changes—additions, deletions, changes in sequence, etc.—will you make to improve the draft before the next peer review? Why will you make these alterations? What <u>specific</u> effect do you hope they will have?

Once you have revised the draft of your outreach piece, you can meet with peers again to gain their feedback on your revision.

IN-CLASS ACTIVITY 4G: PEER REVIEW 2 FOR OUTREACH ESSAY

The Assignment:

Outreach Piece—700 words (2–2.5 pages)

Compose a written piece that draws on your academic research but "reaches out" to a wider <u>public audience</u>. Your document should . . .

- target a specific public audience
- share your research (from Unit 3)

- connect that research to a specific public issue or problem
- present an argument, persuading readers to take a certain action or adopt a certain way of thinking

You will decide which genre to write in, but it must be a public genre (not an academic essay). Possibilities include:

- letter to the editor (for the school newspaper or local newspaper)
- social media post (blog, vlog, GoFundMe, etc.)
- brochure or flyer
- Web site
- Political cartoon

Your piece must make an argument, no matter what genre you write in. Argument, in this context, means . . .

- making an overall **claim** (a big, debatable idea you want readers to consider)
- supporting that claim with **reasons** (smaller ideas that explain the big idea)
- providing **evidence** for those reasons (specifics that firm up those smaller ideas)
- offering **counterarguments** that acknowledge and respond to contrasting perspectives

Sample Pre-Writing

Research question: Why do so many people in the United States not have enough to eat, and what can we as a country do to solve this problem?

Possibilities:

AUDIENCE	GENRE	VENUE/PUBLICATION	CLAIM
Local Voters	Letter to the editor	Lifestyle section of my local newspaper, *LoHud Gannett*	Voters need to understand the food needs of the community and the reason to approve the new food closet as part of the town's public services.
Youth at Various Local High Schools and Colleges	Pamphlet	To hand out to students at the schools	Students need to understand the food needs of the community and volunteer for service at the new food closet.
Local Businesses	Open letter	Through regular mail and on social media platform	Local businesses need to understand the food needs of their community and donate funds or food.

1. Form groups of three. [ONLINE students will complete this activity as In-Class Activity 17b by posting their own drafts and then responding to TWO peers' drafts. ONLINE students will have to upload the peers' drafts and then follow these directions.]

2. Circulate drafts.

3. Assign numbers.

4. Read draft from Writer #1 and then the draft from Writer #2 and fill in the rubric as directed.

EVALUATOR: _____ AUTHOR: _____

FIRST ONE: Evaluator: On your peer's actual essay, annotate (use highlighting/bolding/underlining and written replies) the text. [ONLINE students: Upload your peer's essay and do the mark-up on that copy. Include it with your posted reply.]

Then fill in this evaluation rubric <u>WITH explanations</u> for each of the columns you have checked.

Then return both to the author.

Rubric

CATEGORY	EXCEEDS STANDARDS [20–25 POINTS]	MEETS STANDARDS [17.5–19.75 POINTS]	APPROACHES STAN-DARDS [15–17 POINTS]	DOES NOT MEET STANDARDS [14 POINTS AND BELOW]
Crafts the piece for a specific audience or audiences clearly identifiable				
Follows genre conventions				
Presents a clear and debatable claim				
Supports the claim with reasons and evidence; Draws that support (info and ideas) from credible research sources				
Summarizes, paraphrases, and/or quotes sources effectively; Offers counterarguments				
Documents where information and ideas come from using an appropriate method (for the chosen genre)				

EVALUATOR: _____ AUTHOR: _____

SECOND ONE: Evaluator: On your peer's actual essay, annotate (use highlighting/bolding/underlining and written replies) the text. [ONLINE students: Upload your peer's essay and do the mark-up on that copy. Include it with your posted reply.]

<u>Then</u> fill in this evaluation rubric <u>WITH explanations</u> for each of the columns you have checked.

Then return both to the author.

Rubric

CATEGORY	EXCEEDS STANDARDS [20–25 POINTS]	MEETS STANDARDS [17.5–19.75 POINTS]	APPROACHES STANDARDS [15–17 POINTS]	DOES NOT MEET STANDARDS [14 POINTS AND BELOW]
Crafts the piece for a specific audience or audiences clearly identifiable				
Follows genre conventions				
Presents a clear and debatable claim				
Supports the claim with reasons and evidence; Draws that support (info and ideas) from credible research sources				
Summarizes, paraphrases, and/or quotes sources effectively; Offers counterarguments				
Documents where information and ideas come from using an appropriate method (for the chosen genre)				

Ultimately, you will use this outreach piece as the basis for your presentation for the course.

JOURNAL ENTRY 13: PREPARING FOR YOUR PRESENTATION

See the following links to help you prepare for your final presentation of your outreach project.

"Poster Presentation Basics" by Boise State URC, April 16, 2010:

https://www.youtube.com/watch?v=cRNQjo2IstY

"Giving an Effective Poster Presentation" by George Hess, February 8, 2013:

https://www.youtube.com/watch?v=vMSaFUrk-FA

"How To Create a Research Poster" from NYU Libraries, May 17, 2018:

https://guides.nyu.edu/posters

"How to Prepare an Oral Presentation" by Michigan State University—Undergraduate Research, September 17, 2013:

https://www.youtube.com/watch?v=LzIJFD-ddoI

"Research Talk 101" by Lucia Dettori, DePaul University, June 29, 2007:

https://slideplayer.fr/slide/13917634/

Sketch your plan for your outreach presentation; think about and explain ways you might communicate your work visually. What are some possibilities?

See the directions for this presentation.

Final Exam Outreach Presentation (3–5 minutes)

During Finals Week, you will share with the class your Outreach Piece, in the form of a poster.

Set up your poster in the classroom (or project it from the computer), and then walk around the room, viewing your classmates' posters, and discussing your own poster with others.

Your poster must include:

- A hard copy (or projected copy) of your final Outreach Piece
- Notes and drafts that show your writing process, including . . .
  - ▶ how you decided on your audience, genre, and claim
  - ▶ how the piece differs from your Research Essay
  - ▶ how the piece evolved from draft to draft

MODEL 1—SEARCH ESSAY WITH MLA 8 FORMATTING

What Should We Do about Mandatory Prison Sentences for Drug Use?

Today, the issue of mandatory prison sentences concerns many people. Some believe that the United States has become an industrial prison complex that, because of mandatory sentences for minor drug infractions, is housing hundreds of thousands of people in prison, while others think those in prison deserve their punishment and their incarceration makes our streets safer because fewer people are selling drugs or committing violent acts because of drugs. Considering these ideas has significance to me because so many of my neighbors have vanished and are now living in prison. As a criminal justice major and someone who really liked some of the neighbors now gone, this topic has become ever present in my mind too, especially because the number of people in prison now far exceeds that number in any other nation on the planet. In addition, housing these people in prisons is costing the entire society a great deal, not just in tax dollars, but also in lost revenue from these people who could be working and in lost families broken apart because their fathers, mothers, etc., are in prison. When I began my research this term, I really wanted to know why the United States has so many people in its prisons. As I have progressed through this research process, my question has changed somewhat; now I prefer to know what we can do to alter this prison population explosion. My perspective of the answer too has altered, for I have reached a conclusion I had not fully expected mostly because I entered the conversation with a limited knowledge about the problem.

Even before I began searching for the answer to my question and the problem of mandatory sentencing, I did know a little something about the topic already. For example, I understood that hundreds of thousands of people are in US prisons, and that the US spends more money on prisons than it does on schools because I had learned that information in one of my sociology classes. In addition, through firsthand witnessing, I had comprehended that mostly drug laws are to blame for those high incarceration rates. In fact, I even had a general theory or hypothesis; I imagined that if we just eliminated mandatory sentencing laws regarding drugs, we could end the problem.

In spite of what I already imagined or knew, however, much existed that I did not know or understand fully. Apart from my actual research question, I had to find information about some of the small sub-issues that encompassed my knowledge gaps. These issues included how the mandatory drug-sentencing laws worked, which drugs were included in those laws, exactly how many people in prison were there because of these laws, and what other countries do to keep their prison population smaller than ours. I needed to find out what alternatives existed and succeeded elsewhere.

As I considered these knowledge gaps and the direction I needed to follow in my research, I started my journey of discovery with the texts I discovered in our library's databases and two YouTube documentaries I found on the Internet. Using the search terms "mandatory sentencing and prison population" and "alternatives to mandatory sentencing" and "prisons worldwide versus American" in the databases named *Gale Virtual Reference Library*, *Criminal Justice Periodicals*, and *Social Sciences Full Text*, I soon discovered several helpful articles, including some that were peer-reviewed/scholarly, and several others.

The first of these resources was "Mandatory Sentencing or Mandatory Bigotry?" written by Jillian Towson, PhD, and Mason Tempelton, CSW, and published in *The Journal of Criminal Affairs* on July 12, 2018. These authors' basic claim is that, "Mandatory sentencing is not about drug enforcement at all, but rather, about putting as many black people in jail as possible" (123). In essence, they postulate that the big problem is not so much mandatory sentencing, but actually prejudice and bigotry because too many only black drug dealers and drug-takers are going to jail compared to the number of white drug dealers and users. These authors use data from the Federal Census Bureau as well as studies done by the American Civil Liberties Union as the supporting evidence. As I contemplated this claim and evidence, my own contention surfaced as somewhat contrary to this premise because I think that yes, prejudice exists, and many more black men are arrested than white men because of this bigotry, but if sentencing rules were not so harsh, then these individuals would not be going straight to jail and be put there for so long.

These ideas about jail time stayed in my mind as I discovered another resource, which was entitled "Mandatory Sentencing," and published in *Economist* in June 2015. This article's basic claim is that, "The more men we incarcerate, the greater the impact on US economic growth because we keep taking workers and buyers out of the system. When they can't contribute, we all lose" (13). In essence, the writer contends that in spite of all the jobs generated by prisons' needs, the overall gross national product rate suffers because the number of workers displaced in prison is greater than the number of prison employees. The author uses a lot of statistics, graphs, and previous studies as the supporting evidence. As I contemplated this claim and evidence, my own contention surfaced as still accurate, but I now had an additional reason for the need to eliminate mandatory sentencing.

As I considered these ideas about mandatory sentencing, I found a third resource, "A Global Perspective on Sentencing Reforms," written by Oren Gazal-Ayal and published in *Law and Contemporary Problems in March of 2013*. This author's basic claim is that, "No nation outside of the United States has more people in prison. Other nations use different sentencing to reform criminals and manage drug crimes instead of warehousing them in jails" (76). In essence, he concludes that if the United States followed some of these models, we would have a smaller prison population without losing safety because the punishment would garner reformed people. He uses data, examples, and interviews from eight other industrialized nations across the world as the supporting evidence. As I contemplated this claim and evidence, my own contention surfaced as entirely accurate because I discovered in this article eight other systems that successfully use other kinds of treatments for drug-sellers and drug-users, and these methods actually work better and more humanely than long prison sentences do, an idea that will support my claim fully.

Gradually, my ideas began solidifying and becoming clear, but I continued searching and found a fourth article, "Mandatory Sentencing," in the *Congressional Digest*, published in 2013. This article's basic claim is that, "Mandatory sentencing came out of an era of rampant crime related only to drug trafficking and drug use. It was necessary. But it also served a political expediency for a great many 'tough on crime' candidates" (22). In essence, he postulates that the harsh mandatory drug sentences the US has right now came mostly because politicians wanted to get elected by looking tough on crime and active in the war on drugs. The report uses mostly examples and a lot of quotes from former and current politicians as well as actual data about the numbers as the supporting evidence. As I engaged with this article and thought of the others I had read, I started thinking that although this piece points to a cause of the creation of the harsh sentencing, it does not really offer any solutions, unless I consider not allowing politicians to use laws for their own benefit.

Given these ideas and the research I had already discovered, I chose to find a final, fifth written resource, entitled "Three Strikes and You're Out," written by Carl Schmertmann and published in *Demography* way back in 1998. This author's basic claim is that, "The proportion of people held in prison on drug-related crimes is 3x higher for black males than for white males" (448). In essence, he postulates that the entire justice system is biased, particularly as it deals with drug-related crimes, and uses quite irrefutable data as the supporting evidence. As I pondered this claim and evidence, which is over twenty years old, and compared it to the data from current years, I could see that this trend has not only continued, but it has also increased.

Though I already had a lot of information about the trends, I wanted to be certain I had all of the most current research, so I went to the Internet to find documentaries. I succeeded in finding two: "Are Mandatory Sentences an Injustice?" by *CBS Sunday Morning Show,* produced in 2014 and "The Sentence," produced by HBO Films in 2018. These two resources basically concur in their claims that "Mandatory sentencing stands out as an injustice because there is no consideration for circumstance or amounts and lots of consideration for race" (Valdez and Shank). These videos use a lot of hard data and many interviews with actual prisoners, arresting officers, and judges to support that premise. As I finished watching these last two sources, I began to feel ready to draw my own final conclusions and answers to my research question.

Getting to those conclusions and sources, however, was not necessarily easy. I encountered some difficulties, which included finding many rant-type articles on the Internet. They showed way too much bias to use. In addition, some of what I found in the databases was written over my head; I could not understand these articles very well. Lastly, I found a lot of data regarding the US prison population, but not a lot about what other nations do regarding drug crimes. Nonetheless, I did find information about the mandatory sentencing fairly easily, and along the way, I discovered some interesting surprises, such as the ways the entire idea of these mandatory sentences began. I never knew how much political game-playing created laws that have hurt so many people.

As I worked through the difficulties, the surprises, and the whole process, I finally reached some definitive conclusions. In general, I now believe that mandatory sentences for drug crimes do not succeed in battling the drug problems in the United States and instead, target the wrong people with sentences far too harsh and sentences that have far-reaching effects on our overall economy and on families. I think too that there are other, better alternatives to these mandatory minimum sentences. While scholars such as J. T. Bellham claim that "removing these violent felons from our streets makes life safer for everyone" (qtd. Schmertmann et al. 450), they ignore the fact that most of the people in jail under these mandatory sentencing laws are actually nonviolent offenders—the low-level street dealers and mules, not the big, major drug traffickers who are actually violent. They seem not to understand the actual effects of these mandatory drug crime sentencing laws.

These laws began with good intentions: to end the rise in heroin addiction and resulting homicide increases in the 1970s ("Mandatory Sentencing" 17). Very quickly, however, enacting these mandatory sentences began filling our prisons at a rapid rate, with no adjustment for the fact that by the 1990s and up to the present, conditions had changed. As a result, in the present times, "Half a million Americans are serving long sentences for nonviolent drug offenses [. . .] 48% of the whole prison population" (Frandino). These numbers indicate an alarming trend, especially when we consider who those people are and why they are in prison for ten or twenty years. These individuals include mothers and fathers, young people between the ages of 18 and 24, and mostly individuals selling or possessing reasonably small amounts of drugs. They are not the major drug dealers who possess thousands of ounces of drug product and who kill anyone who threatens the business. Adding another layer to our thinking about this issue is the fact that "80% of those sentenced are black or ethnic, with only 10% of those sentenced being white" (Towson and Templeton 61). Are we to believe that the majority of people who buy and sell drugs are black or ethnic? That concept contradicts, for example, the number of white adolescents we hear about in the news every day who are dying of opioid overdoses and reporting to drug rehabilitation centers. Should we conclude then, that not only are the mandatory sentencing laws imprisoning many people but also doing so unequally, in a prejudicial manner?

Even if we do not agree that enacting the sentencing laws demonstrates an unequal, prejudiced justice system, what effects of these sentencing laws should we consider? I contend that two primary effects of these laws should command our attention: the economic impacts of the laws and the toll on families that these laws take. According to a study conducted by *Economist* in 2015, taking these half-million people out of our workforce and out of our consumer population costs our economy billions of dollars each year ("Jailhouse Nation" 12). Even if we consider that maybe only half of those half-million people might be working and spending in our country, that number of non-working, non-spending people is considerable. And that loss just gets compounded every year they spend in jail and every year that we add people to the prison population. Some would contend that these people probably were not productive workers anyway, that they were just drug dealers, but I would argue that many drug dealers hold other jobs as well, and even if they did not, drug dealers earn money so they can spend money, and spending money keeps our economy going. If we add to this loss to our economy the costs of incarcerating this many people, we see another problem. Depending on the year, keeping these people in prison "costs between 63 and 75 billion dollars each year" (Valdez and Shank), all money that taxpayers send to the government and cannot keep and spend themselves. In addition, there are other costs because of whom we incarcerate. Every time we put a mother or father in jail for a long sentence, something has to be done with their children. Some go into state or foster care, while others go to family members, but in either case, the government then spends money for their care either in foster care payments, welfare checks, or orphan home costs (Frandino). Some say these costs actually save the children by pulling them out of a drug culture family, but I contend that putting children in some of these situations does not always save them and may, in fact, have quite detrimental effects on them. If we are a country that claims to regard family values highly, these drug sentences contradict that concept because by imprisoning all of these mothers and fathers, we are destroying families and family bonds. And if families are the basic unit of any society, by destroying all of these families, what are we doing to our society as a whole?

I believe our society has been thinking of a lot of these drug crimes in the wrong way. Instead of considering these infractions as criminal problems, maybe we should think about them as social problems. If we did so, then we might change our solution to the problem from a punishment approach to a rehabilitation approach. Some, like prosecutor John Stalwart, claim that "Trying to rehabilitate drug addicts and pushers is a losing, expensive proposition" (qtd. Valdez and Shank 82), but others, like psychiatrist Dr. James Bertrandt contend that, "Rehabilitation can work, if tailored to the individual and the specific drug abused. Even if someone needs two or three rounds of treatment, it will still take less time and cost less than ten years in jail" (qtd. Gazal-Ayal 83). While in the most recent year, Congress and the President have addressed decreasing minimum sentences and releasing some prisoners who have already served more than ten years for drug crimes, so far no one has really discussed eliminating the sentences entirely and replacing them with mandatory drug rehabilitation instead. Yet, no fewer than eight other industrialized nations use such an approach successfully. All across Europe, for example, instead of building and filling new prisons with non-violent drug abusers who sell drugs to sustain their own habits, these nations mandate treatment in government-run drug rehabilitation facilities. Their success rate is approximately 80% (Gazal-Ayal 83). In these nations, the cost of drug rehabilitation, "even for those who have to repeat treatment twice, over a 2–3 year period, is 60% lower than the cost of incarcerating them, and they come out productive, whole citizens ready to contribute to the country" (Gazal-Ayal 84). Is the United States so different from these countries that such an effort would not succeed here too? I propose that we at least try this approach before we keep forcing judges to impose mandatory prison sentences. Shouldn't judges have some discretion, based on the individual, the situation, the amount and type of drug, etc.? Shouldn't people have a chance to rehabilitate themselves by curing their drug habits before we lock them into prisons already so overcrowded that we can barely fit any additional people? I conclude we should; the policy of mandatory sentencing for drug crimes needs revising. Yes, the violent drug criminals need to be removed from society, but the non-violent offenders need a different kind of sentencing.

These conclusions represent my learning about the topic within the mere six weeks during which I have studied the question. If I had this process to conduct all over again, I would probably spend more time studying the effects of my solution—rehabilitation—and less time on the effects of mandatory sentencing. I see too that I could have conducted a whole separate study on the possibility of unequal justice in such mandatory sentencing. I maybe could have interviewed some judges too to see what they think, since they are the ones forced by Congressional law to impose these sentences. As I think about the research I have found, I perceive a need for researchers to conduct studies on the effectiveness of drug rehabilitation on the people who get sent to prison. Someone ought to be conducting comparative trials to see if this solution could work. I know that if I had additional time to continue with this research, I would start by searching for such studies myself. Doing so would matter because we cannot just keep warehousing half a million people in our jails because they have drug habits they support by selling drugs on the street. If we really want to end our war on drugs, don't we have to do more than lock people away and make war on our economy and on families? Don't we have to help people to stop buying and using drugs?

Works Cited

Frandino, Joseph L. "Are Mandatory Minimum Sentences an Injustice?" *CBS Sunday Morning*, 5 October, 2014, https://www.bing.com/videos/search?q=mandatory+sentencing%2c+ documentary+about&view=detail&mid=FEA190BC936DE45E7688FE-A190BC936DE45E7688&FORM=VIRE. Accessed 30 March 2019.

Gazal-Ayal, Oren. "A Global Perspective on Sentencing Reforms." *Law & Contemporary Problems*, vol. 76, no. 1, Mar. 2013, pp. 73–87. *EBSCOhost*, search.ebscohost.com/login.aspx?direct=true &db=ssf&AN=88917160&site=ehost-live.

"Jailhouse Nation." *Economist*, vol. 415, no. 8943, June 2015, pp. 11–15. *EBSCOhost*, search.ebscohost.com/login.aspx?direct=true&db=ssf&AN=103359102&site=ehost-live.

"Mandatory Sentencing." *Congressional Digest*, vol. 92, no. 10, Dec. 013, pp. 17–36. *EBSCOhost*, search.ebscohost.com/login.aspx?direct=true&db=ssf&AN=92046482&site= ehost-live.

Schmertmann, Carl P., et al. "Three Strikes and You're Out: Demographic Analysis of Mandatory Prison Sentences." *Demography*, vol. 35, no. 4, Nov. 1998, pp. 445–463. *EBSCOhost*, https://www.doi.org/10.2307/3004013.

Towson, Jillian and Mason Templeton. "Mandatory Sentencing or Mandatory Bigotry?" *The Journal of Criminal Affairs*, vol. 37, no. 4, September 2017, pp. 60–73. *EBSCOhost*, search, ebscohost.com/login.aspx?direct=true &db=ssf&AN=56417160&site=ehost-live.

Valdez, Rudy and Cindy Shank. "The Sentence." *HBO Films*, October 2018, https://www.hbo.com/documentaries/the sentnce.html. Accessed 31 March 2019.

Model Traditional Research Essay in MLA 8 Formatting

Abusing Drugs While Expecting:
Criminal Behavior or Treatment-Needed Behavior?

For many years, some American women have abused narcotics during their pregnancies. These pregnant, substance-abusing women have covered the spectrum, including every race, creed, ethnicity, age, and socioeconomic status, though "these conditions are more often associated with poverty, [so] the poor and minorities are screened more often" (Lewis and Bendersky 20). Everyone knows that the drugs these women use can harm their babies in many ways, but whether or not such women should be prosecuted as child abusers has remained a debatable issue for a really long time, though currently not many are focused upon the problem, and *current* studies are in short supply. Nonetheless, in the past, some prosecutors have believed that such women ought to be incarcerated for child abuse, while others have contended that these women need most to complete a drug treatment and rehabilitation program. Even Congress itself took up the debate, mandating "that pregnant women receive priority enrollment in treatment, specific services such as prenatal care and childcare, and established specialized demonstration" about the effects of prenatal drug abuse (Chavkin et al. 118). But who is right, and should one rule apply to all drug-abusing pregnant women, or do some women deserve prison time while others deserve treatment? Certainly, for the children's sake, we as a society need to decide. On the one hand, I think throwing these women in jail doesn't always succeed in doing anything but punishing the women and taking children away from their mothers, so putting citizens' tax money to work in treatment programs might surface as the best solution for everyone. Educating such women about prenatal care and showing them that having a healthy baby matters a lot might be better than threatening to put them in jail. Yet, I can also understand that some women simply will not learn from or care about such programs and only jail time will keep them from harming additional future babies.

Documented criminal cases related to babies harmed by the mother's drug abuse during pregnancy go back as far as the late 1980s. "Since 1986, at least fifty women across the country have been charged or prosecuted for distributing illegal drugs or alcohol through the umbilical cord" (Grabar 23). At one point, Medicaid insurance even stepped in to keep records of women whose babies were born with fetal alcohol syndrome and addicted to narcotics. Medicaid started tracking the women who delivered these babies (Chavkin et al. 117). But for what purpose did the tracking exist? Only when we consider how these substances affect the fetus during the various stages of pregnancy, how such narcotics affect the child after birth, and how these babies differ from babies born to drug-free mothers can we begin to understand the whole problem and reach any kind of decision regarding the mothers who abuse illicit drugs while pregnant. Likewise, however, we also need to examine the mothers abusing these substances and to examine the results of the differing approaches to the women who abuse substances during pregnancy.

Illegal substance use among expectant mothers does affect the growing life inside of them. "Cocaine easily passes the placenta and the blood brain barrier" (Lewis and Bendersky 22). In other words, the cocaine (or any other narcotic) the mother takes into her body gets absorbed by the fetus. When a woman becomes pregnant, her body and the baby's body are essentially one body. Everything that woman eats, drinks, and even breathes in reaches the fetus. Physically, "'before the umbilical cord is cut, it is really only something arbitrary delivering drugs to that baby, just like a straw or a hypodermic needle'" (Deen qtd. Grabar 23). Just as taking drugs can destroy any woman's body or mind, so too can it destroy a fetus's body and mind. According to the National Institute on Drug Abuse, this habit can actually cause the loss of those babies to miscarriage, stillbirth, or premature birth that ultimately ends in death. Yet, in spite of those deaths, there is an estimate that in the United States, "approximately 375,000 infants are born each year to women who abuse narcotic drugs" (Watson 1). And what can we expect as a result for most of those newborns? Right out of the womb, they may not cry or react in any way because they exist in a sleepy, drugged state; their breathing may be especially shallow, and they may have extremely low birth weights (Garber 24). Some are born addicted to the drug of their mother's choice and experience painful withdrawal. Once these babies survive these difficulties, the next set of effects begins to show, often for the rest of their lives. Cocaine, for example, affects a baby's neurological development, "including a child's attention, arousal, affect, and action" (Lewis and Bendersky 23). In addition, such children often have birth defects, behavioral problems, cognitive deficits, poor information-processing, poor memory, and poor attention skills (NIDA). These types of problems lead to difficulties for children not just in school, but also in all of their lives; the effects do not just go away. These children end up behind most other children in many ways, all because of their mothers' drug abuse during pregnancy. Some scientists maintain that these children can even have "brain structure changes" that will also have life-long consequences (NIDA). These babies will grow, but they likely will never really have what we would call a normal life.

All of these consequences come to innocent beings who had no actual choice in the way their mothers treated them during pregnancy. But what can we say of these mothers? Most of these women are getting late or no prenatal care during their pregnancies. Without such knowledge, these mothers-to-be may not understand fully what damage they do to their unborn children. Some may have some awareness of what might happen, but they forgo prenatal treatment or any other form of help because they fear the system (Jessup et al. 291). In addition, a great many factors lead these women to their drug-abusing behavior in the first place. Many of these women live in poverty, have domestic violence experiences, and live with male-dominant partners who may have started them on their drug habit because they also have a drug habit (295). According to studies done by NIDA, many of these females have grown up in turbulent homes in which one or both parents were alcoholics, in which sexual abuse may have occurred at an early age, and in which loving or careful parental responsibilities did not get managed well. These conditions seem to apply across all races, ethnicities, and social classes (NIDA). We can see, then, that their own drug abuse, while their own choice, also has considerable connection to their histories, histories that had not been addressed in any way before these women, themselves, began abusing drugs or became pregnant.

Regardless of these histories, however, some scholars, prosecutors, and lawmakers believe there is only one way to deal with pregnant drug abusers: to label them child abusers and lock them away in jail. They contend that not everyone with a bad childhood abuses drugs, and not everyone with drug habits keeps using drugs while pregnant. On some level, this argument makes sense, but on another level, it does not because individuals differ in their capacity to handle childhood trauma, and even the level of the trauma varies.

Many do not consider this variation, however. Some states actually have laws dedicated to prosecuting these women. And some of these states as well as their prosecutors, such as Jeff Deen, actually believe imprisonment benefits not only the babies, but also the mothers; they think the convictions are for the mothers' own good, that it saves their lives, and that they will learn a lesson and probably will never give birth to another drugged-out baby again (Grabar 23). Places like Florida have passed laws stating that if a baby is born with drugs in its system, that baby is automatically considered by law an abused child, and physicians are required to report these births to the Florida Department of Health and Rehabilitative Services (23). According to Grabar, South Carolina too requires prosecution in such cases, and as a result, it currently has over 200 cases pending, with others already having been upheld by the State Supreme Court (24). But not all states or prosecutors view this issue in the same way. Massachusetts and Plymouth Superior Court Judge,

Suzanne DelVecchio and Georgia, for example, routinely throw out such indictments and have declared these kinds of cases unconstitutional (Howell 206). These states favor placing these women into treatment programs. Some states even recommend a kind of middle ground by mandating treatment programs.

Treatment programs do accept these women, and they watch them carefully while those women are under their care. These programs can offer mothers "couples and family therapy, prenatal care, childcare, and narcotics anonymous meetings. After the women deliver their babies, they can remain in the program for another six to twelve months, so that the facility's staff can keep a close eye on them" (Watson 6–7). The goal of these programs is to sustain and preserve the family through therapeutic means (Chavkin et al. 118). Advocates for this approach believe that the family unit matters long-term to the child, and putting the mothers in jail damages the possibility of that long-term stability; it destroys the family unit and places the children in others' hands.

But what does the data tell us about the success or failure of any of these approaches? Surprisingly, not a great deal of data regarding the *results* of any of these methods exist. We seem to collect a lot of information about how many mothers abuse drugs while pregnant, how many babies are born drug-addicted, how many of these moms get sent to jail, and how many get put in treatment programs, but we do not seem to do much follow-up on the results of these solutions. Data does seem to show that not enough treatment centers exist, and that for treatment to succeed, it must last longer than seven days (Grabar 24). Otherwise, though, studies have not really been conducted to analyze the effects of any of the three methods of addressing the problem.

Without that hard data, making a valid decision becomes difficult. Nonetheless, I recommend a varied approach. I think that old adage, "A pound of prevention is worth a pound of cure" matters in this situation. Most of these women must see a doctor at some point during their pregnancies. A logical first line of consideration, then, must be these doctors. If the medical caregiver suspects that the woman may be using drugs, that physician should automatically screen her for any substance abuse. While not every urine test is accurate or reliable, enough are that a doctor can immediately start getting the woman and the unborn baby treated. The doctor can educate the woman about the concrete effects of this drug use on the fetus. And, these medical professionals can also advise the woman regarding options available to her. In addition, since many of these women are poor and use the Medicaid program, certainly Medicaid can mandate drug-screening of all pregnant women it serves. If the toxicology report shows drug use, then again, the physician can educate the woman and get her into a treatment program.

Medicaid can play another role once a child is born. It already keeps copies of various records, including birth certificates, medical files on baby and mother, and substance abuse treatment records. As Howell et al. note, "Records that are routinely collected for administrative purposes [. . . can be . . .] merg[ed . . .] to improve the identification of pregnant substance abusers and, more importantly, to provide an enriched data source using variables from all three sources" (206, 207). Keeping track of the women whose babies are born drug-addicted can aid in learning where and how many treatment centers are needed and how to approach these situations. Linking the files can also assist in identifying repeat pregnant drug users and successful outcomes for mothers and babies.

These records can help to determine what course of action should be followed for mother and baby. Some women know the harmful effects their drug abuse will produce and still they continue to use the drugs just so that they can satisfy their addiction; some go through treatment programs and, nonetheless, keep using drugs through every pregnancy. These kinds of women deserve to be incarcerated and have their babies taken away from them because they are unfit parents who will never offer their children safe or healthy lives, because their need for the drug will overrule every other instinct they have. Some women, however, experience drug addiction during pregnancy for the first time; they lack a full awareness and do not necessarily know how to eliminate that addiction. These kinds of women deserve a chance at treatment and keeping their babies.

Even with treatment, addictions are hard to break. They need to be treated on an individual basis, with a plan that meets specific people's needs and lives. Our criminal justice system too needs to consider individual cases in these drug-addicted pregnant women situations and not create sets of laws with a "one-size-fits-all" mentality. Not every woman deserves incarceration, and not every woman deserves to go free, either. Judging which situation should dictate which outcome matters not only to the woman, but also to the baby and to society as a whole.

Works Cited

Chavkin W., et al. "National Survey of the States: Policies and Practices Regarding Drug-Using Pregnant Women." *American Journal of Public Health*, vol. 88, no. 1, Jan. 1998, pp. 117–119. *EBSCOhost*, https://www.doi.org/10.2105/AJPH.88.1.117.

Grabar, Mary. "PREGNANCY POLICE. Sending Women to Jail Is Not the Answer." *Progressive*, vol. 54, no. 12, Dec. 1990, pp. 22–24. *EBSCOhost*, search.ebscohost. com/login.aspx?direct=true&db=a9h&AN=9012172025&site=ehost-live.

Howell, Embry M., et al. "Identifying Pregnant Substance Abusers and Studying their Treatment using Birth Certificates, Medicaid Claims, and State Substance Abuse Treatment Data." *Journal of Drug Issues*, vol. 30, no. 1, 2000, pp. 205–223. *ProQuest*, http://lib-proxy.sunywcc.edu/login?url=https://search.proquest.com/ docview/ 208865837?accountid=14174,doi:http://dx.doi.org/10.1177/002204260003000112.

Jessup, Martha A., et al. "Extrinsic Barriers to Substance Abuse Treatment among Pregnant Drug Dependent Women." *Journal of Drug Issues*, vol. 33, no. 2, 2003, p. 285. *ProQuest*, http://lib-proxy.sunywcc.edu/login?url=https://search.proquest.com/ docview/ 208838164?accountid=14174,doi:http://dx.doi.org/10.1177/002204260303300202.

Lewis, Michael and Margaret Bendersky. "Prenatal Cocaine Exposure and Child Outcome: What Do We Really Know?" *Mothers, Babies, and Cocaine: The Role of Toxins in Development*. Lawrence Erlbaum Associates, Inc., 1995. pp. 19–37.

NIDA. "Health Consequences of Drug Misuse." *National Institute on Drug Abuse*, 23 Mar. 2017, https://www.drugabuse.gov/related-topics/health-consequences-drug-misuse. Accessed 20 Jun. 2017.

Watson, Ronald. *Substance Abuse during Pregnancy and Childhood*. Humana Press Inc., 1995.

Childhood Obesity: A Growing Concern

Marjorie Student

ENG 122

Tiffany Professor

January 17, 2015

Childhood Obesity: A Growing Concern

There are many differences between children today and children 20 years ago. One area of concern not only to researchers and politicians, but to parents as well, is the increase in childhood obesity, which is reaching epidemic proportions. According to the National Health and Nutrition Examination Survey (NHANES) conducted in 2008, the prevalence of obese children in the 6-to-11-year age range alone increased from 6.5% in 1980 to 19.6% in 2008 (Center for Disease Control and Prevention, 2010). Another study conducted by Datamonitor states that two out of five children in the 6-to-13-year age group are overweight or obese. This equates to 40.7% ("Childhood Obesity Expected to be a Growing Concern Through 2014," 2010). There is a wide array of theories on why childhood obesity has climbed, including genetic, medical, environmental, and behavioral reasons.

Although these areas may all play a role in the increasing trend of childhood obesity, it is important to first understand what changes have occurred over the last two decades that would cause a change of this magnitude in children. The obvious cause would be changes that have occurred behaviorally and environmentally. Most simply, children eat more and have a more sedentary lifestyle, which seems very obvious on the surface. It is a well-known fact that lack of exercise and unhealthy eating habits lead to obesity. What is important to reversing this trend is understanding why children eat less healthy foods and are less active. What aspects of life have drawn children into these unhealthy habits? Why are children less active and drawn to foods that are high in fat and sugars, causing childhood obesity to be at its highest point ever? Research on this topic is important, as it is imperative that this trend be reversed. Without a plan, and an understanding of the cause of the increase in childhood obesity, the future health and well-being of these children is at substantial risk. Childhood obesity rates can be reversed with changes to behavior and environmental conditions.

The researcher reviewed both qualitative and quantitative research found in scholarly journals, substantive news and opinion magazines, and research reports found through Proquest, JSTOR, EBSCOhost, Google Scholar, and other scholarly websites, to search for studies and statistics collected by professionals in the field of health and wellness in children. In addition to the Internet, the researcher used the hard copy book *Fed Up! Winning the War Against Childhood Obesity*. The most valuable resources were those that had been conducted and published in the last 3 to 5 years. Recent studies and statistics are

CHAPTER 4

beneficial to the ongoing research needed in this high profile area. It provided the researcher with a point of reference that is relevant to society today.

Many believe that the increasing trend upward in childhood obesity is due to genetics. However, evidence shows that although children may be predisposed at birth to becoming obese, genetics by itself is not the cause for the increase. In order for genetics to be viewed as the reason childhood obesity has increased dramatically, it would require that the genetic makeup of the human race also change. The researcher could not locate any proof of such a claim. Scientists are confident that the increase is based on environmental factors. There has not been enough elapsed time for a new genetic mutation to grab hold of our society and cause children to become obese (Okie, 2005). Therefore, the reason for this trend must be rooted in environmental influences and behavioral changes that have occurred over the last few decades.

In order to prove the theory that changing environmental factors have contributed to the rise in childhood obesity, the researcher has conducted research and come to the conclusion that children are living a sedentary lifestyle and consuming a large amount of calories without burning them off. There is a growing trend of inactivity among children. Children are spending more time indoors and eating unhealthy foods leading to increased obesity.

Research shows that, on average, children watch television or are involved in other screen media 5 to 7 hours per day (Jordan, 2010). During this time, they are exposed to a large number of advertisements for food products that are high in sugar and fat. The presentation of this material sends a message to children that these foods are acceptable as meals, and as a result, this leads them to falsely believe that they are not unhealthy. The more time children spend watching television, the more their body fat percentage increases, contributing to the increase in childhood obesity (Jordan, 2010). In addition to the messages children are receiving from advertisements, evidence shows that while children are engaged in television or gaming activities, they are more likely to snack more frequently, contributing to the increase in childhood obesity.

Although the amount of time spent on watching television and playing video games is disturbing, what really is at question is why. Why are children less active? Changes in the family have occurred over the last 20 years. There are more dual-income families and more single-parent households. These changes can lead to more children being left without supervision and few planned activities. Safety also plays a role in the amount of physical activity that children are involved in. Children in urban environments may not have

CHAPTER 4

areas that are free of traffic or an area of protected space in which to play. In addition, neighborhoods in urban areas may be riddled with crime (U.S. Department of Health and Human Services, n.d.). Not only do crime and traffic impede the ability of children to enjoy outside physical activity as they had in the past, it also inhibits them from obtaining low-impact exercise such as that which could be gained from walking to school or to a friend's home.

Changes in the home over the last two decades have not only played a role in decreasing physical activity, which leads to obesity, but also in reducing the time available to single parents and dual-income families to prepare foods that are nutritionally balanced. Often, parents are left with little option other than to serve their family prepared and processed foods with higher calories and less nutrition.

Evidence shows that families are attempting to do the right things for their children by keeping them safe and providing them with food; however, this tradeoff may not be in the best long-term interest of the children. These changes to society, which have had an impact on the behavioral and environmental factors as they relate to health and wellness, can be reversed with little to no additional effort on the part of families. The end result of the current status quo of eating unhealthily with little to no physical activity is the reason childhood obesity has and undoubtedly will continue to rise.

Many schools have started to implement preventative measures to combat the rise in childhood obesity. However, research shows that school-only interventions do not have enough of an effect (Birch & Ventura, 2009). A whole life approach needs to be implemented. Changes need to take place in the home, external environments, and school. There have been no significant changes to the lunch menus over the last two decades The changes that have occurred, fortunately, have been toward making school meals more nutritionally balanced.

There has, however, been a decline in schools in the area of physical activity. With recess being cut back and physical education classes falling prey to budget cuts, there has been a decline in the amount of time spent on physical movement during school hours. Even with the reduction in school-supervised physical activity alone, it is not so significant as to be a cause for the staggering increase in childhood obesity, but instead may be a contributing factor.

Studies show that the main influences on children occur in the home. This is not only limited to general behavior and attitude. The home influences the whole child, including healthy eating and exercise. Children are akin to video recorders. They record what they see and experience, and assume similar

CHAPTER 4

roles. If the family eats unhealthily and limits activity, the child will as well. It is no different than learning math or science; children have to be taught healthy eating and exercise skills in a similar manner.

Research shows that the best approach to combating obesity in children starts with the parents. In a study in which parents acted as mediators for change, and which did not include their children directly, there was a significant decrease in the weight of the children involved in the study. Parents regulated the foods that were eaten and introduced healthier foods to the children. Parents also participated in regular physical activity, prompting the children to follow suit (Golan, Kaufman, & Shahar, 2006). By having the parents as the main facilitators, children were less likely to rebel against the change to their diet and exercise routine.

Research also shows that there are many reasons as to why children are less active and consume more foods that are high in fat and sodium than children did 20 years ago. Although similar foods were available at that time, the approach to daily living was vastly different. Families typically would eat their meals together at a designated time. Microwaves were not in every home. Prepared foods were not prevalent to the point where you could purchase fully cooked meals at the local supermarket. Fast food takeout was a treat occasionally enjoyed by families. Advertisements on television were not as prominent as they are today, mainly because there were not as many channels.

Since there were not as many channels available to watch 20 years ago, children spent less time engaged in television watching: This prompted them to become more involved in physical activities or other hobbies that utilized the hands. Busy hands cannot aimlessly consume snack foods. In addition, mothers were typically at home with their children and able to monitor their eating habits and involve them in activities. These activities included outdoor supervised play, walking, or other activities to occupy the body and mind.

Time spent preparing balanced foods and incorporating physical activity into the daily routine has significantly diminished, research has shown, and it is necessary for this practice to be introduced into the lives of young children. Parents need to take the reins and be responsible for not only the present health and well-being of their children, but their future as well.

Parents have many concerns in regards to their children, with safety as their top priority. Although this worry is reasonable, parents need to become creative when it comes to getting their children up off the couch and away from the television and computer. It is understandable that parents believe children are safe as long as they are engaged in these activities, but the reality is they are not. These activities are causing their children to be unhealthy not only physically, but mentally as well; they are not learning the key elements of a healthy lifestyle. These elements include both the mind and body. Children need to understand that watching what they eat and the amount of exercise they participate in is a requirement for all of their lives. Children who are obese have a higher risk of being obese as adults, and are at risk for serious health issues including heart disease and diabetes.

The key to reversing the trend of childhood obesity lies in the lifestyle choices that are made by, or in some ways forced upon, families. These choices include the foods that are consumed and the sedentary lifestyles that have become part of the accepted practice. To reverse this trend, families must find ways to cut back the amount of high-calorie, high-fat foods they make available not only to their children, but to themselves as well. Creative measures related to physical activity must also be sought. Video games may be an alternative to outdoor physical play, but parents can reduce the amount of time their children play sedentary games and replace them with video games that require movement in order to play. This allows the combination of both physical movement and the desired activity of playing video games.

The research shows that the reason behind the increase in childhood obesity is based on behavioral and environmental factors that have changed over the last two decades. The approach to combating it does not lie in any one area of the child's environment or activities. It must be approached across the child's entire life, including home and school. Proper foods and exercise that occur in only one of the many environments that a child spends time in will not reverse this trend. Healthy living habits must be encouraged across all domains of a child's life. This will pave the way to a healthy lifestyle, decreasing the percentage of overweight and obese children.

CHAPTER 4

References

Birch, L. L., & Ventura, A. K. (2009). Preventing childhood obesity: What works? *International Journal of Obesity, 33*. doi: 10.1038/ijo.2009.22

Center for Disease Control and Prevention. (2010). *Childhood overweight and obesity*. Retrieved from http://www.cdc.gov/obesity/childhood/index.html

Childhood obesity expected to be a growing concern through 2014. (2010, November/December). *American Fitness, 28*(6), 61.

Golan, M., Kaufman, V., & Shahar, D. (2006). Childhood obesity treatment: Targeting parents exclusively v. parents and children. *The British Journal of Nutrition, 95*(5), 1008–1015.

Jordan, A. (2010). Children's television viewing and childhood obesity. *Pediatric Annals, 39*(9), 569–573. doi: 2137392121

Okie, S. (2005). *Fed up! Winning the war against childhood obesity*. Washington, DC: Joseph Henry Press.

U.S. Department of Health and Human Services Assistant Secretary for Planning and Evaluation. (n.d.). Childhood obesity. Retrieved from http://aspe.hhs.gov/health/reports/child_obesity/

Internet and Distance Education Delivery Models
Jordan Student
EDU 400
Instructor St. Clare
January 1, 2013

CHAPTER 4

Internet and Distance Education Delivery Models

Technological developments over the past 20 years have given people across the globe the ability to interact and obtain information at a tremendous rate. Due to these developments, the field of distance education is also growing at an exponential rate, as is the research conducted on the availability, effectiveness, and best practices of distance learning. This increased interest has led to a variety of options in distance learning systems, and the primary methods for course delivery. Distance education courses are primarily taught via one of three course models: synchronous, asynchronous, or blended.

Synchronous course delivery is conducted in "real time." This means the instructors and students are online at the same time and typically interact via streaming video, live chat, or in a net-meeting format. Students can post or ask questions and receive immediate responses from the course instructor or other students.

In the asynchronous course model, the instruction is conducted when the students and instructor are not online at the same time. These classes typically occur through a distance-learning system that allows the users to post and respond to messages in a specific location within the course. For example, some universities use the asynchronous method to conduct online courses in which students participate in discussion forums, post assignments, and retrieve learning materials. Correspondence with the instructor is often primarily conducted via the online course discussion forums and email.

The blended learning model is a combination of both synchronous and asynchronous delivery. The instructor may have a set lecture time during which all students log into the system to listen and interact with the class. The remainder of the week's instruction may then be conducted asynchronously by having students post additional discussions and questions to a specific location within the learning system.

Regardless of the delivery method, all distance-learning systems include course management. Within the course management system, instructional designers, course authors, and instructors have the ability to edit content, administer assignments, monitor discussions, and interact with learners. The course management features of a distance-learning system are one of the key elements for the successful delivery of a distance education program.

An important factor in selecting a distance-learning system is the ease with which students and instructors can interact and understand the delivery structure. Students' success is often related to their experience with the course technology. If students are to be successful learning at a distance, they must be comfortable with the media used to transmit the content of the course. The distance-learning system should ultimately enhance the learner's experience.

Within distance education, the delivery of information occurs through the use of various communication methods. When the instructor and learners are separated by time and geographic location, asynchronous communication occurs. Asynchronous communication does not require the participants to interact simultaneously. Asynchronous learning tools can be used for a variety of teaching and workplace situations.

In its early use, distance learning involved only the student and instructor. Learners did not have the opportunity to communicate with one another. Technological advancements have fortunately brought much to the field of distance learning. In the teaching arena of online learning, asynchronous communication can be done by way of email, newsgroups for discussions, streaming video, and audio. According to Witt and Mossler (2001):

> The new opportunities that a college degree will . . . [provide are] made possible by the advantages of an online education, including class work on a more flexible schedule, ease of doing research online, ease of collaborating with others at a distance, and access to universities that may be geographically far removed from where [one] lives. Online classes also make it possible for students to learn from working professionals in their fields who may be scattered across the country or around the world. (para. 1)

Asynchronous communications allow learners to select the time and place for class participation. Through emails and other asynchronous learning tools, students can be a part of a learning community, set goals, and complete coursework. In the workplace, professionals can interact without concern for time differences or the high cost of international phone calls. With the asynchronous model, the user has greater control over the acquisition of information and the ability to set a convenient time for completing coursework, training, or job-related activities.

Online synchronous course delivery offers students and instructors the most similar format to a traditional classroom learning experience. While the instructor and students are not located in the same place, they are interacting and communicating at the same time. Within the synchronous delivery system, there are many options for the communication and transmission of

CHAPTER 4

course content. Bach, Haynes, and Smith (2006) state, "Synchronous communication develops its own curios and quite different type of narrative when compared with face to face discussion, and there is often a text based 'stream of consciousness'" (p. 135). Synchronous delivery of course instruction also allows for immediate feedback. In the asynchronous delivery model, learners must often wait for feedback or answers to questions.

An effective synchronous delivery system motivates the learner, provides sufficient time for learner and facilitator interaction, and operates the course at a steady rate, allowing the learners time to reflect and ask questions. Like the asynchronous course delivery model, a successful synchronous delivery system can also provide participants with an effective and challenging learning experience.

While asynchronous and synchronous learning systems each offer a specialized approach to distance learning, a blended learning system can combine the tools of both systems to present an effective and convenient learning experience. According to Watson (2010), "[B]lended learning combines online delivery of educational content with the best features of classroom interaction and live instruction" (p. 4). For example, training for supervisors may be divided into various sections. One section's content may be taught via CD-ROM with the learners interacting through a newsgroup or discussion board. The next section may be taught in the classroom setting. Current blended learning models represent a fundamental transfer in instructional strategies, similar to the way in which online learning demonstrated a change in the delivery and instructional models for learning at a distance (Watson, 2010).

The distance education boom has led many institutions on a search for a management system capable of delivering courses and sharing information while managing the varied and often complex learning tools. As noted by Caplow (2006), the most significant aspects of the course management system include the ability to provide course materials in a web-based format, access online exams, and download or link to course materials, in addition to a system that supports student and faculty interaction in discussions and evaluation. Given the increasing number of options available in distance education, the task of finding a course management system that offers the necessary options, along with the ability to interact with other technology solutions, can be daunting. The decision to implement a courseware management system cannot be pieced together. All distance learning systems, from blended

CHAPTER 4

learning systems to content management, must have the capability and the resources necessary to interact with the course management system.

Learning technologies have opened the doors to a wide variety of options for distance education delivery, and each learning model has benefits and limitations (Picciano, 2001). The Internet and learning technologies provide the means for transmitting content, managing courses, and promoting the interaction of the instructor and learners. When selecting technology for a distance-learning program, the system that provides the best learning approach should be utilized. Around the world, students can join the same class, share information, and learn together. The field of distance education and the various learning systems are continually being revised and improved. The most effective distance learning system is ideally one that provides students with the resources to be successful distance learners.

CHAPTER 4

References

Bach, S., Haynes, P., & Lewis Smith, J. (2006). *Online learning and teaching in higher education* [ebrary Reader version]. Retrieved from http://site.ebrary.com/lib/ashford/Doc?id=10197006

Caplow, J. (2006). Where do I put my course materials? *Quarterly Review of Distance Education, 7*(2), 165–173. doi: EJ875031

Picciano, A. G. (2001). Distance learning: Making connections across virtual space and time. Upper Saddle River, NJ: Prentice Hall.

Watson, J. (2010). Blended learning: The convergence of online and face to face education. *Promising practice in online learning.* Retrieved from http://www.inacol.org

Witt, G. A., & Mossler, R. A. (2010). *Adult development and life assessment.* Retrieved from https://content.ashford.edu/books/4

WHAT'S AFFECTED?

► Health
► Education
► Mental Health
► Economic Stability
► Housing

(US Department of Health and Human Services)

HOW MANY?

According to the US government, 40 million Americans need food assistance everyday, and another 6 million need it occasionally. (Price 557)

Every Wednesday
1:00 – 6:00 p.m.

*Town Hall
Basement,
Room 6A*
*Help pack and distribute food!
OR Donate food!*

HELP END FOOD IN SECURITY

We need you now!

FOOD

Works Cited

Atlantic Marketing Team For Food For America. "America Has A Hunger Problem." *The Atlantic Online (Original Thinking Series)*, June, 2019, https://www.theatlantic.com/sponsored/hunger-2019/america-has-a-hunger-problem/3067/?sr_source=pocket&sr_lift=true&utm_source=pocket&utm_medium=CPC&utm_campaign=simplereach&utm_source=PK_SR_P_3067. Accessed 10 June 2019.

Bridges, Jeff. *A Place at the Table.* Ed. Peter Pringle. Public Affairs, 2013.

Duke Sanford World Food Policy Center. "Food Insecurity," 20 September 2018, *World Food Policy Center at Duke.* https://wfpc.sanford.duke.edu/media/food-insecurity. Accessed 2 February 2019.

Laterman, Kaya. "Hunger on Campus: Pay Tuition Or Eat: Metropolitan Desk." *New York Times*, May 05, 2019. *ProQuest*, http://libproxy.sunywcc.edu/login?url=https:// search.proquest.com/docview/2219855076?accountid=14174.

Price, Tom. "Hunger in America." *CQ Researcher*, vol. 27, no. 24, 7 July 2017. pp. 557–80. www.cqresearcher.com.

US Department of Health and Human Services. "Food Insecurity The Healthy People 2020," *HealthyPeople.gov*, 2019. https://www.healthypeople.gov/2020/topics-objectives/topic/social-determinants-health/interventions-resources/food-insecurity. Accessed 3 March 2019.

WHY MORE FOOD PANTRIES?

Congress has slashed the food assistance programs and issuing of SNAP cards, so fewer people are getting aid and more are going hungry. (Price 560)

WHO?

Approximately **one out of every four children goes hungry in the United States every, single day** (Bridges)

Let's Help Our Neighbors!

Donate your time!

Donate your food.

Don't let a child in need go hungry

WHY?

There is a "web of poverty, racism, and sexism surrounding food insecurity" (Duke Sanford World Food Policy Center).

The Town Food Pantry Open Wednesdays

Town Hall, Room 6A

Help us feed our community, from 1:00 p.m.–6:00 p.m. We need volunteers to sort, bag and distribute food. We need donations of dry goods and canned foods.

At College too...

"**Over 50% of [public university and community college students] are going hungry every day.**" (Laterman MB1)

"*Hunger threatens our minds, our bodies, and our communities.*" (Food for Ameica)

MODEL 2 OUTREACH PIECE

Editorials
LoHud *Journal News*
1 Gannett Plaza
White Plains, New York 10606

Dear Editor:

Yesterday, you ran an article about the horror of drug-addicted, pregnant women and concluded that all of these women should be sent to prison. But I contend you were a bit too hasty in drawing that conclusion. I suggest that our criminal justice system needs to consider individual cases in these drug-addicted pregnant women situations and not create sets of laws with a "one-size-fits-all" mentality. Not every woman deserves incarceration, and not every woman deserves to go free, either. Judging which situation should dictate which outcome matters not only to the woman, but also to the baby and to society as a whole.

I know that, according to sociologist Mary Grabar, some states like Florida and South Carolina think it benefits society to prosecute these women (23), while other states such as Massachusetts and Georgia throw out such cases (Howell 206). I also understand fully that "approximately 375,000 infants are born each year to women who abuse narcotic drugs" (Watson 1), and these poor, innocent babies face painful withdrawal symptoms, breathing problems, low birth weights, birth defects, behavioral problems, and cognitive skill problems (NIDA). But, I also comprehend that some mothers who have not had much prenatal care may not understand what they are doing to their babies and that, as Dr. Jessup tells us, many of the women live in poverty, face regular domestic abuse, live with men who force drugs on them, and often have suffered child abuse (295). Perhaps, then, some compassion is necessary.

That compassion can come in the form of offering treatment programs to these women. These programs can offer mothers "couples and family therapy, prenatal care, childcare, and narcotics anonymous meetings. After the women deliver their babies, they can remain in the program for another six to twelve months, so that the facility's staff can keep a close eye on them" (Watson 6–7). Such programs aim not to punish women and break up families, but, rather, to sustain and preserve the family through therapeutic means (Chavkin et al. 118). If we really do believe the family is the primary unit of society, then wouldn't we prefer to maintain families than to destroy them? Wouldn't we prefer to save the baby and the woman?

Some women know the harmful effects their drug abuse will produce and still, they continue to use the drugs just so that they can satisfy their addiction; some go through treatment programs and, nonetheless, keep using drugs through every pregnancy. These kinds of women deserve to be incarcerated and have their babies taken away from them because they are unfit parents who will never offer their children safe or healthy lives because their need for the drug will overrule every other instinct they have. Some women, however, experience drug addiction during pregnancy for the first time; they lack a full awareness and do not necessarily know how to eliminate that addiction. These kinds of women deserve a chance at treatment and keeping their babies.

Sincerely,

Jill C. Smoot

Works Cited

Chavkin W., et al. "National Survey of the States: Policies and Practices Regarding Drug-Using Pregnant Women." *American Journal of Public Health*, vol. 88, no. 1, Jan. 1998, pp. 117–119. *EBSCOhost*, https://www.doi.org/10.2105/AJPH.88.1.117.

Grabar, Mary. "PREGNANCY POLICE. Sending Women to Jail Is Not the Answer." *Progressive*, vol. 54, no. 12, Dec. 1990, pp. 22–24. *EBSCOhost*, search.ebscohost. com/login.aspx?direct=true&db=a9h&AN=9012172025&site=ehost-live.

Howell, Embry M., et al. "Identifying Pregnant Substance Abusers and Studying their Treatment using Birth Certificates, Medicaid Claims, and State Substance Abuse Treatment Data." *Journal of Drug Issues*, vol. 30, no. 1, 2000, pp. 205–23. *ProQuest*, http://lib-proxy.sunywcc.edu/login?url=https://search.proquest.com/docview/208865837?accountid=14174,doi:http://dx.doi.org/10.1177/002204260003000112.

Jessup, Martha A., et al. "Extrinsic Barriers to Substance Abuse Treatment among Pregnant Drug Dependent Women." *Journal of Drug Issues*, vol. 33, no. 2, 2003, p. 285. *ProQuest*, http://lib-proxy.sunywcc.edu/login?url=https://search.proquest.com/ docview/208838164?accountid=14174,doi:http://dx.doi.org/10.1177/002204260303300202.

NIDA. "Health Consequences of Drug Misuse." *National Institute on Drug Abuse*, 23 Mar. 2017, https://www.drugabuse.gov/related-topics/health-consequences-drug-misuse. Accessed 20 Jun. 2017.

Watson, Ronald. *Substance Abuse during Pregnancy and Childhood*. Humana Press Inc., 1995.

MODEL 3 OUTREACH PIECE

HELP FUND EMSNOW (ELIMINATE MANDATORY SENTENCING NOW)!

© Rob Wilson/Shutterstock.com

We fight for families!
We fight for justice!
We fight to keep non-violent offenders in rehab instead of in prison!

© Garagestock/Shutterstock.com

CHAPTER 4

THE COLD, HARD FACTS

- "Half a million Americans are serving long sentences for nonviolent drug offenses [. . .] 48% of the whole prison population" (Frandino).

- "80% of those sentenced are black or ethnic, with only 10% of those sentenced being white" (Towson and Templeton 61).

- According to a study conducted by *Economist* in 2015, taking these half-million people out of our workforce and out of our consumer population costs our economy billions of dollars each year ("Jailhouse Nation" 12).

- Depending on the year, keeping these people in prison "costs between 63 and 75 billion dollars each year" (Valdez and Shank).

- Every time we put a mother or father in jail for a long sentence, something has to be done with their children. Some go into state or foster care, while others go to family members, but in either case, the government then spends money for their care either in foster care payments, welfare checks, or orphan home costs (Frandino).

© Sakhorn/Shutterstock.com

- While scholars such as J. T. Bellham claim that "removing these violent felons from our streets makes life safer for everyone" (qtd. Schmertmann et al. 450), they ignore the fact that most of the people in jail under these mandatory sentencing laws are actually nonviolent offenders—the low-level street dealers and mules, not the big, major drug traffickers who are actually violent.

Donate whatever you can to help fund the legal team of Emmons, Smith, and Tweeder as they fight to reform these laws!

© Georgios Tsichlis/Shutterstock.com

Works Cited

Frandino, Joseph L. "Are Mandatory Minimum Sentences an Injustice?" *CBS Sunday Morning*, 5 October, 2014, https://www.bing.com/videos/search?q= mandatory+ sentencing%2c+ documentary+about&view=detail&mid=FEA190BC 936DE45E 7688FEA190BC936DE45E7688&FORM=VIRE. Accessed 30 March 2019.

"Jailhouse Nation." *Economist*, vol. 415, no. 8943, June 2015, pp. 11–15. *EBSCOhost*, search. ebscohost.com/login.aspx?direct=true&db=ssf&AN=103359102&site=ehost-live.

Schmertmann, Carl P., et al. "Three Strikes and You're Out: Demographic Analysis of Mandatory Prison Sentences." *Demography*, vol. 35, no. 4, Nov. 1998, pp. 445–63. *EBSCOhost*, https://www.doi.org/10.2307/3004013.

Towson, Jillian and Mason Templeton. "Mandatory Sentencing or Mandatory Bigotry?" *The Journal of Criminal Affairs*, vol. 37, no. 4, & September 2017, pp. 60–73. *EBSCOhost*, search. ebscohost.com/login.aspx?direct=true &db=ssf&AN=56417160&site=ehost-live.

Valdez, Rudy and Cindy Shank. "The Sentence." *HBO Films*, October 2018, https://www.hbo. com/documentaries/the sentnce.html. Accessed 31 March 2019.

O.   Readings and Resources

© Mascha Tace/Shutterstock.com

"How to Integrate Quotations In Essay Writing—APA and MLA," by David Taylor, November 7, 2010:

> https://www.youtube.com/watch?v=_M0F1rOnFUY

"Synthesizing Information" by GCF Learn Free, August 6, 2012:

> https://www.youtube.com/watch?v=7dEGoJdb6O0

"Strategies for Synthesis" by Mary Lourdes Silva, June 12, 2013:

> https://www.youtube.com/watch?v=c7HtCHtQ9w0

"What is Plagiarism?" by mjmfoodie, November 28, 2016:

> https://www.youtube.com/watch?v=zPqKXJbzRP4

"What is Plagiarism and How to Avoid It" by Brock University Library, September 2, 2014:

> https://www.youtube.com/watch?v=Pmab92ghG0M

"Purpose and Genre" by BYU Idaho, 2019:

> http://www.byui.edu/academic-support-centers/writing/video-lessons-and-handouts/purpose-and-genre

"Audience, Purpose, and Genre" by Caitlin Foley, January 26, 2016:

> https://www.youtube.com/watch?v=bXO8jEVQssA

"Genre, Audience, and Purpose" by Kate Green, July 9, 2015:

> https://www.youtube.com/watch?v=oP17FGMrMtk

"Purpose, Audience, and Form (P.A.F.)" by Vicky Maxted, June 2, 2014:

> https://www.youtube.com/watch?v=93eA7cttZCM

"Audience, Purpose, and Tone" by DoE Curriculum, September 29, 2015:

> https://www.youtube.com/watch?v=Z1Nrls4-yH8

"Poster Presentation Basics" by Boise State URC, April 16, 2010:

> https://www.youtube.com/watch?v=cRNQjo2IstY

"Giving an Effective Poster Presentation" by George Hess, February 8, 2013:

> https://www.youtube.com/watch?v=vMSaFUrk-FA

"How To Create a Research Poster" from NYU Libraries, May 17, 2018:

> https://guides.nyu.edu/posters

"How to Prepare an Oral Presentation" by Michigan State University—Undergraduate Research, September 17, 2013:

> https://www.youtube.com/watch?v=LzIJFD-ddoI

"Research Talk 101" by Lucia Dettori, DePaul University, June 29, 2007:

> https://slideplayer.fr/slide/13917634/

P. Grammar Concept: Apostrophes

You will learn grammar best by applying it within the context of your own writing. Use these rules as a guide. Your teacher will probably help you to target examples from your own writing and your peers' writing to help clarify how these rules work.

◇◇

The Apostrophe '

The apostrophe has three uses:

1. **To show possession**
2. **To replace letters**
3. **To form nonstandard plurals**

> ## PUNCTUATION TIP
>
> No other punctuation mark faces as much abuse as the apostrophe. The first problem is failing to use it (thus we see *Walgreens* instead of *Walgreen's*). The second problem is, ironically, using it in words where it doesn't belong *(Open Monday's)*.

To show possession

1. **Use the apostrophe to show possession.**

To know where to place the apostrophe, say the word. Where the word stops, add the apostrophe: the cat—the cat's dish; the cats—the cats' dish.

> Karl's book; both Karls' books (two men named Karl)
>
> everybody's response; someone else's car
>
> city's lights; cities' lights; baby's crib; babies' cribs
>
> the man's hat; the men's hats
>
> the woman's computer; the women's computer
>
> bachelor's degree; master's degree
>
> Paul Smith's house; the Smiths' house
>
> Katie said, "Aren't they at the Smiths'?"
>
> Roger and Bill's book (the one book belongs to both Roger and Bill)
>
> Roger's and Bill's books (each owns a book)
>
> Jean-Luc's singing is enjoyable, and so is Linda's whistling (possessive apostrophe needed for the gerund: a noun that comes from a verb and ends in -*ing*)
>
> the hostess's party; the hostesses' parties
>
> Mrs. Phillips's cell phone

If adding an extra syllable makes the word hard to pronounce, add only the apostrophe.

> Mrs. Phillips' cell phone
>
> Athens' famous sights
>
> for goodness' sake

WARNING!

Don't use the apostrophe with seven possessive pronouns: *yours, his, hers, ours, theirs, its* **(versus the contraction** *it's* = *it is* **or** *it has***), and** *whose* **(versus the contraction** *who's* = *who is* **or** *who has***).**

This book is yours; the car is his or hers; the job is ours; the job is theirs. Its color is green. (It's raining outside; it's been raining all afternoon.) Whose responsibility is this? (Who's going to volunteer? Who's volunteered before?)

To replace letters

2. **Use the apostrophe to replace letters.**

   it's = it is or it has

   shouldn't = should not

   they're = they are

   the class of '91 = the class of 1991

   'til = until

   Hallowe'en = Halloweven

To form nonstandard plurals

3. **Use the apostrophe to form nonstandard plurals: for letters, numbers used as words, words cited as words, abbreviations, and symbols.**

   CAPITAL LETTERS: Watch your P's and Q's. A's win the pennant.

   LOWERCASE LETTERS: Watch your p's and q's.

   NUMBERS USED AS WORDS: He crosses his 7's. (= sevens)

   He often talks about the 1980's. (= nineteen eighties)

   WORDS CITED AS WORDS: Please practice pronouncing your the's.

   ABBREVIATIONS: The professors all have Ph.D.'s.

   SYMBOLS: I saw +'s and -'s in the grade book.

For this third use, leave out the apostrophe if there's no danger of confusion:

Watch your Ps and Qs.

He crosses his 7s.

He talks often about the 1980s.

The professors all have Ph.D.s.

can'ts, don'ts, won'ts

ifs, ands, or buts; ins and outs

But with confusion, use the apostrophe:

As win the pennant! (confusion with *As*)

   A's win the pennant.

Watch your ps and qs. (confusion with a misprint)

   Watch your p's and q's.

Please practice pronouncing your thes. (confusion with a misprint)

   Please practice pronouncing your the's.

I saw +s and -s in the grade book (confusion if symbols unclear)

   I saw +'s and -'s in the grade book.

WARNING!

Remember that most words don't use the apostrophe to form plurals.

WRONG	RIGHT
mens shoe's	men's shoes
open Sunday's	open Sundays
seven month's of the year	seven months of the year

From *The Less-Is-More Handbook: A Guide To College Writing, Second Edition* by Larry Edgerton. Copyright © 2017 by Kendall Hunt Publishing Company. Reprinted by permission.

◇◇

Lessons to Use in the Co-Requisite Classroom During This Unit

A co-requisite Writing and Research course has but one absolute rule: no additional assignments outside of class may be assigned; the work of the Writing and Research course *is* the work of the co-requisite course.

Nonetheless, during co-requisite class times, students should engage in activities that address their noncognitive, cognitive, and skills-related areas. The activities I include here encompass all three categories of learning and coordinate with the work of the Writing and Research course. Of course, students' needs regarding whatever occurs in the Writing and Research course on a particular day may at times take precedence in the co-requisite course, and at times, the class time may function as a writing workshop, but every class session cannot function in these ways, or the students will not acquire what they need from the course. Individual teachers will of course decide what to use, when to use it, and even what adaptations to apply. Some of the activities, each one designed for a single class session, may actually take longer than a single class because co-requisite courses do not operate on the same schedule on every college campus and different students have different kinds of questions about assignments.

"WHO AM I?" ACTIVITY:
The Personality Matrix (Noncognitive)

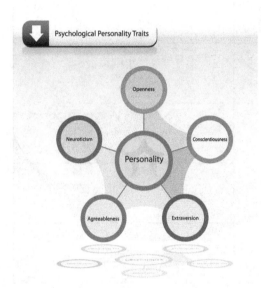

© John T Takai/Shutterstock.com

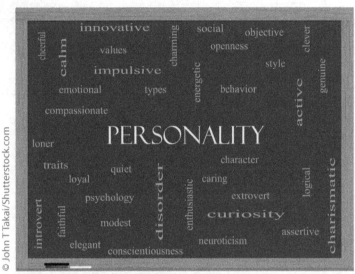

© Keith Bell/Shutterstock.com

1. Examine the two images above. The image on the left shows the five big, general categories psychologists use to categorize all personality traits. The image on the right displays a host of individual traits that might belong to or exemplify the categories on the left.

2. Circle the traits listed on the right image that you believe apply to you. Feel free to add traits you possess but that you do not see on the list. (For example, there is nothing on the list such as "fearful," "shy," "anxious," "gregarious/social," "daring," "adventurous," "spiritual," "physical," etc.)

3. Draw arrows from those traits you have circled or added on the right-side image to the category you think they fit in the image on the left.

4. Now examine what you have created. Do your personality traits spread evenly among the big 5, or do they lie predominantly in one or two realms? What conclusions can you draw about yourself based on these results?

CHAPTER 4

5. Now let's think about these traits in relation to success in the academic world. Form a group of three to four students, discuss the traits, and fill in the chart below.

BIG 5 CATEGORY	TRAITS ASSOCIATED WITH THE CATEGORY	WAYS THESE TRAITS WILL HELP OR HINDER A STUDENT'S ACADEMIC SUCCESS (LABEL AS "HELP" OR "HINDER")
OPENNESS		
CONSCIENTIOUSNESS		
EXTROVERSION		
AGREEABLENESS		
NEUROTOCISM		

6. After you have filled in the chart, send a member or two of your group to the board in the front of the room, and add your group's conclusions to the chart there. If you see other students have used some of the same ideas you did, you need not rewrite them; just put a check mark next to each one, so we know more than one group agreed with the idea. After everyone is done, we'll discuss the consensus as a large group.

7. Now that we have finished thinking and talking, reflect on what you have learned. Are there personality traits you'd like to develop in yourself to engender academic success? Are there some you'd like to alter in yourself for the same reason? How might you go about doing so? Write that reflection here.

Apostrophe Challenge

1. Please put the grammar pages about using apostrophes in front of you, so you can refer to them during the game.
2. You may participate as an individual, or you may work as part of a team of two.
3. Examine the attached student-authored paragraph.
4. Note the highlighted instances of uses of apostrophes.
5. Decide whether or not they are done correctly.
6. See the chart below. Fill in the columns with the answers: Correct or Incorrect, Rule that Applies, Correction if Needed.

The Paragraph

. . . Everyone knows that the drug's these women use can harm their babies' in many ways, but whether or not such women should be prosecuted as child abusers has remained a debatable issue for a really long time, though currently, not many are focused upon the problem, and *current* studie's are in short supply. Nonetheless, in the past, some prosecutors' beliefs encompass the idea that such women ought to be incarcerated for child abuse, while others' have contended that these women need most to complete a drug treatment and rehabilitation program. . . . But who's right, and should one rule apply to all drug-abusing pregnant women's penalty's, or do some women deserve prison time while others deserve treatment? Certainly, for the childrens' sake, we as a society need to decide. But its a tough decision; it's going to require research.

WORD	CORRECT OR INCORRECT	RULE THAT APPLIES	CORRECTION IF NECESSARY
drug's			
babies'			
studie's			
prosecutors'			
others'			
who's			
women's			
penalty's			
childrens'			
its			
it's			

Name_____ Date_____

FINAL SUMMATIVE ATTITUDE ASSESSMENT
CO-REQUISITE COURSE

Using the Likert scale, please answer the following questions by checking the column you feel appropriate.

QUESTION	3—DEFINITELY	2—SOMEWHAT	1—NOT AT ALL
1. After taking this class, I would recommend it to others.			
2. This course has given me a more positive attitude about this subject.			
3. My study habits have improved as a result of taking this course.			
4. I am now better focused in my work to stay on task.			
5. My ability to complete the work assigned to me has improved.			
6. I enjoyed this class, and I am satisfied with my progress after completing this course.			
7. This course enabled me to pass the 3-credit Writing and Research course.			

Please write in the answers you feel appropriate.

QUESTION	YOUR ANSWER
8. What I liked best in this course was . . .	
9. What I liked least about this course was . . .	

10. What I would change about this course includes . . .	
11. Additional comments I would make include . . .	

CHAPTER 4

FROM OUTLINE TO NOTES TO DRAFT ACTIVITY

Directions:

1. On your desk, place your essay outline.

2. Place next to it EITHER your printed note cards or your printed researched sources.

3. Examine the set of notes/highlighted areas of your research articles.

4. Label those notes with an outline topic number and description. You may even decide that some do not fit/cannot be used.

5. IF you are using the articles, then cut up those notes [your highlighted sections] into rectangles.

6. Now spread them out on your desk.

7. Using the outline and your sense of how a draft might work, start moving these note cards around to create a draft. When you think you have some placed properly/logically/sensibly, tape them together in the sequence you have chosen.

8. I have given each of you some blank cards to use to add necessary transitions and explanations and ideas.

9. *What has this exercise taught you about constructing a research essay from your outline and notes?*

CHAPTER 4

Research Essay Brainstorming/Organizing Sheet

SAMPLE:

MY SUBCLAIMS/ CONTRIBUTIONS TO THE PRIMARY ANSWER TO THE QUESTION	SUPPORTING EVIDENCE (QUOTES AND SOURCE AND SUMMARIES/ PARAPHRASES AND SOURCES)	CONTRADICTNG EVIDENCE/ ARGUMENTS (QUOTES AND SUMMARIES/ PARAPHRASES AND SOURCES)
Canada has more weapons but less crime than the U.S.	"Canadians possess an average of 3 guns for every citizen" (Stanger 22). "U.S. citizens possess one gun per every 200 citizens" (Stanger 23).	Canada contains vast areas of open, uninhabited territory (Billings). U.S. populations are heavily concentrated in urban or heavily peopled suburbs (Billings).
Canadian news and other media tend to report hard facts with little hype, whereas U.S. media report everything couched in dire warnings meant to make people afraid and worried.	"The average American newscast of 30 minutes contains a minimum of 6 warnings about any of the following: terror or crime, health, physical appearance or limitations, finances, or environmental hazards" (Trowel 185).	Most news shows offer some "feel-good" stories/human interest stories.
Fear produces stress and anxiety that often find expression or release in explosions—violence. People with weapons use them when they explode.	"When people process fear, their bodies react physically by producing increased levels of cortisol, a chemical that increases aggression levels" (Tansem and Boder 231).	"The vast majority of Americans who own guns never use them for anything more than target-shooting, skeet, and hunting. They never aim at another human being" (Stanger 28).

My Compelling Lead

Canadians possess three times as many guns as United States citizens do, yet Canada has five times fewer murders committed with guns than the United States does (Stanger 22–26). What can possibly cause this difference in violent crime rates? Can we actually find a cause in this comparison? Do the two cultures possess some kind of fundamental difference that accounts for the problem? **I contend that America's steady diet of the culture of fear makes all the difference.** While certainly, geographically, as Billings notes, Canada contains huge swaths of uninhabited land, while the United States seems much heavier in population density, I would argue that difference matters little. Rather, like Trowel, **I conclude America's media produce the kind of fear that constantly engenders anxiety in people, and based on studies of aggression, I see that anxiety can explode in violence.** When even a simple weather report done in exaggerated proportions can send people running in desperate panic to the grocery stores, how can we expect hard-core news to prompt calm?

CHAPTER 4

SO NOW WHAT? WHAT DO I DO NEXT IN MY RESEARCH ARTICLE?

1. Examine your subclaims. What natural sequence/order do you see there? What categories/ subdivisions do they suggest for your essay? Can even these subdivisions be divided further? Those divisions may indeed become separate paragraphs of your essay.

2. WHAT explanations and supporting evidence do you need in each of those subdivisions? (REMEMBER: YOUR ideas drive your article; the research only supports and/or positions you.)

3. What opposing viewpoints must you also mention and discuss/position yourself against in your article?

4. Make outlines of each paragraph with these three questions in mind.

5. Then begin writing those paragraphs, and before you know it, you'll have an article.

EXAMPLE: Subclaim from above: "Fear produces stress and anxiety that often find expression or release in explosions—violence. People with weapons use them when they explode."

 III. Fear Produces Stress and Anxiety, which leads to aggression

   A. Physical-Chemical Components of Fear

     1. Cortisol Levels

       a. Tandem and Border research

       b. Explanation/interpretation of that research

       c. Concrete examples: children in lengthy day care, prisoners

       d. Tudor's research against the claim

       e. My argument in favor of Tandem and Border

     2. Brain Function and Aggression

       a. Changes in brain due to Cortisol (Tandem and Border)

       b. Manifestations of aggression

       c. Interpretations of that research

       d. Counterclaims: Varied levels of aggression (Anderson's research)

       e. My argument addressing both sets of research

   B. How all of this information relates to my overarching claim

ETC. . . .

YOUR TURN:

1. My research question: _____
    _____

2. My answers(s) to the question now that I have completed my research: _____
    _____

MY SUBCLAIMS/ CONTRIBUTIONS TO THE PRIMARY ANSWER TO THE QUESTION	SUPPORTING EVIDENCE (QUOTES AND SOURCES AND SUMMARIES/ PARAPHRASES AND SOURCES)	CONTRADICTNG EVIDENCE/ARGUMENTS (QUOTES AND SUMMARIES/ PARAPHRASES AND SOURCES)

MY COMPELLING LEAD:

Possible Outline:

Formal Outline Template For I-Search Essay

Create a formal outline or a storyboard (a separate template) in which you lay out the organization you would follow if you were to write the actual research article that answers your research question.

Fill in the information in the spaces provided.

I. Introduction

    A. Hook:

    B. Foregrounding/Positioning Statement:

    C. Claim:

II. What I Knew, Assumed, or Imagined:

    A. Idea 1: _____

        1. Detail of Evidence:

        2. Detail of Evidence:

    B. Idea 2: _____

        1. Detail of Evidence:

        2. Detail of Evidence:

    C. Idea 3: _____

        1. Detail of Evidence:

        2. Detail of Evidence:

III. What I Discovered

    A. Idea 1 (Perhaps from source 1): _____

        1. Detail of Evidence:

        2. Detail of Evidence:

        3. Explanation and My Reaction:

    B. Idea 2 (Perhaps from source 2): _____

        1. Detail of Evidence:

        2. Detail of Evidence:

        3. Explanation and My Reaction:

    C. Idea 3 (Perhaps from source 3): _____

        1. Detail of Evidence:

        2. Detail of Evidence:

        3. Explanation and My Reaction:

D. Idea 4 (Perhaps from source 4): _____

    1. Detail of Evidence:

    2. Detail of Evidence:

    3. Explanation and My Reaction:

E. Idea 5 (Perhaps from source 5): _____

    1. Detail of Evidence:

    2. Detail of Evidence:

    3. Explanation and My Reaction:

F. Idea 6 (Perhaps from source 6 and Perhaps an Opposing Argument): _____

    1. Detail of Evidence:

    2. Detail of Evidence:

    3. Explanation and My Reaction:

CHAPTER 4

IV. Reflections (Or What I Learned and What Conclusions I Have Drawn):

    A. Idea 1: _____

        1. Detail of Evidence:

        2. Detail of Evidence:

    B. Idea 2: _____

        1. Detail of Evidence:

        2. Detail of Evidence:

    C. Idea 3: _____

        1. Detail of Evidence:

        2. Detail of Evidence:

    D. What Future Researchers Still Need To Do

        1.

        2.

V. Works Cited

CHAPTER 4

Formal Outline Template for Traditional Research Essay

Create a formal outline or a storyboard (a separate template) in which you lay out the organization you would follow if you were to write the actual research article that answers your research question.

Fill in the information in the spaces provided.

I. Introduction

    A. Hook:

    B. Foregrounding/Positioning Statement:

    C. Thesis Statement:

II. General Reason 1:

    A. Supporting Evidence

        1. Detail of Evidence:

        2. Detail of Evidence:

III. General Reason 2:

    A. Supporting Evidence

        1. Detail of Evidence:

        2. Detail of Evidence:

IV. General Reason 3:

    A. Supporting Evidence

        1. Detail of Evidence:

        2. Detail of Evidence:

V.   General Reason 4:

    A.   Supporting Evidence

        1.   Detail of Evidence:

        2.   Detail of Evidence:

VI.   Opposing Arguments

    A.   What the Opposition Says:

    B.   Counterargument (What I Say):

VII. Conclusion

Concluding Statements:

What Research Remains to be Done:

CHAPTER 4

A POSSIBLE RESEARCH PROJECT/RESEARCH ESSAY/ I-SEARCH ESSAY TEMPLATE

REMINDER: What Are the Components of a Research Project/Essay/I-Search Essay?

Tell the story of your research project, describing what you found, and how your perspective evolved, in a formal, fully-documented essay in MLA style. You'll use your research, what you have learned by completing your annotated bibliography, etc.

Write your essay in narrative form, recording the steps of the discovery process. Do not feel obligated to tell everything, but highlight the findings and happenings that were crucial to your hunt and contributed to your understanding of the topic. Organize your essay into the following sections:

1. **What I Knew, Assumed, or Imagined.** Describe your prior knowledge and understanding of the topic and question, before you began the project. Yes, you may adapt this section from your Proposal.

2. **What I Discovered.** Describe the information and ideas you gathered. Organize this section as a chronological narrative (like a story) recording the steps of the discovery process. Don't share every detail; instead, highlight key findings and happenings, the ones that really impacted your perspective. Feel free to include missteps and mistakes you may have made along the way.

3. **Reflections.** Reflect on what you found and draw some conclusions. Compare what you thought you knew, assumed, or imagined, with what you actually discovered. Discuss what you still hope to learn about this topic/question, and reflect on how you might further share or act on what you have learned.

YES, you may indeed reuse parts—though NOT ALL—of your research proposal! [I have highlighted in blue the different additions/changes from the previous proposal template. NOTE the tense changes.]. You'll also probably use *some* pieces (*not* all) of the annotations you have written in your annotated bibliographies.

Today, the topic/issue/idea/concept/problem (←Choose one) of _____

concerns/interests/intrigues/worries/registers (←Choose one) many people. Some believe

_____,

while others think _____.

Considering these ideas has significance to _____ because _____.

As a _____, this topic has become ever present in my mind too, especially because _____. When I began my research this term, I really wanted to know _____

_____.

As I have progressed through this research process, my question has/has not [← Choose ONE] changed. {IF you state that it has changed, you should state to what it changed.} My perspective of the answer, however, has altered, for I have reached a conclusion I had not fully expected. OR My perspective of the answer has not shifted too much, however, for I have reached a conclusion I had pretty much expected.

Even before I began searching for the answer to my question, I did know a little something about the topic already. For example, I understood _____

_____

because I _____

_____. In addition,

through _____, I had comprehended that _____

_____

_____. In fact, I even had a general theory or hypothesis; I imagined that _____.

In spite of what I already imagined or knew, however, much existed that I did not know or understand fully. Apart from my actual research question, I had to find information about some of the small sub-issues that encompassed my knowledge gaps. These issues included _____

_____.

As I considered these knowledge gaps and the direction I needed to follow in my research, I started my journey of discovery with the texts I discovered in our library's databases. Using the search terms _____ and the databases named _____,

_____, and _____, I soon discovered several helpful articles, including two that were peer-reviewed/scholarly, and three others. The first of these resources was "_____

_____," written by _____ and published in _____ on _____. This author's basic claim is that, "_____

_____" ( ). In essence, he postulates that _____

because _____

_____,

and uses _____ as the supporting evidence. As I contemplated this claim and evidence, my own contention surfaced as _____

because _____

_____.

These ideas stayed in my mind as I discovered another resource, which was entitled "_____

_____," written by _____ and published in _____ on _____. This author's basic claim is that, "_____" ( ). In essence, he postulates that _____

because _____

_____,

and uses _____

_____ as the supporting evidence. As I contemplated this claim and evidence, my own contention surfaced as _____

because _____

_____.

As I considered these ideas, I found a third resource, "_____," written by _____ and published in _____ on _____. This author's basic claim is that, "_____

_____

_____" ( ). In essence, he postulates

that_____

because _____

_____,

and uses _____ as the supporting evidence. As I contemplated this claim and evidence, my own contention surfaced as _____

because _____

_____.

Gradually, my ideas began solidifying and becoming clear, but I continued searching and found a fourth article, "_____," written by _____ and published in _____ on _____. This author's basic claim is that, "_____

_____" ( ). In essence, he postulates

that_____

because _____

_____,

and uses _____

_____ as the

supporting evidence. As I engaged with this article and thought of the others I had read, I started

thinking _____

because _____

_____.

Given these ideas and the research I had already discovered, I chose to find a final, fifth resource, entitled "_____," written by _____ and published in _____ on _____. This author's basic claim is that, "_____" ( ). In essence, he postulates that_____ because _____ _____ , and uses _____ _____ as the supporting evidence. As I pondered this claim and evidence, I began to feel ready to draw my own, final conclusions and answers to my research question.

Getting to those conclusions and sources, however, was not necessarily easy. I encountered some difficulties, which included _____ _____ _____.

Nonetheless, I did find _____ fairly easy, and along the way, I discovered some interesting surprises, such as _____ _____ _____.

As I worked through the difficulties, the surprises, and the whole process, I finally reached some definitive conclusions. In general, I now believe _____ because _____. While _____ (name of a scholar) claims that "_____," I _____ ETC.—Here, you will begin your own argument of **SEVERAL PARAGRAPHS (at least two full pages).** Use citations from your research, BUT, make certain to use your own ideas too. Remember to POSITION YOURSELF IN THE CONVERSATION: They Say, I Say, and Metacommentary/Explanations.

These conclusions represent my learning about the topic within the mere six weeks during which I have studied the question. If I had this process to conduct all over again, I would probably _____. [←Explain here what you'd do the same way and/or what you might change.]. As I think about the research I have found, I perceive a need for researchers to _____. I know that if I had additional time to continue with this research, I would start by _____ _____. Doing so would matter because _____. [← Close with a resounding statement that will linger in your readers' minds.]

Works Cited

[List all sources here in MLA 8 format.]

POSTER BRAINSTORMING SHEET

1. What title should I use? (It probably will not be the title I used for the essay. It will instead be very short and immediately both draw the attention of the audience and encapsulate my primary emphasis.)

2. What are the three to five most interesting findings of my research?

    a.

    b.

    c.

    d.

    e.

3. What graphics (images, charts, graphs, photos, etc.) and quotes can I use to enhance my primary points?

    a.

    b.

    c.

    d.

    e.

4. Where might I want to place specific items on the poster? (What order will I follow?)

5. What talking points will I use to talk to those who view my poster?

    a.

    b.

    c.

CHAPTER 4

RESEARCH TALK BRAINSTORMING SHEET

Introduction

Hello, my name is _____. I am a_____-year student at WCC majoring in _____. I'm going to talk to you today about my research on _____.

Research question and significance

- I wanted to find out _____ [Insert your research question].

- This question interested me because _____, and I think it is an important question because _____.

Research methods/design

- I thought the best way to answer this question would be by _____ _____.

Research activity

Here's what I did:

Results

Here's what I found out:

Significance of results/where this research might lead

- This result matters because . . .

- Now that I've learned this, I see that some other questions to ask are . . .

Conclusion:

MY HANDOUTS/PPT./DEMONSTRATION MATERIALS WILL BE:

CHAPTER 4

SOMETHING NEW ACTIVITY [Noncognitive]

1. Get into a group of three or four students.

2. Send one member of your group to select one of the bags the teacher has brought into class.

3. Each bag contains an apparently random selection of household items. Your job is to make something of them. You must use every item in the bag, though you may trade items with other groups. You may "add" only those items at the front of the room: tape, glue, large paper, etc. WHAT you do is entirely up to your group. You may decide to build something. You may decide to create a skit that uses every item as a prop. You may decide to fashion some artwork or new invention. You may decide to fashion some kind of game or challenge exercise or some social media post. You may choose to join forces with another group and its items.

4. You have thirty minutes to decide what to do and to execute that plan.

5. When the time has expired, you'll perform/show/explain to the rest of the class.

6. After everyone has showcased the creations, we will deconstruct and reflect upon the exercise.

CHAPTER 4

WRITING ACROSS THE CURRICULUM/WRITING IN THE DISCIPLINES TIPS AND CONNECTIONS FOR THIS UNIT

1. For activities 4B and 4C, substitute for the texts connected to your own discipline.

2. Emphasize your discipline's preferred citation format through demonstration, discussion about, and scrutiny of that particular format.

3. Discuss with students the preferred academic essay genre of your field. Offer outline examples and sample essays from that field. For example, a science course might provide from the databases or from online sources an example of an essay that uses the Purpose-method-procedure-conclusion style.

4. Alter the research essay assignment directions to suit the kind of research essay most often done in your discipline. Alter the rubric and peer reviews to correspond with those shifts.

5. Eliminate entirely or replace the research essay entirely with the outreach piece as suits your discipline.

CHAPTER 5

Presenting Our Discoveries and Conclusions

Week 15

© Testing/Shutterstock.com

© Monkey Business Images/Shutterstock.com

One standard additional genre for which academia uses research includes the presentation. Such presentations offer a way for scholars to share their conclusions with others and to interact with other scholars regarding the topic. Students may give presentations to big gatherings in large auditoriums, to moderate-sized groups in a small classroom or conference room, or to very small clusters in a boardroom type setting. In general, these talks may encompass plain *talking/lecturing, poster sessions,* or *multimedia presentations*, or sometimes, some combination of the three because they are not mutually exclusive. They do, however, differ in some ways.

TALKS/LECTURES	POSTER SESSIONS	MULTIMEDIA PRESENTATIONS
The delivery of a lecture about the research and the conclusions reached	The use of text and graphics on a single poster (sometimes paper, sometimes projected on a screen)	The use of a PowerPoint, video, slide show, web page, etc., to convey ideas from the research
May leave room for audience questions	Placed alongside other posters on any number of topics	Projected on screen with minimal commentary from the presenter
May be interactive with a workshop activity after the lecture	Viewers walk from poster to poster to examine them.	Presenter offers an introduction, conclusion, and an invitation for questions (which the presenter answers).
May be part of a panel of presenters on the same topic (very short speaking time followed by question-and-answer session)	Presenter stands by, ready to answer questions OR every 15–20 minutes, talks for 5–10 minutes about the research conclusions.	
May include the use of a PowerPoint as a prop	The poster does most of the talking for the presenter.	
Lasts anywhere from 2 minutes to 60 minutes		

A. Talk Basics

Regardless of the type of presentation you give, you will find that talking to audiences about your research involves some specific considerations.

- Your talk differs from your essay. The essay includes full arguments and details, whereas your *talk offers only the highlights*.
- You want to engage, interest, and excite your audience and command its attention, not bog it down with unnecessary details or impress it with your wisdom.
- You want the audience to understand your primary idea(s) clearly.
- As always, you must consider your audience. What will its members likely know already? What angle will interest its members most? How alert will it be at the time of your delivery?
- Start your talk with the most important concept you want your audience to remember, and hook its members on wanting to know about that idea.

- Use lots of telling examples, particularly the extreme and memorable ones.
- Eliminate explanations of context and background, information overviews, difficulties you may have experienced, etc. Reduce your talk to what you most want the audience to know and remember.
- Eliminate reports on related work, but be prepared to answer questions about it.
- Show energy and enthusiasm for your ideas. Feel free to move around, use hand and arm gestures, and vary your tone and volume.
- Keep eye contact with your audience, not with whatever tools you may have brought along to help present your ideas.
- Practice/rehearse ahead of time to get your timing and expression precise.
- Memorize the first minute of your talk to help get you through any anxiety you may feel at the start.

Whether you address a small or large group, present a talk or a poster, you will find these general rules helpful.

B. Poster Basics

Often, your poster will sit among many other posters at a poster session. Sometimes, the poster is a physical, heavy stock cardboard presentation board, but in these modern times, frequently your poster will be projected through electronic media. Whatever method the poster session uses, your poster should adhere to a few basic guidelines.

- Highlight only the key idea(s) and examples, not get bogged down in details.
- Use an eye-catching, attention-grabbing brief title, which will in all likelihood vary from your essay's title.
- Design the poster so that viewers can see it from about six to ten feet away.
- Use more graphics (graphs, charts, images, photos, etc.) than text.
- When you do use text, use bullets, numbering, and headlines.
- Avoid using too many fonts and colors, and use colors viewers can easily read.
- Use a clean and consistent lay-out that separates sections by columns or spacing.
- In your design, maintain an awareness that viewers' eyes will first see the middle of the poster and then go back to read from the left side to the right side.
- Use salient quotes and data.
- Reserve a section of the poster for your list of sources, and credit only the sources you actually use on the poster.
- Prepare and practice a two-to-five-minute speech that introduces the important ideas of your poster, and then let the poster—and your answers to any questions—do your talking.
- Save your poster as a .pdf, so you can display it electronically no matter what system the session uses for projecting posters.

To create your poster, you can use a variety of programs, including PowerPoint, Adobe Illustrator, Photoshop, InDesign, or Open Source's Impress, for example. Choose the program with which you have the greatest familiarity and facility, so that you do not have to spend a lot of time learning how to use a new program.

C. Multimedia Basics

Your use of multimedia to present your research may stand alone, or it may serve as part of your talk or your poster display. Many of you have probably created such presentations many times in the past, but though you may know the mechanics of composing these creations very well, you may not have practiced some basic rules that can enhance how others receive those presentations.

- Design your presentation based on the required specifications of timing, length, inclusions, etc.
- Remember that your essay and your presentation differ. Use only the most important information, not all of the details.
- Avoid overly complicated—and therefore distracting—backgrounds. Stay with black or white, and remain consistent throughout the presentation.
- Begin with an eye-catching, attention-grabbing but brief title that will probably differ from your essay's title.
- On each frame, emphasize the information, not the subtitle.
- Use graphics wherever and whenever possible.
- Use bullets and phrases, not whole sentences.
- Avoid overloading a frame with too much text. Include no more than three pieces of information per frame.
- Avoid talking over your presentation. The audience cannot both process your visuals and listen to you speak; it will do one or the other.
- Cite and use a list of sources.
- Anticipate and prepare answers for questions the audience may ask.
- Practice running your presentation to make certain of its timing and technological functionality.

Your multimedia presentation should speak for itself, conveying the key ideas you want your audience to remember.

FINAL EXAM OUTREACH PRESENTATION (3–5 MINUTES)

During Finals Week, you will share with the class your Outreach Piece, in the form of a poster.

Set up your poster in the classroom (or project it from the computer), and then walk around the room, viewing your classmates' posters, and discussing your own poster with others.

Your poster must include:

- A hard copy (or projected copy) of your final Outreach Piece
- Notes and drafts that show your writing process, including . . .
  - ▶ how you decided on your audience, genre, and claim
  - ▶ how the piece differs from your Research Essay
  - ▶ how the piece evolved from draft to draft

Earn course points for . . .

- Arriving on time
- Having a complete poster
- Staying the full time to discuss posters with classmates

D. Readings and Resources

© Mascha Tace/Shutterstock.com

"How to Give a Good Research Talk" by Stephanie Weirich, University of Pennsylvania, no date:

https://www.cis.upenn.edu/~sweirich/talks/plmw15-giving-a-talk.pdf

"How to Sound Smart in Your TEDx Talk" by Will Stephen, January 15, 2015:

https://www.youtube.com/watch?v=8S0FDjFBj8o

"TED'S Secret to Great Public Speaking" by Chris Anderson, no date:

https://www.ted.com/talks/chris_anderson_teds_secret_to_great_public_speaking/up-next?language=en

"The Secret Structure of Great Talks" by Nancy Duarte, no date:

https://www.ted.com/talks/nancy_duarte_the_secret_structure_of_great_talks/up-next

"How to Give a Great Research Talk" by Peyton Jones with John Hughes and John Launchbury for Microsoft Research Cambridge, July 26, 2016 [59 minutes]:

https://www.youtube.com/watch?v=sT_-owjKIbA

"How to Avoid Death By PowerPoint," By David JP Phillips, April 14, 2014:

https://www.youtube.com/watch?v=Iwpi1Lm6dFo

WRITING ACROSS THE CURRICULUM/WRITING IN THE DISCIPLINES TIPS AND CONNECTIONS FOR THIS UNIT

1. The week before the presentations begin, show students examples of the kinds of presentations commonly done for your discipline and that you want them to emulate.

APPENDICES

MLA and APA Citations

Where do I start?

Let's start with the two kinds of citations you need to cite sources in a research project:

1. The list of citations you place at the end (called *Works Cited* or *References*)
2. The parenthetical citations you place in the text (called *in-text*)

Let's learn how to format both kinds of citations in two different citation styles.

MLA and APA are the commonest citation styles, and many professors don't care what approach you use as long as it's consistent—no mixing of MLA and APA. The main thing is to give credit to every source that you consult.

What, specifically, is a "source"?

A source is anything you consult to support your project's claims—like a scholarly study that backs up your thesis. Common sources are books and periodicals, but to those you can add a map, the Internet Movie Database, a CD or DVD, a census report, a comic book, an artwork in a museum, a tweet or posting, a YouTube video … You can also add a person, like an expert you interview in person or by email.

So with MLA or APA, you have citation rules for every kind of source?

Just about. This text offers citation models for seventy-nine types of sources, in both MLA and APA, from books to movies to postings. But it's impossible to keep up with every new source. Technology moves too fast.

However, you can use these seventy-nine citation models *as* models for special sources. For example, how do you cite a Blue-ray Disc? Logic says it's just like citing a DVD. Or how do you cite a TED talk?

So you can write citations, MLA and APA both want to know more or less the same information. To gather this information, the eighth edition (2016) of the *MLA Handbook* (often abbreviated *MLA8*) suggests asking the following questions about your source, in this order:

1. **Who's the *author*?**
2. **What's the *title*?**

3. If it's a *part of a whole* (like a story in a book), what's the title of the whole? (MLA calls this whole a "container" because it contains parts.)

4. Who are the other *contributors* (like editors, illustrators, translators, actors)?

5. What *version* is it?

6. What *number* is it?

7. Who's the *publisher* (in other words, who's responsible for it)?

8. *When* was it published?

9. *Where* did you find it (like the page in a book or Web site, the hour/minute/second of a movie frame)?

Once you answer these questions, you can plug the information into a citation—either MLA or APA. You won't always need to answer all nine questions. You answer as many as a reader needs to find the source.

For example, a reader could track down the TED talk with just the following:

MLA

    1.   2 .   3.   8.

Cuddy, Amy. "Your Body Language Shapes Who You Are." TED, June 2012,

                                      9.

www.ted.com/talks/amy_cuddy_your_body_language_shapes_who_you_are.

APA

    1.   8.   2.

Cuddy, A. (2012, June). *Your body language shapes who you are* [Video file].

                                9.

Retrieved from https://www.ted.com/talks/amy_cuddy_your_body_language_shapes_who_you_are

The MLA citation differs from the APA, but the information is approximately the same:

Author? = 1.

Title? = 2.

When published? = 8.

Where found? = 9.

For this source, MLA wants to know the container (**3.**), but APA doesn't. And APA wants to know the source's medium ("Video file"), though MLA doesn't.

So note: Depending on the kind of source, MLA sometimes asks questions about a source that APA doesn't. And vice versa.

If you can't find a specific model in the seventy-nine models below, improvise, using the closest model.

TWO FORMATS TO KNOW BEFORE YOU START:

1. **Page Format—Works Cited and References**
2. **Entry Format—Works Cited and References**

1. Page Format

MLA

1. Start Works Cited on a new page one inch from the top.

2. Double-space from the running head; center Works Cited (don't italicize or underline; use normal capitalization; don't put a period after it).

3. Double-space throughout.

4. Use a hanging indent: for each entry, type the first line flush left; indent each succeeding line one-half inch.

5. Alphabetize each entry by last name; if no author, by first word of title (excluding *A*, *An*, *The*).

APA

1. Start References on a new page one inch from the top.

2. Double-space from the running head; center References (don't italicize or underline; use normal capitalization; don't put a period after it).

3. Double-space throughout.

4. Use a hanging indent: for each entry, type the first line flush left; indent each succeeding line one-half inch.

5. Alphabetize each entry by last name; if no author, by first word of title (excluding *A*, *An*, *The*).

WARNING!

MLA and APA format each entry in very different ways. Do not mix styles.

---

2. Entry Format

MLA

One author

Last name, First name, Middle initial.

Smith, John J.

(Invert author's name; use middle initial if stated; place period after entry.)

Two authors

Last name, First name, Middle initial., and First name Middle initial. Last name.

Smith, John J., and Mary R. Smith.

(Invert first author; separate with commas; place period after entry.)

Three or more authors

Last name, First name, et al.

Smith, John J., et al.

(Invert first author; use first author and et al.*; separate with commas; place period after entry.)*

Corporate (Group) Author

World Health Organization.

(Place period after entry.)

Titles: Book chapters, articles, Web pages

Capitalize the first letter of all words except the following unless they start or conclude a title: **the, a, an**; prepositions: **at, by, between**, etc.; these conjunctions: **for, and, nor, but, or, yet, so**; and **to** in infinitives *(The Way to Win)*.

"Article Title: Subtitle."

"The Slow Death of the Planet: The Next Step."

(Use quotation marks; place period after title if it's the first title in your citation.)

Titles: Books, journals, magazines, newspapers, Web sites

Capitalize the first letter of all words except the following unless they start or conclude a title: **the, a, an**; prepositions: **at, by, between**, etc.; these conjunctions: **for, and, nor, but, or, yet, so**; and **to** in infinitives *(The Way to Win)*.

Book Title: Subtitle.

The Warming of the Planet: A Guide to Climate Change.

(Italicize; place period after title if it's the first title in your citation.)

Place of publication

For books, cite only if an edition is published in another country (e.g., a British or Canadian edition that varies from the American) or if the publisher is not generally known.

London,
(Place comma after entry.)

Publisher

Use full name of publisher but omit *Co., Corp., Inc., Ltd.*, and such words from business titles. However, do abbreviate academic presses:

Farrar, Straus and Giroux, *not* Farrar, Straus, and Giroux, Inc.

UP of Mississippi *(University Press of Mississippi),*

U of Chicago P *(University of Chicago Press),*

(Place comma after entry.)

Publication Date (Year or month/year or day/month/year, depending on source)

1951.

(Ordinarily, place comma after date but see exceptions in Seventy-Nine Citation Models, below.)

APA

One author

Last name, First initial., Middle initial.

Smith, J. J.

(Use middle initial if stated; do not place a second period after entry.)

Two to seven authors

Last name, First initial., Middle initial., & Last name, First initial., Middle initial.

Smith, J. J., & Smith, M.

Smith, J. J., Smith, M., & Jones, P.

(Use comma and ampersand [&]; do not place a second period after entry.)

Eight or more authors

Smith, J. J., Smith, M., Smith, R. J., Smith, P., Smith, A. C., Smith, B. T., … Jones, B.

(List first six authors, ellipsis, last author; do not place a second period after entry.)

Group author

World Health Organization.

(Place period after entry.)

Publication Date

(2017). [Book]

(2017, June). [Magazine]

(2017, 19 June). [Daily newspaper, blog, etc.]

(Place after author; place period after parentheses.)

Titles: Books, book chapters, articles, Web articles, Web pages

Capitalize only the first word and proper nouns in titles and subtitles; capitalize book volume numbers.

Book title: Subtitle.

The warming of the planet: A guide to climate change (Vol. 1).

    (Italicize; place period after entry.)

Article title: Subtitle.

    (Don't italicize or use quotation marks.)

Book chapters, articles, Web articles, Web pages: Subtitle

The slow death of the planet: And then what?

(Place comma after entry unless title includes a punctuation mark.)

Titles: Journals, magazines, newspapers; Web sites, online journals, online newspapers, reference databases

Capitalize the first letter of all words except the following unless they start or conclude a title: **the, a, an,** prepositions, and these conjunctions: **for, and, nor, but, or, yet, so.**

Journal Title,

The Journal of Social Media,

(Italicize; place comma after entry unless title includes a punctuation mark.)

Place of publication

    For nonperiodicals, use first city stated on title page, comma, state postal abbreviation.

    Boston, MA:

    (Place a colon after entry.)

    Omit state with a university press that uses a state name.

    Columbia: University of South Carolina Press.

    (Place colon after city.)

    If publisher is located outside the United States, give country.

    Dublin, Ireland: University College Dublin Press.

    (Place colon after country.)

    Use short form of publisher (leave out *Inc., Co.,* etc.) but write out *Books* or *Press*.

Publisher

    Harvard University Press.

    (Place a period after entry.)

FORMAT GUIDE

Works Cited (MLA) **and** *References (APA)*

Sources exist in three forms:

1. **Only in print**
2. **Both in print and online**
3. **Only online**

Many of the sources you consult will exist both in print and online. It's important, however, not to neglect sources only in print. Old textbooks, obscure government reports, pulp novels and magazines, political and advertising ephemera, archival collections, early audio and visual productions: Many fertile research sources haven't been scanned or uploaded and can't be found online. **Try not to limit your search for sources to what you find on the computer.**

Nevertheless, given that many college research projects rely solely on computer searches, each entry of your Works Cited or References list will probably end with an online address:

MLA

> David, Larry. "Wandering Bear." *Curb Your Enthusiasm*, produced by Jeff Garlin, DVD version, season 4, episode 8, HBO Home Entertainment, 29 Feb. 2004. *Amazon Prime*, www.amazon.com/gp/video/detail/B0172URD64?ref_=aiv_dp_season_select.

APA

> David, L. (Writer-Director). (2004, February 29). Wandering bear [Television series episode]. In Garlin, J. (Producer), *Curb your enthusiasm*. Retrieved from http://www.amazon.com/gp/video/detail/B0172URD64?ref_=aiv_dp_season_select

Therefore, please take note:
Many of the seventy-nine citation models below can be written in one of two ways:

1. **As a print citation**
2. **As an online citation**

MLA

1. For sources that exist both in print and online, begin with the print citation (see 1-63, below) <u>but add</u> the DOI (preferred if available) or URL:

> Last name, First name. *Book Title in Italics: Subtitle If Any.* Publisher, year of publication. *Title of Web Site or Database in Italics*, doi.

Last name, First name. *Book Title in Italics: Subtitle If Any.* Publisher, year of publication. *Title of Web Site or Database in Italics*, URL.

For the DOI (*digital object identifier*, a unique number assigned to a database article, document, or book):

- Find the DOI in the database citation, abstract, or full-text format
- Don't capitalize DOI: doi
- Put a colon after with no space: doi:10.1000/1000000
- Put a period at end of DOI

For the URL (*uniform resource locator*, the address of a Web source):

- Omit *http://* or *https://* but give rest of address
- Put a period at end of URL

If using a library or subscription database, add the name of the database in italics and the DOI or URL:

Last name, First name. "Title in Quotations: Subtitle If Any." *Journal Title in Italics*, vol. 54, no.3, Mar. 2017, pp. 135-54. *Project Muse*, doi:10.1000/1000000.

Last name, First name. "Title in Quotations: Subtitle If Any." *Journal Title in Italics*, vol. 54, no.3, Mar. 2017, pp. 135-54. *ProQuest*, URL.

2. For sources that exist only or primarily online, see 64-79, below.

APA

1. **For sources that exist both in print and online, begin with the print citation (see 1-63, below) <u>but add</u> the DOI:**

   - Find the DOI in the database citation, abstract, or full-text format
   - Don't capitalize DOI: doi
   - Put a colon after with no space: doi:10.1000/1000000
   - Don't put a period at end of DOI

   For books and reports, omit city and publisher and replace with DOI:

   Last name, Initial. (Year of publication). *Title in italics: Subtitle if any.* doi:10.1000/1000000

   For journals, keep all information and add DOI:

   Last name, Initial., & Last name, Initial. (Year of publication). Title without quotations: Subtitle if any. *Journal Title in Italics*, 56, 213-216. doi:10.1000/1000000

   If the source has no DOI, write:

   Retrieved from http:// [rest of URL]

   - Break the URL *before* periods and slashes; don't use hyphens
   - Don't put a period at the end of the URL

For books and reports, omit city and publisher and replace with URL:

Last name, Initial. (Year of publication). *Title in italics: Subtitle if any*. Retrieved from http://[rest of URL]

For journals, keep all information and add URL:

Last name, Initial., & Last name, Initial. (Year of publication). Title without quotations: Subtitle if any. *Journal Title in Italics*, 56, 213-216. Retrieved from http:[rest of URL]

2. For sources that exist only or primarily online, see 64-79, below.

SEVENTY-NINE CITATION TYPES

Book

1. **One Author**
2. **Two Authors**
3. **Two to Seven Authors**
4. **Three or More Authors**
5. **Eight or More Authors**
6. **An Organization as Group Author**
7. **Same Author of More than One Book**
8. **Same Author of More than One Book in Same Year**
9. **Republished (Reprinted) Book**
10. **Second or Later Revised Edition**
11. **One Author with Translator**
12. **One Author with Translator and Editor**
13. **Unknown Author with Translator**
14. **Translation of Part of Book**
15. **Title within Title**
16. **One Work or Collected Works of One Author in One Book with Editor(s)**
17. **Anthology or Scholarly Collection with Editor(s)**
18. **One Work in Anthology or Collected Works with Editor(s)**
19. **Reprinted Article in Scholarly Collection with Editor(s)**
20. **Books in Volumes—with and without Editor(s)**
21. **Book in Series**
22. **Article in Reference Book (Dictionary, Encyclopedia, etc.)**
23. **Foreword, Preface, Introduction, Afterword**
24. **Illustrated Book with Introduction**
25. **Graphic Narrative**
26. **Religious Text (Bible, Qur'an, etc.)**

Master's Thesis or Ph.D. Dissertation

27. Master's Thesis or Ph.D. Dissertation
28. Dissertation Abstract (Citing Abstract Listed in *Dissertation Abstracts International*)

Scholarly Journal

29. Article in Journal Paginated by Volume
30. Article in Journal Paginated by Volume and Issue

Magazine and Newspaper

31. Magazine Article with Author
32. Newspaper Article with Author
33. Unsigned Magazine or Newspaper Article
34. Unsigned Editorial in Magazine or Newspaper
35. Letter to Editor in Magazine or Newspaper
36. Review in Magazine or Newspaper
37. Article in Series in Magazine or Newspaper
38. Advertisement in Magazine or Newspaper
39. Cartoon or Comic Strip

Report, Pamphlet, Conference Proceedings, Paper Presentation, or Poster Session

40. Report or Pamphlet
41. Article (Paper) in Published Conference Proceedings
42. Paper Presentation or Poster Session

Government Publication

43. Government Publication

Print Interview

44. Interview in Magazine or Newspaper

Unpublished Source

45. Letter
46. Manuscript or Typescript Other than Letter

Television, Radio

47. Television Broadcast
48. Radio Broadcast

Film, DVD, Video

49. Film—Seen in Theatre
50. Film—DVD or Videocassette

Sound Recording (CD, LP, Music Download/MP3 File)

51. CD or LP—Composer or Performer Emphasized First
52. Digital File Download: Audio, Image, Video, Movie (e-book, JPEG, MP3, PDF, etc.)

CD-ROM, DVD-ROM, Video or Computer Game, Computer Software

53. CD-ROM or DVD-ROM
54. Video/Computer Game or Specialized Computer Software Program

Podcast

55. Podcast

Lecture, Powerpoint, Speech, Reading

56. Lecture

Oral Interview

57. Oral (Unpublished) Interview
58. Broadcast Interview—Television or Radio

Live Performance

59. Play, Music Concert, Ballet, Opera, Dance

Written Musical Composition

60. Longer Composition: Symphony, Ballet, Opera, etc.
61. Shorter Composition: Song, Short Instrumental Piece, etc.

Artwork (Painting, Drawing, Etching, Sculpture, Photograph, etc.)

62. Artwork

Map or Chart

63. Map or Chart

Entire Web Site

64. Entire Web Site

Section of Web Site

65. Section of Web Site

Article in Online Journal

66. Article in Online Journal

Article from Online Magazine or Newspaper

67. Article from Online Magazine or Newspaper

Online Book

68. Online Book

Online Poem or Short Story

69. Online Poem or Short Story

Online Reference Work

70. Online Reference Work

Wiki

71. Wiki

Blog (Web Log)

72. Entire Blog
73. Posting on a Blog

Postings on a Web Page

E-Mail

Social Media

Youtube and Movie-/Video-Streaming Sites

SEVENTY-NINE CITATION MODELS

Book

1. **One Author**

   MLA

   Last name, First name. *Title in Italics: Subtitle If Any.* Publisher, year of publication.

   Smith, John J. *The Warming of the Planet: A Guide to Climate Change.* Alfred A. Knopf, 2012.

   APA

   Last name, Initial. (Year of publication). *Title in italics: Subtitle if any.* City of publication, State Abbreviation: Publisher.

   Smith, J. J. (2012). *The warming of the planet: A guide to climate change.* New York, NY: Knopf.

   (With DOI, omit city and publisher:

   Smith, J. J. (2012). *The warming of the planet: A guide to climate change.* doi:10.1000/1000000

   See the Rules for Online Sources, page TBD. No period follows DOI in entry.)

2. **Two Authors**

   MLA

   Last name, First name, and First name Last name. *Title in Italics: Subtitle If Any.* Publisher, year of publication.

3. Two to Seven Authors

APA

Last name, Initial., Last name, Initial., & Last name, Initial. (Year of publication). *Title in italics: Subtitle if any*. City of publication, State Abbreviation: Publisher.

4. Three or More Authors

MLA

Last name, First name, et al. *Title in Italics: Subtitle If Any*. Publisher, year of publication.

5. Eight or More Authors

APA

Last name, Initial., Last name, Initial., Last name, Initial., Last name, Initial., Last name, Initial., Last name, Initial., … & Last name, Initial. (Year of publication). *Title in italics: Subtitle if any*. City of publication, State Abbreviation: Publisher.

(After six authors, use ellipsis to omit remaining authors except last author.)

6. An Organization as Group Author

MLA

Group name. *Title in Italics: Subtitle If Any*. Publisher, year of publication.

APA

Group name. (Year of publication). *Title in italics: Subtitle if any*. City of publication, State Abbreviation: Publisher.

7. Same Author of More than One Book

MLA

Last name, First name. *Title in Italics: Subtitle If Any*. Publisher, year of publication.

---. *Title in Italics: Subtitle If Any*. Publisher, year of publication.

(Type three hyphens followed by period; alphabetize by title.)

8. Same Author of More than One Book in Same Year

APA

Last name, Initial. (Year of publication a). *Title in italics: Subtitle if any*. City of publication, State Abbreviation: Publisher.

Same last name, Initial. (Year of publication b). *Title in italics: Subtitle if any*. City of publication, State Abbreviation: Publisher.

(Use lowercase letter for each book published in same year: 2012a, 2012b, etc.)

9. Republished (Reprinted) Book

MLA

Last name, First name. *Title in Italics: Subtitle If Any*. Year of original publication. Publisher, year of new publication.

(If the republished book has been issued under a new title, add reprint information.)

Last name, First name. *Title in Italics: Subtitle If Any*. Publisher, year of new publication, rpt. of *Title in Italics: Subtitle If Any*. Year of original publication.

APA

Last name, Initial. (Year of publication). *Title in italics: Subtitle if any* (Initial. Last name, Ed.). City of publication, State Abbreviation: Publisher. (Original work published [year])
(No period follows.)

10. **Second or Later Revised Edition**

MLA

Last name, First name. *Title in Italics: Subtitle If Any.* 2nd ed., Publisher, year of publication.

APA

Last name, Initial. (Year of publication). *Title in italics: Subtitle if any* (2nd ed.). City of publication, State Abbreviation: Publisher.

11. **One Author with Translator**

MLA

Last name, First name. *Title in Italics: Subtitle If Any.* Translated by First name Last name, Publisher, year of publication.

APA

Last name, Initial. (Year of publication). *Title in italics: Subtitle if any* (Initial. Last name, Trans.). City of publication, State Abbreviation: Publisher. (Original work published [year])
(No period follows.)

12. **One Author with Translator and Editor**

MLA

Last name, First name. *Title in Italics: Subtitle If Any.* Translated by First name Last name, edited by First name Last name, Publisher, year of publication.

For APA, use *Ed.* for one editor and *Eds.* for more than one. (See Model 17.)

APA

Last name, Initial. (Year of publication). *Title in italics: Subtitle if any* (Initial. Last name, Ed.). (Initial. Last name, Trans.). City of publication, State Abbreviation: Publisher.

13. **Unknown Author with Translator**

MLA

Title in Italics: Subtitle If Any. Translated by First name Last name, Publisher, year of publication.

APA

Title in italics: Subtitle if any. (Year of publication). (Initial. Last Name, Trans.). City of publication, State Abbreviation: Publisher.

14. **Translation of Part of Book**

MLA

Last name, First name. "Title in Quotations: Subtitle If Any." Translated by First name Last name, *Title in Italics: Subtitle If Any*, edited by First name Last name and First name Last name, Publisher, year of publication.

APA

Last name, Initial. (Year of publication). Title without quotations: Subtitle if any (Initial. Last name, Trans.). In Initial. Last name & Initial. Last name (Eds.), *Title in italics: Subtitle if any* (pp. 10-15). City of publication, State Abbreviation: Publisher.

15. **Title within Title**

For both MLA and APA, if quoting a title within a title, like *Shakespeare's Pupils: The School of* Hamlet, don't italicize or put into quotations a title that ordinarily would be.

MLA

Last name, First name. *Title in Italics with* Title within Title: *Subtitle If Any*. Publisher, year of publication.

APA

Last name, Initial. (Year of publication). *Title in italics with* Title within title: *Subtitle if any*. City of publication, State Abbreviation: Publisher.

(Capitalize first word of Title within title.)

16. **One Work or Collected Works of One Author in One Book with Editor(s)**

MLA

Last name, First name. *Title in Italics: Subtitle If Any*. Edited by First name Last name, Publisher, year of publication.

APA

Last name, Initial. (Year of publication). *Title in italics: Subtitle if any* (Initial. Last name, Ed.). City of publication, State Abbreviation: Publisher.

17. **Anthology or Scholarly Collection with Editor(s)**

MLA

Last name, First name, and First name Last name, editors. *Title in Italics: Subtitle If Any*. Publisher, year of publication.

APA

Last name, Initial., & Last name, Initial. (Eds.). (Year of publication). *Title in italics: Subtitle if any*. City of publication, State Abbreviation: Publisher.

18. **One Work in Anthology or Collected Works with Editor(s)**

MLA

Last name, First name. "Title of Work in Quotations: Subtitle If Any." *Title of Anthology: Subtitle If Any*, edited by First name Last name, Publisher, year of publication, pp. 254-63.

(Include page numbers of selection after year of publication: pp. 254-63.)

APA

    Last name, Initial. (Year of publication). Title of work without quotations: Subtitle if any. In Initial. Last Name & Initial. Last Name (Eds.), *Title of anthology in italics: Subtitle if any* (pp. 254-263). City of publication, State Abbreviation: Publisher.

19. **Reprinted Article in Scholarly Collection with Editor(s)**

MLA

    Last name, First name. "Title of Article in Quotations: Subtitle If Any." *Title of Journal Where First Printed in Italics*, vol. 18, year of original publication, pp. 40-51, rpt. in *Title in Italics: Subtitle If Any*, edited by First name Last Name, Publisher, year of publication, pp.154-62.

(If the article first appeared in a journal, include journal volume number [18] and page numbers [pp. 40-51] as well as page numbers [pp. 154-62] in book where reprinted [*rpt*.].)

APA

    Last name, Initial. (Year of publication). Title without quotations: Subtitle if any. In Initial. Last Name & Initial. Last Name (Eds.), *Title of collection in italics: Subtitle if any* (pp. 154-162). City of publication, State Abbreviation: Publisher. (Reprinted from *Title in italics: Subtitle if any*, pp. 9-15, by Initial. Last name, Ed., year of publication, City of publication, State Abbreviation: Publisher)

(No period follows.)

20. **Books in Volumes–with and without Editor(s)**

MLA

    Last name, First name. *Title in Italics: Subtitle If Any*. Edited by First name Last name, vol. 2, Publisher, year of publication.

(If your project refers to just one volume, write vol. 2.)

But:

    Last name, First name. *Title in Italics: Subtitle If Any*. 2nd ed., Publisher, year of publication. 4 vols.

(If your project refers to two or more volumes, write *4 vols*., etc..) The in-text citation will state which volume used: 4: 251.)

APA

    Last name, Initial. (Year of publication). *Title in italics: Subtitle if any* (Initial. Last name, Ed.). (Vol. 2). City of publication, State Abbreviation: Publisher.

(If your project refers to just one volume, write Vol. 2.)

    Last name, Initial. (Year of publication). *Title in italics: Subtitle if any* (Initial. Last name, Ed.). (Vols. 1-4). City of publication, State Abbreviation: Publisher.

(If your project refers to more than one volume, write Vols. 1-4.)

21. **Book in Series**

MLA

Last name, First name. *Title in Italics: Subtitle If Any.* Publisher, year of publication. Title of Series 56.

(The series title is not italicized or put into quotations. Include series number if stated.)

APA

Last name, Initial. (Year of publication). *Title in italics: Subtitle if any.* City of publication, State Abbreviation: Publisher. (*Title of Series in Italics 56*)

(Capitalize key words in a Title of Series. Include series number if stated; no period follows.)

22. **Article in Reference Book (Dictionary, Encyclopedia, etc.)**

MLA

Last name, First name. "Title in Quotations: Subtitle If Any." *Title in Italics: Subtitle If Any,* 5th ed., Publisher, 2010, p. 203.

Or

"Title in Quotations: Subtitle If Any." *Title in Italics: Subtitle If Any,* 2nd ed., Publisher, 2011, pp. 1021-2.

(Use title if article has no author.)

APA

Last name, Initial. (Year of publication). Title without quotations: Subtitle if any. In Initial. Last name (Ed.), *Title in italics: Subtitle if any* (Vol. 18, pp. 143-144). City of publication, State Abbreviation: Publisher.

Or

Title without quotations: Subtitle if any. (Year of publication). In Initial. Last name (Ed.), *Title in italics: Subtitle if any* (2nd ed., p. 898). City of publication, State Abbreviation: Publisher.

23. **Foreword, Preface, Introduction, Afterword**

MLA

Last name, First name. Foreword. *Title in Italics: Subtitle If Any,* by First name Last name, Publisher, year of publication, pp. xx-xxvi.

(Include page numbers after year of publication: *pp. xx-xxvi.* **After author's name, include foreword title if given:** Last name, First name. "Title in Quotations: Subtitle If Any." Foreword.**)**

APA

Last name, Initial. (Year of publication). Foreword. In Initial. Last name, *Title in italics: Subtitle if any* (pp. xx-xxvi). City of publication, State Abbreviation: Publisher.

(If specific title is given, write Last name, Initial. (Year of publication). Title without quotations: Subtitle if any [Foreword]. In Initial. Last name, **and then continue rest of reference.)**

24. **Illustrated Book with Introduction**

MLA

Last name, First name. *Title in Italics: Subtitle If Any.* Introduction by First name Last name, illustrated by First name Last name, Publisher, year of publication.

APA

Last name, Initial. (Year of publication). *Title in italics: Subtitle if any* (Initial. Last name, Introd.). (Initial. Last name, Illus.). City of publication, State Abbreviation: Publisher.

25. **Graphic Narrative**

MLA

Last name, First name, artist. *Title in Italics: Subtitle If Any.* Written by First name Last name, Publisher, year of publication.

Or **(depending on whether project primarily discusses artist or writer)**

Last name, First name, writer. *Title in Italics: Subtitle If Any.* Art by First name Last name, Publisher, year of publication.

APA

Last name, Initial. (Artist). (Year of publication). *Title in italics: Subtitle if any* [Graphic novel]. Initial. Last name (Writer). City of publication, State Abbreviation: Publisher.

Or **(depending on whether project primarily discusses artist or writer)**

Last name, Initial. (Writer). (Year of publication). *Title in italics: Subtitle if any* [Graphic novel]. Initial. Last name (Artist). City of publication, State Abbreviation: Publisher.

26. **Religious Text (Bible, Qur'an, etc.)**

MLA

Title in Italics: Subtitle If Any. Translated by name of group, edited by First name Last name and First name Last name, Publisher, year of publication.

(For a large work with many translators, state name of group translating: *World Bible Society.***)**

APA

(Religious and standard classical works are cited in-text parenthetically but not in References. See Guide to Formatting In-Text Citations: MLA and APA, 17 **and** 37.)

Master's Thesis or Ph.D. Dissertation

27. **Master's Thesis or Ph.D. Dissertation**

MLA

Last name, First name. *Title in Italics: Subtitle If Any.* Dissertation. Name of University, year dissertation accepted.

(Use short forms of the university name: U of Iowa, Iowa State U.)

APA

Last name, Initial. (Year dissertation accepted). *Title in italics: Subtitle if any* (Doctoral dissertation, Name of University). Retrieved from http://

(No period follows.)

28. **Dissertation Abstract (Citing Abstract Listed in *Dissertation Abstracts International*)**

MLA

Last name, First name. *Title in Italics: Subtitle If Any.* Dissertation. Name of University, year dissertation accepted, *Dissertation Abstracts International.* vol. 50, no.2, 2005, p. 1321.

(Give *Dissertation Abstracts International* volume number [50], issue number [2], year of publication [2005], and page number [1321]).

APA

Last name, Initial. (2005). Title without quotations: Subtitle if any. *Dissertation Abstracts International: Section B. Sciences and Engineering, 50*(2), 1321.

(Spell out *Dissertation Abstracts International*, stating section letter and category. Italicize volume [50] but not issue number [2].)

Scholarly Journal

> ## WARNING!
>
> MLA gives dates as the following: 27 Sept. 2010. **APA gives dates as the following: 2010, September 27. In MLA, abbreviate all months except May, June, July. In APA, spell out all months.**

29. **Article in Journal Paginated by Volume**

Each issue within a volume continues consecutive page numbering—i.e., each new issue doesn't begin with *page 1*.

APA

Last name, Initial., & Last name, Initial. (Year of publication). Title without quotations: Subtitle if any. *Journal Title in Italics, 56,* 213-216.

(Use normal capitalization with periodical titles: *The Journal of Social Media*. Include volume number [56] and page numbers [213-216]. Note: Don't use *p.* with journals and magazines. Note: Volume number is italicized; don't include issue number.)

30. **Article in Journal Paginated by Volume and Issue**
    Each issue is paginated with a new *page 1*.

    MLA

    > Last name, First name. "Title in Quotations: Subtitle If Any." *Journal Title in Italics*, vol. 54, no. 3, year of publication, pp. 135-54.

    (Include volume number [54], issue number [3], and page numbers [135-54]. If the journal includes only issue numbers, write *Journal Title in Italics*, no. 104, 2010, pp. 1-5.**)**

    APA

    > Last name, Initial. (Year of publication). Title without quotations: Subtitle if any. *Journal Title in Italics*, *54*(3), 135-154.

    (Note: Volume number is italicized, but issue number is not: *54*[3].)

Magazine and Newspaper

31. **Magazine Article with Author**

    For MLA, for a weekly or twice-monthly magazine, include date and page numbers.
    MLA

    > Last name, First name. "Title in Quotations: Subtitle If Any." *Magazine in Italics*, 18 Jan. 2010, pp. 45-51.

    For MLA, for a monthly or every-other-month magazine, include month, year, and page number.

    > Last name, First name. "Title in Quotations: Subtitle If Any." *Magazine in Italics*, Dec. 2010, pp. 75+.

    (For an article that isn't printed on consecutive pages—that is, it skips pages—cite the first page it begins on with a plus sign.)

    For APA, for a weekly or twice-monthly magazine, include volume [56] and also issue number [3] if each issue starts numbering with page 1.

    APA

    > Last name, Initial. (2011, June 18). Title without quotations: Subtitle if any. *Magazine in Italics*, *56*(3), 18-19.

    (Note: Don't use *p*. for page number.)

    For APA, for a monthly or every-other month magazine, include year and month, volume [*91*] and also issue number [2] if each issue starts numbering with page 1.

    APA

    > Last name, Initial. (2011, June). Title without quotations: Subtitle if any. *Magazine in Italics*, *91*(2), 18.

    (Note: volume number is italicized for all magazines, but issue number is not: *91*[2].)

32. **Newspaper Article with Author**

MLA

Last name, First name. "Title in Quotations: Subtitle If Any." *Newspaper in Italics*, 6 June 1995, late ed., pp. D3+.

(Include the section letter [D], the first page the article begins on [3], and the plus sign [+] to show that the article doesn't continue on consecutive pages—that is, the article skips pages.)

APA

Last name, Initial. (1995, June 6). Title without quotations: Subtitle if any. *Newspaper in Italics*, pp. D3, D5, D6.

(Note: If the article doesn't continue on consecutive pages, list each page it appears on. Note: With newspapers, include *p.* or *pp.* for page numbers.)

33. **Unsigned Magazine or Newspaper Article**

For MLA, for magazine follow Model 31 but replace author with title; for newspaper:

MLA

"Title in Quotations: Subtitle If Any." *Newspaper in Italics*, 9 Dec. 1993, late ed., p. B6.

(Add which edition if more than one.)

For APA, for magazine follow Model 31 but replace author with title; for newspaper:

APA

Title without quotations: Subtitle if any. (1993, December 9). *Newspaper in Italics*, p. B6.

34. **Unsigned Editorial in Magazine or Newspaper**

For MLA, for magazine follow Model 31 but replace author with title and add *Editorial* (no italics) plus period after title; for newspaper:

MLA

"Title in Quotations: Subtitle If Any." Editorial. *Newspaper in Italics*, 3 Mar. 2012, p. A8.

For APA, for magazine follow Model 31 but replace author with title and add *Editorial* (no italics) in brackets after title; for newspaper:

APA

Title without quotations: Subtitle if any [Editorial]. (2012, March 3). *Newspaper in Italics*, p. A8.

35. **Letter to Editor in Magazine or Newspaper**

For MLA, for magazine follow Model 31 and add *Letter* (no italics) after name; for newspaper:

MLA

Last name, First name. Letter. "Title in Quotations: Subtitle If Any." *Newspaper in Italics*, 18 Apr. 2009, p. A7.

For APA, for magazine follow Model 31 and add *Letter to the editor* (no italics) in brackets after title; for newspaper:

APA

> Last name, Initial. (2005, March 1). Title without quotations: Subtitle if any [Letter to the editor]. *Newspaper in Italics*, p. A7.

36. Review in Magazine or Newspaper

MLA

> Last name, First name. "Title in Quotations: Subtitle If Any." Review of *Title in Italics: Subtitle If Any*, by First name Last name. *Magazine in Italics*, 8 Sept. 2010, pp. 118-22.

> Last name, First name. "Title in Quotations: Subtitle If Any." Review of *Film in Italics*, directed by First name Last name. *Newspaper in Italics*, 3 Jan. 1974, p. B13.

For APA, for magazine follow Model 31 and add *Review of* (no italics) in brackets after title; for newspaper:

APA

> Last name, Initial. (1974, January 3). Title without quotations: Subtitle if any [Review of the book *Title in italics*, by Initial. Last name]. *Newspaper in Italics*, p. 75.

37. Article in Series in Magazine or Newspaper

For MLA, for newspaper, follow Model 32. If title changes for each installment in a series, add this description: Pt. 3 of a series, Title without Quotations: Subtitle If Any, begun 7 Sept. 2008. For magazine:

MLA

> Last name, First name. "Title in Quotations: Subtitle If Any." *Magazine in Italics*, 28 Sept. 2008, pp. 78-81, pt. 3 of a series, Title without Quotations: Subtitle If Any, begun 7 Sept. 2008.

38. Advertisement in Magazine or Newspaper

For MLA, for magazine or newspaper, use same model, inserting *Advertisement* (no italics).

MLA

> Name of Product Advertised. Advertisement. *Magazine in Italics*, 11 Oct. 1965, p. 18.

39. Cartoon or Comic Strip

For MLA, for magazine or newspaper, insert *Cartoon* or *Comic Strip* (no italics).

MLA

> Last name, First name. "Title If Any in Quotations." Cartoon. *Magazine in Italics*, 3 Feb. 2001. p. 78.

Report, Pamphlet, Conference Proceedings, Paper Presentation, or Poster Session

40. **Report or Pamphlet**

    MLA

    Last name, First name. *Title in Italics: Subtitle If Any.* Publisher, year of publication.

    APA

    Last name, Initial., & Last name, Initial. (Year of publication). *Title in italics: Subtitle if any* (Report No. 555-067). City of publication, State Abbreviation: Publisher.

    (With DOI, omit city, state abbreviation, and publisher.)

41. **Article (Paper) in Published Conference Proceedings**

    MLA

    Last name, First name. "Title in Quotations: Subtitle If Any." *Conference Proceedings in Italics,* edited by First name Last name, City of publication, Publisher, year of publication. pp. 6-12.

    APA

    Last name, Initial. (Year of publication). Title without quotations: Subtitle if any. In Initial. Last name (Ed.), *Conference proceedings in italics* (pp. 6-12). City of publication, State Abbreviation: Publisher.

42. **Paper Presentation or Poster Session**

    MLA

    Last name, First name. "Title in Quotations: Subtitle If Any." Name of Session, Name of Organization, Location, 18 Jan. 2009. Poster session.

    APA

    Last name, Initial. (2010, February). *Title in italics: Subtitle if any.* Paper or poster session presented at the 2010 Name of Organization, City, State Abbreviation.

Government Publication

43. **Government Publication**

    MLA

    Last name, First name. *Title in Italics: Subtitle If Any.* Name of Government Agency Issuing Document, Government Printing Office, year of publication.

    Or (if no author)

    Name of Government Agency Issuing Publication. *Title in Italics: Subtitle If Any,* Government Printing Office, year of publication.

APA

Last name, Initial. (Year of publication). *Title in italics: Subtitle if any*. Washington, DC: Government Printing Office.

Or (if no author)

Name of Government Agency Issuing Publication. (Year of publication). *Title in italics: Subtitle if any*. Washington, DC: Government Printing Office.

Print Interview

44. Interview in Magazine or Newspaper

MLA

Last name, First name. "Title in Quotations: Subtitle If Any." *Magazine in Italics*, 6 Mar. 2009, pp. 56-65.

APA

Last name, Initial. (2009, December). Title without quotations: Subtitle if any. *Magazine in Italics*, 35, 77-87.

Unpublished Source

45. Letter

MLA

Last name, First name. Letter to the author. 8 Nov. 2005. Manuscript.

(Use *manuscript* to show handwritten form; *typescript* to show typed form.)

APA

Last name, Initial. (2005, November 8). [Letter to First name Last name]. Copy in possession of First name Last name.

(Include letter in References if retrievable. Otherwise, include in only parenthetical citation.)

46. Manuscript or Typescript Other than Letter

MLA

Last name, First name. *Title If Any in Italics: Subtitle If Any.* 1951. Typescript, Box 18, Memoirs of First name Last name, Name of Library, City.

(If no title, describe the manuscript/typescript in clear terms: novel, poetry collection, diary, notebooks, memoirs, etc.)

APA

Last name, Initial. (1951). *Title if any in italics: Subtitle if any* [Unpublished memoir]. Smith Memoirs (Box 18). Library, City, State Abbreviation.

(If there is no title or it does not clearly describe the source, immediately after title include bracketed description: unpublished novel, poetry collection, diary, notebook, memoir, etc. If the source has a library description that identifies it, such as Smith Collection or Smith Memoirs, include that after the bracketed description.)

Television, Radio

47. Television Broadcast

MLA

"Title of Episode in Quotations." *Program Series in Italics*, directed by First name Last name, performances by First name Last name, First name Last name, and First name Last name, NBC, WHO, Des Moines, 18 Nov. 2001.

(Give as much information as needed: written by, directed by, performed by, narrated by, etc.)

APA

Last name, Initial. (Writer), & Last name, Initial. (Director). (2001, November 18). Title of episode without quotations [Television series episode]. In Initial. Last name & Initial. Last name (Producers), *Program series in italics*. City, State Abbreviation: Home Box Office.

48. Radio Broadcast

MLA

"Title in Quotations." *Program Series in Italics*, narrated by First name Last name, National Public Radio, WNPR, City, 16 June 2010.

APA

Last name, Initial. (Narrator). (2010, June 16). Title without quotations: Subtitle if any. In Initial. Last name (Executive producer), *Program series in italics* [Radio program]. City, State Abbreviation: National Public Radio.

Film, DVD, Video

49. Film—Seen in Theatre

MLA

Last name, First name, director. *Film Title in Italics*. Performances by First name Last name and First name Last name, Studio, year of release.

(Here emphasizing director first and performers second; studio: M-G-M, Warner Bros., etc.)

Or

Film Title in Italics. Directed by First name Last name, performances by First name Last name and First name Last name, Studio, year of release.

APA

Last name, Initial. (Director), & Last name, Initial. (Producer). (Year of release). *Film title in italics* [Motion picture]. Country of origin: Studio.

(Country of origin = studio's home country.)

50. **Film—DVD or Videocassette**

MLA

Last name, First name, director. *Film Title in Italics.* Performances by First name Last name and First name Last name, year of original release, DVD distributor, year of DVD release, disc 4.

APA

Last name, Initial. (Director), & Last name, Initial. (Producer). (Year of DVD release). *Film title in italics* [DVD]. Country of origin: Studio. (Original release date)

(No period follows.)

Sound Recording (CD, LP)

51. **CD or LP—Composer or Performer Emphasized First**

MLA

Last name, First name. "Title of Selection in Quotations." *Title of CD in Italics*, performance by First name Last name, CD manufacturer, year of release.

APA

Last name, Initial. (Year of copyright). Title of selection without quotations. On *Title of CD in italics* [CD]. City, State Abbreviation: CD manufacturer.

52. **Digital File Download: Audio, Image, Video, Movie (MP3, e-book, JPEG, PDF, etc.)**

MLA

Last name, First name. "Selection in Quotations." *Title in Italics*, year of release. MP3 file.

Last name, First name. *Title in Italics.* Kindle ed., Publisher, year of publication.

APA

Last name, Initial. (Year of release). Title without quotations [MP3]. Available from Organization Name.

CD-ROM, DVD-ROM, Video or Computer Game, Computer Software

53. **CD-ROM or DVD-ROM**

For MLA, for a nonperiodical CD-ROM or DVD-ROM:

MLA

Last name, First name. *Title in Italics.* Version number, Publisher, year of release.

For MLA, for a periodical (journal, magazine, or newspaper) CD-ROM or DVD-ROM:

Last name, First name. "Title in Quotations: Subtitle If Any." *Periodical in Italics.* 9 Mar. 2009, pp. 14+, *Name of CD-ROM in Italics*, Publisher.

APA

> Last name, Initial. (Year of CD-ROM release). Title without quotations: Subtitle if any. On *Title in italics* [CD-ROM]. City of publication, State Abbreviation: Publisher. (Original publication date)

(No period follows.)

54. **Video/Computer Game or Specialized Computer Software Program**
    For both MLA and APA, it isn't necessary to cite common products. Cite only specialized.

    MLA

    > *Title of Software in Italics.* Version Number, Publisher, year of release.

    APA

    > Title of Software in Capitals (Version number) [Computer software]. (Year of release). City of software vendor, State Abbreviation: Software vendor.

Podcast

55. **Podcast**

    For MLA, for downloaded files:

    MLA

    > Last name, First name. "Title in Quotations: Subtitle If Any." *Site Title in Italics*, episode 212, 9 Dec. 2011. MP3 file.

    For MLA, for files available through an open Web site:

    > Last name, First name. "Title in Quotations: Subtitle If Any." *Site Title in Italics*, 8 May 2007, URL.

    APA

    > Last name, Initial. (Producer/Host). (2010, June 18). *Site Title in Italics* [Audio podcast]. Available from Organization Name.

    (Use normal capitalization with Web site titles and italicize.)

Lecture, Powerpoint, Speech, Reading

56. **Lecture**

    MLA

    > Last name, First name. "Title in Quotations: Subtitle If Any." Name of Organization, 5 June 2011, location. Lecture. [*or, if PowerPoint,* Slide 5.]

    (Indicate the type of oral presentation: Lecture, PowerPoint, Reading, Address, Keynote Address, etc.)

APA

Last name, Initial. (2011, June 5). *Title in italics: Subtitle if any.* Lecture presented at Name of Organization. City, State Abbreviation. Retrieved from http://

(Indicate the type of oral presentation: Lecture, Reading, Address, Keynote Address. Include in *References* only if retrievable. No period follows *Retrieved from*.)

Oral Interview

57. Oral (Unpublished) Interview

MLA

Last name, First name. Personal interview. 5 Mar. 2011.

Or

Last name, First name. Telephone interview. 5 Mar. 2011.

(Use Last name, First name of person interviewed: *Obama, Barack*.)

APA

(Use only in-text parenthetical citation since APA does not include nonretrievable sources in *References*. See Guide to Formatting In-Text Citation: MLA and APA, 12 **and** 32.)

58. Broadcast Interview—Television or Radio

MLA

Last name, First name. Interview by First name Last name, *Program Series in Italics*, ABC, WABC, City, 9 May 2004.

APA

Last name, Initial. (Interviewer). (2004, May 9). Interview with First name Last name. *Program series in italics* [Radio program]. City, State Abbreviation: National Public Radio.

(Alphabetize under interviewer's last name.)

Live Performance

59. Play, Music Concert, Ballet, Opera, Dance, Performance Art

MLA

Title in Italics. By First name Last name, directed by First name Last name, performances by First name Last name and First name Last name, Name of Theater, 7 Sept. 2011, City.

(Usual listing of live performance: Emphasizes title first.)

Last name, First name. *Title in Italics.* Directed by First name Last name, performances by First name Last name and First name Last name, Name of Theater, 7 Sept. 2011, City.

(Emphasizes author first.)

APA

Use only in-text parenthetical citation since APA does not include nonretrievable sources in *References*. A typical in-text citation: (Title of live performance, location, date).

Written Musical Composition

60. Longer Composition: Symphony, Ballet, Opera, etc.

MLA

Last name, First name. *Title in Italics*. Year of composition, Publisher, year of publication.

APA

Last name, Initial. (Year of publication). *Title of score in italics* [Opera]. City of publication, State Abbreviation: Publisher. (Year of composition)

(No period follows.)

61. Shorter Composition: Song, Short Instrumental Piece, etc.

MLA

Last name, First name. "Title in Quotations." Year of composition, Publisher, year of publication.

APA

Last name, Initial. (Year of publication). Title without quotations [Song for voice]. City of publication, State Abbreviation: Publisher. (Year of composition)

(No period follows.)

Artwork (Painting, Drawing, Etching, Sculpture, Photograph, etc.)

62. Artwork

MLA

Last name, First name. *Title of Artwork in Italics*. Year of completion, Gallery/Owner, City. Medium.

(Medium = oil on canvas, oil on wood, charcoal, watercolor, etc. If no title, provide brief description: Early twentieth-century oak arts-and-craft chair with barley-twist arm supports.)

APA

Last name, Initial. (Year of completion). *Title of artwork in italics* [Medium]. Gallery/Owner, City, State Abbreviation.

(Medium = oil on canvas, oil on wood, charcoal, watercolor, etc. If no title, provide brief description: Early twentieth-century oak arts-and-craft chair with barley-twist arm supports.)

Map or Chart

63. Map or Chart

MLA

Title of Map in Italics. Map. Publisher, year of publication.

Or

> "Title of Map in Quotations." Map. *Title in Italics*, by First name Last name, Publisher, year of publication. p. 29.

APA

> *Title of map in italics* [Map]. (Year of publication). City of publication, State Abbreviation: Publisher.

> # WARNING!
>
> For MLA, if an online source has no date, don't write *n.d.* Rather, give an indication of possible date: *circa 2011*. Or *2011(?)*.
>
> For APA, if an online source has no date, write *n.d.*

Entire Web Site

64. **Entire Web Site**

    MLA

    > *Site Title in Italics.* 18 May 2012, URL.

    Or

    > Last name, First name, editor. *Site Title in Italics.* Site Sponsor, URL. Accessed 30 May 2012.

    (If author or editor is given, begin with that. If site sponsor is important to identify source, add that. Give access date for source material regularly updated. Period follows.)

    APA

    > *Site Title in Italics.* (2012, May 18). Retrieved from http://

    Or

    > Last name, Initial. (Ed.). (2012, May 18). *Site Title in Italics.* Retrieved from http://

    (No period follows.)

Section of Web Site

65. **Section of Web Site**

    MLA

    > "Title in Quotations." *Site Title in Italics*, URL. Accessed 30 June 2012.

    (Give access date for source material regularly updated. Period follows.)

    Or

    > Last name, First name. "Title in Quotations." *Site Title in Italics*, 18 May 2012, URL.

APA

Title without quotations. (2012, May 18). *Site Title in Italics*. Retrieved from http://

Or

Last name, Initial. (2012, May 18). Title without quotations. *Site Title in Italics*. Retrieved from http://

(No period follows.)

Article in Online Journal

66. Article in Online Journal

MLA

Last name, First name. "Title in Quotations: Subtitle If Any." *Journal Title in Italics*, vol. 8, no. 4, 2010, pp. 15-28, DOI or URL.

APA

Last name, Initial., & Last name, Initial. (2010). Title without quotations: Subtitle if any. *Journal Title in Italics*, 8(4), 15-28. Retrieved from http://

(No period follows.)

Article from Online Magazine or Newspaper

67. Article from Online Magazine or Newspaper

MLA

Last name, First name. "Title in Quotations: Subtitle If Any." *Magazine Title in Italics*, 31 Dec. 2010, DOI or URL.

APA

Last name, Initial. (2011, July 3). Title without quotations: Subtitle if any. Newspaper *Title in Italics*. Retrieved from http://

(No period follows.)

Online Book

68. Online Book

MLA

Last name, First name. *Title in Italics: Subtitle If Any*. Publisher, year of original publication. *Site Title or Database in Italics*, DOI or URL.

APA

Last name, Initial. (Year of original publication). *Title in italics: Subtitle if any*. Retrieved from http://

Or

    Last name, Initial. (Year of original publication). *Title in italics: Subtitle if any.*
      doi:10.1000/1000000

(No period follows.)

Online Poem or Short Story

69. **Online Poem or Short Story**

    MLA

    Last name, First name. "Title in Quotations." Publisher, year of original publication. *Site Title or Database in Italics*, DOI or URL. Site Sponsor, Publisher, year of site publication, URL.

    APA

    Last name, Initial. (Year of original publication). Title without quotations. *Site Title in Italics.* Retrieved from http://

(No period follows.)

Online Reference Work

70. **Online Reference Work**

    MLA

    "Title of Entry in Quotations." *Site Title in Italics*, year of publication, DOI or URL.

    APA

    Title of entry without quotations. (n.d.) In *Title in italics* (2nd ed.). Retrieved from http://

(No period follows.)

Wiki

71. **Wiki**

    MLA

    "Title with Quotations." *Wiki Title in Italics*, 14 Apr. 2009, URL. Accessed 9 Sept. 2009.

(Give access date for source material regularly updated. Period follows.)

    APA

    Title without quotations. (2009, April 14). Retrieved September 9, 2009, from Name of Wiki: http://

(Give access date for source material regularly updated. No period follows.)

Blog (Web Log)

72. Entire Blog

MLA

Last name, First name. *Blog Title in Italics*. 19 Feb. 2012, URL. Accessed 21 Mar. 2012.

(Give access date for source material regularly updated. Period follows.)

APA

Last name, Initial. (2012, February 19). *Blog Title in Italics* [Web log]. Retrieved March 21, 2012, from http://

(Give access date for source material regularly updated. No period follows.)

73. Posting on a Blog

MLA

Last name, First name. "Title in Quotations." *Blog Title in Italics*, June 2017, 2:15 a.m., URL. Accessed 9 Sept. 2012.

(Give access date for source material regularly updated. Period follows.)

APA

Last name, Initial. (2012, June 4). Title without quotations [Web log post]. Retrieved September 9, 2012, from http://

(Give access date for source material regularly updated. No period follows.)

Posting on a Web Page

74. Discussion Group Posting

MLA

Online Name *or* Last Name, First name. "Title in Quotations." *Discussion Group in Italics*, Site Sponsor, 2 Aug. 2011, 1:14 p.m., URL. Accessed 4 Aug. 2011.

(Give access date for source material regularly updated. Period follows.)

APA

Last name, Initial. (2011, August 2). Title without quotations [Online discussion group post]. Retrieved August 4, 2011, from http://

(Give access date for source material regularly updated. No period follows.)

75. Comment Posted on Web Page

MLA

Name [*Or* Last name, First Name]. Comment on "Title in Quotations." *Site Title in Italics*, 29 Aug. 2017, 3:31 a.m., URL.

APA

Last name, Initial. (2017, August 29, 3:31 a.m.). Title without quotations [Online comment post]. Retrieved from http://

E-mail

76. E-mail

MLA

Last name, First name. "Re: Subject in Quotations." Received by First name Last name, 18 Mar. 2017.

APA

APA considers e-mail a nonretrievable source and hence includes it only for in-in-text citations, not for References.

Social Media

77. Social Media (Twitter, Facebook, Google+, Etc.)

In MLA, pseudonyms and usernames are acceptable.

MLA

@Name [*Or* Last name, First name]. "Entire tweet in quotations, #Subject." *Twitter*, 23 May 2017, 8:53 a.m., twitter.com address.

APA

Last name, Initial [@Name]. (2017, 23 May). Entire tweet [Tweet]. Retrieved from http://twitter.com

(No period follows.)

YouTube and Movie-/Video-Streaming Sites

78. YouTube

MLA

[*If author*] Last name, First name. "Title in Quotations." *YouTube*, uploaded by First name Last name, upload date if given, **URL.** Accessed 8 Mar. 2017.

(Give access date for source material regularly updated. Period follows.)

APA

YouTube user name. (upload date if given; if not given, n.d.) Title [YouTube Channel]. Retrieved March 8, 2017, from http://youtube.com

(Give access date for source material regularly updated. No period follows.)

79. **Movie-/Video-Streaming Sites (Netflix, Hulu, Amazon Prime, etc.)**

For any movie or video Web-streaming source like YouTube, follow the YouTube model, adding relevant information (e.g., for television, episode and season) as needed.

MLA

David, Larry. "Wandering Bear." *Curb Your Enthusiasm*, produced by Jeff Garlin, DVD version, season 4, episode 8, HBO Home Entertainment, 29 Feb. 2004. *Amazon Prime*, www.amazon.com/gp/video/detail/B0172URD64?ref_=aiv_dp_season_select.

(Period follows.)

APA

David, L. (Writer-Director). (2004, February 29). Wandering bear [Television series episode]. In Garlin, J. (Producer), *Curb your enthusiasm*. Retrieved from http://www.amazon.com/gp/video/detail/B0172URD64?ref_=aiv_dp_season_select

(No period follows.)

How to Format In-Text Citations

General Rules

For giving in-text credit to sources of information for your project, you must write a citation. You write this citation inside parentheses; it can have several forms, depending on whether you use MLA or APA and whether you do or don't state the author's name in a sentence in the text.

If you *do* state the author's name in the text:

MLA

On the one hand, as film scholar David Webber claims, D.W. Griffith is the racist who in *The Birth of a Nation* glorified the Ku Klux Klan (12).

Citation = parentheses with page number only.

(12)

APA

On the one hand, as film scholar David Webber (2015) has claimed, D.W. Griffith is the racist who in *The Birth of a Nation* glorified the Ku Klux Klan.

Citation = parentheses after author's name with date of publication

(2015).

If you *don't* state the author's name in the text—and save it till the parentheses:

MLA

On the other hand, Griffith is the pioneer technician whose "brilliant editing set the standard for films to come" (Webber 12).

Citation = author's last name plus page number—no comma.

(Webber 12)

APA

On the other hand, Griffith is the pioneer technician whose "brilliant editing set the standard for films to come" (Webber, 2015, p. 12).

When using quotations or making specific references, add p. (page) or para. (paragraph).

(Webber, 2015, p. 12) *or* (Webber, 2015, para. 13)

Otherwise, write the following:

Citation = author's last name plus year of publication—separated by comma

(Webber, 2015).

And note:

When you refer to sources, MLA uses present-tense signal phrases ("claims"); APA uses past-tense or present-perfect ("has claimed").

Specific Rules

All your in-text citations won't be a simple author and page (MLA) or author and year (APA). Complexities develop putting together various combinations—one author, more than one author, unknown author, etc. —with various kinds of publications—book, anthology, the Bible, e-mail, etc.

Guide to Formatting In-Text Citations

MLA and APA

A. You *Do* State the Author in the Text

1. **One Author Stated in Text**
2. **Two or More Sources by Same Author Stated in Text**
3. Two Authors Stated in Text (MLA)
4. Two Authors Stated in Text (APA)
5. Three or More Authors Stated in Text (MLA)

A. You *Do* State the Author in the Text

1. One Author Stated in Text

MLA: According to Elliott, the rising whooping crane population has encountered several "life-threatening setbacks" (47).

For APA, use *p.* plus page number for quoted words but also specific but unquoted references to a text.

APA: Elliott (2012) shows that the rising whooping crane population has encountered several "life-threatening setbacks" (p. 47).

2. Two or More Sources by Same Author Stated in Text

For MLA, use a short version of title in citation to distinguish source from author's other works.

MLA: The newest models, argues Dvorsky, will be "accessible from your cell phone" ("Appliances" 26).

For APA, if more than one publication by author in the same year, letter the sources in the citation and in References.

APA: A current projection (Dvorsky, 2012a) claims that the newest models will be "accessible from your cell phone" (p. 26).

3. Two Authors Stated in Text (MLA)

MLA: A pioneering study by Harkins and Stafford explores how nineteenth-century artist William Daniell undertook a series of sketching voyages around the coast of Great Britain to gain admittance to the Royal Academy (18).

4. Two Authors Stated in Text (APA)

Use *and* (not *&*) in text.

APA: A pioneering study by Harkins and Stafford (1997) explores how nineteenth-century artist William Daniell undertook a series of sketching voyages around the coast of Great Britain to gain admittance to the Royal Academy.

5. Three or More Authors Stated in Text (MLA)

Use the first author plus *et al.* (without italics).

MLA: Bobbs et al. claim that passing a single-payer system will cause a dramatic fall in insurance costs (184-86).

6. Three to Five Authors Stated in Text (APA)

List all authors in first citation; in later citations, use first author plus *et al.* (without italics).

APA: Bobbs, Fitch, Gunderman, and Hernandez (2005) claim that passing a single-payer system will cause a dramatic fall in insurance costs.

and

APA: According to the study by Bobbs et al. (2005), the single-payer system has been successfully instituted in Massachusetts.

7. Six or More Authors Stated in Text (APA)

APA: An investigation by Henshaw et al. (2010) of Milwaukee's redlining has revealed a sordid history of racial intolerance.

8. **An Organization as Group Author Stated in Text**

    MLA: The World Health Organization has published a study demonstrating that malnutrition has ravaged the sub-Saharan continent (43).

    For APA, in first citation, spell out group author with parenthetical abbreviation (WHO); in later citations, abbreviate: WHO (2008).

    APA: The World Health Organization (WHO) has published a study (2008) demonstrating that malnutrition has ravaged the sub-Saharan continent.

9. **Two or More Separate Sources Stated in Text**

    For both MLA and APA, separate with semicolon.

    MLA: The dissertation by Claussen and the book by McBride and Peters simultaneously point out that Ned Rorem made "major creative breakthroughs" while living in Africa (313; 128).

    For APA, in parenthetical citation, use *&* instead of *and* when referring to paired authors.

    APA: The dissertation by Claussen (2011) and the book by McBride and Peters (2011) simultaneously point out that Ned Rorem made "major creative breakthroughs" while living in Africa (p. 313; p. 128).

10. **Nonprint (Web, Social Media, etc.) Author Stated in Text**

    Cite page number if using a PDF format; otherwise, identify according to available identifiers:

    For MLA, author or title and/or section (*sec.* or *secs.*) or paragraph number (*par.* or *pars.*) following a heading. For a movie or video, if referring to a frame, shot, or scene, give the time in hours/minutes/seconds.

    MLA: "Great Depression Games" reminds us that Monopoly is no doubt Parker Brothers' most famous game from the 1930s (Parker Brothers heading, par. 6).

    MLA: Movie director Schoenberg shows a dog tormented by a trio of Italian schoolboys (01:03:14-54).

    For APA, author or title and/or section (*section* or *sections*) or paragraph number (*para.* or *paras.*) following a heading. For a movie or video, if referring to a frame, shot, or scene, give the time in hours/minutes/seconds.

    APA: "Great Depression Games" (2012) reminds us that Monopoly is no doubt Parker Brothers' most famous game from the 1930s (Parker Brothers heading, para. 6).

    APA: Movie director Schoenberg (2015, 01:03:14-54) shows a dog tormented by a trio of Italian schoolboys).

11. **Lecture or Public Presentation Author Stated in Text**

    For both MLA and APA, if more than one lecture or presentation, use identifying date.

    MLA: Dr. Baldridge claims that Istanbul as a source of romantic imagery has made its way into a number of spy novels (9 Sept. 2012).

    APA: Dr. Baldridge (lecture, 2012, September 9) claims that Istanbul as a source of romantic imagery has made its way into a number of spy novels.

12. **Personal Interview, Telephone Interview, or E-mail Author Stated in Text**

For MLA, if more than one communication from same source, use identifying date.

MLA: To summarize Stanton-Crosby, significant advances have been made in treating macular degeneration with blood-vessel inhibitors (24 June 2009).

For APA, any nonretrievable source like e-mail or personal interview is cited within the text but not included in References. Identify as *personal communication* (no italics) with date.

APA: To summarize C.K. Stanton-Crosby (personal communication, June 24, 2009), significant advances have been made in treating macular degeneration with blood-vessel inhibitors.

13. **Republished Author Stated in Text**

For MLA and APA, with a text that has gone through many editions, give the page number of the text consulted but also a chapter, part, or line number.

MLA: In *Gulliver's Travels*, Swift tells how Gulliver says of a farmer whom he encounters, "[He] by this time was convinced I must be a rationale Creature" (87; pt. 2, ch. 1).

For APA, with a text that has gone through many editions, also give original publication date as well as date of text consulted. (Abbreviate *Part* but not *Chapter*.)

APA: In *Gulliver's Travels*, Swift (1735/1976) tells how Gulliver says of a farmer whom he encounters, "[He] by this time was convinced I must be a rationale Creature" (Pt. 2, Chapter 1, p. 87).

14. **Author of Multivolume Work Stated in Text**

For MLA, give both volume and page number (don't write *volume* or *page*).

MLA: We are told by Stanley, "Among our Egyptians there was one called Ali Effendi, a captain, who complained of heart disease" (2: 226).

For APA, give both volume and page number (but write *Vol.* and *p.*).

APA: We are told by Stanley (1890), "Among our Egyptians there was one called Ali Effendi, a captain, who complained of heart disease" (Vol. 2, p. 226).

15. **Author in Anthology Stated in Text**

MLA: Whittington's "Swamp Search" is typical of the crime stories published in *The Black Lizard Anthology of Crime* for pulp lines like "She had me all clobbered, but I wanted her worse than ever" (33).

For APA, with a text that has gone through many editions, also give original publication date as well as date of text consulted.

APA: Whittington's "Swamp Search" (1957/1987) is typical of the crime stories published in *The Black Lizard Anthology of Crime* for pulp lines like "She had me all clobbered, but I wanted her worse than ever" (p. 33).

16. **Unknown Author Stated in Text**

MLA: "Nursing Home Laws Needed" blows the whistle on how the nursing home industry often escapes "rigorous oversight" (2).

APA: "Nursing Home Laws Needed" (2009) blows the whistle on how the nursing home industry often escapes "rigorous oversight" (p. 2).

17. **A Religious Work (Bible, Qur'an, etc.): Unknown Author Stated in Text**

For MLA and APA, use the edition/translation. Spell out names in text.

> MLA: Lamentations 5.10 gives the reader yet another metaphor: "Our skin is as hot as an oven with the burning heat of famine" (*The Holy Bible, New Revised Standard Version*).

For APA, cite classical work like the Bible in the text but not in References; don't italicize.

> APA: Lamentations 5:10 (The Holy Bible, New Revised Standard Version) gives the reader yet another metaphor: "Our skin is as hot as an oven with the burning heat of famine."

18. **An Indirect Source: Author Stated in Text**

For MLA and APA, give page number in parentheses. Do not abbreviate *quoted*.

> MLA: As quoted in Murray, Hamwell often insists that, in the words of the famous Irish playwright, "I can resist everything except temptation" (334).

> APA: As cited in Murray (1982), Hamwell often insists that, in the words of the famous Irish playwright, "I can resist everything except temptation" (p. 334).

19. **Encyclopedia or Other Reference Book: Author Stated in Text**

For both MLA and APA, if the reference book doesn't provide the author of an entry, use entry title ("Lemon").

> MLA: The history note on "Lemon" on the etymology of the word reveals the tree's origins in the Middle East.

> APA: The history note on "Lemon" (1992) on the etymology of the word reveals the tree's origins in the Middle East.

20. **A Long Quotation: Author Stated in Text**

For MLA, set off quotations longer than four typed lines:

- indent *one inch* from flush left
- double-space
- don't use quotation marks unless the passage quotes a quotation
- don't indent the first line unless (1) the passage is longer than one paragraph and (2) the first paragraph in the original is indented
- indent each new paragraph *one-fourth inch*
- place a period at the end of the quotation, and then one space after, type the parenthetical citation: page number (no period follows)

> Klare notes that historians will credit Algeria for the recent unrest in the Middle East:
>
> > On January 5, young protestors in Algiers, Oran, and other major cities blocked roads, attacked police stations and burned stores in demonstrations against soaring food prices. Other concerns–high unemployment, pervasive corruption, lack of housing–also aroused their ire, but food costs provided the original impulse. As the epicenter of youthful protest moved elsewhere … the food price issue was subordinated … but it never disappeared. (7–8)

For APA, set off quotations forty words or more:

- indent *one-half inch* from flush left
- double-space
- don't use quotation marks unless the passage quotes a quotation
- indent each new paragraph one more *one-half inch*
- place a period at the end of the quotation, and then one space after, type the parenthetical citation: page number (no period follows)

> Klare (2011) notes that historians will credit Algeria for the recent unrest in the Middle East:
>
> > On January 5, young protestors in Algiers, Oran, and other major cities blocked roads, attacked police stations and burned stores in demonstrations against soaring food prices. Other concerns–high unemployment, pervasive corruption, lack of housing–also aroused their ire, but food costs provided the original impulse. As the epicenter of youthful protest moved elsewhere … the food price issue was subordinated … but it never disappeared. (pp. 7–8)

B. **You *Don't* State the Author's Name in the Text**

21. **One Author Not Stated in Text**

    MLA: The rising whooping crane population has encountered several "life-threatening set-backs" (Elliott 47).

    For APA, use *p.* plus page number for quoted words but also specific (but unquoted) references to a text.

    APA: The rising whooping crane population has encountered several "life-threatening set-backs" (Elliott, 2012, p. 47).

22. **Two or More Sources by Same Author Not Stated in Text**

    For MLA, use a short version of title in citation to distinguish source from author's other works.

    MLA: The newest models will be "accessible from your cell phone" (Dvorsky, "Appliances" 26).

    For APA, if more than one publication by author in the same year, letter the sources in the citation and in References.

    APA: The newest models will be "accessible from your cell phone" (Dvorsky, 2012a, p. 26).

23. **Two Authors Not Stated in Text (MLA)**

    MLA: Nineteenth-century artist William Daniell undertook a series of sketching voyages around the coast of Great Britain to gain admittance to the Royal Academy (Harkins and Stafford 18).

24. **Two Authors Not Stated in Text (APA)**

    Use the *&* to replace *and* in citation.

    APA: Nineteenth-century artist William Daniell undertook a series of sketching voyages around the coast of Great Britain to gain admittance to the Royal Academy (Harkins & Stafford, 1997).

25. **Three or More Authors Not Stated in Text (MLA)**

    Use the first author plus *et al.* (without italics).

    MLA: Passing a single-payer system will cause a dramatic fall in insurance costs (Bobbs et al. 184-86).

26. **Three to Five Authors Not Stated in Text (APA)**

    List all authors in first citation; in later citations, use first author plus *et al.* (without italics). Use *&* to replace *and* in citation.

    APA: Passing a single-payer system will cause a dramatic fall in insurance costs (Bobbs, Fitch, Gunderman, & Hernandez, 2005).

27. **Six or More Authors Not Stated in Text (APA)**

    APA: An investigation of Milwaukee's redlining has revealed a sordid history of racial intolerance (Henshaw et al., 2010).

28. **An Organization as Group Author Not Stated in Text**

   MLA: Malnutrition has ravaged the sub-Saharan continent (World Health Organization 43).

   For APA, in first citation, spell out group author with bracketed abbreviation [WHO]; in later citations, abbreviate: (WHO, 2008).

   APA: Malnutrition has ravaged the sub-Saharan continent (World Health Organization [WHO], 2008).

29. **Two or More Separate Sources Not Stated in Text**

   For both MLA and APA, separate with semicolon. Alphabetize sources.

   MLA: Two simultaneous studies both point out that Ned Rorem made "major creative breakthroughs" while living in Africa (Claussen 313; McBride and Peters 128).

   For APA, in parenthetical citation, use & instead of *and* when referring to paired authors.

   APA: Two simultaneous studies both point out that Ned Rorem made "major creative breakthroughs" while living in Africa (Claussen, 2011, p. 313; McBride & Peters, 2011, p. 128).

30. **Nonprint (Web, Social Media, etc.) Author Not Stated in Text**

   Cite page number if using a PDF format; otherwise, identify according to available identifiers:

   For MLA, author or title and/or section (*sec.* or *secs.*) or paragraph number (*par.* or *pars.*) following a heading. For a movie or video, if referring to a frame, shot, or scene, author or title plus give the time in hours/minutes/seconds.

   MLA: Monopoly is no doubt Parker Brothers' most famous game from the 1930s ("Great Depression Games," Parker Brothers heading, par. 6).

   MLA: The movie's shot startling for its brutality, we watch a dog tormented by a trio of Italian schoolboys (Schoenberg, 01:03:14-54).

   For APA, author or title and/or section (*section* or *sections*) or paragraph number (*para.* or *paras.*) following a heading. For a movie or video, if referring to a frame, shot, or scene, author or title plus give the time in hours/minutes/seconds.

   APA: Monopoly is no doubt Parker Brothers' most famous game from the 1930s ("Great Depression Games," 2012, Parker Brothers heading, para. 6).

   APA: The movie's shot startling for its brutality, we watch a dog tormented by a trio of Italian schoolboys (Schoenberg, 2015, 01:03:14-54).

31. **Lecture or Public Presentation Author Not Stated in Text**

   For both MLA and APA, use name of lecturer or presenter. If more than one lecture or presentation, use identifying date.

   MLA: Istanbul as a source of romantic imagery has made its way into a number of spy novels (Baldridge, 9 Sept. 2012).

   APA: Istanbul as a source of romantic imagery has made its way into a number of spy novels (Baldridge, 2012, September 9).

32. Personal Interview, Telephone Interview, or E-mail Author Not Stated in Text

For MLA, use author's last name. If more than one communication from same source, use identifying date.

> **MLA:** Significant advances have been made in treating macular degeneration with blood-vessel inhibitors (Stanton-Crosby, 24 June 2009).

For APA, any nonretrievable source like e-mail or personal interview is cited within the text but not included in References. Use author's initials and don't invert name. Identify as *personal communication* (no italics) with date.

> **APA:** Significant advances have been made in treating macular degeneration with blood-vessel inhibitors (C. K. Stanton-Crosby, personal communication, June 24, 2009).

33. Republished Author Not Stated in Text

For MLA and APA, with a text that has gone through many editions, give the page number of the text consulted but also a chapter, part, or line number.

> **MLA:** In *Gulliver's Travels*, Gulliver says of a farmer whom he encounters, "[He] by this time was convinced I must be a rationale Creature" (Swift 87; pt. 2, ch. 1).

For APA, with a text that has gone through many editions, also give original publication date as well as date of text consulted. (Abbreviate *Part* but not *Chapter*.)

> **APA:** In *Gulliver's Travels*, Gulliver says of a farmer whom he encounters, "[He] by this time was convinced I must be a rationale Creature" (Swift 1735/1976, Pt. 2, Chapter 1, p. 87).

34. Author of Multivolume Work Not Stated in Text

For MLA, give both volume and page number (don't write *volume* or *page*).

> **MLA:** We are told, "Among our Egyptians there was one called Ali Effendi, a captain, who complained of heart disease" (Stanley 2: 226).

For APA, give both volume and page number (but write *Vol.* and *p.*).

> **APA:** We are told, "Among our Egyptians there was one called Ali Effendi, a captain, who complained of heart disease" (Stanley, 1890, Vol. 2, p. 226).

35. Author in Anthology Not Stated in Text

For both MLA and APA, use the author of the piece consulted, not the editor of the anthology; use the page number from the anthology.

> **MLA:** "Swamp Search" is typical of the crime stories published in *The Black Lizard Anthology of Crime* for pulp lines like "She had me all clobbered, but I wanted her worse than ever" (Whittington 33).

For APA, with a text that has gone through many editions, also give original publication date as well as date of text consulted.

> **APA:** "Swamp Search" is typical of the crime stories published in *The Black Lizard Anthology of Crime* for pulp lines like "She had me all clobbered, but I wanted her worse than ever" (Whittington, 1957/1987, p. 33).

36. **Unknown Author Not Stated in Text**

For MLA, use full or short form of a title.

> **MLA:** The nursing home industry often escapes "rigorous oversight" ("Nursing Home Laws Needed" 2).

For APA, shorten a title to two or three words, leaving out *The, A,* and *An.* Use quotation marks or italics as appropriate; capitalize key words for parenthetical citation but not for References.

> **APA:** The nursing home industry often escapes "rigorous oversight" ("Nursing Home Laws," 2009, p. 2).

37. **A Religious Work (Bible, Qur'an, etc.): Unknown Author Not Stated in Text**

For MLA and APA, use the edition/translation plus book, chapter, and verse. Spell out names in text, but in citation, abbreviate books with long names.

> **MLA:** The reader is given yet another metaphor: "Our skin is as hot as an oven with the burning heat of famine" (*The Holy Bible, New Revised Standard Version*, Lam. 5.10).

For APA, cite classical work like the Bible in the text but not in References; no page numbers required because such texts are normally numbered; don't italicize.

> **APA:** The reader is given yet another metaphor: "Our skin is as hot as an oven with the burning heat of famine" (The Holy Bible, New Revised Standard Version, Lam. 5:10).

38. **An Indirect Source: Author Not Stated in Text**

For MLA, use *qtd. in* ("quoted in") to show that your source is quoting or paraphrasing another source.

> **MLA:** Hamwell often insists that, in the words of the famous Irish playwright, "I can resist everything except temptation" (qtd. in Murray 334).

For APA, use *as cited in* to show that your source is quoting or paraphrasing another source.

> **APA:** Hamwell often insists that, in the words of the famous Irish playwright, "I can resist everything except temptation" (as cited in Murray, 1982, p. 334).

39. **Encyclopedia or Other Reference Book: Author Not Stated in Text**

For both MLA and APA, if the reference book doesn't provide the author of an entry, put the entry title in quotations (and alphabetize by title in Works Cited or References). Don't use page numbers for reference books that list entries alphabetically.

> **MLA:** The history note on the etymology of the word reveals the tree's origins in the Middle East ("Lemon").

> **APA:** The history note on the etymology of the word reveals the tree's origins in the Middle East ("Lemon," 1992).

40. **A Long Quotation: Author Not Stated in Text**

For MLA, set off quotations longer than four typed lines:

- indent *one-half inch* from left margin
- double-space

- don't use quotation marks unless the passage quotes a quotation
- don't indent the first line even if the first paragraph in the original is indented
- indent each new paragraph *one-fourth inch*, place a period at the end of the quotation and then one space after, type the parenthetical citation: author and page number (no period follows)

> It may turn out that historians will credit Algeria for the recent unrest in the Middle East:
>
> > On January 5, young protestors in Algiers, Oran, and other major cities blocked roads, attacked police stations and burned stores in demonstrations against soaring food prices. Other concerns–high unemployment, pervasive corruption, lack of housing–also aroused their ire, but food costs provided the original impulse. As the epicenter of youthful protest moved elsewhere … the food price issue was subordinated … but it never disappeared. (Klare 7-8)

For APA, set off quotations forty words or more:

- indent *one-half inch* from flush left
- double-space
- don't use quotation marks unless the passage quotes a quotation
- indent each new paragraph one more *one-half inch*
- place a period at the end of the quotation and then the parenthetical citation: author, date, and page number (no period follows)

> It may turn out that historians will credit Algeria for the recent unrest in the Middle East:
>
> > On January 5, young protestors in Algiers, Oran, and other major cities blocked roads, attacked police stations and burned stores in demonstrations against soaring food prices. Other concerns–high unemployment, pervasive corruption, lack of housing–also aroused their ire, but food costs provided the original impulse. As the epicenter of youthful protest moved elsewhere … the food price issue was subordinated … but it never disappeared. (Klare, 2011, pp. 7-8)

Endnotes And Footnotes

Occasionally, as you put a project together, you may want to say something more about a point. But a problem develops: If you bring up the new material, it won't fit the flow of your project. It will veer off at a tangent.

But scholars have developed a solution for such tangents: endnotes and footnotes.

The endnote (which comes at the end of the project) or the footnote (which comes at the foot of the page) will allow you to expand on a point without breaking into the forward, logical movement of your prose. Here's how to handle endnotes (MLA calls them "Notes") and footnotes (APA calls them "Footnotes"):

For referring to endnotes or footnotes,

1. **Use superscripts.**

2. **Number notes (endnotes or footnotes) in the same order that they appear in the text. Note that APA uses the superscript to number notes (no period follows).**

3. **Superscripts follow all punctuation except the dash. With the dash—like here[1]—the superscript comes before.**

MLA: Ortiz makes no such claim.[1]

Notes

1. In fact, Ortiz argues to the contrary. See Ortiz in *The Way to the Border* (2009) and earlier articles that clearly state his position on immigration policies.

APA: Ortiz makes no such claim.[1]

Footnotes

[1]In fact, Ortiz argues to the contrary. See Ortiz in *The Way to the Border* (2009) and earlier articles that clearly state his position on immigration policies.

◇◇◇

Word Confusions

ability—being able to do something ("the ability to learn languages")
capacity—an amount that can be contained ("the flour canister's capacity")

about—approximately ("I made about fifty dollars.")
around—circling ("I flew around the house.")

accept—agree to something
except—exclude somebody or something

adapt—adjust to a situation
adept—skillful at something
adopt—borrow or take as your own

adverse—opposing ("The drug caused adverse effects.")
averse—disinclined, unwilling ("The boy is averse to hard work.")

advice—a recommendation
advise—make a recommendation

affect (verb)—to change
effect (noun)—the result ("How does this effect affect you?")

aid—help ("We offered aid.")
aide—helper ("He had a hard-working aide.")

all most—all of them, very much ("They were all most pleased with the food.")
almost—not quite all ("Almost everybody was pleased with the food.")

all ready—completely prepared ("He's all ready to go.")
already—previously ("He's already gone.")

all right—correct spelling
alright—misspelling

all together—together in a group ("We are all together.")
altogether—completely or entirely ("We are altogether displeased.")

all ways—in every way ("They wanted in all ways to do a good job.")
always—at all times ("They always wanted to do a good job.")

allot—distribute
a lot—much or many (no such word as *alot*)

From *The Less-Is-More Handbook: A Guide To College Writing, Second Edition* by Larry Edgerton. Copyright © 2017 by Kendall Hunt Publishing Company. Reprinted by permission.

allude—hint at; not say straight out
elude—evade or get away
refer—say straight out

allusion—reference to something
delusion—false belief, often a symptom of madness
illusion—mistaken impression

almost—not quite ("Almost everybody was there.")
most—majority of ("Most men agreed.")

alternate—one thing after another ("on alternate days")
alternative—available as another possibility ("an alternative juror")

alumna—female singular graduate
alumnae—female plural graduates
alumnus—male singular graduate
alumni—male and/or female plural graduates

among—use for three or more ("Among the triplets, Bob is the smartest.")
between—use for two ("Between the twins, Bob is the smarter.")

amount—what you measure (like sugar)
number—what you count (like coins)

ante—before ("antecedent")
anti—against ("antiwar")

anxious—worried about something
eager—looking forward with enthusiasm

any one—member of a group ("Any one of the family can go.")
anyone—any person ("Anyone can go.")

any time—at some point ("At any time did you visit the doctor?")
anytime—whenever ("Come at anytime.")

any way—any method ("Is there any way you can help?")
anyway—in any case ("Anyway, we don't have the money for a trip.")
anyways—misspelling of *anyway*

a part—part of something (like a slice of pie: "I want a part of that pie.")
apart—separate from ("He sat apart from the group.")

appraise—estimate the worth
apprise—keep somebody up to date about whatever

apt—natural inclination for something
liable—responsible; obligated by law
likely—something will probably happen

argue about—debate something ("Don't argue about politics.")
argue with—debate something with somebody ("Don't argue with him about politics.")

as—while ("I listened to music as I washed the dishes.")
because—for the reason that ("I took a new job because I needed the money.")

assure—give a guarantee to somebody
ensure—make safe or certain
insure—protect against loss (using insurance)

a while (noun)—use with <u>preposition</u> ("Rest <u>for</u> a while.")
awhile (adverb)—use with verb ("Rest awhile.")

bad—an adjective describing a noun ("a bad book")
badly—an adverb describing a verb, an adjective, or another adverb ("writes badly"; "badly written"; "badly over")

based in—don't use when you mean *based on*
based off of—don't use when you mean *based on*
based on—rests on; uses as a basis ("The movie was based on a play by Shakespeare.")
based upon—same as *based on*

beside—next to ("The dog sat beside Sheila.")
besides—in addition to ("Besides a dog, Sheila has a cat.")

biannual—twice a year
biennial—every other year

bimonthly—every two months or twice a month
semimonthly—twice a month

bloc—group of countries ("the Soviet bloc")
block—piece of something (wood, stone, etc.); a unit ("city block")

boarder—somebody who lives in a boarding house
border—the line between two states

born—what happens to a child
borne—to be carried ("She was borne by her servants.")

breath—air drawn in and out; the noun ("I took a breath.")
breathe—draw air in and out; the verb ("I will breathe a sigh of relief.")

bring—You bring something HERE.
take—You take something THERE.

callous—unsympathetic
callus—hardened skin

can—have the ability to do something ("I can sing.")
may—ask permission ("May I sing?")
could—feel inclined to ("We could see a movie this weekend.") or past tense of *can* ("We could have accomplished that.")

capital—main, chief; seat of government; uppercase letter; assets (chiefly monetary)
capitol—statehouse where legislature meets

cement—it goes into concrete
concrete—a mixture of cement, sand, gravel, and water ("the concrete road or sidewalk")

censer—a device in a church for burning incense
censor—somebody who judges something
censure—what the judge does; to show disapproval

center around—wrong use (illogical because you can't be *around* the center; you're *on* the center)
center on—correct use ("The plan centered on one premise.")

childish—similar or suitable to a child (a putdown: "You're being childish.")
childlike—like a child (more positive, a compliment: "Your painting is childlike.")

cite—quote a source
sight—vision
site—a location

climactic—deals with a climax ("the climactic end of Act III")
climatic—deals with the weather ("the climatic changes at the North Pole")

coarse—rough to the touch
course—what you take in college

collaborate—work with somebody
corroborate—confirm something
compare to—finding the likeness of one thing in another (comparing the journey of life to a journey down a river)
compare with—placing one thing by another to show similarities and differences (comparing Bach with Mozart)

compel—forced to act against your will ("The general compelled his troops to fight back.")
impel—responding to an inner motive ("Curiosity impelled him to snoop.")

complected—no such word
complexioned—use this one ("dark complexioned")

complement—completing or supplementing ("Your idea complements mine.")
compliment—saying something nice about somebody or something ("I complimented his idea.")

comply to—don't use
comply with—do as asked or ordered ("comply with the rules")

compose—make up or constitute ("The quartet is composed of four cellists.")
comprise—include ("The quartet comprises four cellists.")

confidant(e)—male or female in whom one confides ("The boy is her confidant; the girl is her confidante.")
confident—self-assured, bold ("She felt confident.")

connotation—what a word suggests; its associations
denotation—what the dictionary says the word specifically means

conscience—what makes you feel guilty
conscious—what you are when you're not asleep

consist in—have as its main feature ("Success consists in hard work.")
consist of—be made up of ("The suite consists of three rooms.")

continual—constantly recurrent (like a ringing phone)
continuous—uninterrupted (like a whistling teakettle)

correspond to—similar to ("The prime minister corresponds to the president.")
correspond with—exchange mail with ("We corresponded with each other.")

could care less—wrong form; makes no sense (How can you *care less*?)
couldn't care less—use this form ("I couldn't *care less*.")

council—group of people
counsel—advice or a lawyer
consul—an ambassador

councilor—a member of a council
counselor—a lawyer or advisor

couple—don't use (as in "I borrowed a couple dollars.")
couple of—use this phrase ("I borrowed a couple of dollars.")

credibility—believability ("She had credibility with the court.")
credulity—willingness to believe too easily ("His credulity was laughable.")

credible—believable, trustworthy
creditable—praiseworthy
credulous—too trusting, innocent, gullible

criterion—the singular ("This criterion is clear.")
criteria—the plural ("These criteria are clear.")

criticize—use as a verb ("Criticize the memo.")
critique—don't use as a verb ("I'll critique your memo."); use as a noun ("She wrote a good critique.")

datum—the singular ("This datum is here.")
data—the plural ("These data are here.")

decent—proper, respectable, good ("She has decent table manners.")
descent—downward slope, going down ("She made the descent to the bottom.")

defiantly—resistantly, disobediently ("He defiantly refused to go tonight.")
definitely—clearly, unmistakably ("He definitely refused to go tonight.")

depart for—leave for a destination ("We will depart for Rhode Island.")
depart from—leave a destination ("We will depart from Rhode Island.")

deprecate—criticize
depreciate—lose value

desert (noun)—dry, barren land, like Death Valley
desert (verb)—abandon; leave with no intention of returning
deserts (noun)—getting what is deserved ("She got her just deserts.")
dessert—the course that follows the meal, like apple pie and ice cream

detract—take away a part; to lessen quantity/value ("The billboard detracts from the park's beauty.")
distract—draw away the attention of ("The loud clock distracts him from reading.")

differ about—disagree about something ("They differ about politics but not about morality.")
differ from—is different from ("Singing differs from humming.")
differ in—have similarities but also differences ("Cats and dogs have fur, four legs, and a tail but differ in head shapes and behavior.")
differ on—have a different view of ("Bob and Bill differ on the interpretation.")

differ over—have a different view of ("Bob and Bill differ over the interpretation.")
differ with—disagree with someone ("Bob differs with Bill on abortion.")

different from—preferred in formal or academic writing
different than—generally avoid in formal or academic writing

disassemble—take something apart (e.g., a machine)
dissemble—pretend or lie

disburse—pay out
disperse—scatter

discomfit—make uneasy, embarrass; thwart, foil ("She was discomfited by his suggestion.")
discomfort—make uncomfortable; distress ("She was discomforted by the lumpy mattress.")

discreet—keeping your mouth shut ("Please be discreet.")
discrete—something that's separate ("That is a discrete problem.")

disinterested—impartial (like a judge)
uninterested—having no interest in something

distinct—clear ("a distinct possibility")
distinctive—individual ("a distinctive style")

dominant—dominating, controlling ("the dominant male in the herd")
dominate—influence or control ("He dominates the herd.")

due to—attributable to (use only after a *to be* verb: am/is/was/were/will be: "His loss *was* due to budget issues.")
because of—by reason of; on account of (use in sentences when *due to* isn't appropriate—i.e., after verbs other than *to be* verbs: "He lost because of budget issues.")
on account of—by reason of; because of (use in sentences when *due* to isn't appropriate—i.e., with verbs other than *to be* verbs: "He lost on account of budget issues.")

each other—between two people
eachother—misspelling of *each other*
one another—among three people or more

effective—performing its function well ("an effective teaching model")
efficient—not wasting resources ("an efficient engine")

e.g.—for example (from the Latin *exempli gratia*); use with commas ("a popular truck, e.g., F-150")
i.e.—that is (from the Latin *id est*; use with commas) ("the 'god of the sea,' i.e., Poseidon")

electric—producing, carrying, or started by electricity ("an electric wire")
electrical—pertaining to but not carrying electricity ("an electrical engineer")

elicit (verb)—draw forth ("elicit an answer")
illicit—illegal ("illicit drug trade")

emigrate—leave a place ("emigrate from Canada")
immigrate—go into a place ("immigrate to Canada")

eminent—prominent ("an eminent lawyer")
immanent—existing within a reality; inherent ("God was immanent in the world.")
imminent—impending ("the imminent storm")

end in—conclude in a feeling or state of mind ("Their marriage ended in misery.")
end with—conclude with some event ("The world will end with an explosion.")

endemic—commonly found in one area ("AIDS is endemic in Africa.")
epidemic—rapidly widespread in one area ("the AIDS epidemic in South Africa")
pandemic—widespread over more than one area ("AIDS is pandemic in the world.")

enormity—great wickedness or very serious crime ("the enormity of his abuse")
enormousness—very large or huge ("the enormousness of the warehouse")

enthuse—no such word ("I am enthused.")
enthusiastic—use this form ("I am enthusiastic.")

envelop—enclose or encase
envelope—what you put the letter into

every day—each day of the week
everyday—common, ordinary ("Every day I wear my everyday clothes.")

every one—member of a group ("Every one of the group was there.")
everyone—everybody ("I saw everyone.")

except—not including ("everyone except Peter")
except for—don't use this redundancy ("everyone except for Peter")

famous—favorably well-known ("famous actor")
infamous—having or deserving a bad reputation; unfavorably well-known ("infamous drunk")
notorious—unfavorably well-known ("notorious liar")
prominent—conspicuous, important, well-known ("prominent lawyer")

farther—refers to physical distance (i.e., to space: "farther down the road")
further—refers to non physical or figurative distance (i.e., time, degree, extent, addition: "a further comment")

fewer—refers to number ("fewer sugar cubes")
less—refers to amount/quantity ("less sugar")

flammable and inflammable—can catch on fire
nonflammable—can't catch on fire

flaunt—show off ("She flaunted her wealth.")
flout—be disrespectful to authority ("He flouted the law.")

flounder—make mistakes; become confused while trying to act; stumble ("The political candidate floundered in the first debate.")
founder—sink (like a ship); fail ("He foundered on the reef of procrastination.")

forego—precede ("The flag-bearer will forego the parade.")
forgo—give up or go without ("We will forgo eating in restaurants.")

foreword—introduction to a book
forward—at or near the front

formally—something to do with a proper occasion
formerly—in the past

former—refers to the first of two of something ("Of Coke and Pepsi, I prefer the former.")
first—refers to the first of three or more things ("Of Coke, Pepsi, and Dr. Pepper, I prefer the first.")

from—use with people ("I borrowed five dollars from Marco.")
off—don't use with people (as in "I borrowed five dollars off Marco.")

good—an adjective describing a noun ("a good book"); refers to psychological health ("I feel good; my spirits are high.")
well—an adverb describing a verb ("He writes well."); refers to physical health ("I feel well; I'm over my cold."); can also describe an adjective ("well-written book") or another adverb ("well inside the strike zone")

graduated—successfully complete a course of study; use with *from* ("He graduated from Harvard," not "He graduated Harvard.")
was graduated—alternative expression but slightly less acceptable for extra word; also use with *from*

hanged—what happened to a murderer ("We hanged the killer.")
hung—what happened to a picture ("We hung the picture.")

healthful—conducive to good health ("Exercise is healthful.")
healthy—state of health ("He feels healthy.")

historic—a memorable event, worth a place in a history book ("historic home run")
historical—any routine event in history ("historical census data")

holey—full of holes
holy—sacred
wholly—completely

holistic—concerned with a complete system
wholistic—misspelling

home—(as a verb, use with *in*) guided to a target, moved toward ("The pigeon homed in on the apartment building.")
hone—sharpen ("He honed his knife on an oiled stone.")

hopefully—illogical; avoid this form ("Hopefully, it will rain": Rain comes down with hope?)
I hope—use this form ("I hope it will rain.")

human—of people (use as an <u>adjective</u>, not as a noun: <u>human</u> beings, not humans)
humane—compassionate toward people

hyper—high, above, above normal ("His blood pressure shows hypertension.")
hypo—low, beneath, below normal ("His blood pressure shows hypotension.")

if—introduces a <u>dependent clause</u> in a conditional sentence ("<u>If car manufacturers built safer cars</u>, then we would have fewer accidents.")
whether—introduces alternatives ("I didn't know whether it would rain or snow.")

imply—what the speaker does ("The speaker implied I was an idiot.")
infer—what the listener does ("I inferred the speaker thought I was an idiot.")

impressed by—be taken with something or someone ("I'm impressed by you.")
impressed on—fix firmly in mind ("He impressed on them the need for accuracy.")
impressed with—impress one thing with another ("The paper was impressed with a watermark.")

in—inside something ("We swam in the pool.")

in to—enter something (use with a <u>two-part verb</u>: "We <u>came in</u> to swim in the pool.")

into—enter something ("We jumped into the pool.")

in behalf of—in the interest of, for the benefit of ("They held the concert in behalf of the earthquake victims.")

on behalf of—as a representative of, in aid of ("He spoke on behalf of his client.")

in regard to—okay to use ("in regard to your letter")

in regards to—not okay to use

as regards—okay to use

incidence—the rate at which something happens or affects things ("a high incidence of bankruptcy")

incidents—events ("several incidents of theft")

independent from—don't use this phrase

independent of—use this phrase ("That company is independent of this company.")

individual—doesn't mean *people*; means a particular person/thing ("an individual student")

person—means people ("She's a helpful person.")

ingenious—something that's clever ("an ingenious rhyme")

ingenuous—simple or naïve ("an ingenuous country boy")

intense—strong in degree or quality ("intense cold")

intensive—taking effort, concentrated ("intensive review")

intents—practical purposes ("for all intents and purposes")

inter (office, state, etc.)—between offices, states, etc. ("inter-California-Oregon mail")

intra (office, state, etc.)—within offices, states, etc. ("intra-California mail")

intervene between—come between two sides ("She intervened between the boxers.")

intervene in—come into a dispute involving more than two sides ("She intervened in the battle.")

invest in—put money, time, or effort into something or somebody ("We invested in her career.")

invest with—endow with a quality ("She invested the child with hope.")

irregardless—no such word

disregardless—no such word

regardless—use this one

it's—contraction for *it is* or *it has* ("It's hot today.")

its—possessive ("its color")

last—after all others; use with three or more ("He was last in the parade.")

later—a time after this one ("a later event")

latest—most recent ("her latest movie role")

latter—the last in a list ("the latter president"); mentioned after another; use with two (Of the two e-mails, it was the latter.")

lie—recline (use like *sit*: "Please lie down.")

lay—place or put something down (use like *set*: "Please lay it down.")

lead (noun)—a metal or pencil graphite
lead (verb)—guide (present tense: "I lead groups of tourists.")
led—guided (past tense: "I led groups of tourists.")

leave—go away from ("He wants to leave the state.")
let—allow to, permit ("Let him leave the state.")

lend—give somebody something
loan—what you lend (you lend a loan)

liable—responsible; obligated by law
libel (verb)—defame
libel (noun)—printed defamatory statement

like—use when no verb follows it ("We work like dogs.")
as—use when a <u>verb</u> follows it ("We work as hard as workers <u>did</u> in the past.")
as if—use when a <u>verb</u> follows them ("We work as if we <u>owned</u> the place.")

loath—reluctant
loathe—to hate

loose—free or unfastened ("loose change")
lose—misplace something ("Lose your change?")

luxuriant—a lot of growth ("luxuriant foliage")
luxurious—very comfortable ("luxurious house")

marshal—high-ranking officer (noun: "Marshal Smith"); arrange in proper fashion; assemble (verb: "marshal your argument")
martial—warlike ("martial law")

masterful—domineering ("a masterful leader")
masterly—of a master; skillful ("a masterly performance")

mastery of—complete knowledge of a subject ("She had mastery of geometry.")
mastery over—complete control over a person ("She had mastery over her servant.")

material—substances that make up something ("building material")
matériel—equipment, apparatus, and supplies ("military matériel")

may—suggests permission or possibility; use in present ("We may go.")
might—suggests permission or possibility; use in past ("We thought we might go.")

may be—a verb showing possibility ("I may be going.")
maybe—perhaps ("Maybe I'll go.")

meantime (noun)—between times ("in the meantime")
meanwhile (adverb)—at the same time ("Meanwhile, he drove his car.")

memento—souvenir ("memento of her trip to Russia"); reminder of ("memento mori")
momento—misspelling and mispronunciation of *memento*

militate—act as a strong influence ("Two problems militated against the senator's success.")
mitigate—make less intense, serious, or severe ("His depression was mitigated by winning money.")

miner—a person who mines: coal miner
minor—somebody who's under age

moot—debatable ("They hit a moot point in the argument.")
mute—silent ("The boy was mute.")

moral—a lesson ("The fable offered a moral."); a standard of behavior ("Have you no morals?")
morale—how you feel ("Our morale is high.")

more important—a short version of *what is more important* ("More important, Ken needs to over-see the Singapore branch.")
more importantly—in a more important way ("The doctor handled this case more importantly than any other.")

more than—in a greater degree than something else ("I saw more than twenty eagles.")
over—don't use when you mean *more than*

mucous—of or like mucus; (adjective: "A mucous membrane lines the mouth.")
mucus—moist, sticky substance lubricating and covering body's inner hollow organs; (noun: "Mucus aids in protecting the lungs.")

nauseated—feel sick ("I am nauseated.")
nauseous—thing that sickens ("This horror film is nauseous; it makes me nauseated.")

no body—refers to a group ("No body of work is as important as Shakespeare's.")
nobody—refers to no person ("Nobody was able to attend.")

no one—not a single one; none ("No one of the elms was infested.")
noone—misspelling of *no one*
none—not a single one; no one ("None of the cake was eaten.")

observance—celebrating a date ("observance of Memorial Day")
observation—paying attention to something ("observation of climate change")

of—misspelling of *'ve* in contractions like *could've, would've,* etc.
've—correct spelling of contracted *have*

off—use this word ("He jumped off the shed.")
off of—don't use this redundancy

on—at a position above ("We sat on the bench.")
on to—continued on (use with a <u>two-part verb</u>: "We <u>walked on</u> to the store.")
onto—to a position on ("The boy jumped onto the chair.")

opposite—on the other side of; use *to, from,* or only *opposite* ("Her house is opposite to mine." *Or* "His house is opposite mine.")
opposite of—on the other side of (use when *opposite* is a noun followed by *of* ("The style of that house is the opposite of mine.")

oral—what you say out loud ("oral instructions")
verbal—of the word, written or spoken ("He was more verbal than visual.")

over all—over an area ("Snow fell over all the town.")
overall—taken as a whole ("Overall, I loved the movie.")

overdo—do in excess
overdue—past due

over time—through a period of time ("We visited over time.")
overtime—time worked beyond regular hours ("We worked overtime.")

palate—roof of the mouth ("burned his palate on pizza")

palette—artist's board for mixing colors; also used metaphorically ("I like his palette.")

pallet—forklift platform for lifting and storing goods ("the cases of corn on the pallet"); a makeshift bed, often of straw ("slept on a pallet")

part from—separate oneself from a person or organization ("Jason parted from the Boy Scouts.")

part with—separate oneself from a thing ("Jason parted with his Boy Scout badges.")

passed—past tense of *pass*, to go or overtake ("I passed him in the street.")

past—belonging to the time before ("He was interested in the past.")

peace—lack of conflict

piece—a fragment

pedal—a foot lever (noun); push with foot, as on a bicycle (verb)

peddle—to sell

people—use when you're talking about big groups ("three hundred people")

persons—use when you're talking about small groups ("three persons")

persecute—treat cruelly without cause

prosecute—start criminal action against

perquisite—profit or privilege in addition to salary ("The job had many perquisites.")

prerequisite—required as a condition for something ("The class was a prerequisite.")

personal—of a person

personnel—employees

perspective—a view of something ("a new perspective on an old idea")

prospective—future, possible ("a prospective student")

petit—generally means *small*: petit jury, petit larceny, petit mal, petit point

petite—with small, dainty build ("a petite gymnast")

phenomenon—singular extraordinary occurrence ("this phenomenon")

phenomena—plural extraordinary occurrences ("these phenomena")

pore over—study, pay close attention to ("pored over the calculus book")

pour over—flow over ("cream to pour over oatmeal")

practicable—feasible; something you can do ("If I train, the marathon is practicable.")

practical—useful; proved through experience ("practical advice")

precede—come before ("Washington precedes Lincoln.")

proceed—move forward; advance ("Washington proceeded to cross the Delaware.")

precedence—established priority ("This has precedence.")

precedents—noun plural used for legal example ("The lawyer cited two precedents.")

predominant—main person with authority, power, or influence ("Tiger Woods is today's predominant golfer.")

predominate—be greater than others in number or intensity ("Tiger Woods predominates in golf.")

preventative—don't use; careful writing prefers *preventive*

preventive—preventing something ("preventive medicine")

principal—head of something; main person
principle—a rule

prophecy (noun)—a prediction
prophesy (verb)—make the prediction ("This is the prophecy I prophesy.")

prostate—the gland
prostrate—stretched out on the floor ("He was prostrate with prostate pain.")

proved—use as a past tense verb ("It has been proved.")
proven—use as an adjective ("a proven fact")

purposefully—with purpose and determination ("He strode purposefully.")
purposely—intentionally ("He purposely let himself get caught.")

quiet—with little or no sound
quite—to a considerable degree ("It was quite quiet in the library.")

raise—lift or bring something up (like children)
rise—get up ("I rise at six o'clock.")

rack—shelf, framework to stretch out, or destruction (noun: "the hat on the rack"); inflict with great
    torment (verb: "racked with pain"; "rack your brains")
wrack—noun: damage or destruction ("wrack and ruin"); a wreck, seaweed cast on shore used as
    manure (*Note*: Both "rack and ruin" and "wrack and ruin" are correct.)

rap—knock or speak
wrap—cover

rational—reasonable, sane, able to reason
rationale—logical basis for something

real—an adjective describing a <u>noun</u> ("a real <u>experience</u>")
really—an adverb describing a verb, adjective, or another adverb ("really exercised"; "really tall";
    "really well")

reason is because—avoid this expression; replace with *because*
reason is that—use this expression or *because* ("The reason I'm late is that . . ." or "I'm late
    because . . .")

regretfully—feeling regret ("I regretfully decline.")
regrettably—it is to be regretted ("The accident regrettably happened.")

rend—tear something apart ("a heart-rending story")
render—boil something down ("rendered the jam")

residence—home
residents—inhabitants

respectfully—having respect for somebody
respectively—in the order mentioned

restive—stubborn, impatient ("Middle school is full of restive children.")
restless—always agitated, uneasy ("The sky was restless before the tornado.")

right—correct
rite—ceremony
write—form words on a surface

role—a part to play
roll—to tumble; a list

root—part of a plant
rout—defeat
route—a direction to take

seasonable—appropriate to a season ("a seasonable fall frost")
seasonal—of a season ("I had a seasonal job.")

sensual—pleasing to the body (has sexual overtones: "A massage is sensual.")
sensuous—refers to the senses (without sexual overtones: "The smell of coffee is sensuous.")
sexual—refers to sex ("a sexual experience")

set—place or put something down (use like *lay*: "Please set it down.")
sit—take a position with the buttocks (use like *lie*: "Please sit down.")

shear—cut ("shear the sheep")
sheer—thin (as of fabric); steep ("sheer cliff")

some body—member of a group ("Find some body of evidence to support your theory.")
somebody—unspecified person ("Ask somebody to go.")

some day—at some point in time; use with a <u>preposition</u> ("Please pick an appointment time <u>for</u> some day next week.")
someday—in the future ("We hope to have an appointment someday soon.")

some one—member of a group ("Ask some one of the scouts to go.")
someone—unspecified person ("Ask someone to go.")

some time—an unspecified quantity of time ("I needed some time to myself.")
sometime—at an unstated, indefinite time ("I'll call you sometime.")
sometimes—at some times but not all times ("Sometimes he was sad.")

spacious—large, roomy ("a spacious room")
specious—logical at first but lacking merit ("a specious argument")

speak to—tell somebody something ("I will speak to the meeting.")
speak with—discuss something with somebody ("I will speak with the senator.")

stationary—something that doesn't move
stationery—what you write on

straight—not curved or bent ("a straight line")
strait—narrow, restricted, as of a waterway ("the Strait of Gibraltar")

stratum—singular layer of something
strata—plural layers of something

style—don't use in the following ("this style painting")
style of—use ("this style of painting")

suit—a set of clothes or a case in court
suite—a set of rooms or furniture

sure—an adjective describing a noun ("a sure thing")
sure and—avoid; use *sure to* ("You must be sure to go.")
surely—an adverb describing a verb, an adjective, or another adverb ("surely won the game"; "surely tall"; "surely more")

suspect of—have doubts about something ("She is suspected of a felony.")
suspect with—don't use ("She is suspected with a felony.")

than—use to compare things ("I'm taller than Bill.")
then—at that time ("I was taller then.")

their—possessive ("their house")
there—location ("over there")
they're—contraction for *they are* ("They're here.")

thesis—singular idea or dissertation
theses—plural ideas or dissertations

thorough—absolutely complete ("a thorough job of cleaning")
through—from one end or side to the other ("I ran through the tunnel.")

to—shows location ("Go to the store.")
too—excessively ("It's too hot.")
two—number ("two brothers")

tortuous—winding, twisting (like a road)
torturous—painful

toward—American preference ("I'm driving toward town.")
towards—British (or American Midwestern) "preference ("I'm driving towards town.")

true to—according to a standard ("true to their beliefs")
true with—according to a measurement ("The door should be true with the frame.")

try and—avoid ("You must try and be good.")
try to—use this form ("You must try to be good.")

turbid—cloudy, muddy (like water)
turgid—inflated, stiff

type—don't use in the following ("this type painting")
type of—use ("this type of painting")

unconscience—misspelling of *unconscious*
unconscious—not aware ("He was unconscious.")

until—use
till—use
'til—okay to use but *till* preferred
'till—don't use

up—to a position above ("We went up the hill.")
up on—to a position above (use with a <u>two-part verb</u>; "He <u>ended up on</u> the chair.")
upon—on ("The old man fell upon the floor.")
on—at a position above ("We sat on the bench.")

venal—capable of being corrupted (as by bribery)
venial—a sin you can excuse

verbage—no such word
verbiage—excessive number of words ("His style was marked by verbiage."); don't use as a synonym
     for *words* ("Can you produce the verbiage for the report?")

vice—wicked conduct; a habit
vise—the clamp on a workbench

waive—set aside
wave—a swell of water; what you do with your hand

wangle—get something by manipulating somebody
wrangle—bicker with somebody or herd livestock

weather—atmospheric conditions
whether—introduces alternatives ("I didn't know whether I would go or stay home.")

what—don't use in the following ("What use is that old lawnmower?")
of what—use ("Of what use is that old lawnmower?")

when—use for a situation ("a time when I fell in love")
where—use for a place ("a city where I fell in love")

while—period of time (noun: "wait for a while"); spend time pleasantly (verb: "while away the hours
     reading mystery novels")
wile—trickery to deceive or attract ("The snake used his wile to persuade Eve.")

who's—contraction for *who is* or *who has* ("Who's here?" "Who's gone to work?")
whose—possessive ("Whose house is that?")

woman—female singular ("She is a woman.")
women—female plural ("I'm taking a women's studies course.")

wreak—inflict, cause something to happen ("The hail wreaked havoc on the corn crop.")
wreck—destroy ("The crew wrecked the building.")

yore—of long ago ("days of yore")
your—possessive ("your house")
you're—contraction of *you are* ("You're funny.")

From *The Less-Is-More Handbook: A Guide To College Writing, Second Edition* by Larry Edgerton. Copyright © 2017 by Kendall Hunt Publishing Company. Reprinted by permission.

◇◇

Sample Syllabus Template

Rawpixel.com/Shutterstock.com

Course Section: ENG 101: CRN #

Meeting Schedule: Days: Time:

Location:

Instructor:

E-mail: Through Blackboard or

Phone:

    Office:
    Office Hours:

Mondays:

Tuesdays:

Wednesdays:

Thursdays:

Fridays:

Course Description

In English 101, you will conduct research and write proposals, annotated bibliographies, and research essays. You will develop research topics and questions; identify, summarize, analyze, evaluate, and synthesize relevant sources; and present arguments based on your findings. You will document where information and ideas come from by using MLA style. You will enter academic conversations by doing research that builds upon existing knowledge.

Prerequisite:

Required Texts and Materials

Buy or rent this **E-TEXT** <u>immediately</u>, from the bookstore. You'll need the e-text version so that you can acquire the code necessary to participate in the required reading, assignments, and exercises.

Reinventing the Freshman Writing and Research Course
ISBN #: 987-1-5249-9302-3

*You may choose to have a "print-on-demand" version at additional cost.

- <u>An active college e-mail address.</u> I will send regular e-mails with important information about the class, our schedule, etc.—and I will send these only to your college e-mail address. You will be held responsible for knowing this information, so if you don't know how to log in to your college e-mail, contact the Help Desk ASAP and get in the habit of checking this e-mail account daily.

- <u>Access to Blackboard.</u> You must check Blackboard DAILY to learn about homework assignments, submit your work, and generally stay in touch with me and with the course. Our Blackboard site is the authoritative source for information about the course: what's due, when it's due, and so on. I sometimes post messages on Blackboard between class sessions, and you will be responsible for this information.

Course Overview

UNIT 1: **Entering the Academic World**	**UNIT 2:** **Finding a Research Topic and Question**

Growth Mindset
- I can learn anything I want to
- When I'm frustrated, I persevere
- I want to challenge myself
- When I fail, I learn
- Tell me I try hard
- If you succeed, I'm inspired
- My effort and attitude determine everything

Fixed Mindset
- I'm either good at it, or I'm not
- When I'm frustrated, I give up
- I don't like to be challenged
- When I fail, I'm no good
- Tell me I'm smart
- If you succeed, I feel threatened
- My abilities determine everything

desdemona72/Shutterstock.com

What is an academic mindset?

How can mindset impact my writing and growth in college?

Read published essays on how the brain works, how we learn, and how we learn to write.

Write a formal letter to the instructor, reflecting on your mindset toward writing.

Ileezhun/Shutterstock.com

About what do academics and intellectuals write? How do they construct arguments?

Read published essays that will open up possibilities for our own original research.

Write a formal Proposal that sketches out the original research you will conduct in Unit 3.

UNIT 3:
Finding and Assessing Existing Academic Dialogues

Golden Sikorka/Shutterstock.com

What do experts say about an issue in which I'm interested? What different perspectives are there, and how do they compare?

Read sources on a topic/question you choose, borrowing information and/or ideas.

Write an annotated bibliography for the sources you have discovered about the topic and question you have selected.

UNIT 4:
Formalizing Our Contribution to the Dialogue: Research Project or Essay and Outreach Piece

Aurielaki/Shutterstock.com   iQoncept/Shutterstock.com

Write a Research Essay on an issue and question of your choice that tells the story of your research process, documenting what you learned.

Read examples of successful writing in the genre in which you choose to compose.

How does the issue I have researched impact my community? How can I persuade people to think or act?

Write an argument to a public audience, in a genre of your choice (*i.e.,* Letter to the Editor), that persuades readers to act or to think differently about the issue you researched in Unit 3.

Learning Outcomes

By the end of *Writing and Research*, students will:

1. Demonstrate an understanding of writing as a multistage process, devising strategies for pre-writing, composing, revising, editing, and proofreading and using writing for inquiry, learning, thinking, and communicating.

2. Produce texts that present ideas effectively and fluently:
   a. Include a clear focus, controlling idea, or question.
   b. Support ideas with reasoning and evidence.
   c. Summarize others' ideas clearly, accurately, thoroughly, and concisely.
   d. Integrate their own ideas with those of others.
   e. Organize ideas to clarify and support the controlling idea or question and to best suit the targeted audience.
   f. Write with adequate command of language and its grammatical and mechanical conventions.

3. Use appropriate research methods.
   a. Develop and refine a research topic and question.
   b. Evaluate the credibility, reliability, and applicability of sources.
   c. Identify, analyze, and evaluate arguments in sources.
   d. Document where information and ideas come from in the style appropriate for the discipline.

4. Develop the foundations for creative, independent, and critical thinking that considers a multiplicity of perspectives and disciplines.

Measurement Instruments for ALL Objectives:
See Project and Points Section, Next Page

Rawpixel.com/Shutterstock.com

Projects & Point System

PROJECT	DESCRIPTION	POINTS
Preparation	Earn 10 points for completing the preparation for each class. Preparations (posts, journals) will include quizzes, posts (informal writing exercises that offer practice with specific skills and strategies), and journals (online activities to guide you through the course).	300 (10 points x 30 preps)
Peer Reviews	Peer reviews are class activities in which you will exchange writing with classmates, giving and receiving feedback. (Online students will engage in this activity through discussion forum posts.)	160 (16 points x 10 reviews)
Mindset Letter	A formal letter to the instructor reflecting on what you learned about your mindset toward writing.	150
Research Proposal	A document that articulates your idea for your independent research.	150
Annotated Bibliography	A document that evaluates your researched sources	150
Research Essay	After doing independent and original research on a topic/question of your choosing, you will reflect on the research process in a formal essay.	150
Outreach Essay	An argument to a public audience, in a genre of your choice (i.e.. letter to the editor, etc.), that persuades your readers to act or to think differently about the topic you researched.	150
Total Points Available		1,200+

Final Grade Equivalents

FINAL GRADE	POINTS	FINAL GRADE	POINTS
A	1,080+	C	840–899
B+	1,020–1,079	D	720–839
B	960–1,019	F	719 or below
C+	900–959		

The College's Grading Policy

GRADE	PERCENT (%)
A [4.0]	90%–100%
B+ [3.5]	85%–89%
B [3.0]	80%–84%
C+ [2.5]	75%–79%
C [2.0]	70%–74%
D [1.0]	60%–69%
F [0.0]	59% and below
FN [0.0]	Failure for insufficient attendance

IN OTHER WORDS: SLO's and Measurements in Another Format

SLO/Objectives—Upon successful completion, students will be able to:	This outcome will be **measured** by the following instruments (exercises, tools, observations):
SLO 1: Demonstrate an understanding of writing as a multistage process, devising strategies for pre-writing, composing, revising, editing, and proofreading and using writing for inquiry, learning, thinking, and communicating.	Research Proposal, Annotated Bibliography (or Literature Review), Research Essays, peer review, and journals, together totaling a minimum of 4,000 words, equivalent to 16 double-spaced pages
SLO 2: Produce texts that present ideas effectively	Mindset Letter, Research proposal, Annotated Bibliography (or Literature Review), and Research Essays, together totaling a minimum of 4,000 words, equivalent to 16 double-spaced pages
Objective 1 Focus on a controlling idea or question	
Objective 2 Support ideas with reasoning and evidence	
Objective 3 Summarize others' ideas clearly, accurately, and thoroughly	
Objective 4 Integrate their own ideas with the ideas of others	
Objectve 5 Write with adequate command of language and its grammatical and mechanical conventions.	
Objective 6 Organize ideas to clarify and support a controlling idea or question	
SLO 3: Use appropriate research methods	Research Proposal, Annotated Bibliography (or Literature Review), and Research Essays, together totaling a minimum of 4,000 words, equivalent to 16 double-spaced pages
Objective 1 Develop and refine a research topic and question.	
Objective 2 Evaluate the credibility and reliability of sources.	
Objective 3 Identify, analyze, and evaluate arguments in sources.	
Objective 4 Document where information and ideas come from in the style appropriate to the discipline.	
SLO 4: Develop the foundations for creative, independent, and critical thinking that considers a multiplicity of perspectives and disciplines.	Research Proposal, Annotated Bibliography (or Literature Review), and Research Essays, together totaling a minimum of 4,000 words, equivalent to 16 double-spaced pages

The Calendar/Weekly Schedule

Please note that this calendar is a "preview" of our schedule this semester and will probably change. Blackboard is the authoritative source for our schedule, and especially our class-by-class schedule. You must check our Blackboard site to learn what you need to do for each upcoming class session.

WEEK	DATE	UNIT	TOPICS	READINGS	ASSESSMENTS
1		1	Welcome; Developing a growth mindset; College-level writing, reading, and thinking	Chapter 1, section a; Dweck's "What is Mindset?," "How Does Mindset Affect Success?," and "Test Your Mindset"; Scott's "Fixed Mindset vs. Growth Mindset"; Duckworth's "The Key to Success: Grit?"; "Lamott's "Shitty First Drafts"	In-Class Activity 1A, 1B, and 1C; Journal Entries 1, 2, and 3
2			Developing a growth mindset toward writing, etc.; Entering class academic dialogue (including peer review) and active reading strategies	Chapter 1, sections b, c, and d; Ohlin's "Five Ways to Develop Growth Mindset Using Resilience"; Rose's "Blue Collar Brilliance"; Bahrampour's "Find your Passion? That's bad advice, scientists say"; Cherry's "Gardner's Theory of Multiple Intelligences"	Draft 1 of Mindset Reflective Letter; In-Class Activities 1D and 1F (Peer Review 1); Journal Entries 4 and 5
3			Entering the class academic dialogue, etc.; Defining college-level research	Chapter 1, sections e, f, and h and "Transitions"; any <u>one</u> reading <u>from each</u> of five sections (total 5 readings): "On Education"; "On Technology and Us"; "On Negotiating Cultural, Political, and Other Differences"; "On a College Education"; "On Food"	Draft 2 of Mindset Reflective Letter; In-Class Activities 1G (Peer Review 2) and 1 H **Final Mindset Reflective Letter**
4		2	Finding a research topic and question; determining significance	Chapter 2, sections a, b, and c; any two readings <u>from each</u> of five sections (total 10 readings): "On Education"; "On Technology and Us"; "On Negotiating Cultural, Political, and Other Differences"; "On a College Education"; "On Food"	In-Class Activities 2A and 2B; Journal Entry 6A/6B

5			Determining a research plan; Writing proposals	Chapter 2, sections d, e, f, and h; any two readings <u>from each</u> of five sections (total 10 readings): "On Education"; "On Technology and Us"; "On Negotiating Cultural, Political, and Other Differences"; "On a College Education"; "On Food"	Draft 1 of Research Proposal; In-Class Activity 2C and 2E (Peer Review 3); Journal Entry 7
6			Writing proposals, etc.; Where to search	Any one reading <u>from each</u> of five sections (total 5 readings): "On Education"; "On Technology and Us"; "On Negotiating Cultural, Political, and Other Differences"; "On a College Education"; "On Food"	Draft 2 of Research Proposal; In-Class Activity 2F (peer Review 4) and 2D **Final Research Proposal**
7		3	Using databases vs. using Internet searches; Summarizing sources; Library visit	Chapter 3, sections a, b, c, and j	In-Class Activities 3A and 3B; Journal Entries 8 and 9
8			Finding and evaluating sources; Opposition positions	Chapter 3, sections d, e, and f	Draft 1 Annotated Bibliography; In-Class Activities 3B, 3C, and 3F (Peer Review 5); Journal 10
9			Writing annotated bibliographies; Tentative claims	Chapter 3, sections d, e, f	Draft 2 Annotated Bibliography; In-Class Activities 3G (Peer Review 6) and 3D **Final Annotated Bibliography**
10		4	Types of evidence and argument structures; Plagiarizing, quoting, paraphrasing, and summarizing	Chapter 4, sections a, b, c, d, and e	In-Class Activities 4A and 4B
11			Synthesizing; Establishing balance; Using citations	Chapter 4, sections f, g, h, i, and j	In-Class Activity 4C
12			Targeting purpose and audience; Outlining; Drafting and revising	Chapter 4, sections k, m, and p	Draft 1 Research Essay; In-Class Activity 4D (Peer Review 7); Journal Entry 11

13			Rhetoric: Genre, Audience, and Purpose; Using the research for outreach piece	Chapter 4, sections I and n; NYU Libraries' "How to Create a Research Poster"	Draft 2 Research Essay; Draft 1 Outreach Piece; In-Class Activities 4E (Peer Review 8) and 4F (Peer Review 9); Journal 12 **Final Research Essay**
14			Presentation basics	Chapter 5; Weirich's "How to Give a Good Research Talk"; Stephen's "How to Sound Smart in Your TEDx Talk"; Anderson's "TED's Secret to Great Public Speaking"; Duarte's "The Secret Structure of Great Talks"; Jones' "How to Give a Great Research Talk"; Phillips's "How to Avoid Death by PowerPoint"	Draft 2 Outreach Piece; In-Class Activity 4G (Peer Review 10); Journal 13 **Final Outreach Essay**
15		5	Finals Week: Outreach Presentations		**Outreach Presentation**

Contract for English 101

To participate in English 101, I agree to . . .
(write your initials beside each item if you agree)

	In face-to-face classes: Attend class regularly—not missing more than a week's worth of classes (in other words, no more than 2 classes). In online classes: Attend class regularly by logging in at least twice each week—not missing more than one week's worth of log-on time.
	In face-to-face classes: Arrive to class on time. I understand that arriving late is disruptive and that I cannot enter class more than ten minutes after class has started.
	Complete and submit writing tasks when they are due. I understand that late work will be penalized by 10 points per day, and that no late work will be accepted more than a week after the due date.
	In face-to-face classes: Complete all journal entries on time and bring a copy of each journal entry to class on the day that entry is due. I understand that I cannot earn points for attending class if I do not have my journal entry completed and with me in class. In online classes: Complete all journal entries on time, and post a copy of each journal entry on the day that entry is due. I understand that I cannot earn points for attending class if I do not have my journal entry completed and posted for others to read.
	Be prepared for every class session. This means completing, and bringing with me to class [or posting online], all materials (journal entries, readings, drafts, etc.) that were involved in preparing for that class session.
	In face-to-face classes: Bring to class any and all readings completed for that particular class session. If reading an electronic copy, I agree to print out the reading—or selected passages that I believe are important. In online classes: Complete all assigned reading prior to the activities done online that pertain to that reading.
	Participate in all in-class exercises and activities. I understand that if I do not participate in class activities, I will lose my attendance and participation points for that day.
	Submit only my own original work and never plagiarize. I understand that plagiarism includes submitting others' work as my own. I understand that plagiarism also includes borrowing information or ideas from others and failing to give credit—to acknowledge that they are borrowed, and from whom they are borrowed. I understand that plagiarism is a serious academic offense and that if I plagiarize, I will fail the assignment and be reported to college administration, and that if I plagiarize a second time, I will fail the course.
	In face-to-face classes: Refrain from using electronic devices including phones, tablets, and computers, except when instructed, or after seeking permission to use these for class purposes only. If I must use my device, I agree to leave the classroom to do so: "Take the call in the hall."

On the lines below, please print your name, then sign and date. You will submit this signed contract to the instructor, but do make a copy for your records.

_____ (Print)

_____ (Sign and date)

Support

Tutoring

You may go for assistance in writing to the Writing Center.

ROOM: _____

PHONE NUMBER: _____

You may also use _____, the Writing Center's online version of writing tutoring. Go to the following link: _____ (Insert link appropriate for your school).

You may also use NETTUTOR, a link available on the home page of our Blackboard shell.

IMBEDDED LIBRARIAN
Ask the librarian a question through our Blackboard e-mail.

HELP FROM ME:
If you need my assistance, have questions, etc., please feel free to contact me!

College Academic Honesty Policy

Definition from Handbook

For complete College definitions and examples of plagiarism and academic dishonesty, please see the following links:

Definition of Plagiarism

Plagiarism—deliberate and knowing use of someone else's work or ideas as one's own. Examples of plagiarism are: quoting a source verbatim, or paraphrasing text from a given source, without properly citing the source; turning in a research paper that was written by someone else; or in any other way passing off someone else's work as one's own; or failing to give credit for ideas or materials taken from someone else.

Consequences of Academic Dishonesty

College Policy Regarding Class Cancellation for Weather, etc.

College Services for Students with Disabilities:

Part 2: Additional Information Required by the College and the Department but Perhaps Not of Particular Interest To You

1. Course #: ENGLISH 101

2. NAME OF ORIGINATOR or REVISOR:

   NAME OF COURSE: Writing and Research

3. CURRENT DATE: _____.

   Please indicate whether this is a NEW COURSE or a REVISION:

   REVISION _____ DATE OF PRIOR REVISION: _____

4. NUMBER OF CREDITS: <u>3</u>

5. NUMBER OF CONTACT HOURS PER WEEK: <u>3</u>

6. APPROXIMATE FREQUENCY OF OFFERING THIS COURSE: Every semester

7. PREREQUISITES or ENTRY LEVEL SKILLS or PLACEMENT SCORES: _____

8. COREQUISITES: None

9. PLACE OF THIS COURSE IN CURRICULUM:

   ___ Required for Curriculum (name) _____. __X__ College Core ___ Elective

   ___ Part of Required/Recommended Sequence with (Number of Course) _____

10. IS THIS COURSE DESIGNED FOR TRANSFER TOWARD A SPECIFIC MAJOR?

    __X__ Yes _____ No MAJOR(S) _____

11. INSTRUCTIONAL METHODS: List the different instructional methods you might use in the course of the semester. List supplementary learning options, if any.

    A major intent of instruction is to put students in active control of their learning—using, analyzing, and evaluating language within different contexts to build on what they already know. Ideally, while not limited to the activities on this list, the instructor will act as an informed and challenging coach by engaging students in several of the following activities:
    a. Collaborative small group discussion and writing.
    b. Whole class discussion.
    c. Process modeling.
    d. Student presentations.
    e. Student–instructor conferencing (in class/in office).

f. Word processing with computers.
g. Writing/reading journals.
h. Building and revising portfolios.
i. Using various media for illustration and analogy.
j. The Library's online Research Path Tutorial for Internet Research.
k. Use electronic resources such as Blackboard, Smart Board, and online pedagogical aids (OWL, writing web sites, etc.)

12. The College's **Key Values**: These skills, abilities, knowledge, and attitudes cross disciplines and prepare our students to be life-long learners.

STUDENT LEARNING OUTCOME/OBJECTIVE(S)	RELATED COURSE SLO
If any of the following *values* pertain to this course, indicate which of the above course SLO's address those values. *Please see related objectives for each SLO on last page.*	
Skills & Abilities	
Value 1: Communication Skills: Reading, Writing & Speech	**SLO 1, SLO 2, SLO 3**
Value 2: Critical Thinking and Problem-Solving Skills—The student will be able to:	**SLO 2, SLO 3**
Value 3: Information and Technology Literacy Skills—The student will be able to:	**SLO 2, SLO 3**
Knowledge & Attitudes	
Value 4: Learning to be a successful learner	**ALL SLO's**
Value 5: Global Awareness and a Sense of Community and Responsibility	**SLO 2, SLO 3**

APPENDIX A
ESSAY ASSIGNMENT DESCRIPTIONS, DIRECTIONS, AND GRADING RUBRICS

"MY MINDSET REFLECTIVE LETTER" ESSAY—700 WORDS (2–2.5 PAGES)

Reflect on your own beliefs about *yourself as writer*. How have your experiences as writer affected those beliefs? How have those views changed over time and as a result of the work we have been engaged in during these first couple of weeks of class?

Write a letter to me, your teacher, describing your mindset about writing. What is your own mindset toward writing—and especially toward academic writing—and how can you improve that mindset? Discuss how specific readings (Dweck, Duckworth, Rose, Gardner, and/or Lamott) have influenced how you think about your own writing abilities and how you might cultivate new ways of thinking about yourself as a writer. How might those ways of thinking affect your experience of this course and of college in general?

Your letter should be . . .

* *In first-person*: This letter is about your mindset, so you will use "I."

* *Organized chronologically*: Begin by describing how you thought about your writing before this semester, and then explain how specific readings and exercises have influenced your thinking. End the essay by describing the way you think now and what influence you believe that thinking will have on your college/academic writing experience.

* *Addressed to me, your teacher*: Follow the outlined conventions and formatting of a formal letter, and adopt a formal (or semi-formal) tone. Your purpose is to convince me, your teacher and reader, that you have thought seriously about the material and about how you might use it to improve your learning. For a sample, see the model at the end of this chapter.

* *Well-documented*: Integrate the ideas and information from at least two of the readings of this unit. (See a complete list at the end of this chapter.) Use signal phrases such as "According to Carol S. Dweck," or "Mike Rose notes that," etc., to acknowledge where ideas, information, and borrowed words come from. Enclose all borrowed words in quotation marks (" ").

You will write this journal entry as draft 1.

After your first peer review, you will revise the essay. Then you will meet with peers again. After that discussion, you will revise the essay a third and final time to submit for a grade.

MY MINDSET REFLECTIVE LETTER ESSAY EVALUATION RUBRIC

CATEGORY	EXCEEDS STANDARDS [20–25 POINTS]	MEETS STANDARDS [17.5–19.75 POINTS]	APPROACHES STANDARDS [15–17 POINTS]	DOES NOT MEET STANDARDS [14 POINTS AND BELOW]
Reflection Writer's thinking shows depth and rigor?				
Integration Writer integrates ideas/info from readings?				
Focus Writer stays on task and on topic?				
Organization Writer organizes ideas effectively?				
Documentation Writer uses signal phrases and quotation marks?				
Correctness Writer avoids errors that confuse or distract?				

RESEARCH PROPOSAL—700 WORDS (2–2.5 PAGES)

Compose a 700-word formal document that describes your plan for the Unit 4 Research Essay and Project.

What question do you plan to address, and how will you go about finding an answer?

Your Research Proposal must include the following sections:

TOPIC & QUESTION

Describe the topic and the specific question you hope to address.

WHAT I KNOW, ASSUME, OR IMAGINE (CONTEXT/ FORE-GROUNDING/ BACKGROUND/ SCOPE)

What do you already know about the topic and question? What do others in general think about the topic? What don't you already know about the topic and question? What do you hope to learn?

SOURCE

- Identify a published essay on your topic question. (You may use one of the readings in our text.)

- Summarize the essay's argument (identifying the claim and key reasons/evidence). If helpful, use some of the templates we used in doing our class activities on summary and response.

- State your own view, and explain how it compares to the argument presented. If helpful, use some of the templates we used in doing our class activities on summary and response.

SIGNIFICANCE

Address the questions, "Why does this topic/question matter to me? Why should it matter to anyone else? To whom does it matter?"

PLAN

What kinds of sources could be helpful to answer your question? What will you be looking for in terms of credible and useful sources?

Your audience here is I, your instructor. Persuade me that you have an interesting, but focused and manageable, research plan in mind.

Rubric

CRITERIA	YES [25 POINTS]	NO [0 POINTS]
Topic and Question Author identifies a focused, manageable topic and a specific question.		
What I Know, Assume, or Imagine Author explains what he/she already knows and what he/she does not know about the topic and question as well as what he/she hopes to learn and, in general, what others commonly think (scope).		
Source Author identifies a published essay on the topic/question. Author summarizes the essay's argument (identifying the claim and key reasons/evidence). Author states his/her own view, and explains how it compares to the argument presented.		
Significance Author identifies and explains both the personal and larger significance of her/his topic and question.		
Plan Author articulates a detailed plan for accomplishing her/his research project, including the types of sources and databases, etc., to be examined.		
Correctness Author writes clearly and correctly, making few if any errors that confuse the reader. Writer uses MLA formatting correctly.		

Annotated Bibliography Directions

Context. You have spent the last few weeks thinking and researching. Your annotated bibliography gives you an opportunity to take stock of your sources so that you see what sources you have, whether or not they are reliable and relevant, how you might use them in your research essay and project, and what sources you still need to find.

What Is an Annotated Bibliography? There are many different types of annotated bibliographies and professors use the term in a variety of ways. Essentially, though, an annotated bibliography is a document that lists sources on a particular topic/question and offers a brief discussion of each source, summarizing that source and discussing how it connects to the other sources and to the researcher's own thinking-in-progress, including her working thesis.

Why Write an Annotated Bibliography? Creating an annotated bibliography gives structure and purpose to the (otherwise messy) research process. Writing an annotated bibliography requires you, the researcher, to read, think about, and analyze each of your sources, so that you are clear about how you will use them. Often while working on an annotated bibliography, a researcher realizes he/she cannot use a source and/or needs additional (or different) sources. This kind of setback can be frustrating, but necessary as you, the researcher, figure out what you really want to know—and argue.

What Are the Components of an Annotated Bibliography?

- An Overview: This paragraph or two will:
  - ▶ Explain your topic, question, and claim or working thesis (A "working" thesis is what your thesis would be if you were to write the paper right now. It's called "working" because it might change.). *[Often, you can use a part of your already written proposal to create this section.]
  - ▶ Summarize what you have found out so far from your sources and what you still want/need to find out.

- Then, list each of your sources in MLA format and, below EVERY source, write one to two paragraphs in which you:
  - ▶ Using terms from the CRAAP Test, explain why this is a relevant and reliable source (You will not include sources that are not relevant or reliable).
  - ▶ Summarize the basic claim of the source. What did the author(s) say? Use the call and response and summary patterns we have studied.
  - ▶ Respond to the source. What do "you" say? Use the call and response and summary patterns we have studied. You might agree, disagree, raise questions, etc.
  - ▶ Explain how you will use this source in your research essay. Be specific.
  - ▶ Synthesize. Explain the way this work fits with—or challenges—other information you have about the topic.

Use MLA Citation in the Appendix of your text (or actually written in your sources or found in the database citation tools). Citations are important because they help researchers organize and share information about sources in a standardized way. There are many online resources that will help you create citations for your sources, including a thorough guide at the Purdue Online Writing Lab.

How many sources do I need? You need enough sources to address your research question from a variety of perspectives; **six is the minimum.**

Annotated Bibliography Rubric

CRITERIA	A—EXCELLENT	B—VERY GOOD	C—AVERAGE	F—UNACCEPTABLE
Selection of Sources	Sources discussed are numerous and varied. Together, they are more than sufficient to address the writer's question.	Sources discussed are numerous and/or varied. Together, they are sufficient to address the writer's question.	Sources discussed are sufficient to address the writer's question.	Author includes too few sources, or sources that are not varied. These sources are insufficient to address the writer's question.
Overview	Overview articulates a clear and focused topic and question, and describes in-depth how the sources gathered address that question.	Overview articulates a clear and focused topic and question, and describes how the sources gathered address that question.	Overview articulates a topic and question, and describes how the sources gathered address that question.	Overview does not articulate a clear and focused topic and question—or the overview is not included at all.
Source Evaluation	Author persuasively argues that all sources are reliable and relevant to her/his topic.	Author argues that sources are reliable and relevant to her/his topic.	Author discusses whether sources are reliable and relevant.	Author does not discuss whether sources are reliable and/or reputable.
Source Summary	Author presents a summary of each source that is clear, thorough, accurate, and unbiased.	Author presents a summary of most sources that is clear, thorough, accurate, and unbiased.	Summaries are sometimes clear, thorough, accurate, and unbiased.	Summaries are not clear, thorough, accurate, or unbiased—or are not present at all.
Response to Sources	Author consistently articulates a response to the sources' claims that is nuanced and in-depth.	Author articulates a response to the sources' claims that is nuanced and in-depth.	Author articulates a response to the sources' claims.	Author does not offer a response to the sources' claims.
Source Synthesis	Author identifies complex interrelationships among sources, often probing sources down to the assumption-level, in order to identify points of convergence and divergence.	Author identifies complex interrelationships among sources.	Author identifies interrelationships among sources.	Author does not identify interrelationships among sources.
MLA Style	Author consistently follows MLA format.	Author follows MLA format.	Author mostly follows MLA format.	Author rarely or does not follow MLA format.
Correctness	No errors that confuse or distract. Author uses word choice, punctuation, and sentence structure effectively.	Only a few errors that confuse or distract. Author uses word choice, punctuation, and sentence structure effectively.	Many errors that confuse or distract. Words, punctuation, and sentence structure are ineffective or inappropriate to the writing task.	Many errors that confuse or distract.

THE I-SEARCH RESEARCH ESSAY—1,750 WORDS (5–6 PAGES)

In a formal, fully-documented MLA 8-style essay, tell the story of your research project. Describe what you found, and how your perspective evolved.

Write your essay in narrative form, recording the steps of the discovery process. Do not feel obligated to tell everything, but highlight the findings and happenings that were crucial to your hunt and contributed to your understanding of the topic. Organize your essay into the following sections:

1. **What I Knew, Assumed, or Imagined.** Describe your prior knowledge and understanding of the topic and question, before you began the project. Yes, you may adapt this section from your Proposal.

2. **What I Discovered.** Describe the information and ideas you gathered. Organize this section as a chronological narrative (like a story) recording the steps of the discovery process. Don't share every detail; instead, highlight key findings and happenings, the ones that really impacted your perspective. Feel free to include missteps and mistakes you may have made along the way.

3. **Reflections**. Reflect on what you found and draw some conclusions. Compare what you thought you knew, assumed, or imagined, with what you actually discovered. Discuss what you still hope to learn about this topic/question, and reflect on how you might further share or act on what you have learned.

While your essay should be personal and reflective, it should be crafted for readers both real (me, your instructor) and imagined (others interested in your topic, but who may lack your newfound expertise). This consideration means you'll need to write clearly and engagingly, explain ideas and information thoroughly, and of course document everything.

Rubric

When evaluating your essay, I will ask the following questions.

Focus	Does the writer remain focused on a specific topic and question?
Summary	Does the writer summarize sources clearly, accurately, and thoroughly?
Evaluation	Does the writer present evaluations of source credibility and reliability?
Synthesis	Does the writer discuss connections and disconnections among multiple sources?
Organization	Does the writer organize ideas effectively? Does the writer use paragraphing, topic sentences, transitions?
Reflection	Does the writer show how her thinking has evolved, explaining how she thought at the beginning of the project, and how that thinking changed as they researched and wrote?
Documentation	Does the writer use correct MLA signal phrases, in-text citations, and Works Cited page?
Correctness	Does the writer avoid errors that confuse or distract?

This prompt was adapted from: Olson, Carol Booth. "A Sample Prompt, Scoring Guide, and Model Paper for the I-Search." *Practical Ideas for Teaching Writing as a Process*. Diane Publishing, 1996.

OR

TRADITIONAL RESEARCH ARTICLE ESSAY DIRECTIONS— 1,750 WORDS (5–6 PAGES)

Context: You have engaged in a process of exploration and discovery of your research topic. You began with a proposal in which you posed a question that was meaningful to you. Your annotated bibliography discussed various ideas from an array of sources and opinions. You are now ready for the "culminating event," to write an article in which you will discuss your research, draw conclusions, and offer a persuasive argument.

What Is a Research Article? A research article discusses the results of original research and contributes something new to the body of knowledge in a given area. Your goal in writing a research article is to express an informed argument or thesis and to try to persuade the reader to care about your findings and to accept your conclusions on your original question.

(How) and Why Write a Research Article? Craft this persuasive article for a general audience, an audience who might be interested in this particular topic, but lacks your expertise. In other words, pitch the article to someone like me, or like your classmates.

Your role as a researcher is to deepen others' understanding of an issue, problem, or question, while also offering your own original perspective. Present yourself as an expert who can educate your audience on this topic. After all, you have been researching and writing about this topic for many weeks now, so you are a legitimate local expert.

What Are the Components of a Research Article? In terms of its format, your article should include:

- a title
- a body in which you present your research and conclusions:
  - ▶ an original claim supported by reasoning and evidence
  - ▶ discussions of how your claim responds to the research you have done
  - ▶ some reflection on what remains to be researched relative to this question
- a Works Cited page in MLA style (or, if you prefer, some other formal documentation style)

I-Search Essay OR Traditional Research Essay Rubric

CRITERIA	EXCEEDS STAN-DARDS (A TO B+)	MEETS STANDARDS (B TO C)	APPROACHES STANDARDS (D)	DOES NOT MEET STANDARDS (F)
Focus Writer identifies a focused and manageable topic and research question or problem. Writer has a clear, thoughtful, and substantive claim in response to the research question or problem. Writer places the claim and its significance within the context of the broader conversation going on about the topic.			.	
Organization of Argument and Evidence Writer builds a logical and clearly organized argument in support of the claim. Topic sentences unify paragraphs. Transitions clearly indicate relationships between ideas. Evidence, including quotations, is effectively introduced, explained, and contextualized.				

CRITERIA	EXCEEDS STAN-DARDS (A TO B+)	MEETS STANDARDS (B TO C)	APPROACHES STANDARDS (D)	DOES NOT MEET STANDARDS (F)
Analysis of Research Writer gathers numerous, varied, and reliable sources to develop evidence in support of a claim. Writer applies source information that advances the claim. Writer effectively summarizes, paraphrases, and quotes from research materials. Writer effectively acknowledges multiple perspectives on a claim, including potential objections to the claim. Writer shows awareness of interrelationships among sources.				
Documentation Writer attributes evidence to sources using MLA documentation style, including in-text citations and a Works Cited list.				
Revision Writer's work demonstrates revision for clarity, organization, and depth of thought.* (*When based on comparison of rubric scores for final version vs. initial draft)				
Editing Writer effectively edits the essay; the writing does not confuse or distract.				

OUTREACH PIECE—700 WORDS (2–2.5 PAGES)

Compose a written piece that draws on your academic research but "reaches out" to a wider <u>public audience</u>. Your document should . . .

- target a specific public audience
- share your research
- connect that research to a specific public issue or problem
- present an argument, persuading readers to take a certain action or adopt a certain way of thinking

You will decide which genre to write in, but it must be a public genre (<u>not</u> an academic essay). Possibilities include:

- letter to the editor (for the school newspaper or local newspaper)
- social media post (blog, vlog, GoFundMe, etc.)
- brochure or flyer
- web site
- political cartoon

No matter what genre you choose, your piece must make an argument. Argument, in this context, means . . .

- making an overall **claim** (a big, debatable idea you want readers to consider)
- supporting that claim with **reasons** (smaller ideas that explain the big idea)
- providing **evidence** for those reasons (specifics that firm up those smaller ideas)
- offering **counterarguments** that acknowledge and respond to contrasting perspectives

Sample Pre-Writing

Research question: Why do so many people in the United States not have enough to eat, and what can we as a country do to solve this problem?

Possibilities:

AUDIENCE	GENRE	VENUE/PUBLICATION	CLAIM
Local Voters	Letter to the editor	Lifestyle Section of my local newspaper, *LoHud Gannett*	Voters need to understand the food needs of the community and the reason to approve the new food closet as part of the town's public services.
Youth at Various Local High Schools and Colleges	Pamphlet	To hand out to students at the schools	Students need to understand the food needs of the community and volunteer for service at the new food closet.
Local Businesses	Open letter	Through regular mail and on social media platform	Local businesses need to understand the food needs of their community and donate funds or food.

Grading

When evaluating your piece, I will ask the following questions. Does the writer:

- Craft the piece for a specific audience or audiences?
- Follow genre conventions?
- Present a clear and debatable claim?
- Support the claim with reasons and evidence?
- Draw support (info and ideas) from credible research sources?
- Summarize, paraphrase, and/or quote sources effectively?
- Offer counterarguments?
- Document where information and ideas come from using an appropriate method (for the chosen genre)?

Rubric

CATEGORY	EXCEEDS STANDARDS	MEETS STANDARDS	APPROACHES STANDARDS	DOES NOT MEET STANDARDS
Crafts the piece for a specific audience or audiences clearly identifiable				
Follows genre conventions				
Presents a clear and debatable claim				
Supports the claim with reasons and evidence; Draws that support (info and ideas) from credible research sources				
Summarizes, paraphrases, and/or quotes sources effectively; Offers counterarguments				
Documents where information and ideas come from using an appropriate method (for the chosen genre)				

FINAL EXAM OUTREACH PRESENTATION (3–5 MINUTES)

During Finals Week, you will share with the class your Outreach Piece, in the form of a poster.

Set up your poster in the classroom (or project it from the computer), and then walk around the room, viewing your classmates' posters, and discussing your own poster with others.

Your poster must include:
- A hard copy (or projected copy) of your final Outreach Piece
- Notes and drafts that show your writing process, including . . .
  - ► How you decided on your audience, genre, and claim
  - ► How the piece differs from your Research Essay
  - ► How the piece evolved from draft to draft

Earn course points for . . .
- Arriving on time
- Having a complete poster
- Staying the full time to discuss posters with classmates

Journal Entry Rubric

CATEGORY AND SLO ADDRESSED	EXCEEDS STANDARDS (2.5 POINTS)	MEETS STANDARDS (2 POINTS)	APPROACHES STANDARDS (1.5 POINTS)	DOES NOT MEET STANDARDS (0–1 POINT)
Response answers the questions with clarity of expression.	Writer addresses all parts of the question thoroughly in clear, understandable prose.	Writer addresses the question with reasonable clarity.	Writer does not fully answer the question and lacks some clarity.	Writer does not address the question or barely addresses it and lacks any clarity.
Response demonstrates critical thinking.	Writer demonstrates thoughtful and critical analysis and utilizes engaged consideration of others' ideas to form his/her own.	Writer demonstrates some analysis and some consideration of others' ideas to form her/his own.	Writer demonstrates little thoughtful and critical analysis and does not utilize consideration of others' ideas to form her/his own.	Writer demonstrates no critical analysis and mostly merely summarizes others' ideas and does not form his/her own.
Response demonstrates originality and creativity.	Writer creates his/her own thoughtful, original ideas.	Writer attempts to create his/her own ideas.	Writer mostly parrots others' ideas with little creation of his/her own ideas.	Writer merely summarizes others' ideas.
Response incorporates or addresses in some way others' perspectives.	Writer incorporates others' positions in her/his discussion.	Writer acknowledges at least one other person's position in her/his discussion.	Writer attempts to reference at least one other person's position in her/his discussion but fails to acknowledge that contribution or position her/his own argument against it.	Writer does not even acknowledge others' positions in her/his discussion.
OVERALL SCORE:	EXCEEDS STANDARDS	MEETS STANDARDS	APPROACHES STANDARDS	DOES NOT MEET STANDARDS

Peer Review Rubric

CRITERIA	YES [4 POINTS]	NO [0 POINTS]
ATTENDANCE Author attended the full class session. [Or ONLINE: Author participated in reviewing two peers' drafts.]		
PREPARATION WITH FULL DRAFT Author came to class with <u>TWO</u> HARD COPIES/PRINTED copies of the full draft. [Or ONLINE: Author posted a full draft on time.]		
RESPONSE Author completed earnestly and fully the peer evaluation sheet <u>for at least two peers</u> and offered significant commentary, including at least a few very specific and detailed comments about the strengths of the essay, about the ways the essay does or does not meet the goals and criteria of the assignment, and about ways to improve/revise the essay.		
FULL PARTICIPATION Author used the full time allotted in a focused, dedicated manner. [Or ONLINE: Author fully and thoughtfully evaluated two peers' drafts.]		

Sample Side-by-Side Schedule

			ENGLISH 101			ENG 99
WEEK	DATE	UNIT	TOPICS	READINGS	ASSESSMENT	ASSESSMENT
1		1	Welcome; Developing a growth mindset; College-level writing, reading, and thinking	Chapter 1, section a; Dweck's "What is Mindset?," "How Does Mindset Affect Success?," and "Test Your Mindset"; Scott's "Fixed Mindset vs. Growth Mindset"; Duckworth's "The Key to Success: Grit?"; Lamott's "Shitty First Drafts"	In-Class Activity 1A, 1B, and 1C; Journal Entries 1, 2, and 3	Hierarchy of Needs Noncognitive Activity; First Day Reflection; First Day Activity 2
2			Developing a growth mindset toward writing, etc.; Entering class academic dialogue (including peer review) and active reading strategies	Chapter 1, sections b, c, and d; Ohlin's "Five Ways to Develop Growth Mindset Using Resilience"; Rose's "Blue Collar Brilliance"; Bahrampour's "Find your Passion? That's bad advice, scientists say"; Cherry's "Gardner's Theory of Multiple Intelligences"	Draft 1 of Mindset Reflective Letter; In-Class Activities 1D and 1F (Peer Review 1); Journal Entries 4 and 5	Analyze texts activity; Sentence structure activity
3			Entering the class academic dialogue, etc.; Defining college-level research	Chapter 1, sections e, f, and h and "Transitions"; any <u>one</u> reading <u>from each</u> of five sections (total 5 readings): "On Education"; "On Technology and Us"; "On Negotiating Cultural, Political, and Other Differences"; "On a College Education"; "On Food"	Draft 2 of Mindset Reflective Letter; In-Class Activities 1G (Peer Review 2) and 1 H **Final Mindset Reflective Letter**	Round-Robin draft activity; Values noncognitive activity

4		2	Finding a research topic and question; determining significance	Chapter 2, sections a, b, and c; any two readings <u>from each</u> of five sections (total 10 readings): "On Education"; "On Technology and Us"; "On Negotiating Cultural, Political, and Other Differences"; "On a College Education"; "On Food"	In-Class Activities 2A and 2B; Journal Entry 6A/6B	Obstacles to our success noncognitive activity; Research proposal and question activity; Preliminaries for writing proposal activity
5			Determining a research plan; Writing proposals	Chapter 2, sections d, e, f, and h; any two readings <u>from each</u> of five sections (total 10 readings): "On Education"; "On Technology and Us"; "On Negotiating Cultural, Political, and Other Differences"; "On a College Education"; "On Food"	Draft 1 of Research Proposal; In-Class Activity 2C and 2E (Peer Review 3); Journal Entry 7	Use/Abuse subject–verb agreement activity; Research plan and significance activity; Research proposal template activity
6			Writing proposals, etc.; Where to search	Any one reading <u>from each</u> of five sections (total 5 readings): "On Education"; "On Technology and Us"; "On Negotiating Cultural, Political, and Other Differences"; "On a College Education"; "On Food"	Draft 2 of Research Proposal; In-Class Activity 2F (peer Review 4) and 2D **Final Research Proposal**	Round-Robin with research proposal activity; Our support structures and/or time management noncognitive activity
7		3	Using databases vs. using Internet searches; Summarizing sources; Library visit	Chapter 3, sections a, b, c, and j	In-Class Activities 3A and 3B; Journal Entries 8 and 9	Library visit; Fear of failure noncognitive activity; More summary practice activity; Judging Internet sites activity

8			Finding and evaluating sources; opposition positions	Chapter 3, sections d, e, and f	Draft 1 Annotated Bibliography; In-Class Activities 3B, 3C, and 3F (Peer Review 5); Journal 10	Pronoun roulette activity; Mid-term attitude assessment; Annotated bibliography activity (and template activity)
9			Writing annotated bibliographies; Tentative claims	Chapter 3, sections d, e, and f	Draft 2 Annotated Bibliography; In-Class Activities 3G (Peer Review 6) and 3D **Final Annotated Bibliography**	Refutation/counterargument activity; Stress assessment and/or do I act on impulse noncognitive activity
10		4	Types of evidence and argument structures; Plagiarizing, quoting, paraphrasing, and summarizing	Chapter 4, sections a, b, c, d, and e	In-Class Activities 4A and 4B	Who am I and/or Something new noncognitive activity; Apostrophe challenge activity
11			Synthesizing; Establishing balance; Using citations	Chapter 4, sections f, g, h, I, and j	In-Class Activity 4C	Outline to notes activity; Outlining template
12			Targeting purpose and audience; Outlining; Drafting and revising	Chapter 4, sections k, m, and p	Draft 1 Research Essay; In-Class Activity 4D (Peer Review 7); Journal Entry 11	Research essay brainstorming activity; Essay template work
13			Rhetoric: Genre, Audience, and Purpose; Using the research for outreach piece	Chapter 4, sections I and n; NYU Libraries' "How to Create a Research Poster"	Draft 2 Research Essay; Draft 1 Outreach Piece; In-Class Activities 4E (Peer Review 8) and 4F (Peer Review 9); Journal 12 **Final Research Essay**	Research essay drafting and peer swapping activity; Review of outreach piece expectations

| 14 | | | Presentation basics | Chapter 5; Weirich's "How to Give a Good Research Talk"; Stephen's "How to Sound Smart in Your TEDx Talk"; Anderson's "TED's Secret to Great Public Speaking"; Duarte's "The Secret Structure of Great Talks"; Jones's "How to Give a Great Research Talk"; Phillips's "How to Avoid Death by PowerPoint" | Draft 2 Outreach Piece; In-Class Activity 4G (Peer Review 10); Journal 13 **Final Outreach Essay** | Final summative assessment; Poster brainstorming activity; Research talk activity |
| 15 | | | Finals Week: Outreach Presentation | | **Outreach Presentation** | **Outreach Presentation** |

Some Rules for Co-Requisite Courses

Some Course Rules and Guidelines for Co-Requisite Courses

1. **It is an ENG 101 *companion* course, so students get NO additional assignments; if we see they need practice in something, we do so in class and in line with whatever assignment they are working on in ENG 101.**

2. Start every co-requisite class with a little bit of writing. These students need to get comfortable with writing and with the idea that they ARE writers.

3. In every class, ask students what questions they have about ENG 101 work. Often, their responses may dictate what at least some of the time in the class addresses.

4. Discuss grammar and mechanics ONLY in the context of writing.

5. Very often, class sessions are like workshopping sessions. Sometimes, they work with their own hard copies, and at other times, we are projecting some work they submitted, and we workshop it together as a whole.

6. Sometimes, use class time for ENG 101 drafting work, so teachers can move to each individual and target that student's particular needs.

7. As in all teaching, we make our concrete lesson plans, but students offer those opportunities for teachable moments, upon which we must act. A co-requisite class is a very individualized course. With only ten students in the class, there is lots of opportunity to address individual needs even within a prescribed whole class lesson.

8. Use a lot of students' own work as well as samples taken from published work. BUT, never forget that creating their own texts is that with which they struggle most. At a certain point, engaging with their own writing matters most.

9. These students need help with databases, so do some work on figuring out search terms, best choices in databases, etc. Do so by actually drawing from the students' actual topics. Schedule the library session early, and maybe include a second one.

10. Addressing the noncognitive issues students face becomes very important in this classroom; these issues often impede the students' success.

11. Encourage—or require, depending on students' circumstances—time in the college's writing tutorial/writing center.

Active Learning Strategies

Berkeley Center for Teaching & Learning

Active Learning Strategies

Active Learning Strategies help to initiate learners and faculty into effective ways to help learners engage in activities based on ideas about how people learn. Multiple active learning strategies may be used in each of the active learning designs. Here's an annotated list of active learning strategies.

1. **Sit and talk with peers nearby**
   Think-Pair-Share.

2. **Define "Think-Pair-Share."** Explain to students that a Think-Pair-Share allows them to activate their prior knowledge and share ideas about content or beliefs with peers. This structure gives students a chance to organize their ideas—first in their own minds, then in a smaller group setting before sharing with the entire group. In a Think-Pair-Share, students Think individually about the question or idea(s) put forth, Pair up with someone to discuss their thinking, and then Share their conversation with their table group, and then finally with the whole group.

3. **Display Think-Pair-Share prompts about a concept or topic.** Give students one to two minutes to think about the prompt on their own. Then discuss with a partner for another few minutes.

4. **Facilitate a whole group discussion.**
   - Listen to their responses.
   - Ask students to elaborate on their thinking by providing explanations, evidence, or clarifications. Suggested probing questions:
     - What makes you think that?
     - Please give an example from your experience.
     - What do you mean?
   - Try to stay neutral in your reaction to students' comments.
   - Invite others to react and respond to ideas by providing alternative viewpoints, agreements, or disagreements. Suggested probing questions:
     - Can anyone add something to that comment?
     - Who would like to share an alternative opinion?

Quick Write

A prompt is posed for students to respond to in writing. Taking only five minutes or so, this is a quick way to accomplish one or more of the following: determine whether or not students have done the homework assignment, engage students in thinking about the topic that will be covered in the session, provide the opportunity for students to access their prior knowledge on a topic. The quick write can be graded to encourage students to do their reading assignment, or collected to serve as an attendance check.

Turn and Talk

In a turn and talk, a question is posed to the class and students simply turn to the person next to them to discuss. This can serve as a comfortable way for students to share their ideas with others and set the stage for them sharing with the larger group. The instructor doesn't need to hear all (or any) of the ideas shared—the important aspect of this strategy is for the peers to share and for individuals to access their prior knowledge about a topic. Example prompt: Ask students to turn to someone next to them and discuss their responses to the following question. Tell them to take two minutes to discuss this with their partner, with each person getting some time to talk.

- Part of the challenge of communicating climate change with the public is that there is disparity between what scientists and the non-scientist public think and know about climate change.
- Why do you think there is such a disparity?

Polling

Having students vote anonymously on what they perceive as the best explanation/answer to a question, followed by opportunities to discuss their ideas with peers, and then to vote again leads to greater learning of the material. It is important to have students discuss why they think their explanation is the most accurate and also why the other explanations proposed are not accurate. It is also important that the teacher looks at the polling results and listens to the reasoning of the students in order to determine what further explanations and summary might need to be made in lecture. There are various tools that can be used for polling, including Clickers, Socrative.com, and Poll.Everywhere.com.

Individual Plus Group Quizzes

Give students a quiz that they complete individually and turn in to be graded. Immediately following the individual quiz, put students in small groups and have them take the quiz again, but this time they discuss the answers in their group and turn it in for a group score. Both quizzes are graded and if the group score is higher, the two grades are averaged. The group score can't hurt someone if they have a higher individual score. This encourages individual accountability, and also helps students to better understand the material as they discuss it with peers. In this way, they keep up with the material, rather than realizing they don't totally understand it when they reach the midterm.

Tests/Quizzes with Common Preconceptions as Distracters

Design assessments to include common preconceptions (or misconceptions) that students often hold. Allow students to answer the question on their own and then discuss their answer and rationale with a partner. Have them answer the question again after the peer discussion. Elicit a whole group discussion about why the correct answer is correct and why the others are not. Common misconceptions students have about STEM topics and concepts can be found at AAAS, and assessment questions including common misconceptions as distracters can be found at Brain candy.

Jigsaws

Students work in small groups to read information that has been organized into sections. Each student in the group reads one section of the material and then shares that information with the rest of their group. As they read and share information, they refer to prompts such as: what do you think each idea means? What is the big idea? How can this idea be applied to help understand the concept(s)? What questions do you have about what you read? What do you agree/not agree with?

There are various permutations of jigsaws. One such model includes expert and cooperative groups: Each group can be assigned a particular aspect/part of the overall information—they read it individually and then discuss in their small "expert" group to make sure they all understand it. Then new "cooperative" groups are formed made up of one to two students from each of the original expert groups. In this way, the new groups have an "expert" representative from each of the original groups so that all of the information is now represented in the new cooperative group. The "expert" has had a chance to practice sharing and hearing other viewpoints about the information in their original group, and therefore likely feels more comfortable sharing in the new group.

Sorting Strips

Small bits of information are separated into strips so that students can sort the strips into various categories, or organize them into a sequence depending on the topic. This strategy encourages discussion of competing ideas or organizations or order in which a process would take place. In this case, it is often the discussion and sharing of ideas that is the most important outcome of the activity.

Partial Outlines/PPTs Provided for Lecture

Research has shown that students have a better understanding, do better on exams, and stay more engaged with the content during lecture when they are provided with partial, rather than complete, lecture notes or PowerPoints.

Pausing in Lecture

These strategies work toward inserting wait time in lectures for students to reflect on, discuss, and apply ideas just presented and to encourage them to engage actively in the lecture rather than passively taking notes. These strategies also help students to understand what they do and don't understand about the lecture.

- Ask students to not take notes as you work through a problem on the board with the class, followed by five minutes for them to copy down the board and discuss the problem/chemical reaction/process with peers.
- Pause six to ten seconds after asking a question before calling on a student to respond. Have students do a quick write about a concept just covered in lecture (e.g., their understanding, two questions they have about the concept as presented, what they would like to know more about,

etc.). Optional, collect the quick write to help you better understand what they understood from the lecture and the questions they have and to keep them engaged.

- Turn and talks—ask peers to talk to each other about what they do and don't understand and/or share with each other what they wrote down in their notes about a particular concept just covered in lecture. Encourage students to add to their notes from the discussion.

- Have students apply their understanding of a concept just covered by working with a small group around a huddle board. Optional, have a few groups share their work and elicit reactions and reviews from other students. Summarize findings and scientific normative explanations.

- Have students do think-pair-shares or polling to keep their mind engaged in the topic and to share their ideas with their peers for greater meaning-making opportunities.

Posters and Gallery Walk

Give groups of students an assignment that they need to work on together and present their ideas on a sheet of chart paper. Once they have completed their poster, have them display it on the wall, much like at a scientific poster session. One person from their group will stay with the poster and help to explain it as the class circulates to look at all of the posters. Students take turns standing by their poster so that each of them has the chance to visit the other groups' posters. This sets up a more interactive way of presenting as compared to PowerPoint presentations.

Fish Bowl

A fish bowl allows a small group of students to engage in a discussion about ideas or concepts that have alternative explanations while the rest of the class observes and takes notes. An inner circle of students engages in the discussion, while the rest of the class either sits in an outer circle, or remains in their regular seats and observes. If you have your class organized into small groups, then the members of each group can tap their respective teammate and replace them in the inner circle to expand on or provide additional evidence to support an explanation. Optional: the entire class needs to take part in the inner circle conversation by the end of the class period.

Idea Lineup

The idea lineup is a structure that allows a teacher to use the diversity of perspectives in the classroom to generate heterogeneous groups of students for discussion. This diversity of thinking is a good place from which to develop a classroom climate that supports argumentation. More student-initiated science talk happens when students are connected with peers who have opposing perspectives (Clark & Sampson 2007). The question should be one about which students have enough prior knowledge/experience to have some evidence to bring to bear in the discussions which ensue.

How it works: The teacher provides a question that (s)he knows may have a continuum of responses, especially if it is asked prior to collecting significant amounts of evidence or before students have the opportunity to synthesize the evidence they have already collected.

The question is displayed prominently for students to consider. Students are directed to position themselves on a line to indicate their level of agreement in response to the question. After the students line up, have students talk to the person next to them so they can clarify their own thinking on why they positioned themselves on the line in a particular spot.

Student positions on the line typically indicate a diversity of thinking. The teacher can then use their positions to form groups of students with differing ideas about the question. Students then discuss their thinking and reasoning for their responses with the peers with whom they have been matched. Students should be prompted to listen carefully to each other's claims and evidence and respond with evidence to counter or support the claims of other students in their group. A group claims and evidence chart or small whiteboards can be used to collect student thinking.

If the activity is used prior to an investigation, students can use the ideas from the initial discussion to continually weigh against the evidence they gather from their investigations. If the activity is used after an investigation, but prior to a whole-group meaning-making discussion, ideas from the small group discussions can be used to prepare for a whole group discussion.

Four Corners

Four corners is used for the same reasons as the idea lineup. The only difference is that students are considering several claims (responses to a question). For example, a teacher might ask, "Where does most of the mass in a plant come from?" Claims for consideration might include, "soil," "air," "water," and "sunlight."

How it works: The teacher displays the question prominently for all to consider. Each corner of the classroom is assigned one claim, also prominently displayed. Students are asked to go to the corner of the classroom that has the claim they agree with most. If they think more than one answer is correct, they should just pick one of the corners they agree with. If they don't agree with any claims, they should go to the middle of the room. Once in their corners, students should discuss with others why they chose that corner to help clarify their thinking. Have them share and record evidence that supports that claim and why the other claims are not supported. Optional: have them visit the other corners to see what others thought about the ideas and the evidence they put forth.

Just as in the idea lineup, the teacher can use the student positions around the room to form groups with a diversity of ideas. The rest of the instructions are the same as for the idea lineup.

https://teaching.berkeley.edu/active-learning-strategies

BIBLIOGRAPHIES

Descriptive Annotated Bibliography

Bailey, Thomas R., Shanna Smith Jaggars, and Davis Jenkins. *Redesigning America's Community Colleges: A Clearer Path to Student Success.* Cambridge, Massachusetts: Harvard University Press, 2015.

In this text, community college scholar Thomas R. Bailey pairs with education researchers and practitioners Shanna Smith Jaggars and Davis Jenkins to advocate for changing the entire community college structure from what they term the "cafeteria style model" to what they label the "guided pathway model." They declare their model aimed at garnering improved student success rates through a concerted, deliberate integration of clearly outlined programs of study with all student services. Using data from the Community College Research Center at Columbia University, they offer the rationale for the change, comparisons between the two models, and a detailed plan for implementation of the new model. (I note that inspired by this text and research, many US community colleges and Title V grants have embraced this design.)

Bean, John C. *Engaging Ideas: The Professor's Guide to Integrating Writing, Critical Thinking, and Active Learning in the Classroom.* 2nd ed., San Francisco, California: Jossey-Bass A Wiley Imprint, 2011.

A professor of English at Seattle University and a leading scholar in composition and argument, John C. Bean presents a text designed to offer practical, hands-on instruction in how to use writing to spur critical thinking. A proponent of active learning to promote deep learning, Dr. Bean provides rationale and explanations and offers clear designs for everything from syllabus materials and assignments to grading and coaching. Based in research and practice, this text delivers content applicable across all disciplines of study.

Behrens, Laurence, and Leonard J. Rosen. *Writing and Reading Across the Curriculum.* Philadelphia, Pennsylvania: Pearson, 2016.

Focusing on research and its related skills of analysis, evaluation, and synthesis, Laurence Behrens (University of California) and Leonard J. Rosen (Bentley College), practicing professors of writing, provide an interdisciplinary teaching-of-writing text. It encompasses writing instruction, reading exercises, and a host of cross-disciplinary readings like those students might encounter in their non-English courses. In its thirteenth edition, this book offers updated, current readings to engage students as well as concrete lessons and practice assignments.

Cohen, Arthur M., and Florence B. Brawer. *The American Community College*. 5th ed., San Francisco, California: John Wiley and Sons, Inc., 2008.

Veterans of the study of every aspect of the American community college, in this fifth edition of their quintessential and comprehensive text, Arthur C. Cohen and Florence B. Brawer provide an analysis of the history, evolution, and current dynamics of the community college in the United States. Filled with data, examples, and sections divided by fourteen categories covering everything from expectations to student demographics to faculty and administration to curriculum to the role of the community college in society, this book offers the definitive primer for anyone involved with or interested in US community colleges.

Conference on College Composition and Communication Executive Committee. "CCCC Position Statement on Undergraduate Research in Writing: Principles and Best Practices." National Council for the Teaching of English, March 2017, https://cccc.ncte.org/cccc/resources/positions/undergraduate-research.

Just one of the many policy statements the CCCC writes and approves by vote every year, this statement recommends undergraduate writing research (in writing and communication through writing) as a high impact educational practice that engages students in intellectual inquiry. It also advocates that it become "well-defined and well-supported [. . .] by the allocation of available campus resources." Lastly, it offers a full list and explanation of principles and best teaching practices. While these ideas focus on undergraduate researchers studying writing itself, the ideas provide a broad enough spectrum to apply to any undergraduate research writing.

Conference on College Composition and Communication Executive Committee. "Statement of WAC Principles and Practices." National Council for the Teaching of English, December 2014, https://cccc.ncte.org/resources/positions/WAC-principles.

Another of CCCC's statement of best practices and principles for teaching writing, this position policy details specific practices to follow to make writing an interdisciplinary study embraced by more than English professors but still engaged with high level thinking and writing.

Cox, Michelle, Jeffrey Galin, and Dan Melzer. *Sustainable WAC: A Whole Systems Approach to Launching and Developing Writing Across the Curriculum Programs*. Urbana, Illinois: NCTE Publications, 2018.

Directors of various Writing Across the Curriculum (WAC) programs, scholars, and practitioners, Cox, Galin, and Melzer discuss the theoretical framework of WAC programs and provide information regarding how to develop—and importantly, sustain—such programs. Illustrated through theories and strategies on meaningful change within systems as well as narratives from WAC directors from all over the United States, the text outlines ways to start, re-energize, and maintain WAC programs at any college. Rather than take a one-way-fits-all approach, this book recognizes that the specific contexts of any educational institution must govern the implementation of these programs.

Davis, Robert L., and Mark F. Shadle. *Teaching Multiwriting Researching and Composing with Multiple Genres, Media, Disciplines, and Cultures.* Carbondale, Illinois: Southern Illinois University Press, 2007.

These professors offer an unconventional approach to defining and teaching writing. They champion a movement away from traditional concepts of college composition and genre in favor of multiwriting, which they define as beyond mere multi-genre writing to encompass instead an opening of students and their essays not only to mixed genres, but also to mixed media, cultures, and disciplines. The text offers a multitude of examples, exercises, and assignment and project ideas and asks readers to think about whether or not our canonized genres and modes of writing have become outmoded and out of touch with the modern and culturally diverse demographics of our student populations.

Drake, Eron, and Dina Battaglia. "Teaching and Learning in Active Learning Classrooms Recommendations, Research, and Resources." Faculty Center for Innovative Teaching Central Michigan University, March 18, 2014. https://www.scribd.com/document/259486222/Teaching-and-Learning-in-Active-Learning-Classrooms-FaCIT-CMU-Research-Recommendations-And-Resources.

Leading members of the Faculty Center for Innovative Teaching at Central Michigan University, these professors provide classroom-tested strategies for teaching in ways that engage students actively in critical thinking and learning. With links to other resources and an offer of contact information so readers can ask questions, this text provides practical guidance for college classroom teaching.

Dweck, Carol S., PhD. *mindset The New Psychology of Success.* New York, New York: Random House, 2016.

Stanford University psychologist Carol S. Dweck, PhD, explains the concepts of what she calls "growth mindset" and "fixed mindset" and their relationship to success and accomplishment in school, work, sports, management, parenting, teaching, loving, business, and any other field of endeavor. She explores these concepts as they apply to individuals as well as to group cultures, she makes recommendations about how to develop growth mindset in self and others, and she explains how to identify and avoid what she labels "false growth mindset." Filled with references, vignettes, and practice examples, though not designed specifically for teachers, the text gives teachers a way to help students see themselves as successful learners.

Gardner, Howard. *Frames of Mind The Theory of Multiple Intelligences.* New York, New York: Basic Books, 2011.

Howard Gardner, Professor of Cognition and Education at the Harvard Graduate School of Education and Senior Director of Project Zero, champions the idea that individuals do not possess a single—and finite—intellectual capacity, but, rather, that each individual can claim a number of different types of intelligences that together create a unique cognitive capacity. Dividing his text into three parts—"Background," "Theory," "Implications and Applications"—Gardner discusses the history of thinking about intelligence, his theories about multiple intelligences, and his ideas regarding how we might apply such theories in understanding how we become educated and in actually applying that understanding in our classrooms. Replete with concrete examples and years of research, the text immerses us in theory that readers can use.

Graff, Gerald, Cathy Birkenstein, and Russell Durst. *They Say I Say*. 4th ed., New York, New York: W.W. Norton and Company, 2018.

These three professors offer classroom-tested approaches to teaching research writing as an academic dialogue into which our students can position themselves. They provide a template approach that asks students not to report their research, but, rather, to make their own contribution to the scholarly dialogue. Covering the particulars of incorporating what scholars (they) say with what students (I) say and providing examples of how to do so, this classroom text talks plainly to students about the variations research conclusions might offer.

Joyce, Marilyn Z., and Julie I. Tallman. *Making the Writing and Research Connection with the I-Search Process*, 2nd ed. How-To-Do-It-Manuals for Librarians, Book No. 143. New York, New York: Neal-Schulman Publishers, 2006.

Librarians Marilyn Z. Joyce and Julie I. Tallman expand grade-level application for and explain and update Ken Macrorie's 1988 approach to writing research papers. Like Macrorie, they emphasize the process and the vital nature of having students connect to and have an interest in their topic choice to produce improved research and improved writing. This text offers templates and examples, promotes collaboration, and includes a cross-disciplinary section.

Kester, Jessica, *et al.* "Improving Success, Increasing Access: Bringing HIPs to Open Enrollment Institutions through WAC/WID." *Across the Disciplines A Journal of Language, Learning, and Academic Writing*, Special Issue 13, Is 4 (2016) 1–17. https://wac.colostate.edu/docs/atd/special/hip/kesteretal2016.pdf.

This article responds to the fact that although repeated studies have demonstrated that WAC/WID (Writing Across the Disciplines/Writing in the Disciplines) programs consistently improve community college students' success rates, only about one-third of US community colleges actually have such programs in place. Creating their own empirical study, these scholars use the open-access Daytona State College to determine WAC/WID impacts on student success and faculty development, focusing particularly on the historically underserved and at-risk population. They conclude that such programs can and do have positive effects on students and faculty, but that at community colleges, institutional barriers obstruct that possibility.

Kuh, George D., and Carol Geary Schneider. *High-Impact Educational Practices: What They Are, Who Has Access To Them, And Why They Matter*. Washington, DC: American Association of Colleges and Universities, 2008.

A data-driven text, this book defines and explains eleven teaching and learning practices that their research from the National Survey of Student Engagement along with other data such as campus case studies demonstrates offer great benefits to all college students, but especially to underserved students. Kuh and Schneider also discuss why these practices (HIPs) have such positive impacts, how their effects might vary with different kinds of students, and why these educational practices need to be implemented in a systematic way. Covering first-year seminars, common learning experiences, learning communities, writing-intensive courses, collaborative assignments and projects, undergraduate research, global learning, e-portfolios, service and community-based learning, internships, and capstone courses and projects, Kuh and Schneider provide concrete rationale and theory for the need to utilize these eleven practices.

Macrorie, Ken. *The I-Search Paper*. Portsmouth, New Hampshire: Heinemann, 1989.

Ken Macrorie designed this inquiry-based, personally meaningful approach to teaching research writing for his own freshman composition class. A step-by-step discussion of how to emphasize process with topics in which students feel invested includes examples and implementation guidelines.

Olson, Carol Booth, editor. *Practical Ideas for Teaching Writing as a Process at the High School and College Levels*. Sacramento, California: California State Department of Education, 1996.

A scholar of education, Dr. Carol Booth Olson offers in this text a compilation of assignments and assessments for high school and college-level courses. Practical and explicit, these assignments showcase the writing process in its many stages and encompasses everything from the very brief writing assignment to the I-Search essay.

Rose, Mike. *Why School? Reclaiming Education for All of Us*. New York, New York: The New Press, 2009.

A research professor in the Social Research Methodology division of UCLA's Graduate School of Education and widely-published writer, Mike Rose discusses the subject of what our schools ought to do to enact a vision of democracy. Filled with examples from his own experience, his experiences with students, and his research, the text brings to life answers to questions about our definitions of intelligence, education, and educational opportunity in the United States.

Tinberg, Howard, and Jean-Paul Nadeau. *The Community College Writer Exceeding Expectations*. Edwardsville, Illinois: Southern Illinois University Press, 2010.

This text reports on a study of first-semester writing programs at four community colleges in the United States. Tinberg and Nadeau, both professors at Bristol Community College, tell us about their method, purpose, rationale, and conclusions, but in the midst of their explanations, they allow many student voices and writing samples and discuss faculty and student responses to surveys. Ultimately, they give us a list of six "characteristics as essential to effective design of assignments for our students" (116) and contemplate what future research regarding writing in classes other than the English classroom needs to be done.

Verschelden, Cia. *Bandwidth Recovery Helping Students Reclaim Cognitive Resources Lost to Poverty, Racism, and Social Marginalization*. Sterling, Virginia: Stylus Publishing in Association with Association of American Colleges and Universities, 2017.

Executive Director of Institutional Assessment at the University of Central Oklahoma and advocate for social justice and equity, Cia Verschelden provides educators who work with low income and minority students a new way to see them: through the lens of the obstacles that impede their learning. She contends that their ability and preparation are not to blame for their failure. Rather, their reduced cognitive and emotional resources due to the conditions of their lives that quite literally block their learning must shoulder that blame. She explains and offers examples of the concept and then provides a host of tools for educators to use to restore those cognitive and emotional resources.

Yancy, Kathleen Blake, ed. *Delivering College Composition The Fifth Canon*. Portsmouth, New Hampshire: Boyton/Cook Publishers, Inc. 2006.

A well-known and often honored and quoted scholar in the field of rhetoric and composition studies and the director of just such a graduate program, Kathleen Blake Yancy in this text takes up the question of how we educators actually deliver our college composition courses. Using the work of thirteen other scholars bookended by her own commentary, and studying programs at such diverse institutions as a research university, a private college, a community college, an historically black college, a cyber school, and a high school with advanced placement classes, Yancy posits—and proves—the premise that today's twenty-first century delivery of composition classes does indeed differ from the past's courses because of "digital technology, ways of defining the teacher, and because of new ways of understanding both curricular and physical spaces" (ix). She advocates that readers consider these differences seriously and "make them matter" (ix) not only in how we deliver our courses, but also in terms of how we even define writing.

Bibliography for Readings and Resources

Academic Earth. "How the Internet is Changing Our Brains." 2019, Video with Transcript, 2:05. https://academicearth.org/electives/internet-changing-your-brain/.

Anderson, Chris. "TED's Secret to Great Public Speaking." TED Talks, March 2016. Video, 7:49. https://www.ted.com/talks/chris_anderson_teds_secret_to_great_public_speaking/up-next?language=en.

Anderson, Janna, and Lee Rainie. "The Future of Truth and Misinformation Online. The Pew Research Center, October 19, 2017. https://www.pewinternet.org/2017/10/19/the-future-of-truth-and-misinformation-online/.

Apigo, Maritez. "How to Write an Effective Summary Paragraph," December 5, 2015. Video, 3:30. https://www.youtube.com/watch?v=WZFI6dvgOzU.

Atlantic's Marketing Team for Feeding America. "America Has a Hunger Problem." Think Original Series, 2019. Multimedia Advertising Campaign. https://www.theatlantic.com/sponsored/hunger-2019/america-has-a-hunger-problem/3067/?sr_source=pocket&sr_lift=true&utm_source=pocket&utm_medium=CPC&utm_campaign=simplereach&utm_source=PK_SR_P_3067

"Audience, Purpose, and Tone." Tasmanian Government DoE (Department of Education), September 29, 2015. Video, 2:45. https://www.youtube.com/watch?v=Z1Nrls4-yH8.

Bahrampour, Tara. "'Find your passion?' That's bad advice, scientists say." *Washington Post,* July 23, 2018. https://www.washingtonpost.com/news/inspired-life/wp/2018

Boise State URC. "Poster Presentation Basics." Boise State Undergraduate Research Center, April 16, 2010. Video, 5:10. https://www.youtube.com/watch?v=cRNQjo2lstY.

Brandenburg, Broughton. "Chapter 1 The Impetus and the Method." In *Imported Americans the story of the experiences of a disguised American and his wife studying the immigration question,* 1–6. New York: Frederick A. Stokes Company Publishers, 1904. https://www.gutenberg.org/files/57517/57517-h/57517-h.htm.

Brigham Young University Idaho. "Addressing Opposing Viewpoints." Brigham Young University Idaho Academic Support Center, 2019. Video, 5:50. http://www.byui.edu/academic-support-centers/writing/video-lessons-and-handouts/addressing-opposing-viewpoints.

Brigham Young University Idaho. "Purpose and Genre." Brigham Young University Idaho Academic Support Center, 2019. Video, 7:48. http://www.byui.edu/academic-support-centers/writing/video-lessons-and-handouts/purpose-and-genre.

Brock University Library. "What is Plagiarism and How to Avoid It," September 2, 2014. Video, 1:50. https://www.youtube.com/watch?v=Pmab92ghG0M.

Carnegie Melon University. "Environmental Issues: Green Computing." Carnegie Melon University MySecureCyberSpace: Environmental Issues, 2019. http://www.carnegiecyberacademy.com/facultyPages/environment/issues.html.

Cherry, Kendra. "Gardner's Theory of Multiple Intelligences." The Very Well Mind, April 3, 2019. https://www.verywellmind.com/gardners-theory-of-multiple-intelligences-2795161.

Dettori, Lucia. "Research Talk 101." DePaul University, June 29, 2007. Slide-Player Show. https://slideplayer.fr/slide/13917634/.

Dewey, John. "I The School and Social Progress." In The School and Society, 19–46. Illinois: The University of Chicago Press, 1900. https://www.gutenberg.org/files/53910/53910-h/53910-h.htm.

Dooley, Samantha. "Population Control, The Environmental Fix No One Wants to Talk About." World Crunch Los Echos, May 16, 2018. https://www.worldcrunch.com/opinion-analysis/population-control-the-environmental-fix-no-one-wants-to-talk-about.

Duarte, Nancy. "The Secret Structure of Great Talks." TED Talks, November 2011. Video, 18:03. https://www.ted.com/talks/nancy_duarte_the_secret_structure_ of_great_talks/up-next.

Duckworth, Angela. "The Key to Success: Grit?" TED Talks, April 2013. Video, 6:02. http://www.ted.com/talks/angela_lee_duckworth_the_key_to_success_grit?language=en.

Dweck, Carol S., PhD. "How Does Mindset Affect Success?" Mindset Online. 2006–2010. https://www.mindsetworks.com/science/Impact

Dweck, Carol S., PhD. "Test Your Mindset." Mindset Online. 2006–2010. http://blog.mindsetworks.com/what-s-my-mindset?view=quiz.

Dweck, Carol S., PhD. "What is Mindset?' Mindset Online. 2006–2010. https://www.mindsetworks.com/science/.

Environmental Literacy Council. "Landfills. Environmental Literacy Council, 2015. https://enviroliteracy.org/environment-society/waste-management/landfills/.

Ferdman, Roberto A. "The disturbing ways that fast food chains disproportionly target black kids." Washington Post, November 12, 2014. https://www.washingtonpost.com/news/wonk/wp/2014/11/12/the-disturbing-ways-that-fast-food-chains-disproportionately-target-black-kids/?noredirect=on&utm_term=.95af5a6bd144.

Foley, Caitlin. "Audience, Purpose, and Genre," January 26, 2016. Video, 8:12. https://www.youtube.com/watch?v=bXO8jEVQssA.

Gable, John. "Bridging America's Divide: Can the Internet Help?" The Huffington Post, April 23, 2017. https://www.huffpost.com/entry/bridging-americas-divide_b_9752176.

Goodwill Community Foundation. "Synthesizing Information." Goodwill Community Foundation Learn Free, August 6, 2012. Video, 2:30. https://www. youtube.com/watch?v=7dEGoJdb6O0.

Green, Kate. "Genre, Audience, and Purpose," July 9, 2015. Video, 2:58. https://www.youtube.com/watch?v=oP17FGMrMtk.

Gustin, Georgina. "Your Food Choices Can Have a Big Climate Impact, So Be Picky, New Study Says." Inside Climate News, May 31, 2018. https://insideclimatenews.org/news/31052018/environmental-impacts-food-production-climate-change-meat-vegetarian-vegan-diets-global-warming-study.

Hess, George. "Giving an Effective Poster Presentation." North Carolina State University Project Posters, February 8, 2013. Video, 11:55. https://www.youtube.com/watch?v=vMSaFUrk-FA.

Hoffower, Hillary. "College is more expensive than it's ever been, and the 5 reasons why suggest it's only going to get worse." *Business Insider,* July 8, 2018. https://www.businessinsider.com/why-is-college-so-expensive-2018-4.

Hornaday, William T. "Part 1. Extermination Chapter 1 The Formar Abundance of Wild Life." In *Our Vanishing Wild Life,* 1–6. New York: Charles Scribner's Sons, 1913. https://www.gutenberg.org/files/13249/13249-h/13249-h.htm.

"Is College Education Worth it?" ProCon.org, May 20, 2019. https://college-education.procon.org/.

Jilani, Zaid. "Is Diversity Good for the Bottom Line?" *The Greater Good Magazine,* January 7, 2019. https://greatergood.berkeley.edu/article/item/is_diversity_good_for_the_bottom_line.

Jilani, Zaid. "What Makes a Good Interaction Between Divided Groups?" *The Greater Good Magazine,* May 14, 2019. https://greatergood.berkeley.edu/article/item/what_makes_a_good_interaction_between_divided_groups.

Johmann, Caroline. "Making a Claim," October 4, 2014. Video, 2:14. https://www.youtube.com/watch?v=5-tOeh8n8yQ.

Jones, Peyton with John Hughes and John Launchbury. "How to Give a Great Research Talk." Microsoft Research Cambridge, July 26, 2016. Video, 0:59. https://www.youtube.com/watch?v=sT_-owjKlbA.

Keogh. "Big Fail: The Internet hasn't helped democracy." *The Conversation,* October 15, 2019. https://theconversation.com/big-fail-the-internet-hasnt-helped-democracy-104817.

Lamott, Ann. "Shitty First Drafts." Presented by University of Kentucky, August 6, 2012. https://wrd.as.uky.edu/sites/default/files/1-Shitty%20First%20Drafts.pdf.

Learning Network of *The New York Times.* "401 Prompts for Argumentative Writing." The Learning Network of *The New York Times,* March 1, 2017. https://www.nytimes.com/2017/03/01/learning/lesson-plans/401-prompts-for-argumentative-writing.html.

"The Link Between our Health and the Environment." *Earth Talk in Scientific American,* 2019. https://www.scientificamerican.com/article/environment-and-our-health/?redirect=1.

Lyiscott, Jamila. "Bridging Cultural Gaps: 3 Ways to Speak English." TED Talks, February 2014. Video, 4:18. https://www.ted.com/talks/jamila_lyiscott_3_ways_to_speak_english?referrer=playlist-bridging_cultural_differences.

Maxted, Vicky. "Purpose, Audience, and Form (P.A.F.)," June 2, 2014. Video, 12:29. https://www.youtube.com/watch?v=93eA7cttZCM.

Michigan State University. "How to Prepare an Oral Presentation." Michigan State University—Undergraduate Research, September 17, 2013. Video, 4:08. https://www.youtube.com/watch?v=LzIJFD-ddoI.

Mir, Elina, and Caroline Novas. "Social Media and Adolescents' and Young Adults' Mental Health." National Center for Health Research, 2019. http://www.center4research.org/social-media-affects-mental-health/.

MJMFoodie. "What is Plagiarism?," November 28, 2016. Video, 2:45. https://www.youtube.com/watch?v=zPqKXJbzRP4.

Moss, Michael. "The Extraordinary Science of Addictive Junk Food." *New York Times Sunday Magazine,* February 20, 2013. https://www.nytimes.com/2013/02/24/magazine/the-extraordinary-science-of-junk-food.html.

Mudd, Michael. "How to Force Ethics on the Food Industry." *New York Times Sunday Review,* March 16, 2013. https://www.nytimes.com/2013/03/17/opinion/sunday/how-to-force-ethics-on-the-food-industry.html.

National Aeronautics and Space Administration. "The Causes of Climate Change." NASA, May 17, 2019. https://climate.nasa.gov/causes/.

National Climate Assessment Program. "Extreme Weather." National Climate Assessment Program, 2014. https://nca2014.globalchange.gov/highlights/report-findings/extreme-weather.

New York University Libraries. "How To Create a Research Poster." New York University Libraries, May 17, 2018. https://guides.nyu.edu/posters.

Nicholson, Jeremy. "Pros and Cons of Online Dating." *Psychology Today,* April 30, 2014. https://www.psychologytoday.com/us/blog/the-attraction-doctor/201404/pros-and-cons-online-dating.

Ohlin, Birgit. "5 Ways to Develop Growth Mindset Using Grit and Resilience." *Positive Psychology Program,* April 28, 2018. https://positivepsychologyprogram.com/5-ways-develop-grit-resilience/.

Park, Alice. "Sugar is Definitely Toxic, a New Study Says." *Time Magazine,* October 29, 2015. http://time.com/4087775/sugar-is-definitely-toxic-a-new-study-says/.

Paulson, Amanda. "Does everyone need a college degree? Maybe not, says Harvard study." *Christian Science Monitor,* February 2, 2011. https://www.csmonitor.com/USA/Education/2011/0202/Does-everyone-need-a-college-degree-Maybe-not-says-Harvard-study.

Penfield Library. "Google vs. Databases." Penfield Library of SUNY Oswego University, February 3, 2014. Video, 2:56. https://www.youtube.com/watch?v=lMYZiUv47x8.

Phillips, David J. P. "How to Avoid Death by PowerPoint." TED Talks Stockholm, April 14, 2014. Video, 20:31. https://www.youtube.com/watch?v=Iwpi1Lm6dFo.

Public Broadcasting Station. "Is Your Meat Safe?—Antibiotic Debate Overview." From *Frontline* televised by Public Broadcasting Station in 2014. Telecast Script. https://www.pbs.org/wgbh/pages/frontline/shows/meat/safe/overview.html.

Rose, Mike. "Blue Collar Brilliance." *The American Scholar,* June 1, 2009. https://theamericanscholar.org/blue-collar-brilliance/#.XDNbjfx7lN0.

Rushkoff, Douglas. "Chapter 3 The opportunity for renaissance." In *Open Source Democracy How online communication is changing offline politics,* N.P. Gutenberg EBook through Demos Open Access, 2003. http://www.gutenberg.org/cache/epub/10753/pg10753-images.html.

Salt, Henry S. "Why Vegetarian?" In *The Logic of Vegetarianism Essays and Dialogues,* 4–13. London: George Bell and Sons, 1906. https://www.gutenberg.org/files/49949/49949-h/49949-h.ht.

Scott, S. J. "Fixed Mindset vs. Growth Mindset: What Characteristics Are Critical to Success?" *Develop Good Habits A Better Life One Habit at a Time,* April 24, 2019. https://www.developgoodhabits.com/fixed-mindset-vs-growth-mindset/.

Selingo, Jeffrey J. "How much is too much to pay for college?" *Washington Post,* February 24, 2018. https://www.washingtonpost.com/news/grade-point/wp/2018/02/24/how-much-is-too-much-to-pay-for college/?noredirect=on&utm_term =.cadf2dfbab1f.

Silva, Mary Lourdes. "Strategies for Synthesis," June 12, 2013. Video, 12:19. https://www.youtube.com/watch?v=c7HtCHtQ9w0.

Smith, Beth. "The Value of GE or the Answer to 'Why do I Need to Take This Class?'" *Rostrum*, by the Academic Senate for California Community Colleges, September 2012. https://www.asccc.org/content/value-ge-or-answer-why-do-i-need-take-class.

Smrt, Shaun. "How to Write a Summary." Smrt English Live Class, November 15, 2012. Video, https://www.youtube.com/watch?v=eGWO1ldEhtQ.

Southern Illinois University Writing Center. "Summarizing: Five Keys To Writing Effective Summaries." SIU Writing Center Handouts, 2019. https://write.siu.edu/_common/documents/handouts/summarizing.pdf.

Stegner, Wallace. "Wilderness Letter (1960)." *The Wilderness Society Newsletter*, December 28, 2009. https://psych.utah.edu/_resources/documents/psych4130/Stenger_W.pdf

Stephen, Will. "How to Sound Smart in Your TED Talk." TED Talks, January 15, 2015. Video, 5:55. https://www.youtube.com/watch?v=8S0FDjFBj8o.

Stern, Barbara Slater. "A Comparison of Online and Face-To-Face Instruction in an Undergraduate Foundations of American Education Course." *Contemporary Issues in Technology and Teacher Education (CITE) Journal*, 2016. https://www.citejournal.org/volume-4/issue-2-04/general/a-comparison-of-online-and-face-to-face-instruction-in-an-undergraduate-foundations-of-american-education-course/.

Suttie, Jill. "How Good People Can Fight Bias." *The Greater Good Magazine,* December 7, 2018. https://greatergood.berkeley.edu/article/item/how_good_people_can_fight_bias.

Svoboda, Elizabeth. "These Kids Are Learning How To Have Bipartisan Conversations." *The Greater Good Magazine*, December 4, 2018. https://greatergood.berkeley.edu/article/item/these_kids_are_learning_how_to_have_bipartisan_conversations.

Taylor, David. "APA-MLA Annotated Bibliography: Complete Guide To Writing Annotated Bibliography," Part 1, July 16, 2016. Video, 5:47. https://www.youtube.com/watch?v=iW4eXLAtOhk.

Taylor, David. "APA-MLA Annotated Bibliography: Complete Guide To Writing Annotated Bibliography," Part 2, June 26, 2016. Video, 4:59. https://www.youtube.com/watch?v=w3A_wEMvnFA.

Taylor, David. "How to Integrate Quotations in Essay Writing—APA and MLA," November 7, 2010. Video, 2:52. https://www.youtube.com/watch?v=_M0F1rOnFUY.

United States Department of Agriculture. "Food Waste Challenge." USDA Office of the Chief Economist. 2013–2019. https://www.usda.gov/oce/foodwaste/faqs.htm.

Weirich, Stephanie. "How To Give a Good Research Talk." University of Pennsylvania. N.D. PowerPoint Presentation. https://www.cis.upenn.edu/~sweirich/talks/plmw15-giving-a-talk.pdf.

"Where GMO's Hide in Your Food." *Consumer Reports*, October 2014. Video, 3:29. https://www.consumerreports.org/cro/2014/10/where-gmos-hide-in-your-food/index.htm.

World Health Organization. "Health Care Waste." World Health Organization, February 8, 2018. https://www.who.int/news-room/fact-sheets/detail/health-care-waste.

Yavapai College Library. "What Are Databases and Why You Need Them," September 29, 2011. Video, 2:34. https://www.youtube.com/watch?v=Q2GMtluaNzU.

About the Author

A former 7–12 public school English teacher, teaching fellow at Fordham University, and adjunct at Pace University before coming to SUNY Westchester Community College, **Patricia Sehulster** earned her PhD in American literature at Fordham University, New York. Her academic publications include essays for *The Western Journal of Black Studies*, *The Journal of Black Studies*, *A.T.Q.: 19th Century American Literature and Culture*, *The Facts on File Companion to the American Short Story*, *Literary Themes for Students: War and Peace*, *The Facts on File Companion to the American Novel*, *Teaching English in the Two-Year College*, and *Kate Chopin in Context: New Approaches*. She has presented at conferences including the Guided Pathways Institute III, the Successful Teaching Conference, the NYU National Symposium, Information Literacy and the (New) Student Learner, and Using E-Portfolios to Assess Student Learning. Professor Sehulster also serves as a peer reviewer for *Teaching English in the Two-Year College*, *African American Review*, and Pearson Higher Education. In 2011–2012, she received the SUNY Chancellor's Award for Excellence in Service and the SUNY Westchester Community College Foundation Award for Excellence in Service and in 2017–2018, the SUNY Chancellor's Award for Excellence in Scholarship and Creative Work and the SUNY Westchester Community College Foundation Award for Excellence in Scholarship. She is also a published freelance writer and editor of long and short mainstream fiction and nonfiction, and her works have appeared in such publications as *Troika; Dogsongs; Reader's Break; Elements; Ink; Poor Katie's Almanac; Behind the Yellow Wallpaper: New Tales of Madness Anthology; First Came Fear New Tales of Horror Anthology; Salon Style An Online Literary Journal; Salon Style: An Anthology of Fiction, Poetry, and Art; Offshore: Northeast Boating; Boston Parents' Paper; Big Apple Parent; Children's Writer; Family Times; Naturally Women Magazine;* and *Camping Today*.

CPSIA information can be obtained
at www.ICGtesting.com
Printed in the USA
LVHW061752061120
670971LV00005B/8